LA/ACCESS

Richard Saul Wurman

S0-AGI-527

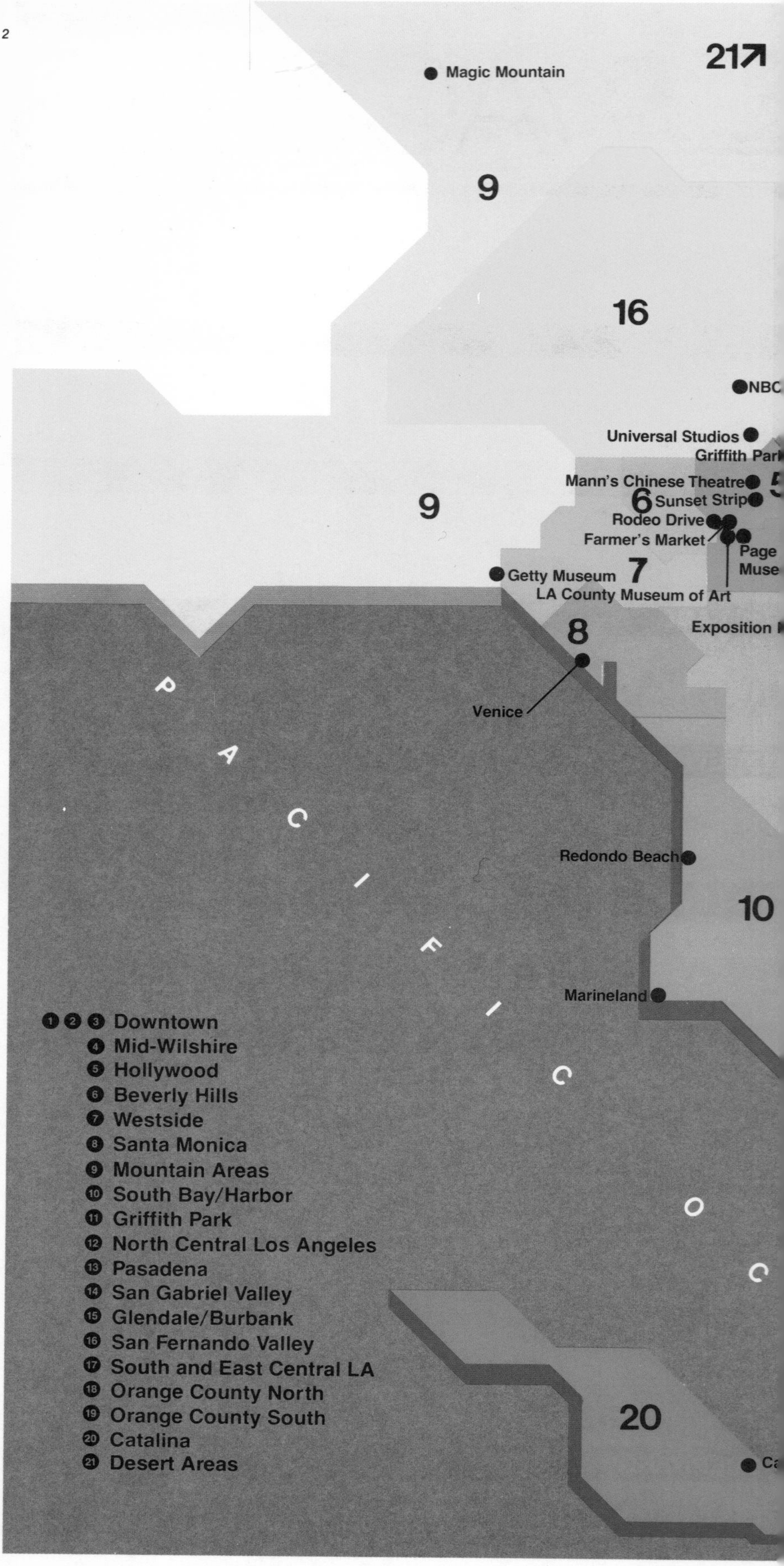

2

Magic Mountain

21↗

9

16

●NBC

Universal Studios ●
Griffith Park
Mann's Chinese Theatre●
6 Sunset Strip●
Rodeo Drive●●
Farmer's Market●●
Page
Muse
● Getty Museum 7
LA County Museum of Art

8

Exposition

9

Venice

Redondo Beach●

10

Marineland●

P
A
C
I
F
I
C

O

C

❶❷❸ Downtown
❹ Mid-Wilshire
❺ Hollywood
❻ Beverly Hills
❼ Westside
❽ Santa Monica
❾ Mountain Areas
❿ South Bay/Harbor
⓫ Griffith Park
⓬ North Central Los Angeles
⓭ Pasadena
⓮ San Gabriel Valley
⓯ Glendale/Burbank
⓰ San Fernando Valley
⓱ South and East Central LA
⓲ Orange County North
⓳ Orange County South
⓴ Catalina
㉑ Desert Areas

20

● Ca

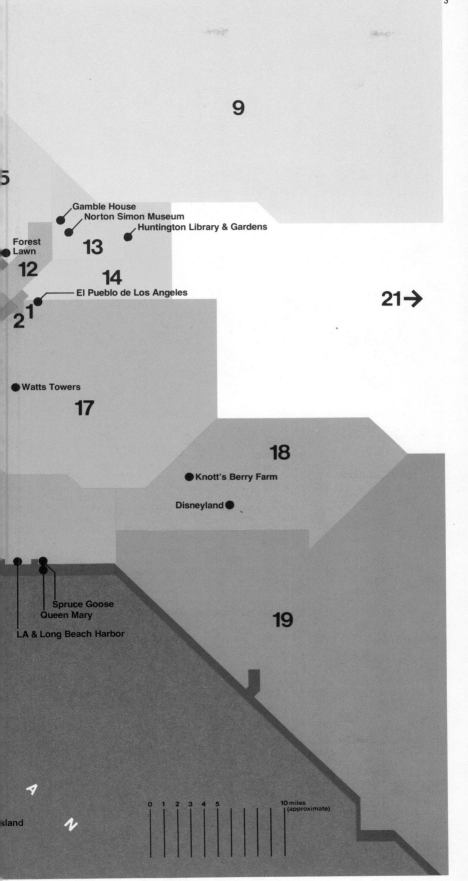

9

5

Gamble House
Norton Simon Museum
Huntington Library & Gardens

Forest
Lawn

13

12

14

El Pueblo de Los Angeles

21→

2 1

Watts Towers

17

18

Knott's Berry Farm

Disneyland

Spruce Goose
Queen Mary

LA & Long Beach Harbor

19

0 1 2 3 4 5   10 miles
                        (approximate)

sland

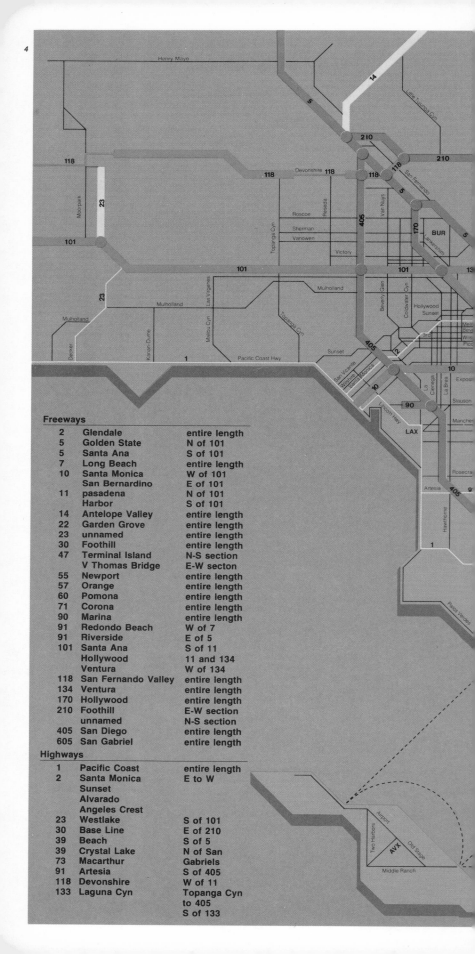

4

Freeways

2	Glendale	entire length
5	Golden State	N of 101
5	Santa Ana	S of 101
7	Long Beach	entire length
10	Santa Monica	W of 101
	San Bernardino	E of 101
11	pasadena	N of 101
	Harbor	S of 101
14	Antelope Valley	entire length
22	Garden Grove	entire length
23	unnamed	entire length
30	Foothill	entire length
47	Terminal Island	N-S section
	V Thomas Bridge	E-W secton
55	Newport	entire length
57	Orange	entire length
60	Pomona	entire length
71	Corona	entire length
90	Marina	entire length
91	Redondo Beach	W of 7
91	Riverside	E of 5
101	Santa Ana	S of 11
	Hollywood	11 and 134
	Ventura	W of 134
118	San Fernando Valley	entire length
134	Ventura	entire length
170	Hollywood	entire length
210	Foothill	E-W section
	unnamed	N-S section
405	San Diego	entire length
605	San Gabriel	entire length

Highways

1	Pacific Coast	entire length
2	Santa Monica	E to W
	Sunset	
	Alvarado	
	Angeles Crest	
23	Westlake	S of 101
30	Base Line	E of 210
39	Beach	S of 5
39	Crystal Lake	N of San
73	Macarthur	Gabriels
91	Artesia	S of 405
118	Devonshire	W of 11
133	Laguna Cyn	Topanga Cyn
		to 405
		S of 133

Fort Tejon

2

2

2

Angeles Forest Hwy

Angeles Crest Hwy

Tujunga Cyn

Mt Wilson Forest Hwy

2

San Gabriel Cyn

San Antonio Cyn

2 210

134 134 210

Colorado

210

210

Base Line 30

30 Foothill

605

Garey

Central

Euclid

2

11 11

5

11 Huntington

11

7 7

10 10

10

10

57

71

10

60 60

605

60

57

60

71

5

605

Whittier

60

80

71

Hacienda

Century

Imperial Hwy

7

605

Imperial Hwy

90

57

Carbon Cyn

71

Atlantic

Artesia

5

91 91

91

605

91

91

91

90

90 91

91

7

Lincoln Hwy

57

55

405

Atlantic

Garfield

Lakewood

605

Katela

Beach

5

Santiago Cyn

47 7

405

22

22

22

5

55

1

Ocean

Pacific Coast Hwy 1

5

405

Beach

Brookhurst

Harbor

55

405

133

405

SNA

133

55

Macarthur 73

1

133

Laguna Cyn 133

Pacific Coast Hwy

1

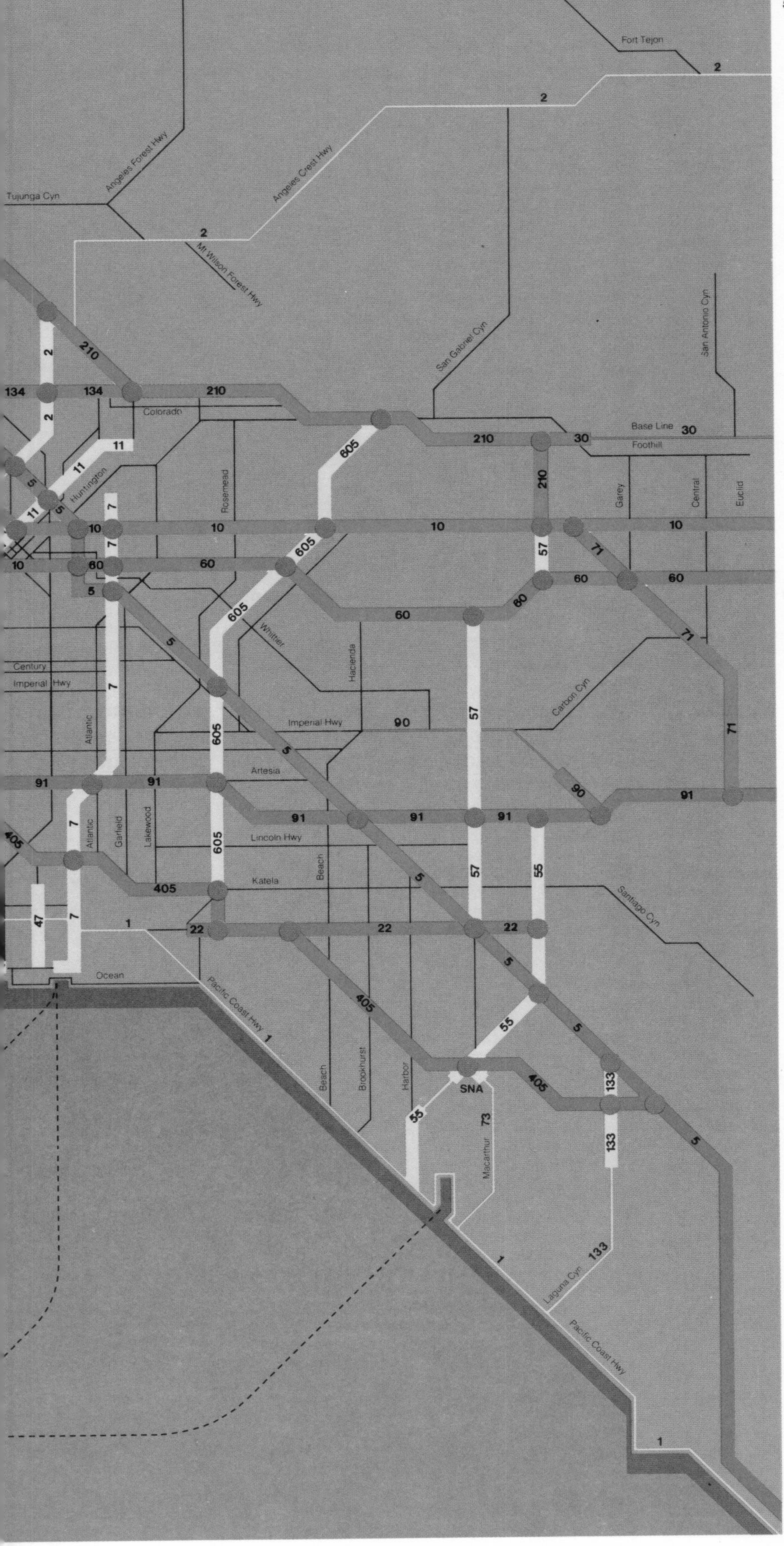

We have separated the complex and large Los Angeles downtown area into three more accessible subdivisions: Area 1—Civic Center; Area 2—Business and Financial; and Area 3—Commercial and Exposition Park-USC.

Each subdivision is organized as a tour of easy walks. For casual visitors and Angelenos alike, downtown is a center for daytime civic and commercial business. The streets are crowded and active by day, less so at night. Most stores close at the same evening hour office workers begin to head home. Over 210,000 workers commute to downtown everyday, and daily traffic is more than 350,000 cars. The resident population downtown has been steadily dwindling—from 23,000 in 1970 to 19,700 in 1977. Several major new developments are beginning to reverse this trend. Access to downtown is easy from the airport, with a bus service that circulates regularly to all major hotels. If you arrive by car it is best to park in your hotel garage or in one of the municipal garages such as City Hall Mall East or Pershing Square. Many garages close overnight; check with the attendant. Small orange and brown striped buses called *minibuses* are an excellent way to get around the central area during the day. They run along a simple loop through downtown. If you need to take a taxi, a dispatch call is recommended since cruising taxis are uncommon in Los Angeles.

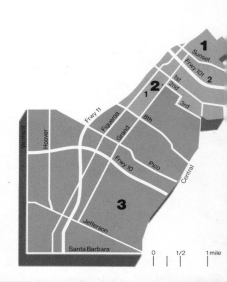

1   DOWNTOWN/CIVIC CENTER

Despite the myth that Los Angeles has no center, there has always been a downtown LA. Since the founding of the city on September 1781, the central urban core has remained close to its origin near Olvera Street. Within this small portion of downtown remains traces of all stages in the city's development.

Buildings from nearly every era in the past 200 years (from the oldest to one of the newest) demonstrate the long historical lineage evident in the neighborhood between Olvera Street and City Hall. The oldest area, dating back to the founding, is the Spanish. Los Angeles became a Mexican city in 1822 when Mexico won its independence from Spain. In 1850, the Stars and Stripes went up over Los Angeles, and a small stream of Yankee immigrants began arriving. When the railroad arrived in 1869, the trickle of immigrants became a torrent, upsetting the fragile balance of the small town's center. Newer immigrants clustered in settlements in the eastern portion of downtown; the established and more affluent natives began to shift their residences southwestward. Over the years, the constant influx of newcomers took its toll, and the neighborhood around City Hall became a civic embarrassment. Only gradually, beginning in the 1930s, did the community take steps toward redevelopment. The first priority was sprucing up the last vestige of the original Spanish pueblo, Olvera Street. Later the city created the Community Redevelopment Agency (CRA) to manage the downtown slum-clearance project, and, after 1949, it began to acquire properties for renovation and renewal. Three areas of cultural importance within Area 1 were singled out by the CRA: Little Tokyo, Chinatown, and El Pueblo de Los Angeles State Historic Park. Today a multitude of ethnic groups continue to be part of Los Angeles life and bring excitement and vitality not only to the Civic Center area but also to Los Angeles as a whole. The visitor can sample from Chinese, Korean, Japanese, Filipino, Mexican, and South American cultures within a few square miles.

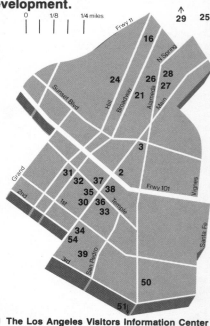

1 The Los Angeles Visitors Information Center is a valuable resource for tourists. Printed information on a number of Southern California attractions is available here, as well as a courteous and helpful staff who can answer questions. Travel counselors speak seven languages: English, French, German, Japanese, Spanish, Italian, and Portuguese. *M-F, 10AM-6PM; Sa, 11AM-5PM. ARCO Plaza, 505 S. Flower St. 628-3101*

HISTORICAL MEXICAN AREA. Los Angeles is home to one of the largest Spanish-speaking constituencies in the Western Hemisphere outside of Mexico City. In 1980, the city had an estimated 750,000 Hispanics, the largest minority group in Los Angeles. Within Los Angeles County are well over one million Hispanics. There are two areas of Latino activity downtown, one for the locals and one for the tourists. The tourists' center for traditional Mexican culture is Olvera Street in Area 1. The locals' center is Broadway in Area 3.

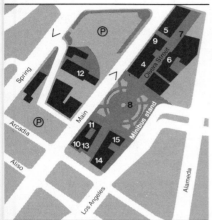

Olvera Street and El Pueblo de Los Angeles State Historical Park. Between Sunset Boulevard, Main Street, the Plaza, and Los Angeles Street. *Visitor Information Center: 130 Paseo del Plaza (next to Firehouse). 628-1274. Free guided tours begin from Visitor Center, Tu-Sa, 10AM, 12PM, and 1PM. Admission free.* The founding site of the City of Los Angeles, consisting of the Plaza, Olvera Street, and a number of historically and architecturally significant buildings. Olvera Street is named for Augustin Olvera, a Los Angeles County judge and supervisor. Rebuilt in 1930 as a re-creation of a typical Mexican marketplace, Olvera Street is a major attraction that has been described as the *first Disneyland*. The brick-paved block is lined with shops and *puestos* (stalls) which sell Mexican handicrafts and confections. You may purchase the candles you've seen dipped at shop 332 or the glass figurine you've seen formed in shop 61. Imported Mexican crafts are available in the various stalls. Food is served at a number of stands and cafes along the street.

La Luz del Dia. You can watch women skilled in the fast-disappearing art of making tortillas by hand. *Closed M. $. 624 N. Main Street.* For dessert, go to the Plaza where a fruit vendor sells peeled mangos, papayas, and other tropical fruit. The confectioners in the center of Olvera Street carry Mexican sweets, such as candied squash or brown sugar cones. Delicious Mexican donuts (*churros*) can be found at the bakery near the north center side of the street. Mariachis and dancers entertain while the audience enjoys Mexican dishes at **Casa La Golondrina**. *Closed W and Th. $$. 17 W. Olvera Street (in the cellar of the Pelanconi House). 628-4349*

Fandangos declared illegal without a license, except for weddings and national days.
1839

6 Avila Adobe. Built by Don Francisco Avila, one-time mayor of the pueblo. Once the town's poshest house, it is now the city's oldest adobe. Although portions of it are restored and reconstructed in concrete, the original 2½-foot thick walls date back to 1818. The simple one-story structure is of typical Mexican design, with a garden patio in the rear. On display inside are furnishings typical of an early California family of wealth, ca. 1840. *Open Tu-F, 10AM-3PM; Sa-Su, 10AM-4:30PM. Admission free. 10 Olvera St.*

7 Zanja Madre (Mother Ditch). The path of a triple row of bricks cutting diagonally through Olvera Street marks the Zanja Madre, the town's first water system, built in 1783 to carry water from the Los Angeles River near Elysian Park. Because the city's life has always depended on a reliable water-delivery system, this inconspicuous marker represents a major site in the history of Los Angeles.

5 Pelanconi House. One of the first brick buildings in Los Angeles. The two-story balconied structure was built as a residence with a large wine cellar. It is named for its second owner, Antonio Pelanconi. *17 W. Olvera St.*

On the southeastern end of Olvera Street is El Pueblo State Historic Park. Once the center of **8** pueblo life in the 1830-1840s, the **Plaza** and **9 Kiosko** today are the setting for several public festivals which bring back the spirit of the Mexican era. Most notable are Cinco de Mayo (May 5—a Mexican holiday), the Blessing of the Animals (the Saturday before Easter), and Las Posadas (during the week before Christmas). The Kiosko, a hexagonal band shell with filigreed grillwork, is the site of summer concerts.

9 Sepulveda House. Built by Eliosa Martinez de Sepulveda as a combined hotel and boarding house, circa 1887. Constructed in red brick, this two-story structure with upper bay windows is a rare example of a Victorian commercial structure. *624 N. Main St.*

10 Masonic Temple. The first lodge constructed in the city, built in 1858. It is a compact, two-story masonry structure with a cast iron balcony and three arched openings on each floor. Its design is derived from the Italian Renaissance. *Open W-F. 10AM-3PM. Admission free. 416 N. Main St.*

11 Pico House. Built in 1869 by Pio Pico, the last Mexican governor of California. The three-story Italian palazzi-styled structure attracted wealthy visitors to the city. During its heyday the Pico House was the finest hotel in California south of San Francisco. *424 N. Main St.*

Restaurants red
Architecture blue
Narrative/Museums/Shops black
Gardens/Parks/Piers green

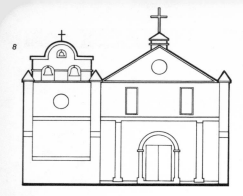

12 Plaza Church (Church of Our Lady the Queen of the Angels). Restored, enlarged, and remodeled several times, the Old Plaza Church was originally a simple adobe built by Franciscan padres and local Indians between 1818-1822. The first structure to be built in the pueblo was the jail and it was rushed to completion. However, it took the town 40 years to build the church. It is the oldest religious structure in Los Angeles. *Open 24 hours daily. 535 N. Main St.*

13 Merced Theatre. In 1870, architect Ezra Kysor designed this 400-seat auditorium as a more elaborate version of the Pico House next door. Originally, a covered portico greeted carriages in the front and the second-story theater connected with the Pico House. *420 N. Main St.*

14 Garnier Block. Built by Philippe Garnier in 1890 as commercial stores and apartments for the city's Chinese businessmen. It is constructed of buff brick with sandstone trim and has an unusual cornice of Victorian Romanesque design. *415 N. Los Angeles St.*

15 Old Plaza Firehouse. A simple, Victorian brick structure built in 1884. The castle-like roof line gives the building a defensive character. It is now a museum containing early fire-fighting equipment and photographs of l9th-century fire stations. *Open daily, M-F, 10AM-3PM; Sa-Su, 10AM-4:30PM. Admission free*

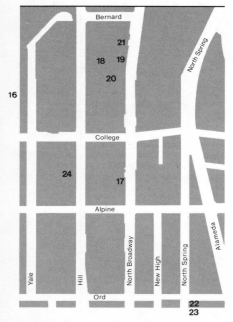

16 NEW CHINATOWN: Centered on 700-1000 N. Broadway in an area roughly bordered by Ord, Alameda, Bernard and Yale Streets. The Chinese community in Los Angeles dates back to the Gold Rush. The community of two Chinese living in Los Angeles in 1850 had increased to 2,000 by 1900. About 15,000 people now live in Chinatown, and the area is the cultural center for over 150,000 Chinese-Americans living in the Southland.

Chinese New Year is celebrated in this part of the city with parades, beauty pageants, and lots of holiday food. The date varies from year to year as the Chinese follow a lunar calendar, but New Year usually falls in February or March. The original settlement on Alameda was moved northwest in the 1930s because of the construction of Union Station. Civic leaders saw the tourist potential in a *New Chinatown*; in 1938 the theme buildings on the 900 block of North Broadway were constructed. The entrance gate has an inscription on the back side with a dedication to the mother of one of the architects. All of the buildings in the complex are romanticized Chinese designs with exaggerated curving roof lines and abundant ornament. In addition to its tourist charms, the area functions as a major provisioning center for the Chinese community. A visit to a Chinatown market can become a game of *animal, mineral or vegetable?* Chickens squawk, ducks quack, fish swim—you know the food is fresh. Gift shops sell everything from the real Hong Kong to the really fine. Try: **Sam Ward Co.,** *959 N. Hill St.,* for chinaware; **Fong's,** *939-43 Chung King Rd.,* for art; **Sule One Co.,** *122 Ord St.,* for fine antiques and furniture; **Jin Hing & Co.,** *412 Bamboo Lane,* for jade; **Sincere Importing,** *483 Gin Ling Way,* for baskets.

Restaurants? If it's true that an hour later you're hungry, consider it a blessing—it gives you a chance to have another superb meal.
17 Possibilities are: **Green Jade,** *747 N.*
18 *Broadway;* **General Lee's,** *475 Gin Ling Way;*
19 **The Mandarin,** *970 N. Broadway;* **Grand Star,**
21 *943 Sun Mun Way;* **Hunan,** *980 N. Broadway.*

22 Mon Kee. ☆ ☆ Even without linen tablecloths or high prices, this is considered among the very best seafood restaurants in LA. It is certainly the only seafood restaurant, Chinese or otherwise, where most of what you eat is swimming around in giant tanks minutes before it is placed before you. Bring your own wine and expect to wait. *Lunch and dinner daily. $$. 679 N. Spring St. 628-6717*

23 Young Sing. Down the block from Mon Kee, with the same tank-fresh seafood. It lacks the reputation of Mon Kee, but then again, it also lacks the crowds. *Lunch and dinner daily. $$. 643 N. Spring St. 623-1724*

24 Miriwa specializes in tea cakes (*dim sum*) for lunch. They are wheeled by your table on carts; stop the waiter, point to your choices, and pay by the number of empty dishes at the end. Turn the lid of your tea pot upside down to indicate that you've run dry and need more. *750 N. Hill St.*

25 San Antonio Winery. Another look at the city's past. A working winery in an old industrial section of town. The three-acre site includes tasting rooms and a restaurant. Self-guided tours include the original buildings made from wooden boxcars in 1917. Food as well as wine is on the menu at the restaurant, with Italian sandwiches the specialty. *Open daily. $. 737 Lamar St. 223-1401*

26 Philippe's Original Sandwich Shop. Across the street from Terminal Annex. Legend has it that the French-dip sandwich was invented here in 1908. Since then, the faithful come for simple honest food and 10-cent coffee. The crowd, waiting for a seat at the linoleum-topped tables on the sawdusted floor, is a cross section of LA society from ballplayers to stockbrokers. (Be sure to have your sandwich double-dipped.) *Open daily, 6AM-10PM. $. 1001 N. Alameda St. 628-3781*

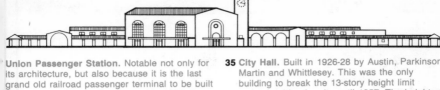

Union Passenger Station. Notable not only for its architecture, but also because it is the last grand old railroad passenger terminal to be built in the United States. Constructed in 1939, the structure was built by the Southern Pacific, Union Pacific, and Santa Fe Railroads. The design by John and Donald Parkinson is an interpretation of Spanish Mission architecture that combines enormous scale with Moderne and Moorish details. The wood-beamed ceiling of the waiting room is 52 feet high, the floors are of marble, and deep-scalloped archways lead to two outside patios that are brilliant with the colors of California flowers and foliage. Currently the terminal is being developed by the city and state as a major regional transportation center. *800 N. Alameda St. 683-6873*

Main Post Office (Terminal Annex). The main mail distribution center for Los Angeles. Inside the building are 1930s Works Progress Administration (WPA) murals by Boris Deutsch depicting the history of communication. *Windows open M-F, 8AM-4PM. Building, mail drops, and stamp-vending machines open daily, 24 hours.*

Woman's Building. Imaginative remodeling changed the three-story brick warehouse into a gallery. Featured are exhibitions of feminist art, as well as a print workshop, classes, lectures, and public seminars. *Hours vary—call before visiting. Admission fee. 1700 N. Spring St. 221-6161*

THE CIVIC CENTER. Bounded by Temple, Main, First, and Spring Streets. The number of buildings clustered in the area make it the largest governmental center in the United States next to Washington, D.C. The large scale of the architecture makes it an impressive civic complex.

1 Hall of Records. Designed in 1961 by architect Richard Neutra. *227 N. Broadway. 974-6616*

2 Criminal Courts Building. Home of the Municipal Court of the Los Angeles Judicial District, County of Los Angeles and State of California. It was designed in 1925 by the Allied Architects of Los Angeles. *210 W. Temple. 972-6111*

3 Parker Center. Named for a former chief of police, William Parker, it is the headquarters of the Los Angeles Police Department. The center was built in 1955. *150 N. Los Angeles St. 485-2121*

4 Los Angeles Times. Designed in 1935 by Gordon Kaufmann. The beige limestone and bronze grillwork of the original Moderne building intermesh with the bronze steel and glass addition of 1974 by William Pereira and Associates. A free tour is offered that allows you to see the making of the newspaper from press room to printing. *Tours: M-F at 3PM; admission free; children must be 10 and over; meet guide at the First St. entrance. 202 W. First St. 972-5000*

7 Federal Courthouse Building. Home of the United States District Court. The WPA-style structure was designed in 1940 by G. Stanley Underwood. *312 N. Spring St. 688-2000*

Restaurants red
Architecture blue
Narrative/Museums/Shops black
Gardens/Parks/Piers green

---

35 City Hall. Built in 1926-28 by Austin, Parkinson, Martin and Whittlesey. This was the only building to break the 13-story height limit maintained by the city until 1957. The height of the 27-story structure was made possible by public vote. The monumental building presents an image befitting a major metropolitan center. Although the stepped, pyramidal tower incoporates Greek, Roman, and Renaissance design elements, the total outcome is purely American. Inside, luxurious marble columns and an inlaid-tile dome lend an almost religious effect to the entrance rotunda. An observation deck, located on the 27th floor, affords a splendid view. A 45-minute escorted tour gives a capsule history of Los Angeles and California. *Tours by reservation only; call 485-4423 at least two days in advance. Tours given M-F, 10-11AM. Observation deck open M-F, 8AM-5PM. Tours and deck free. 200 N. Spring St.*

36 Los Angeles Mall. Built by architects Stanton and Stockwell in 1973-75, the well-landscaped multi-level mall has four underground parking levels, a ground plaza housing shops and restaurants, and a pedestrian crossing bridge above Temple Street. *Main St. between First and Temple Sts.*

38 Children's Museum. A touch and play museum designed especially for children. Exhibits on such topics as the city's streets, crafts of the past, and a kid's television station encourage participation. Classes and workshops are regularly scheduled; call the museum for current availability. *Open W, 2:30-4:30PM; Sa-Su, 10AM-4:30PM; hours extended during school vacation periods. Admission fee. 310 N. Main St. (Los Angeles Mall, street-level.) 687-8800*

39 LITTLE TOKYO. Centered around First Street from Main to Alameda Streets, Little Tokyo, just east of the Civic Center, is the heart of Southern California's Japanese-American community of over 110,000. First settled 100 years ago, the community began to flourish after World War I, but was devastated by the forced evacuation of Japanese-Americans from the Pacific Coast during World War II. Little Tokyo has emerged in the past decade as an active and cohesive area. The district is a mix of late 19th-century commercial buildings and modern structures. Nisei Week, held in August, is a major community event, with a parade, street decorations, festival food, and public demonstrations of such Japanese arts as flower arranging, sumi brush painting, and the tea ceremony.

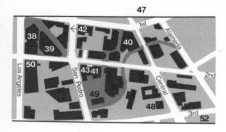

The vigorous redevelopment of the community
40 is exemplified by the **New Otani Hotel.**
Designed by Kajima and Associates and
opened in 1977, the hotel features both
American and Japanese style rooms. A
shopping arcade carries luxury goods. Try the
Kinokuniya Bookstore for books on Japanese
culture. Marukyo carries textiles, kimonos, and
futons. In the center of the main lobby is the
40 Canary Garden, a pleasant luncheon spot.
special feature is a roof-top garden on the fifth
level, where you can stroll through a gradually
maturing Japanese garden. The Genji Bar at
this level is a lovely place to watch twilight
40 deepen. **A Thousand Cranes,** ☆ the hotel's
luxury restaurant, has individual rooms for sushi,
tempura, and teppan grill. *Japanese. Open
daily. $$$. First and Los Angeles Sts. 629-1200*

41 Oiwake. The sushi bar is like many others in
Little Tokyo. But it is the only restaurant with
live *minyo*—Japanese country and western
music. Customers are welcome to come up on
stage and sing along with the band, which
colors its songs with every instrument from
Chinese bells to marracas. *Dinner Tu-Su. Shows
weekends only. $$. 511 E. First St. 628-2678*

42 Weller Court, at the corner of Weller and
Second Streets, is a recently completed
shopping and dining arcade. The major tenant
is Matsuzakaya, a branch of Japan's oldest and
largest department store.

43 Japanese Village Plaza Mall, has a rural
feeling created by using inset stone paths and
ponds. The design, by David Hyun Associates,
completed in 1979, utilizes white stucco with
exposed wood framing to set off the blue
sanchu tile roofs. The complex is identified by
its fire tower, a traditional fireman's lookout that
faces First Street. *The mall is bounded by First
and Second Sts. and Central Ave. For
information call 620-8861*

43 Mitsuru Children's Shop brings Japanese
monster movies to life with battery-operated
creatures that shoot missiles from their hands
to the great delight of children. *107 Japanese
Village Plaza Mall.*

43 Sumida Gallery specializes in contemporary
and antique prints and artifacts. *129 Japanese
Village Plaza Mall*

44 Rafu Bussan, across the street, carries an
unusually large selection of laquer-ware and
ceramics. *326 E. Second St.*

Eating in Little Tokyo ranges from simple to
elegant. Moderately-priced restaurants usually
have plastic models of the dishes they serve in
the window. If your tongue fails you, take the
waiter outside and point. The recent Southern
California sushi craze started here; to
understand sushi's popularity as both cuisine
and entertainment, a visit to some sushi bars is
recommended. Private tatami rooms, where you
sit on the floor and dine Japanese style, are
available by reservation in many restaurants.

45 Horikawa. ☆ One of the largest dining spots in
the area and one of the finest in the city,
featuring five different rooms for specialities.
*Open daily. No lunch Sa, Su. $$$. 111 S. San
Pedro. 680-9355*

46 Tokyo Kaikan. A re-creation of an old
Japanese inn. Excellent sushi bar and teppan
bar. *Lunch 11:30AM-2PM, dinner 5PM-10PM.
Closed Su. No Lunch Sa. $$. 225 S. San Pedro.
489-1333*

43 Naniwa Sushi Restaurant. One of the better
sushi bars in the area; the dining room serves
other Japanese dishes. *Open 7 days. $$.
137 Japanese Village Plaza Mall. 623-3661*

Two nearby Buddhist temples are of
architectural interest:

47 Nishi Hongwangji Buddhist Temple. A 1925
structure. It is a unique combination of modern
construction and traditional Japanese forms.
The fine torii canopy above the entrance is
made of concrete rather than the customary
wood. *119 N. Central Ave.*

48 Higashi Hongwangji Buddhist Temple. A
traditional structure, designed by Kajima
Associates for the Jodo Shinshu Sect. A broad
flight of stairs leads to the entrance; the
dominant blue-tile roof is protected by two
golden dragons. *505 E. Third St. 626-4200*

**49 The Japanese American Cultural and
Community Center** offers regularly changing
exhibitions in the gallery of the recently opened
building. The schedule also includes classes in
Japanese culture, senior-citizen group meetings,
and other activities of interest to the community.
The James Irvine Garden, beside the building,
is a spot for meditation and refreshment. *The
gates are usually closed, but you may obtain
access by phoning 628-2725 or stopping by
Room 503 in the Cultural Center. The garden
was designed and planted by volunteers with
materials donated by gardeners, nurseries and
landscapers. 244 S. San Pedro. 628-2725*

DOWNTOWN ART. Low rents and large spaces
in previously unused buildings recently have
attracted a number of artists to downtown. The
current situation is in transition; a number of
small galleries have opened and closed. Check
with the established places listed here for
current viewing information.

50 Los Angeles Institute of Contemporary Art.
A new branch of the main LAICA (located at
2020 S. Robertson Blvd.) This alternative space
shows contemporary art in all mediums.
Performance and music events are sometimes
offered in the evenings. *M-F, 12-4PM.
Admission free. 815 Traction Ave. 680-1427*

51 Cirrus Gallery. A commercial gallery that
features fine contemporary work. Cirrus
Editions, located at the same address, is a
major publisher of fine-art prints by Southern
California artists. *Tu-F, 11AM-5PM; Sa, 12-4PM.
542 S. Alameda Ave. 680-3473*

51 Lowinsky and Arai Gallery. A gallery
specializing in contemporary and vintage
photography. *Tu-Sa, 12-5PM. 542 S. Alameda.
687-8943*

52 Banyan Gallery. Located in a remodeled brick
warehouse. Two galleries display contemporary
and traditional textiles and folk art. *W-Su,
12-6PM. 319 S. Towne Ave. 680-4368*

53 Mizuno Gallery. Work by major contemporary
artists. *Tu-Sa, 12-6PM. 210 E. Second St.
625-2491*

Restaurants red
Architecture blue

St. Vibiana's Cathedral. Designed in 1876 by Ezra F. Kysor, architect of the Pico House and Merced Theatre. Modeled after a Spanish Baroque church in Barcelona, the facade's classical pilasters and volutes are crowned with a tower and cupola. Inside, relics of the Early Christian martyr, St. Vibiana, are preserved in a marble sarcophagus.

DOWNTOWN MINIBUS: Maximum access at a mini price. 25 cents buys you transportation to Olvera Street, Little Tokyo, Chinatown, City Hall, the World Trade Center, ARCO Plaza, and many other downtown points of interest. Watch for buses every 10 minutes or less during the day. Board where you see signs showing the line 202 route.

DOWNTOWN/BUSINESS AND FINANCIAL   2

Sometimes called the new *Gold Coast* of Los Angeles, this area is the high-rise pride of the Los Angeles urban renaissance. From the Music Center to the City's tallest buildings, Area 2 contains the newest and biggest category of LA landmarks.

And it isn't finished yet. Work will soon begin on an elaborate high-rise development now known as *California Center.* The center will house major shopping, business, residence, hotel, and theater facilities, and a new museum of modern art on the site bounded by Grand Avenue, Fourth, Hill, Olive, and upper Second streets. It is scheduled for completion in 1989 and will finish the redevelopment of Bunker Hill.

Prior to the turn of the century, Bunker Hill was the most desirable residential neighborhood in the city, its Victorian gingerbread mansions looking down on what was then the city's business district. Over the years the neighborhood fell into disrepair. In the late 1950s, the dilapidated Victorian structures, many of which had been converted into seedy boarding houses, were demolished, and the top of the hill was leveled. The resulting open space, plus the elimination in 1957 of the 13-story height limitation on buildings, enticed several major corporations to locate their new headquarters on Bunker Hill, thus giving the western portion of downtown Los Angeles a skyscraper skyline.

Flower Street is the main avenue within Area 2; since 1970, it has been the center of the city's banking and financial trade. The local financial-building boom is shaped by two factors: the widespread popularity of branch banking in Southern California, and the emergence of Los Angeles as the West Coast business channel to the Orient. Not only are there at least 120 different banks in Los Angeles and Orange Counties, but there are over 800 branch offices in Los Angeles alone. Of the six largest banks in California, four have built high-rise headquarters, while the other two maintain their Southern California headquarters here. The Southland ranks third nationally in total bank deposits.

This flourishing bank business in Southern California is paralleled by the steady growth of investment interchange between Los Angeles and what is known as the Pacific Rim Community. A number of buildings downtown have been purchased by foreign investors, and it is not unusual to see local companies listing branch offices in Tokyo, Hong Kong, and Singapore.

Narrative/Museums/Shops black
Gardens/Parks/Piers green

1 THE MUSIC CENTER. The main location for theater and concerts in the downtown area. The three-building complex, designed by Welton Becket and Associates and finished in 1969, sits on a broad plaza centered by a reflecting pool with a sculpture by Jacques Lipchitz. The Academy Awards ceremony is held at the Music Center every April; bleachers are set up in the center plaza for fans.

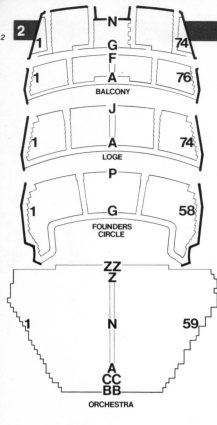

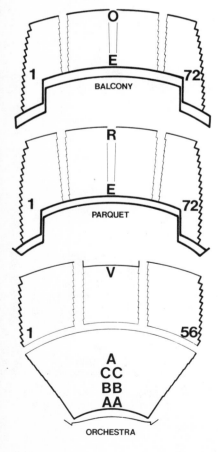

2 Dorothy Chandler Pavilion. (Seats 3250). Named after the wife of the late Los Angeles Times publisher, Dorothy Chandler spearheaded the effort to give Los Angeles a proper cultural forum. The Los Angeles Philharmonic Orchestra season is held in the Pavilion from September to June. Music Center of Los Angeles County. *135 N. Grand Ave. 972-7211*

3 Ahmanson Theatre (Seats 2100). The Ahmanson Theatre, at the north of the complex, offers musical comedy and drama. With the Pavilion, it houses the Los Angeles Civic Light Opera and various special concerts. Music Center of Los Angeles County. *135 N. Grand Ave. 972-7211*

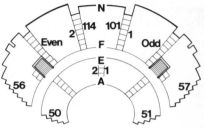

4 Mark Taper Forum. (Seats 750). The Mark Taper Forum is the most intimate of the three halls, featuring contemporary drama and chamber music in an acoustically excellent theater-in-the-round setting. The Ahmanson and the Taper are the homes of the Centre Theatre Group, a widely respected repertory company.

Preconcert dining is emphasized by several
5 downtown restaurants. **Francois, in the ARCO Plaza,** *505 S. Flower St., 680-2727,* offers a
6 theater-goer's special, as does **Bernard's** at the Biltmore Hotel, *515 S. Olive St., 624-0183.*
7 **The Birch Tree,** *445 S. Figueroa, 620-0567,* has free parking and a bus to the Music
8 Center, as does **Crossroads**, located in the *World Trade Center, 350 S. Figueroa, 629-4124.*
5 Within the Music Center complex, the **Hungry Tiger**, located on the *first floor of the Pavilion*, offers moderately-priced fare in a modern
5 atmosphere. At the top, the **Pavilion Restaurant**, *972-7333,* offers elegant dining among crystal chandeliers and quartz columns. The gourmet buffet is beautiful and delicious.

9 Department of Water and Power Building. Across from the Music Center, the headquarters for the largest utility in the United States. Designed by A.C. Martin in 1964, the glass and steel building is an elegant stack of horizontal levels. It is especially attractive when seen aglow at night, a luminous beacon for the area. The surrounding moat is not only beautiful, but also serves as a heat sink for the building's air-conditioning system. *111 N. Hope St.*

10 Bunker Hill Towers. Fine residential living has been provided by the three high-rise towers designed by Robert Alexander in 1968. These were the first residential structures on redeveloped Bunker Hill. *800 W. First St. (bounded by First, Second, and Figueroa Sts.)*

8 World Trade Center. Pedestrian bridges link it to the Bonaventure Hotel and the Bunker Hill Towers. Built in 1974-77, the center is international in its shopping range and provides a convenient location to exchange foreign currency or to apply for a U.S. passport. *333 S. Flower St.*

Dorothy Chandler Pavilion inaugurated.
1964

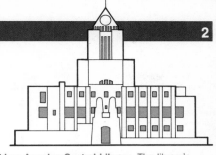

Security Pacific National Bank Headquarters Building and Plaza. The well detailed, 55-story tower was designed by the A.C. Martin firm in 1974. The northern end of the main lobby is the site of art exhibitions which usually feature group shows. Be sure to take a look at the large red stabile sculpture by Alexander Calder on the Hope Street side of the building. *Gallery Hours: M-Sa, 10AM-4PM. 333 S. Hope St.*

Atlantic Richfield Tower and Bank of America Tower. Twin 52-story charcoal granite sheathed towers designed by A.C. Martin and completed in 1972. At the rear of the southern side of the Atlantic Richfield Tower, two 20-foot-high art deco bronze doors, which were formerly in the old Richfield Building, have been installed.

ARCO Plaza. Located beneath the towers. Escalators at Fifth and Flower and Sixth and Flower lead to seven acres of subterranean shopping and dining. The interior is finished in richly colored tile; a glass stairway connects B level with the center of C level where exhibitions and demonstrations are held. Among the shops are Gary's, a fine men's clothier; Joel's, for fashionable moderately-priced women's wear; the Upstairs Gallery, a commercial art gallery; and B. Dalton Booksellers.

Los Angeles Visitors Information Center, mentioned in the Downtown Introduction, offers advice, free maps and brochures, and emergency assistance for visitors. The **RTD Center** gives information about the Los Angeles bus lines and sells bus passes.

Among the restaurants in the Plaza are:
O'Shaughnessy's. A stone-walled castle on C level serving steaks and hearty food. The bar here is a favorite with downtown workers. *Closed Sa-Su. $$. 629-2565*

Francois. A beautiful Belle Epoque style dining room where solicitous service and fine French cuisine create an atmosphere of refinement. *Closed Sa-Su. $$$. 680-2727*

ARCO Center for Visual Art. A non-profit gallery sponsored as a public service by Atlantic Richfield Company. Exhibitions of contemporary art in all mediums are offered in two galleries. *M-F, 10AM-6PM; Sa, 11AM-5PM. Admission free. 488-0038*

Upstairs, in the center of the **Plaza,** is the red helical sculpture by Herbert Bayer entitled **Double Ascension.** *The Plaza is open M-F, 9AM-6PM; Sa, 11AM-5PM. 505 S. Flower St. 625-2132*

3 The California Club. Next to the library is the roof-terraced Renaissance-style private club built in 1928-29 by architect Robert Farquhar. Members only.

4 Rainbow Hotel. A moderately-priced hotel recommended to those on a budget. *536 S. Hope St. 627-9941*

5 Linder Plaza is a 15-story building and plaza distinctively separated from neighboring buildings by its flat grey metallic surface and curved corner meant to create the image of an aircraft wing. *888 W. Sixth St.*

Funicular railway from 3rd & Hill up to Bunker Hill opens. Price for a ride on the Angel's Flight? 1 cent.
1901

Restaurants red
Architecture blue
Narrative/Museums/Shops black
Gardens/Parks/Piers green

12 Los Angeles Central Library. The library's multicolored tiled pyramid peak makes it an easily spotted landmark. It is a mixture of Byzantine, Egyptian, Roman, and other styles typical of the exotic tastes of the period. Designed by Bertram Goodhue and Carleton Winslow, Sr. in 1925, it is a city and national landmark. Inside are many decorative works of art including murals in the children's wing by N.C. Wyeth. *Closed Su. Open M-Th, 10AM-8PM; F-Sa, 10AM-5:30PM. 630 W. Fifth St. 626-7461*

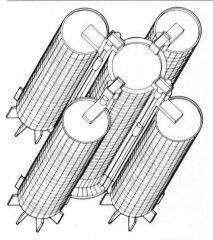

16 Bonaventure Hotel. The five mirrored-glass cylinders of this futuristic hotel make it the most eye-catching of the new downtown high-rises. Designed by John Portman and opened in 1978, the silvery silos contain luxury rooms and suites. The hotel lobby is located in the square base of the building, which may be entered from either Flower Steet or Figueroa Street. It is ringed by circular reflecting pools, glass-walled elevators, and winding staircases. Eight levels of arcades containing shops and several restaurants ascend on the inside. The circular structure, dazzling glass core, shimmering water, and overhead skylight make the interior kaleidoscopic. The Bonaventure is one of the most stunning buildings in the city. *404 S. Figueroa St. 624-1000*

The restaurants of the Bonaventure are: **Top Of Five.** A luxurious seat from which to enjoy the 360-degree panorama of Los Angeles as the floor revolves. The location on the 35th floor insures that, on a clear day, you will see all the way to the ocean. *Continental. Open daily. $$/$$$*
34th Lounge. A cocktail lounge located on the 34th floor which offers the same stunning view as it revolves.
Beaudry's. Better than usual hotel dining in elegant surroundings. *Continental. Open daily. $$$/$$$$*
Plaza Express. Located on the fifth floor, this deli serves interesting hot and cold sandwiches and entrees. *American. Open daily. $*
Inagiku. ☆ An elegant Japanese restaurant which specializes in tempura, as well as offering a teppan grill and handsome sushi bar. Tatami rooms are available by reservation. *Open daily. $$/$$$. 8th Floor. 614-0820*

17 Mayflower Hotel. A medium-priced hotel that is popular with Japanese and European visitors. There is a 24-hour coffee shop on the first floor. *535 S. Grand Ave. 624-1331*

18 United California Bank. The tallest building in Los Angeles is this 62-story steel and glass tower designed by Charles Luckman and Associates in 1973. *707 Wilshire Blvd.*

19 Caravan Book Store. A fine antiquarian bookseller. *550 S. Grand Ave. 626-9944*

20 Casey's Bar. Simple fare served in a setting of white-tile floors, dark paneling, and tin ceilings. This is the most popular after-work meeting place for young downtown workers. On Friday nights a band plays dance music; Tuesday through Thursday there is ragtime piano music. *American. Closed Su. Lunch only, Sa. $/$$. 613 S. Grand Ave. 629-2353*

21 The Broadway Plaza and Hyatt Regency Hotel. The double, 32-story glass towers of the Hyatt Regency Hotel on the east and office building on the west sit atop the brick base of the Broadway Plaza shopping mall. Shops are reached from Seventh Street via a high, skylit central atrium with tiled pool. Inside are over 30 stores including: The Broadway, a major department store; Silverwoods, a fine men's clothing store; Judy's and Joseph Magnin's, stores catering to the chic young woman; Radio Shack, for electronic gear, and Waldenbooks. *700 W. Seventh St.*

Angel's Flight. A revolving restaurant that offers fine food with a fabulous view. *Open 7 days. No lunch, Sa-S. $$. 683-1234*

Hyatt Regency. A luxury hotel located in one of the towers. All rooms feature city views and tasteful decor. *711 S. Hope St. 683-1234*

21 Pavan. ☆ Hyatt's attempt to bring chic, up-town dining to their downtown hotel. The modern deco peach and mauve room soothes the eye. So does the *nouvelle cuisine*, although it does not always please the palate. *Closed Sunday. M-Sa, lunch 11:30AM-2PM, dinner 6-10PM. Reservations necessary. Gentlemen requested to wear jackets. $$$$. 711 S. Hope St. 683-1234*

21 Pasquini's Expresso Bar. A sunlit, walk-down cafe. Tasty antipasto and pasta are served from the counter at lunchtime. *Italian. Closed Sa-Su. Breakfast and lunch only. 701-1/2 W. Seventh St. 628-5261*

22 Clifton's Silver Spoon Cafeteria. Occupying a turn-of-the-century building that once housed downtown's most prestigious jeweler, Clifton's manages the seemingly impossible: it is an elegant cafeteria. The basement Soup Kitchen serves inventive soups and salads. Also in the basement is the Meditation Room which offers food for thought. *American. Closed Sa-Su. Breakfast and lunch only. $. 515 W. Seventh St. 485-1726*

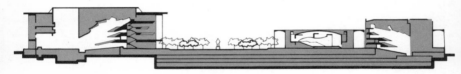

Music Center. See Area 2 for phone number and information.

Left: **Dorothy Chandler Pavilion** *Center:* **Mark Taper Forum** *Right:* **Ahmanson Theater**

3 DOWNTOWN/COMMERCIAL AND EXPOSITION PARK

The meeting place of industry, education, and culture, Area 3 has an intriguing complexity. The northern portion of the section is a mixture of shops and hotels; the eastern part has commercial, wholesale, manufacturing, and distribution sites, while in the south, Exposition Park and the University of Southern California provide a green oasis in a prevailing landscape of treeless commercial streets and vintage but dilapidated housing.

As with any region of such varied uses, the population composition is diverse and changes according to the time of day. Most of the area around Pershing Square is active during regular business hours, but almost deserted at night. Near the Coliseum and Shrine Auditorium, nighttime traffic jams often occur due to the confluence of football and concert fans. The streets of the wholesale distribution centers are quiet until after midnight, then hundreds of trucks fill the roadways. And in the early dawn hours, movie crews are likely to be anywhere downtown, filming on the deserted streets. If you feel you've seen this part of downtown before, you're probably right—it is a favorite location for film and TV production crews.

Restaurants red
Architecture blue

The Biltmore Hotel. Dramatically reflects a rich blending of classical architecture with contemporary luxury. Designed in the style of the Spanish Italian Renaissance era by architects Schultze and Weaver, the Biltmore opened in 1923 to national acclaim, and was designated a Historical Cultural Landmark in 1969 by the Los Angeles Cultural Heritage Board. Today, restored beyond its initial elegance and grandeur by architect/owner Gene Summers, the Biltmore has integrated the original elaborate art and architecture with contemporary art forms, (a Jim Dine repository) furnishings, and designs, creating a single aesthetic from two chronologically diverse styles. Perhaps the best services available at any hotel (at a premium price) can be found on the Biltmore Club Floor.

Within the hotel are:

Bernard's. ☆ ☆ ☆ One of the finest restaurants in the city. The dramatically lit paneled interior, exquisite table appointments, and solicitous service befit the elegant *nouvelle cuisine* menu. *Closed Su, no lunch Sa. $$$/$$$$. 515 S. Olive St. 624-1011*

Grand Avenue Bar. ☆ Midst marble tables from Italy, Mies van der Rohe chairs in plum velvet, exotic plants and works of art that change seasonally, there is a uniquely designed bar that serves vintage wines by the glass. An exquisite and reasonably priced cold buffet luncheon M-F, evening hors d'oeuvre menu. *Closed Sa-Su. $$$. 624-1011*

Pershing Square. In 1866, five acres of the original pueblo land grant were set aside for a public space. The new square replaced the older plaza near Olvera Street in popularity as it recognized the population shift toward the southwest. In 1918, the square was renamed for Gen. John J. Pershing. Today, extensive paving and light landscaping top several levels of underground parking. *Bounded by Olive, Fifth, Hill, and Sixth Sts.*

LACE. Los Angeles Contemporary Exhibitions. *Eat Your Heart Out*, an annual St. Valentine's extravaganza was founded by this downtown art space which provides diverse gallery and community art programs. Significant film, video and audio pieces; performance, music and installation pieces as well as sculpture, drawings, and paintings by emerging and well-known regional and non-regional artists have been presented since 1977. The artist-based organization also has a slide registry for downtown artists and an art periodical library for the public. *Open M-Sa, 11AM-5PM; Su 1PM-5PM. Third floor, 204 S. Broadway. 620-0104*

City renames Central Park "Pershing Square" in honor of Armistice.
1918

Narrative/Museums/Shops black
Gardens/Parks/Piers green

4 Bradbury Building. Acclaimed as one of the most significant buildings in Los Angeles' architectural heritage. In 1893, architectural draftsman George Herbert Wyman was given the commission for this extraordinary work. A message from his dead brother received via a ouija board encouraged him to take the job. Externally, the five-story buff brick office building is inconspicuous. Inside, under the glass skylight, the open court is awe-inspiring. Wood paneling, dark foliate grillwork, winding open stairs and open-cage elevators, marble, and brickwork are all accentuated by the filtered light. *Open to the public M-Sa. Admission fee. 304 S. Broadway.*

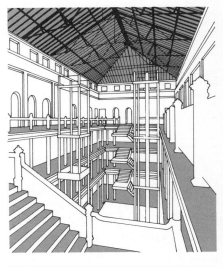

5 Grand Central Public Market. An indoor bazaar that extends from Broadway to Hill Street. A favorite with budget-conscious shoppers and recent immigrants to the Los Angeles area, it is crowded (over 30,000 people a day pass through), frenzied, and picturesque. The stalls sell all types of food, and ready-made Mexican specialities are available for on-premises eating. Plastic wrap doesn't exist in Grand Central; butchers use waxed paper, fruit and vegetable vendors select your produce from beautiful piles (don't help yourself here) and brown bag it. If you're hungry, try a taco or lamb sandwich at stall 43. Thirsty? The juice bar on the Hill Street side has 75 possibilities to choose from. If you're really overwhelmed, have your blood pressure checked at the Health Food counter. *Open M-Sa, 9AM-6PM. 317 S. Broadway. 624-2378*

6 Al Carbon Restaurant. Just south of the market. You're given meat and a tortilla at one end of the counter; choose the sauce from an array at the other end. *343 S. Hill St.*

7 Oviatt Building. Designed in 1927 by architects Walker and Eisen as the most prestigious men's store in the downtown area. The combination of Lalique glass, silver and gold grillwork, and zigzag decorative paving creates a shimmering effect of glamor and delicacy. It is currently a brightly restored office building. *617 S. Olive St.*

7 Rex. ☆ ☆ ☆ This grand Italian restaurant done in authentic Art Deco detail in the authentically Art Deco Oviatt Building is one of the most dramatically beautiful restaurants in the country. With his *nuova cucina*, restaurateur Mauro Vincenti has succeeded in modernizing Italian cuisine, just as the French modernized haute cuisine with *nouvelle*. Be sure to have a dance upstairs on the black marble dance floor in the bar. *Italian. Lunch M-F. Dinner M-Sa. $$$$. 617 S. Olive St. 627-2300*

Broadway has become the main shopping street for the LA Hispanic community. Latin music livens the atmosphere, and bustling, Spanish-speaking crowds make this one of the most intensely urban-feeling areas in town.

8 BROADWAY. In the early 1920s, the Pantages and Orpheum circuits made the decision to open their new theaters for moving pictures on Broadway. A number of theaters from that era still remain, most still showing films (although they are usually 7th or 8th run); many will allow you to peek into or enter the lobby. A full palette of architectural styles ranging from ersatz French Renaissance to pseudo-Mayan awaits you. The **Million Dollar Theater** opened in 1917 (Baroque); the **Arcade Theatre** opened in 1910 (English music-hall motif); the **Cameo Theatre**, opened in 1910, is the best remaining example of a nickelodeon; the **Los Angeles Theatre** opened in 1931 (*French Renaissance with a fervor*); the **Palace Theatre** opened in 1910 (Hollywood Rococo); the **Tower Theatre** was opened in 1927 as the first theater built for talkies. The interior is a replica of the lobby of the Paris Opera. The **Orpheum** opened in 1925 (Louis XIII Baroque). *Broadway between Third and Eighth Sts.*

The Eastern Columbia Building is a 13-story tower of turquoise terra-cotta with dark blue and gold trim. Designed in 1930, it is ornamented by an angular zigzag Moderne motif with a medieval twist. *849 S. Broadway*

9 The Broadway Arcade Building creates an enormous skylit space between Broadway and Spring Street. The Spanish Renaissance block and arcade serve to unify the commercial, entertainment, and financial districts of the area. *542 S. Broadway*

9 The Alexandria Hotel was built in 1906 by John Parkinson as the largest and finest hotel in the city. The **Palm Court**, with its enormous stained-glass ceiling, is cited as a City Monument because it recalls the hotel's past glory when it was a haven for celebrities and notables. *501 S. Spring St.*

9 Irwin's. Classic American fare the way it was meant to be served—casual atmosphere, quality food. Hefty menu with everything from bacon-and-egg breakfasts to sandwich lunches and steak dinners. *American. Breakfast 7AM, lunch 11AM, dinner 4:30PM-8PM. $/$$. 528 S. Spring St. 498-7340*

10 Pacific Coast Stock Exchange. This 1929-1930 structure, designed by Samuel Lunden in association with the Parkinson firm, is one of the most beautiful exchanges in the country. Its trading room is second in size only to New York's. Throughout the structure, classical architectural elements are mixed with Egyptian and Medieval designs. Especially noteworthy are the massive bronze doors with their interlacing patterns. Above the deep-set entrance, the relief sculpture by S. Cartaino represents Finance bringing together Science and Industry. *Viewing gallery open M-F, 7AM-2:30PM. Admission free. 618 S. Spring St.*

11 Cole's Buffet. This downtown eatery is the legendary birthplace of the French Dip sandwich. A favorite of LA's work force for years. Corned beef, roast beef, pastrami and, of course, French Dip sandwiches. A real bargain. *Daily 10AM-7PM. $. 118 E. 6th St. 622-4090*

Restaurants red
Architecture blue
Narrative/Museums/Shops black
Gardens/Parks/Piers green

12 Los Angeles Conservancy. Non-profit historic preservation organization offering a variety of excellent programs and events exploring this architecturally rich area. Downtown walking tours are weekly with specially scheduled neighborhood walks, bus tours and film programs. For calendar of events and information, call *623-CITY. 849 S. Broadway, Suite 1225*

8 Jewelry Center. The Los Angeles jewelry trade is centered in the new International Jewelry Center on the northeast corner of 6th and Hill Streets and the older Jeweler's Trade Building at 607 S. Hill. In addition, Hill Street from 6th Street down to and around the corner of 7th Street is lined with sparkling shops. Be sure to take a look into the lavish Pantages Theatre, on the southwest corner of 7th and Hill, which is being used as a jewelry center. Prices in this area are generally 20-50% lower than conventional jewelry stores.

13 Garment District. Los Angeles has been a major center for garment manufacture since the 1930s. First gaining fame for ladies sportswear (Cole of California, Catalina, and Rose Marie Reid transformed the nation's beaches), the current products fit everyone. Jobbers and discount stores offering bargains on everything from children's wear to leather coats line Los Angeles Street from Seventh Street down to Washington Boulevard. The **California Mart** on the southwest corner of 9th and Los Angeles Streets houses manufacturer's representatives, most open to the trade only.

13 Feast Restaurant. On the first floor of the California Mart. A good place for lunch and glamor watching. Some of the rag traders are their own best advertisement.

13 Sam's Deli offers a good Greek salad and a walnut cake that revives flagging energy. *121 East 9th St.*

14 Wholesale Produce Market. The bounty of San Joaquin and Imperial Counties floods out of the cornucopia of the Produce Market *every weekday from 3AM to noon.* Produce is sold by the lug or bushel only. The market has two main sections:

14 Produce Court, *off 9th Street just west of*
14 Central Avenue; and **Merchants Street,** *off 8th Street just west of Central Avenue.*

14 Vickman's is a cafeteria-counter restaurant that's been satisfying trenchermen appetites since 1930. Bakery goods are made fresh on premises. *American. Open M-Sa, 3AM-3PM. $. 1228 E. Eighth St. 622-3852*

Also located in this area, between 9th and 11th Streets on San Pedro, are several Chinese
15 restaurants, among which the **New Moon** and
15 Man Fook Low are recommended.

LA'S TALLEST
Nowhere else in the city is there such a concentration of high rises. Despite LA's reputation as a horizontal city, some of the tallest buildings in the world are in this area. Highest is the 62 story United California Bank building, 13th tallest building in the world. It is one foot shorter than Water Tower Place in Chicago, and slightly higher than the Transamerica Pyramid in San Francisco.

	meters	feet
United California Bank 1973	262	858
Security Pacific National Bank 1973	225	738
Crocker Bank 1982	213	700
Atlantic Richfield Towers 1971	213	699
Wells Fargo Bank 1981	190	625
Bonaventure Hotel 1976	123	400

Wholesale Flower Market. Warm and sunny Southern California weather insures a constant supply of flowers. Like the Produce Market, the action here begins at 3AM. The **Flower Market** at *766 Wall Street* and the **Grower's Wholesale Florists** at *755 Wall Street* are huge halls of flowers reflecting the seasons that Southern California doesn't have. Most stalls sell to the trade only, but Wall Street is lined with smaller merchants who offer potted plants to the public at substantial discounts. *Wall Street between Seventh and Eighth Sts.*

Transamerica Center. This 32-story commercial structure has an observation deck which is *open M-F, 10-11AM and 2-4PM. Admission is free. 1150 S. Olive St. 742-2111*

The Tower Restaurant. ☆☆ This would be one of the best restaurants in town without the view, but with it...the experience is sublime. *French. Closed Su. No lunch Sa. $$$/$$$$. 746-1554*

The Original Pantry. Steaks, coleslaw, remarkable sourdough bread, and the best hashbrowns in town since 1924. They never close, not even to redecorate. The Pantry publishes a small annual report dealing with the massive volume of food consumed there; we recommend you become a statistic. *Open daily, 24 hours. $. 877 S. Figueroa St. 972-9279*

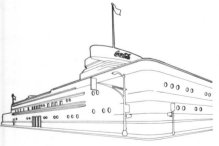

Coca-Cola Building. This part of Central Avenue seems to have been set to sea because of Robert V. Derah's 1935-37 transformation of five bland industrial buildings into a gigantic ocean liner. The streamlined forms, hatch covers, portholes, and imposing flying bridge bring a little salt air to the land of asphalt. Inset at the corners are two enormous coke bottles, making Derrah a pop-art pioneer 30 years before the style was created. *1334 S. Central Ave.*

19 Herald Examiner Building. William Randolph Hearst commissioned Julia Morgan to design this newspaper building in 1903. Morgan, the first woman trained at the Ecole des Beaux Arts in Paris and the designer of Hearst's San Simeon castle, created a Spanish Mission Revival design inspired by the California Building from the 1893 Chicago World's Fair. *1111 S. Broadway. 748-1212*

20 Figueroa Hotel. A budget priced hotel that is patronized by a number of touring performers such as the New York City Opera Company and American Ballet Theatre. The enormous swimming pool has a garden setting and the *cafe is open 24 hours a day. 939 S. Figueroa St. 627-8971*

20 Variety Arts Center. Vaudeville lives in a 1924 building that is home to the Society for the Preservation of the Variety Arts. Since 1977, the group has promoted and encouraged the lively arts of the music hall. A number of entertainment facilities are on the premises. The **Theatre Roof Garden** is a nightclub presenting a stage show on Friday and Saturday with dining and dancing. The **Variety Arts Theatre** hosts plays and revues. **Tin Pan Alley Cabaret Theatre** offers a musical showcase accompanied by a light supper Wednesday through Saturday nights. The **Ed Wynn Bar** is filled with mementos from the career of the famous vaudevillian. Although this is a private club, *visitors are admitted on payment of a small entry fee. 940 S. Figueroa St. 923-9100*

21 Los Angeles Convention Center Holiday Inn. Convenient to the commercial centers of downtown, this medium-priced hotel is popular with business travelers. There is a swimming pool and live entertainment in the evening. *1020 S. Figueroa St. 748-1291*

22 Los Angeles Convention Center. This municipal facility opened in 1971. A 211,000-square-foot main exhibition hall and auxiliary rooms are used for conventions, trade shows, and other public events. *1201 S. Figueroa. 748-8531*

23 Stimson House. Originally designed for prominent lumberman Douglas Stimson, the Queen Anne type house has a tower and a number of Medieval fortress-like details. Now occupied by the Convent of the Infant of Prague and not open to the public. *2421 S. Figueroa*

24 Patriotic Hall. The building, noticeable from the Harbor and Santa Monica Freeways, is a tall Renaissance palazzi-styled structure with an upper colonnaded terrace. *1816 S. Figueroa St.*

23 St. Vincent de Paul Roman Catholic Church. In 1923, oilman Edward Doheny donated the funds for this church. Architect Albert C. Martin designed it in the ornate Spanish style known as *Churrigueresque*, patterned after Baroque scrolled silverwork. The interior is decorated in brightly colored tiles and contains ceiling decorations painted by Giovanni Smeraldi. Doheny planned that the church would be set at a 45-degree angle on the lot so continuing development would not detract from the building's beauty. *621 W. Adams Blvd.*

Restaurants red
Architecture blue
Narrative/Museums/Shops black
Gardens/Parks/Piers green

25 Automobile Club of Southern California. Advocating the good life on wheels since 1903, the Automobile Club has done much to shape the mobile habits of Southern California. Services offered to members include insurance, towing, travel assistance and availability of club publications on Southern California attractions and road conditions, for both AAA and club members. Wall maps can be purchased by nonmembers. *Open M-F 8:45AM-5PM; Sa 8:45AM-1PM. 2601 S. Figueroa. 741-3111*

26 Olympic Auditorium. Opened in 1925 when boxing was king, the Italian Renaissance-style building seats 10,000. *Wrestling every Wednesday and Friday at 8PM; boxing Thursday at 8PM. 1801 S. Grand Ave. 749-5171*

23 Doheny Mansion and **Chester Place.** Chester Place is one block of a 15-acre residential park. Thirteen grand and expensive houses were built here at the turn of the century. The Doheny Mansion is considered the finest structure on the block. It was designed by Theodore Eisen and Sumner Hunt for Oliver Posey in 1900; shortly after construction, oilman Edward Doheny bought the home. Few alterations have been made to the French Gothic chateau exterior. The house is now owned by the Sisters of St. Joseph of Carondelet. *Tours by appointment only. 8 Chester Pl. 746-0450*

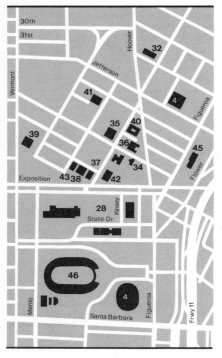

27 EXPOSITION PARK. The location of the Memorial Coliseum, Sports Arena, Museums of Science, Industry, Space and Natural History, a community clubhouse, and several landscaped areas, including the rose garden. Bounded by Exposition Boulevard, Menlo Street, Figueroa Street, and Santa Barbara Boulevard. Exposition Park began as a casual, open-air market grounds, and in 1872 was formally deeded as an agricultural park for farmers to exhibit their products. Fairs and carnivals on the grounds were organized by the Southern California Agricultural Society, including occasional sponsorship of races on the lot to the rear of the park. The lot was used as a track for horse racing and, on a few occasions, was the site of camel races. Toward the turn of the century it was home to bicycle and automobile competitions. During the park's decline in the early 1890s, it became a hang-out for society's lower elements and home to three saloons. The transformation of the rowdy agricultural park into a major state, county, and city museum center was accomplished by Judge William Miller Bowen. The park's romantic attractions made truants of much of Judge Bowen's neighboring Sunday school classes. One Sunday he followed his class to discover their secret destination and utilized his shocking discovery to spearhead a drive to create a landmark of worthwhile cultural significance on the saloon site. By 1910, work on the County Museum of Natural History had begun.

28 Exposition Park Rose Garden. A sunken garden containing over 16,000 rose bushes representing over 190 varieties. It is centered by a latticework gazebo. When the roses are in bloom, this is the most fragrant spot in town. *Admission free. Open daily, 7AM-5PM. 900 Exposition Blvd.*

29 California State Museum of Science and Industry. One of the best places in the city to take children. Lively and touchable displays in 14 permanent exhibition halls illuminate such diverse topics as electricity, animal husbandry (a giant incubator hatches 150 chicks a day), and communications. A number of displays are sponsored by private industry and have a sophisticated level of graphic design. The IBM mathematics exhibit created by Charles Eames makes math accessible with soap bubbles and moving demonstrations. The General Motors Turning Wheel exhibit features a cut-away Chevrolet to show how a modern internal-combustion engine works. Upstairs are two new exhibits including one of the history of computing replete with bilingual talking computers. Participation is emphasized in many displays, with buttons to push and levers to pull. The **Hall of Health**, next door to the main building, shows the functioning of the human body, including explanations of the five senses, the reproductive system, and the nervous system.

29 The Dental Exhibition Hall is located next to the Hall of Health. One of the liveliest parts of the museum's program is the temporary exhibition schedule. Over 60 presentations annually showcase a wide range of topics.

30 The Space Museum, a branch of the Museum of Science and Industry, is across the street in the old Armory Building, originally built in 1913 to house the California National Guard. The structure is now full of missiles and other air and space equipment on loan from NASA and other sources. *Open daily 10AM-5PM. Admission free. 700 State Dr. 794-0101*

Los Angeles County Museum of Natural History. Opened in 1913 in a Spanish Renaissance style structure by Hudson and Munsell. The interior is beautifully detailed, with an inlaid marble floor, travertine columns, and ornate plaster domes. Over 35 halls and galleries display permanent and temporary exhibitions. Among the most notable permanent collections are: marine and bird life, minerals and gems, reptile and mammal fossils (including several dinosaurs), insects, and pre-Columbian mezo-American artifacts. The Hall of American History displays machinery and memorabilia from the American past. Another room is full of restored automobiles. The museum has a bookstore, a fine gift shop, and a cafeteria serving low-priced meals. *Closed M. Tu-Su, 10AM-5PM. Admission fee. First Tuesday of each month is free-admission day; special hours for that day only, 12-9PM. Bookstore and gift shop, 10AM-4:30PM; cafeteria, 10AM-4PM. Free travel films Saturday, 2PM; free chamber music concerts Sunday, 2PM. 900 Exposition Blvd. 746-3775*

Hebrew Union College and Skirball Museum. An institute of Jewish higher learning, opened in 1954. The Frances-Henry Library of Judaica contains a special collection of material on the American Jewish experience. Skirball Museum has a collection of archeological and biblical Judaica, including textiles, coins, ritual objects and marriage contracts. One gallery displays a biblical environment entitled *A Walk Through the Past* that is a delight for children. Changing temporary exhibitions are also offered. *Open M-F, 9AM-5PM. Library open M-F, 9AM-5PM; Su, 10AM-5PM. Skirball Museum open Tu-F, 11AM-4PM; Su, 10AM-5PM. Admission free. 3077 University Ave. 749-3424*

UNIVERSITY OF SOUTHERN CALIFORNIA. Founded in 1880, USC is the oldest major independent coeducational nonsectarian university on the West Coast. The student body has grown from 53 at the founding to the current 27,000. Numbered among the internationally known professional schools are: architecture, law, medicine, dentistry, social work, education, public administration, engineering, gerontology, performing arts, pharmacology, and international relations. The downtown campus has 191 buildings on 152 acres. *Campus open daily year-round; specific buildings open daily 9AM-5PM. Between Jefferson, Exposition, Figueroa, and Vermont. 743-2388*

Among the notable structures are:

Widney Hall, the oldest university building in Southern California, dating from 1880. The 2-story clapboard building was designed by Ezra F. Kysor and Octavius Morgan. In 1920-21, John and Donald B. Parkinson master-planned the campus with Romanesque-style buildings. Their three-story brick **Bovard Administration Building** is at the heart of the campus. Directly across from it is the **Doheny Memorial Library** designed by Samuel Lunden with Cram and Ferguson in 1932. The Romanesque design has an impressive vaulted lobby.

The Mudd Memorial Hall of Philosophy, designed by Ralph Flewelling in 1929, houses rare books and incunabula from the 13th through 15th century. Medieval scholastic charm is achieved by such features as the cloistered courtyard and decorative gargoyles.

Restaurants red
Architecture blue
Narrative/Museums/Shops black
Gardens/Parks/Piers green

38 The Harris College of Architecture and Fine
38 Arts Building houses the **Fischer Art Gallery.** The 1939 building is also by Ralph Flewelling. Here he employs a Regency Moderne style adopting the red and white color scheme of the older Romanesque buildings.

38 The Armand Hammer Collection of 18th and 19th-century Dutch paintings is permanently exhibited in one of the three galleries. Annual student exhibitions are shown, as well as temporary exhibitions. *Open M-F, 12-5PM; closed weekends except during special exhibitions. Admission free. 823 Exposition Blvd. 743-2799*

39 The Gerontology Center (1972) by Edward
40 Durrell Stone and the **Von Kleinsmid Center for International and Public Affairs** (1961) by William Pereira are two contemporary structures that maintain the red-brick and cream-trim tradition. Both of these buildings have classical arcades and interior courtyards. An interesting
41 modern structure houses the **Schoenberg Institute,** a study center devoted to composer Arnold Schoenberg's life and works. It is the site of delightful free concerts of modern music.

42 Other noteworthy buildings are the **Hoffman Hall** of the School of Business (1967) by I.M.
43 Pei and the **Watt Hall of Architecture and Fine Arts** (1973) by Sam Hurst with Killingsworth, Brady and Associates.

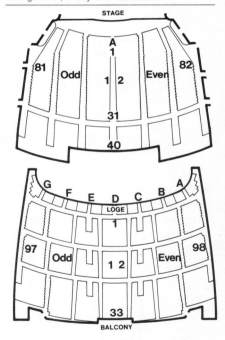

44 The Shrine Auditorium. (Seats 6,485). *Neo-penal Baghdad* is the description of the architecture given by Martin Bernheimer, music critic of the *Los Angeles Times.* Built in 1925 by the Al Malaikah Temple, the Shrine Auditorium was the city's largest until construction of the Music Center in 1964. The grandiose auditorium ceiling imitates the swag roof of a tent. *3228 Royal St. 748-5116. Box office at 655 S. Hill St. 749-5123*

45 The University Hilton. Located across the street from USC's Davidson Conference Center, this luxury hotel offers a spa, swimming pool, and a number of fine eating spots. *3540 S. Figueroa St. 748-4141*

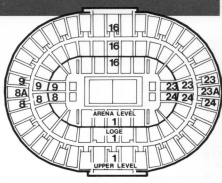

46 Los Angeles Memorial Coliseum. (Seats 91,000). Designed by John and Donald Parkinson in 1921 to seat 75,000 spectators, and subsequently enlarged to host the 1932 Olympics. The stadium is home to the USC football team and the 1984 Olympics. Other sports events, concerts, and public festivities are held here regularly. The Memorial Court of Honor at the Peristyle end of the stadium contains bronze plaques commemorating famous events and people connected with the Coliseum. *3911 S. Figueroa.* 747-7111

47 Sports Arena. (Seats 16,000). This sister facility to the Coliseum was designed by Welton Becket and Associates and opened in 1958. The elliptical structure is used as a multi-purpose indoor sports and entertainment facility. The main auditorium is home to the USC basketball team, as well as host to ice shows, track meets, car shows, concerts, rodeos, and conventions. *3939 S. Figueroa.* 748-6131

4 MID-WILSHIRE

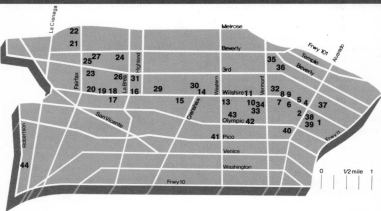

Wilshire Boulevard predates the founding of the city, existing first as a path followed by the Yang-Na Indians from their Elysian Hills settlement to the tar pits of Hancock Park where they obtained pitch to waterproof their homes.

Today's Wilshire runs 16 miles from the center of downtown to the Pacific Ocean in Santa Monica. The Wilshire District was the harbinger of decentralization in Los Angeles. The street traverses ethnically and economically diverse neighborhoods: from the Harbor Freeway to Lafayette Park is a settlement of thousands of new immigrants from Central America, Mexico, the Philippines, Southeast Asia, and Korea; professional firms line the boulevard with new high-rises from Lafayette Park to La Brea Avenue; and finally, the *Miracle Mile* shopping district, a development of the 1930s, is located from La Brea to La Cienega Boulevard. Both the boulevard and the area are named after H. Gaylord Wilshire (1861-1927), a real-estate entrepreneur from Ohio who made and lost fortunes in orange and walnut farming, gold mining, patent therapeutic electric belts, and real-estate development. During the real-estate boom of the 1880s, Wilshire created a tract through which ran an unpaved road, naming it for himself.

Oil fever captured the city shortly after Edward Doheny struck oil near Second Street and Glendale. (Amazingly, Doheny did it with a shovel, digging 16 feet into the hillside to discover a small pool of oil). By 1905, the neighborhood was dotted with oil wells. Many fortunes were made from the black resource beneath Wilshire, including that of the Hancock family who owned a farm around the well-known tar pits near Wilshire and Fairfax. The Hancock Park-Wilshire field was rapidly exhausted; the tar pits and a few disguised modern wells are the only remains of the once-booming local economy.

Freeway Overpass. Between Figueroa and Beaudry Streets, Wilshire Boulevard passes over the Harbor Freeway. There is a particularly good view from this spot of the *stack* interchange, where the Hollywood, Harbor/Pasadena, and San Bernardino Freeways interlace to form the hub of the Southern California Freeway system.

Restaurants red
Architecture blue
Narrative/Museums/Shops black
Gardens/Parks/Piers green

Los Angeles County Museum of Art inaugurated.
1964

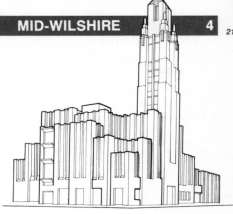

Edward's Steak House. Sawdust on the floor, Tiffany-style shades over the lights, good steaks on the table. A winning combination for over 25 years. *American. Open 7 days. No lunch, Sa-Su. $/$$. 733 S. Alvarado. 385-0051*

Langer's Delicatessen. ☆ Good enough to have been reviewed in the *New York Times*. One of the last places on earth where they slice the pastrami by hand. *Jewish. Open 7 days. $/$$. 704 S. Alvarado. 483-8050*

MacArthur Park. This 32-acre site, originally known as Westlake Park and rechristened in 1942 in honor of the famous general, is one of the first public parks in the Los Angeles area. Originally laid out in 1890, it currently contains over 80 species of rare plants and trees. The park has a lake with paddle boats for rent, a small band shell used for summer entertainment, snack bars, and children's play areas. The park is not recommended for nighttime strolls. *Wilshire Blvd. between Alvarado and Park View.*

Otis Art Institute of Parsons School of Design. With sister institutions in New York and Paris, this is one of the foremost art schools on the West Coast. Offering BFA, MFA and AAS degrees for courses in Fine Arts, Fashion Design, Graphic Design and Interior Architecture, the school also exhibits avant-garde contemporary art in the Gallery at the corner of Park View Avenue and Wilshire Blvd. *Gallery hours: M-Sa, 10:30AM-5PM. 2401 Wilshire Blvd. 387-5288*

La Fonda. Los Camperos, one of the finest mariachi groups anywhere, entertains in this popular spot. The margaritas are especially good and the atmosphere one of the most festive in town. *Mexican. Open 7 days. No lunch Sa-Su. $$. 2501 Wilshire Blvd. 380-5055*

Granada Building. The Granada Building is an extraordinary 1927 version of Spanish colonial architecture combined with Mission-style arches and arcades. It was designed for architects, designers, and artists who desired courtyard-studio offices. *672 S. Lafayette Park Pl.*

Sheraton Town House. A luxury hotel in the middle of the city with tennis courts, swimming pool, sauna, and gardens. Lanai suites have private patios overlooking the pool, and are a good value. *2961 Wilshire Blvd. 382-7171*

Lafayette Park. This is another one of the oldest public parks in Los Angeles. It includes a recreation and senior citizens' center, tennis courts, and a picnic area. A scent garden, with numerous fragrant flowers, is maintained for the blind. *2830 W. Sixth St., 2800 Wilshire Blvd.*

CNA Building and the **First Congregational Church.** A juxtaposition of architectural and landscape elements, the mirror-glass 1972 CNA building reflects the sky (actually disappearing at times) and the 1932 English Gothic-styled First Congregational Church across the street. *Sixth and Commonwealth Sts.*

Ambassador Hotel. Built in 1921 at the then phenomenal cost of $5 million, the luxury hotel is located on 23 acres of tropical landscaping. It has been a favorite stopping place for political and entertainment celebrities throughout its history. The Palm Bar is a beautiful place for afternoon drinks. *3400 Wilshire Blvd. 387-7011*

7 Bullock's Wilshire. One of the glistening jewels of Wilshire Boulevard, the art deco tower of Bullock's Wilshire rises with an air that suggests the imminent arrival of chauffeured Pierce Arrows at its rear porte cochere. The establishment opened its doors in 1929 as the first *suburban* department store in the city. Counting on trade from the nearby silk-stocking communities of Hancock Park and Fremont Place, John G. Bullock gambled that proximity and elegance could persuade the wealthy to leave the then-fashionable downtown Broadway shopping district. He was right. John and Donald Parkinson were the architects. Bullock's Wilshire is still one of the most elegant stores in the city. The fifth-floor **Tea Room** serves the delicate food dear to a lady's heart in a lovely garden atmosphere. Cocktails are also available. Luncheon fashion shows are frequently presented; call ahead for reservations. *American. Open M-Sa. Lunch only. $$. 3050 Wilshire Blvd. 382-6161*

11 Wilshire Hyatt Hotel. A luxury hotel featuring a swimming pool and use of a nearby health club. *3515 Wilshire Blvd. 381-7411*

12 St. Basil's Catholic Church. Designed by Bozidar Von Serda for the architectural firm of Albert C. Martin and built in 1967-68. The cement construction with stained-glass windows and bronze doors by Calire Falkenstein contains in its massive walls the 14 Stations of the Cross by Franco Asseto. The procession toward the Calvary was modelled in 28 days with 5600 pounds of clay converted into reverse plaster castings, each 110 sq. ft. and 2500 pounds with one-foot-thick wood reinforcements to sustain the weight of the cement. *View daily between 1PM-4PM. 3611 Wilshire Blvd. 381-6191*

13 Wiltern-Pellisier Building (Franklin Life Building). One of the finest art deco structures in the city. The exterior of the 1930 building is turquoise terra-cotta with zigzag Moderne ornament. In the summer of 1983, the restored Wiltern Theater reopens as a cultural/performing arts center with 2500 seats to serve the greater Los Angeles community. *3790 Wilshire Blvd.*

14 Perino's. ☆ ☆ Bastion of propriety, epitome of elegance and refinement since 1932. The faithful who dine here expect perfection and get it. *Gentlemen requested to wear jackets. French. Closed Su. No lunch Sa. $$$$. 4101 Wilshire Blvd. 383-1221*

15 Wilshire Ebell Theatre and Club. The excellent period design of these 1924 Renaissance-style buildings has made them the frequent setting for filming by television and movie companies. The theater is noted for its cultural and educational programs. *Theater: 4401 W. Eighth St. 939-1128*
Club: 4400 Wilshire Blvd.

15 Fremont Place. An elegant residential neighborhood; entry to the privately-owned streets is through massive gates on the south side of the 4400-4500 blocks of Wilshire Boulevard. Not open to the public.

MIRACLE MILE

In the 1930s, the Hancock family sold its holdings to a promoter named A.W. Ross, who conceived the name to attract motoring shoppers to a row of newly-built fashionable stores on the boulevard. Promotion soon made the Mile a success.

16 Khorram Building. A richly-ornamented black and gold zigzag Moderne building from 1929. *5209 Wilshire Blvd.*

17 Lew Mitchell's Orient Express. Copper and brass accents and modern rattan furniture. A sleek setting for Chinese cuisine that runs the gamut from fried calamari to grilled shark. *Chinese. Lunch M-F; dinner daily. $$$$. 5400 Wilshire Blvd. 935-6000*

18 Shanghai Winter Garden. An elegant Chinese restaurant, the inside embellished with carvings. The chef knows the dishes of the noble kitchens. *Chinese. Open daily. No lunch Sa-Su. $$/$$$. 5651 Wilshire Blvd. 934-0505*

19 Prudential Building. The 1948 Prudential complex is an excellent example of late International style in Los Angeles. In front is a bronze sculpture entitled *Primavera* by Aristides Demetrios. *5757 Wilshire Blvd.*

20A La Brea Tar Pits and **George C. Page Museum of La Brea Discoveries.** Mention of the natural seepage of tar (in Spanish, *la brea*) from these pits occurs as early as the 1769 diary which Father Crespi kept during his first journey through the area with Portola. The Indians, padres, and early settlers of Los Angeles used the tar to seal their boats and roofs. In 1906, geologists discovered that the pits contained the largest collection of Pleistocene fossils ever found in a single location—over 200 varieties of mammals, plants, birds, reptiles, and insects are entombed here. Some were enticed by the thin film of water hiding the gooey preservative, and then were trapped. Excavation of fossils continues in several fenced enclaves in the park. One area houses a laboratory where you can watch volunteers perform the painstaking process of sorting and cleaning. You will also notice large colonies of abandoned Easter bunnies living in the fenced areas.

B The museum is located at the eastern end of the park, opened in 1964. The museum is hidden on three sides in a grassy knoll. At the top of the knoll a walkway allows you to peer through the steel-frame roof into the atrium rock garden below. Floating above the walkway is a pictorial bas-relief of life at the park when mastodons and sabertooth tigers came to the ponds to drink. Inside, many exhibitions, films, and demonstrations tell about the evolution of the tar pits. Children will be delighted by two astonishing holographic displays that magically give flesh to the bones of a tiger and a woman found in the pits and a participatory demonstration of how sticky tar really is. The museum shop sells gifts and books. *Admission free. Closed M. Open Tu-Su, 10AM-5PM. Museum: 5801 Wilshire Blvd. 931-8082*

Attempt made to construct sidewalks out of tar from pits at Rancho la Brea.
1860

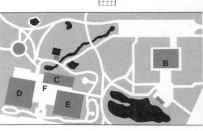

20 Los Angeles County Museum of Art. Designed by William Pereira and Associates and opened in 1964. Three buildings make up the museum: the Ahmanson Gallery on the west; the Hammer Gallery in the center; and **D** the Leo S. Bing Theatre on the east. The Ahmanson Gallery houses the museum's permanent collections, with East Indian and Islamic holdings that are among the finest in America. The Western European Painting and Sculpture, American Painting and Sculpture, Ancient Near Eastern, Oriental, and textile and costume collections are also notable. The Gilbert Collection of Monumental Silver is very popular. Primitive, Modern, Medieval, and **C** Classical art are also displayed. The Hammer Gallery is used for temporary exhibitions, always of high calibre and often organized by **E** the museum itself. The Bing wing contains a theater that is used for regularly scheduled film series (call the museum for current schedule), lectures, and concerts. The Monday evening concerts of contemporary music held during the winter are a Los Angeles institution. In addition, the Bing houses a cafeteria and the Art Rental Gallery where works by local artists are available for rental or sale. Jewelry objects, posters, and art books may be purchased in the **F** museum shop in the dark glass building at the center of the plaza level. On weekends, the plaza turns into a festival with mimes, musicians, and other outdoor performers. There are plans for two additions to the museum in the near future: Ahmanson Gallery by architects William L. Pereira & Assoc., opens October, 1982 and will provide walkway access to the Hammer Gallery, and Atlantic Richfield Gallery for Modern Art by architects Hardy Holzman Pfeiffer & Assoc., will increase by half the total museum exhibition space in 1985. Tours of the permanent collection are available; check at information desk at the Ahmanson. *Hours: Tu-F, 10AM-5PM; Sa-Su, 10AM-6PM. Closed M, Thanksgiving, Christmas, New Year's Day. Admission fee for nonmembers. 5909 Wilshire Blvd. Recorded info, 937-2590; general info, 857-6111*

---

20 Craft and Folk Art Museum/The Egg & The Eye Restaurant. A small museum that features changing exhibitions of ethnic and contemporary folk art. The museum shop, on the first floor, sells fine crafts as well as books. The Egg & The Eye Restaurant, on the upper level, specializes in omelettes (over 50 varieties, as well as an invitation to compose your own), salads, and desserts. *Hours: Tu-Sa, 11AM-8:30PM; Su, 10AM-6PM. Closed M. Admission free, donation suggested. 5814 Wilshire Blvd. 937-5544*

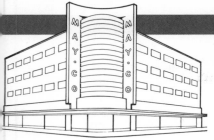

May Co. Department Store. A streamlined 1940 building that combines a simple rectangular box with an immense gilded cylinder set into the northeast corner. *6067 Wilshire Blvd. 938-4211*

Fairfax Avenue. The center for the Jewish community of Los Angeles since World War II. Although the majority of Los Angeles Jews currently reside on the West Side and in the San Fernando Valley, the Eastern European Jewish tradition continues as a strong influence in this area. Elderly men congregate on street corners to discuss business and politics, Hassids and a large number of Orthodox Jews walk to worship on Friday night and Saturday, other days women carry shopping bags to the butcher, greengrocer, and bakery.

21 Canter's Fairfax Restaurant Delicatessen and Bakery. The largest and liveliest of the delis on Fairfax. The inside has remained untouched since Doris Day was a girl. Waitresses not only bring your food, they also make sure you eat it. *Jewish. Open daily, 24 hours. $/$$. 419 N. Fairfax Ave. 651-2030*

22 Silent Movie Theatre. Chaplin, Valentino, Laurel and Hardy among others regularly show up on the screen here in prints owned and maintained by the theater. The wooden-seated auditorium is without frills and has something of a honky-tonk atmosphere. *Hours: M-Sa, 7-10PM. Admission fee; children under 12 free. 611 N. Fairfax. 653-2389*

23 Park LaBrea Housing and Towers (Metropolitan Life Housing and Towers). A large, Moderne Regency style complex of garden apartment units built in 1924 and covering 176 acres. *Bounded by Third, Cochran, Sixth, and Fairfax Sts.*

24 Pan Pacific Auditorium. So streamlined, it looks as if it could travel 50 miles per hour, this huge green 1935 building is a perfect, albeit stationary example of the futuristic auto and aircraft-based forms of the Moderne style of the 1930s. *7600 Beverly Blvd.*

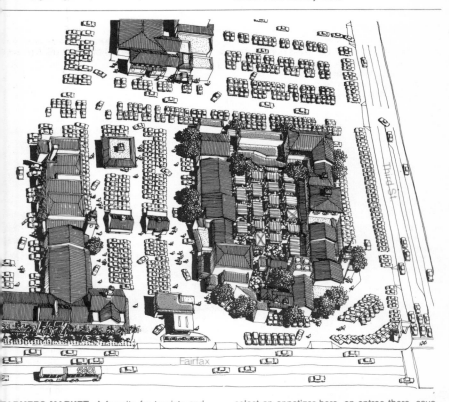

FARMERS MARKET. A favorite for tourists and locals alike, over 40,000 people visit the Farmers Market on an average day. The bustling atmosphere within the colorful maze of shops, market stalls, and food stands is alive with tempting sights and smells. The ultimate cornucopia, there are no blemished peaches or brown bananas in the Farmers Market. Established in 1934 as a cooperative market where local farmers sold their produce, today there are over 160 vendors. Stores offer a range of products from exotic crafts to basic household supplies. Twenty-six different restaurants offer food from around the world: try waffles, Chinese food, pizza, capuccino, or a delicious concoction from the juice bar; browse,

select an appetizer here, an entree there, save room for pastry, and sit under umbrellas and awnings outside to enjoy it all. The market section provides fine vegetables, cheeses, meats, pastries, baked goods, and exotic imported foodstuffs. Mr. K's Gourmet Foods and Coffee (stall 430) sells hard-to-obtain spices and teas; try Kludjian and Stone Tropical Fruits (stall 324) for fruits that you may never even have heard of. Several of the fruit and nut stalls make up and ship gift boxes, as do several of the confectioneries where you can watch candy being made. Don't rush through the Farmers Market; the spirit is relax and enjoy. *The market is open June-September, 9AM-8PM; October-May, 9AM-6:30PM. Closed Su. 6333 W. Third St.*

Seating chart: STAGE / ODD / EVEN / BALCONY

26 Scottish Rite Auditorium. (Seats 1,730). *4357 Wilshire Blvd. 937-2566*

26 Loehmann's. This discount clothing store is a woman's best friend, carrying an extensive selection of loungewear, suits, casual and formal wear, and accessories. Quality merchandise discounted 30% and more. Haute couture in the Backroom. *6220 W. 3rd St. (also at 19389 Victory Blvd. in Reseda). 933-5675*

27 CBS Television City. Built in 1951-52 by the architectural firm of Pereira & Luckman. Age limits for admittance to programs varies and is specified on the face of each ticket which can be picked up at the CBS information window. *Open 7 days, 9AM-5PM. Closed major holidays. 7800 Beverly Blvd. 852-2624. Groups of 20 or more, 852-2455*

28 Regina's. ☆ Buenos Aires has its share of Italian restaurants. Now LA has several Argentine restaurants, Italian style, and this is the best. There is an emphasis on beef, and a lot of food for your money. *Italian-Argentine. Lunch Tu-F; dinner Tu-Su. $$$. 371 N. Western Ave. 462-2525*

28 El Cholo. A Mexican classic that dates back 50 years. Gable and Lombard used to eat here. Today, patrons don't mind waiting in the lounge for a table, as it has the look and feel of a Mexican hacienda and whopping margaritas. *Mexican. Lunch and dinner daily; Su brunch. $$. 1121 S. Western Ave. 734-2773. Also in La Habra and Newport Beach.*

28 Pink's Famous Chili Dogs. Hot dogs, hamburgers and tamales, but the chili dogs are what make it world famous. *American. Open daily, 8AM-3AM. $. 711 N. La Brea Ave. 931-4223*

29 Hancock Park/Windsor Square/Larchmont Village/Wilton Historic District. Capt. G. Allan Hancock, son of Henry Hancock who bought Rancho LaBrea in 1860, began this exclusive residential section. The palatial mansions have been owned by the Doheny, Huntington, Van Nuys, Janss, Banning, Crocker, and other notable California families. The Hancock Park-Windsor Square area, roughly bounded by Highland and Melrose Avenues and Wilshire and Larchmont Boulevards, began development in the 1910s.

30 Getty House. This 1921 English half-timbered house was given to the city in 1977 by Getty Oil Company. It is used as the official mayor's home. Private residence. *605 S. Irving Blvd.*

29 Larchmont Village. Between First Street and Beverly Boulevard, a shopping street that serves the commercial needs of the community. It has the charm of a small town Main Street. Nearby is the Wilton Historic District, a more modest area with a number of California bungalows dating from 1907 to 1925.

31 Robaire's. One of the oldest bistro-style French restaurants in town. A reliable value. *French. Closed M. No lunch. $$. 348 S. La Brea. 931-1246*

32 Cassell's Patio Hamburgers. ☆ You'll wonder why we've sent you here until you taste the freshly-ground prime-beef hamburger; note the sesame bun stands up for its rights; and realize that the mayonnaise is homemade and the lemonade recently squeezed. *American. Closed Su. Lunch only. $. 3300 W. Sixth St. 480-8668*

33 The Windsor. Classic luxury: burnished paneling, a wall full of awards, attentive service, and a menu of staggering magnitude. *French/Continental. Open daily. No lunch Sa-Su. $$$/$$$$. 3198 W. Seventh St. 382-1261*

34 Hotel Chancellor. An excellent budget-priced hotel, popular with European and Japanese visitors. *3191 W. Seventh St. 383-1183*

34 The Cove. A romantic spot complete with strolling violinists. Traditional German dishes are well prepared, as are the salads. *German/Continental. Open daily. No lunch Sa-Su. $$$. 3191 W. Seventh St. 388-0361*

35 Hamayoshi. ☆ Immaculate sushi bar at the front, beautifully appointed back rooms. Private tatami rooms are available by reservation; be sure to be on time. *Japanese. Closed Su. No lunch Sa. $$. 3350 W. First St. 384-2914*

36 Shibucho. The menu is restricted to sushi and sashimi of remarkably high quality. Natural wood detailing and pebble floors create a traditional Japanese interior. *Japanese. Open daily. Dinner only. Open late. $$. 3114 Beverly Blvd. 387-8498*

37 Pacific Dining Car. ☆ ☆ Prime beef aged on the premises, a remarkable wine cellar, and a fine spinach salad. The front dining room was once a railroad car. *American. Open 7 days. Breakfast served. $$$/$$$$. 1310 W. Sixth St. 483-6000*

38 Mary Andrews Clark Memorial Residence of the YWCA. An enormous French chateau located at the corner of Loma and Third Streets, it was built for the YWCA by William Andrews Clark, former senator from Montana, as a memorial to his mother in 1913. It was designed by Arthur Benton. *306 Loma Dr.*

39 800 and 1000 Blocks of South Bonnie Brae Street. In the late 19th century, Los Angeles experienced a building and population boom. Westlake (now MacArthur Park) emerged as a residential section in that era. Here are found some of the city's finest Victorian houses. 818 So. Bonnie Brae is a regal example of a Queen Anne house displaying an immense veranda, elaborate woodwork, and several types of columns and piers. 824 So. Bonnie Brae is remarkable for its Islamic domed tower. The 1000 block is richer yet with well-preserved Victorian houses at numbers 1026, 1033, 1035, 1036-38, 1047, and 1053 So. Bonnie Brae.

Restaurants red
Architecture blue
Narrative/Museums/Shops black
Gardens/Parks/Piers green

Olympian Hotel. An aviary full of exotic birds, tropical foliage, and statuary fills the center of this medium-priced hotel. It has a swimming pool and offers guests a free downtown shuttle bus service. *1903 W. Olympic Blvd. 385-7141*

Carmina's. Freshly baked tortillas, cocido to restore you, salsa to get you going. Mexican cooking at its best. *Open daily. $. 2500 West Pico Blvd. 480-8184*

Korea Town. The Los Angeles melting pot has recently been enriched by a large influx of Korean immigrants. Located in an area bounded roughly by Vermont, Pico, Eighth and Western, these new Angelenos have revitalized this area. Rambling old bungalows have been repainted and store fronts provisioned with Korean foodstuffs and identified by distinctive angular calligraphy. The market at the corner of Eighth Street and Normandie Avenue is a technicolor delight, with vividly painted columns, rafters and trim, blue-tile roof, and stacks of sacks and bottles.

42 VIP Palace. A peacock of a restaurant; shiny red and gold inside and out. Barbecue beef is a Korean specialty; it is very spicy and very delicious. *Open daily. $/$$. 3014 W. Olympic Blvd. 388-9292*

43 Dong Il Jang. Refined atmosphere of natural wood and subdued lighting. Your order of beef or chicken is cooked on a grill hidden under the removable table top. *Japanese/Korean. Open daily. $$. 3455 W. Eighth St. 383-5757*

44 Los Angeles Institute of Contemporary Art (LAICA). An exhibition space which emphasizes avant-garde work by Southern California artists. The bookstore sells books, catalogs, and art magazines. *Open T-Sa, 12-6PM. Admission free. 2020 S. Robertson Blvd. 559-5033*

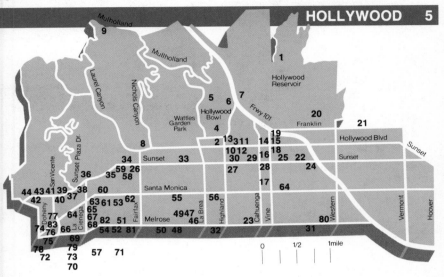

HOLLYWOOD 5

Land of tinsel, dreams, and fantasy, destination of the starry-eyed and ambitious, Hollywood has provided grist for countless stories from *Day of the Locust* to *The Loved One*.

Famous stars have been billed as Hollywood's main attraction—but don't look for them here; most live in Beverly Hills, Bel Air, and Malibu.

The gap between fantasy and reality is large—the Hollywood seen in films doesn't exist. What does exist is an area divided economically and geographically into two communities: the flatlands and the hills. The flatlands, covered with dozens of film, music, stage, television, and photographic production facilities, provide a strong economic base for technicians and creative workers. Hollywood Boulevard, from Vine Street to La Brea Avenue, thrives by night; it is often referred to as the Times Square of the West. The residents of this area include a large number of new immigrants from dozens of countries, especially from the areas of Southeast Asia and the Middle East. The steep hills are home to the literary and artistic contingent. The *good life* is a daily reality in neighborhoods such as Beachwood, Nichols, and Laurel Canyons. This is a world of tree-lined, winding streets and rural-chic homes, surrounded by wild chaparral-covered foothills.

Originally a campground for the Cahuenga Indians, Hollywood was later included in the Rancho La Brea land grant. Because of its proximity to the Cahuenga Pass, the main route to the north, Cahuenga served as a way station on the Camino Real, and after California's entry into the Union, as a major stop on the Butterfield Stage route. In comparison to its recent image, the early years of the town were staid and upright. The film capital of the world started out as a farming community in the Cahuenga Valley. Mrs. Horace H. Wilcox, wife of the founder of Hollywood, named the area after the suburban Chicago summer home of a friend. The first Yankee homesteaders were Midwestern Methodist prohibitionists who arrived in the 1880s. These church-going farmers supplied downtown Los Angeles with watermelons, green peppers, lemons, oranges, figs, and other fruits and vegetables.

Towering canopies of eucalyptus trees spread over the main roads, and deer often ventured down onto Hollywood Boulevard in the early morning. It was in this rural atmosphere that the nearly 500 residents decided to incorporate as a city in 1903.

The residents were more occupied with the problems of heavy sheep traffic passing through their town to the stockyards of downtown LA than with Thomas Edison's *living pictures* being shown barely eight miles away on Broadway. In 1911, the tranquility of the quiet community was shattered when the Horsely Brothers rented an abandoned tavern at the corner of Sunset and Gower (now a shopping center named Gower Gulch) to film moving pictures. The rowdy and boisterous crew of actors, carpenters, and film makers enlarged rapidly, straining the water and sewer resources of the community. In 1911, residents agreed to be annexed to the City of Los Angeles.

1 Hollywoodland Gates and Sign.
Hollywoodland, a residential project begun in 1923, is located on the lower slopes of Mt. Lee. Two Gothic sandstone gates at Beachwood Drive and Westshire Streets announce the entrance to the subdivision. Near the summit of Mt. Lee, fifty-foot high letters spell out HOLLYWOOD. The original sign advertised the name of the subdivision. In 1945, the deteriorating sign and its acreage were deeded to the Hollywood Chamber of Commerce who took down the -LAND to create a civic advertisement. A new sign costing $250,000 was erected in 1978. The sign has been a universal symbol for Hollywood and for Los Angeles in general. *Gates at Beachwood and Westshire. Sign visible further north.*

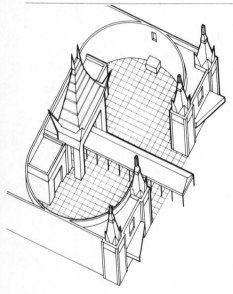

2 Mann's Chinese Theatre. The fantasy and shrewd showmanship of Hollywood came together in the Chinese Theatre, opened by Sid Grauman with great hoopla for the premiere of Cecil B. DeMille's *King of Kings* on May 18, 1927. The theater is best known for the courtyard filled with the impressions of more than 160 movie stars' footprints, handprints, and signatures in concrete, a tradition which began at the first premiere when Norma Talmadge accidentally stepped in wet cement. The structure is also significant for its design. Architects Meyer and Holler created an exotic, almost tropical interpretation of the Chinese temple with extravagantly turned up *dragon-tail* edges. The two side wings are capped on their corners by obelisks of dubious Chinese origins. The dramatic style, majestic scale, vivid coloring, and court enclosure make this a memorable space. *6925 Hollywood Blvd. 464-8111*

2 C.C. Brown's Ice Cream. When playing the *What would you have for your last meal on Earth?* game, a lot of people specify a C.C. Brown hot-fudge sundae for dessert. The creamiest, most delicious hot fudge in the world—rich vanilla ice cream, toasted almonds—served up in a decor that recalls the day in 1929 when the parlor first opened its doors. *American desserts. Closed Su. $. 7007 Hollywood Blvd. 462-9262*

3 Hollywood Wax Museum. If you happen to miss the real thing at Hollywood and Vine, you can always find celebrities here. Established over 40 years ago, the guest register spans Mary Pickford to Cher. The Oscar Movie Theatre has an ongoing trailer of Academy Award winners. *Open daily, 10AM-midnight. Admission fee. 6767 Hollywood Blvd. 462-8860*

4 Yamashiro Restaurant and Bernheimer's Gardens. See one of the most glorious views in the city from a replica of a Japanese mountain palace-retreat designed by Franklin M. Small in 1913. (Yama shiro means *castle on the hill*). The original owners, Adolphe and Eugene Bernheimer, were importers of Oriental art and this elaborate setting was their home. Because of its authentic design, the home and gardens are often used as sets for films. *Japanese/American. Open daily. No lunch Sa-Su. $$. 1999 N. Sycamore Ave. off Franklin Ave. 466-5125*

5 Freeman House. Frank Lloyd Wright's Freeman House is tucked into one of the Hollywood Hills overlooking the Hollywood Bowl. Built in 1924, this is one of his concrete-block structures displaying Mayan influences. Private residence. *1962 Glencoe Way*

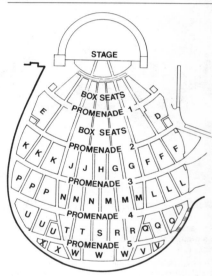

6 Hollywood Bowl. (Seats 17,619). Nestled in a 116-acre park at the foot of the Hollywood Hills, surrounded by trees and shrubbery, the Bowl is an outdoor amphitheatre. The Los Angeles Philharmonic plays programs ranging from classical favorites to pop at *Symphonies Under the Stars* from July through September. Other performers present jazz, rock, folk, and country music. One of the most pleasant ways to enjoy the Bowl is to arrive early for a picnic in one of the many sylvan spots on the grounds; bring your own or buy an inexpensive prepackaged dinner at the Bowl. There is also a restaurant which serves moderately-priced suppers al fresco on the patio. On-grounds parking at the Bowl is somewhat limited; lots along Highland take care of the overflow. Parking farther up the Cahuenga Pass offers a bus back to the Bowl. You'll be doing a fair amount of uphill walking wherever you park, so wear comfortable shoes. There are 14 special park-and-ride buses to the Bowl from points throughout the LA Basin. Call 876-8742 for information. Seating in the theater is on wooden bleacher-style seats that go high up the hill at the back. Thanks to amplification, the acoustics are fair all the way to the back. Evenings get cold in the foothills; bring a warm sweater. If you're in the bleachers, a cushion or blanket to sit on makes for a more comfortable evening. During the concert you'll notice two light beams crossed overhead. These warn small planes away and give concertgoers a protected feeling. *Grounds open daily, July-September, 9AM-dusk. 2301 N. Highland Ave. 876-8742*

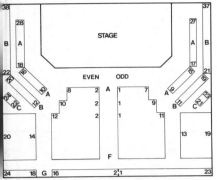

Los Angeles Actors Theatre. (Seats 174). *1089 N. Oxford Ave. 464-5500 (after 1PM).*

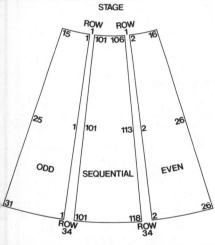

John Anson Ford Theater. (Seats 1,300). *2580 Cahuenga Blvd. 974-1343*

Two of the most interesting residences in Los Angeles may be seen by taking a detour west on Hollywood Boulevard and then north on Laurel Canyon Boulevard to Mulholland Drive. This will also give you a chance to see the hip rural community in Laurel Canyon and a stunning view of the Los Angeles Basin and San Fernando Valley from Mulholland Drive.

Storer House. This Mayan-styled concrete block house was designed by Frank Lloyd Wright in 1923. Within the structure, a two-story living room opens out onto front and rear terraces. Private residence. *8161 Hollywood Blvd.*

Chemosphere Malin House. This daring circular structure built by John Lautner in 1960 stands supported by a single pedestal on the side of one of the Hollywood Hills. The best view of the stucture is from the opposite hill on Torreyson Place, or from Woodrow Wilson Drive. Private residence. *7776 Torreyson Drive.*

Restaurants red
Architecture blue

Narrative/Museums/Shops black
Gardens/Parks/Piers green

Back down Hollywood Boulevard you will find under your feet the **Walk of Fame**, a procession of pink and charcoal terrazzo stars embedded in the sidewalk. They have been sponsored by the Hollywood Chamber of Commerce since 1961 to remember those who put the city on the map. Little insignias above the name help you remember the field of fame: movie camera, TV set, television, record. There are currently over 1,100 stars. *Hollywood Blvd. from Sycamore to Gower and Vine St. from Yucca to Sunset.*

10 Egyptian Theatre. An example of architecture-goes-to-the-movies. Sid Grauman was responsible for this plaster Temple of Thebes, which has seen many changes, including a new multi-theater addition, since the halcyon days when usherettes were dressed as Cleopatra. *6708 Hollywood Blvd. 467-6167*

11 Musso and Frank Grill. Hollywood's oldest restaurant, open since 1919. Reassuring in its paneled permanence and lack of change, with a comfortable counter for solitary diners. Waiters may be brusque unless they know you. *American. Closed Su. $$$. 6667 Hollywood Blvd. 467-7788*

Hollywood Boulevard is one of the main centers of the Los Angeles book trade. A number of book shops line Hollywood Boulevard from Whitley to McCadden Place. New, old, and special-interest material is sold. Many stores stay open until late evening, offering an opportunity for pleasant after-dinner browsing. Among the best are:

3 B. Dalton Bookseller. The largest bookstore on the boulevard. Be sure to check the discounted and remaindered books on the third floor. *6743 Hollywood Blvd.*

12 Larry Edmunds. Movie books and memorabilia. *6658 Hollywood Blvd.*

11 Book City. An enormous collection of new and used books on all topics. *6627 Hollywood Blvd.*

11 Cherokee Book Shop. First editions; comics. *6607 Hollywood Blvd.*

13 Don the Beachcomber. Dancing. The progenitor of Polynesian restaurants. The rum drinks are sensational. *Polynesian. Open daily. $$. 1727 N. McCadden Pl. 469-3968*

12 Frederick's of Hollywood. Immortalized in pulp fiction and male fantasies. Frederick's has transcended fashion and created a unique, timeless style. *6608 Hollywood Blvd.*

10 Universal News Agency. One of the best sources of hometown (whether Bangor or Bangkok) newspapers and international magazines. *1655 N. Las Palmas Ave.*

14 Tick Tock Tearoom. The restaurant takes its name from an enormous collection of clocks on the walls; the decor and atmosphere are genteel. Much loved by the very old and the very young. *Midwestern American. Closed M-Tu. $$. 1716 N. Cahuenga Blvd. 463-7576*

15 Hollywood and Vine. An intersection that makes you wonder about the power of publicity. Nothing every really happened here; it's just a pass-by spot. But in the days when nearly every major studio was located nearby, the passersby were often the famous and beautiful.

"...Hollywood Boulevard: The Golden Road, Hardened Artery, Santa Claus Lane, Main Street in Slacks..."

Hedda Hopper
1941

EVEN 2 | **N G** | **ODD 1**

MEZZANINE

EVEN 2 | **F A** | **1 ODD**

LOGE

T
24 | 2 | 114 | 101 | 1 | 23
A
BB
AA

ORCHESTRA

16 Huntington Hartford Theatre. (Seats 1038). A midsized theater which presents one-man shows, dramatic plays, and musical reviews. *1615 N. Vine St. 642-6666*

---

16 Martoni's. A comfortable old restaurant convenient to Hollywood theaters, serving the hearty peasant food of southern Italy. Herbs and *arrugola* grown in the owner's garden. *Italian. Lunch M-F; dinner M-Sa 'til 1AM. $$. 1523 N. Cahuenga Blvd. 466-3441*

17 Au Petit Cafe. The wellhead of many of the local French restaurants, offering haute cuisine in a cozy atmosphere. *French, Closed Su. No lunch Sa. $$$/$$$$. 1230 N. Vine St. 469-7176*

18 Vine Street Bar and Grill. A strikingly modern contrast to Musso's and the Brown Derby, the Vine Street is good for pre- or post-theater dining, even with inconsistent Italian cuisine. You can make a splendid meal of the complimentary hors d'oeuvres during *Happy Hour. Italian. Lunch M-F; dinner M-Sa. $$$. 1610 N. Vine St. 463-4050*

18 The Hollywood Brown Derby. The famous caricatures are still in place, covering the walls of the Celebrity Room. Red plush, tufted booths and crystal chandeliers add to the glamorous air. The delicious Cobb Salad deserves its reputation. *Open daily. $$/$$$. 1628 Vine St. 469-5151*

5 HOLLYWOOD

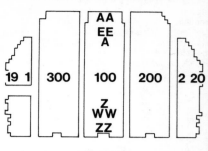

STAGE

AA EE A

19 | 1 | 300 | 100 | 200 | 2 | 20

Z WW ZZ

MEZZANINE

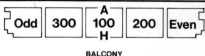

A
Odd | 300 | 100 | 200 | Even
H

BALCONY

A
27 | 1 | 300 | 100 | 200 | 2 | 26
G

Pantages Theatre. (Seats 2,900). Constructed in 1929, this Moderne building designed by B. Marcus Priteen has zigzag grillwork; Egyptian figures peer down from the roofline. The interior is a sensational example of Art Deco decoration by Anthony Heinsbergen. Home to the Academy Awards presentation for many years, the theater is now used for stage plays and musicals. *6233 Hollywood Blvd. 462-3104*

TV SHOW TICKETS
ABC Network Shows · 557-7777
CBS Network Shows · 852-2624
NBC Network Shows · 840-4444
Metromedia TV · 462-7111; ext. 1921
TICKETS
Ticketron General Information · 670-2311

Specific Reservations 9A-5P
M-F Tickets available at most
Sears, Broadway and
Montgomery Ward Stores. · 642-5700

☆ ☆

1 Jan 1925: Joan Crawford came to Hollywood from Kansas City

10 Jan 1938: Capra invites public to write in votes for best picture/best acting, to be considered by AMPAS Committee

2 Feb 1914: Chaplin's first film released: **Making a Living**

7 Feb 1914: Chaplin introduces the costume which became his trademark in **Kid Auto Races at Venice**. *Items gathered hastily from various dressing rooms include Ford Sterling's shoes (worn on opposite feet so that they would stay on) and Fatty Arbuckle's trousers*

13 Feb 1914: Mary Pickford announces her retirement

1 March 1925: Will Hays formed Central Casting, actor's employment agency. Hays Code: in effect, censorship of US films

6 March 1937: **A Star is Born** *released, the first modern technicolor comedy*

10 March 1910: **In Old Hollywood** *released, first Hollywood-made film shot in two days*

28 March 1920: Douglas Fairbanks and Mary Pickford marry

31 March 1935: Richard Chamberlain born in Beverly Hills

2 April 1974: Streaker at Academy Awards Ceremony entered in tux wearing press badge

8 April 1932: John Gavin born in Los Angeles

17 April 1919: D. W. Griffith, Mary Pickford, Douglas Fairbanks and Charlie Chaplin form United Artists Corporation

2 May 1933: Twentieth Century incorporated

9 May 1946: Candice Bergen born in Beverly Hills

16 May 1929: First Academy Awards Ceremonies

17 May 1924: MGM (Metro-Goldwyn-Mayer) founded

31 May 1930: Clint Eastwood born in San Francisco. After success as a High School and Army athlete, he worked as a movie extra. His first film was in 1955, **Revenge of the Creature** *but he became a star through his TV series* **Rawhide**

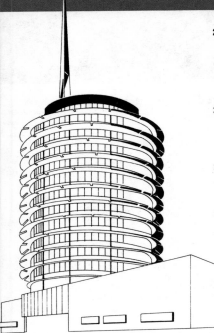

Capitol Records Tower. The Capitol Records Tower is considered the first round office tower. Designed by Welton Becket in 1954, one story has it that the inspiration for the unusual shape was a suggestion by Capitol's president, the composer Johnny Mercer. Mercer, along with singer Nat *King* Cole, came up with the idea of imitating a record shape. *1750 Vine St.*

Samuels-Navarro House. Once owned by actor Ramon Navarro, this house was designed by Lloyd Wright, son of Frank Lloyd Wright, in 1928. The house stretches horizontally along a natural ridge ending with a swimming pool (now enclosed) at one end and a private garden at the other. Pressed copper trims the white stucco surface. Private residence. *5699 Valley Oak Dr.*

21 Sowden House. This unusual home was designed by Frank Lloyd Wright; construction was supervised by his son. A star-shaped opening appears in the cast concrete blockwork over the dark cavernous entrance, offset by plain stucco walls on either side. Private residence. *5121 Franklin Ave.*

21 Fujiya Market. A sashimi alternative. For $6 you get sashimi, a glob of mustard and a cut cucumber at one-third the price you can pay for similar main course fare at any chic Sushi Bar. *Corner Virgil and Clinton.*

22 The Old Spaghetti Factory. Antiques, pictures, geo-gaws galore plus—surprise—spaghetti. Great for kids. *Italian. Open 7 days. No lunch Sa-Su. $. 5939 Sunset Blvd. 469-7140*

23 Le St. Germain. ☆ ☆ The atmosphere of an elegant French country inn, a chef of imagination schooled in the classics. Waiters recite the menu for the evening. *French. Closed Su. No lunch Sa. $$$/$$$$. 5955 Melrose Ave. 467-1108*

25 The Hollywood Palladium. Famous since 1940, the Palladium has swung to the sounds of the Dorsey Brothers, Glen Miller, Stan Kenton, and Lawrence Welk. Current attractions vary from dancing to conventions, but big names still make frequent appearances. Full bar and a la carte dinners offered. *6215 Sunset Blvd. 466-4311*

26 Crown Books. 10,000 titles, each at a discount. Two stores: *Ventura Blvd. and Laurel Canyon, 506-5744, and Sunset and Fairfax, 851-9183*

27 Hampton's. The hamburger place for gourmets. Beef is ground fresh daily and cooked to order. Enjoy the bountiful salad bar and the live music during Sunday brunch. *American. Dinner daily. $/$$. 1342 N. Highland Ave. 469-1090. In Burbank at 4301 Riverside Dr. 845-3009*

28 Cinerama Dome. A startling cellular construction, originally built to accommodate the extra-wide screen of the Cinerama process. The acoustics and sight lines of the theater are remarkably good. *6360 Sunset Blvd. 466-3401*

1 July 1925: Land purchased by Walt Disney on Hyperion Avenue in Silverlake becomes company's new facilities and birthplace of Mickey Mouse (1928) and later, Pluto, Goofy, Donald Duck and Snow White

8 Aug 1921: Esther Williams born in Los Angeles. Although a swimmer and not an actress, she became a major star for eleven years.

8 Aug 1937: Dustin Hoffman (named for a silent screen actor, Dustin Fornum) born in Los Angeles, originally planned to become a concert pianist, became a star overnight in The Graduate, 1968

18 Aug 1937: Charles Robert Redford, Jr. born in Santa Monica

5 Sept 1953: Grauman's Chinese Theater (now Mann's) installed its first marquee sign in house's 25-year history.

1 Oct 1911: First Hollywood studio established. City was picked by coin toss, and a derelict roadhouse on Sunset Boulevard was rented. Today it is the site of CBS radio and TV station KNX (6121 Sunset Blvd.)

7 Oct 1945: A labor dispute and a strike was to be the beginning of a communist purge by the House Un-American Activities Comittee, which affected the careers of 19 "unfriendly witnesses" and 300-plus actors, dirctors and writers

20 Oct 1947: House Un-American Activities Committee hearings began, lasting two weeks and including the "Hollywood Ten"

24 Nov 1947: Fifty of the leading motion picture executives adopt the blacklist and suspend the "Hollywood Ten"

26 Nov 1942: Casablanca opens in Hollywood

28 Nov 1925: Gloria Grahame (Hallward) born in Los Angeles

21 Dec 1937: Premiere of Walt Disney's Snow White and the Seven Dwarfs at the Carthay Theater in Los Angeles, first full-length animated feature

25 Dec 1928: First Western talkie, In Old Arizona, premiered in Los Angeles, proved outdoor sound movies successful, and revived interest in westerns

24 Sculpture, Metro-Media Building. A structural engineer's dream, *Starsteps* is an awesome and breathtaking 40,000-pound steel sculpture by Chicagoan John David Mooney, commissioned for the 1981 Bicentennial Celebration. An elaborate computerized lighting system changes seasonally and provides subtly modulating lighting changes on the 35-foot piece 4 times an hour. *Sunset at Wilton and Hollywood Freeway 101, on top of the Metromedia Building.*

29 South Town Soul Food. Substantial soul food in a casual atmosphere. A favorite with the Motown Record people from around the corner. *Southern American. Open daily, 24 hours. $. 1515 N. Wilcox Ave. 464-9677*

30 Crossroads of the World. The architectural theme of a ship (center building) sailing into various foreign ports (the surrounding French, Spanish, and English shops) was a major tourist attraction when it was built in 1936. The small-scale fantasy buildings were the creation of architect Robert V. Derrah, who was also responsible for the Coca-Cola building in central Los Angeles. *6671 Sunset Blvd.*

31 Lucy's El Adobe. A favorite haunt of Governor Jerry Brown, especially during his Linda Ronstadt days. (She still orders to-go when she craves enchiladas.) *Mexican. Lunch and dinner M-Sa. $$. 5536 Melrose Ave. 462-9421*

32 Emilio's Ristorante. ☆ With a central fountain, statuary, and more than its share of Chianti bottles perched on the backs of the red leather booths, Emilio's is more than a little theatrical. The food reflects that same tendency for overabundance: there are a zillion dishes to choose from and lots on the plate. Forget the menu and ask Emilio to create something special—that's when he shines. *Italian. Dinner daily. $$/$$$. 6602 Melrose Ave. 935-4922*

THE SUNSET STRIP is a small, unincorporated area that adjoins the western section of Hollywood. Free of certain legal restrictions enforced in the City of Los Angeles, the Strip has traditionally been a nightlife center, the location of famous clubs like Ciro's and the Mocambo. In the '30s and '40s, many Hollywood stars used to stop off here for some relaxation on their way home to Beverly Hills from a day's work at the studios. A steady stream of limousines would drop off glamorous carousers for dining, drinking, and dancing. In the '60s, the Strip was a haven for hipsters and flower children. Rock clubs now predominate. This section of Sunset Boulevard is the art gallery of the entertainment industry. The work of graphic designers and sign painters is constantly displayed on the enormous custom billboards, referred to in the industry as *vanity boards*, elevated above small stucco buildings.

33 Dar Maghreb. ☆ A stunning Moroccan setting, as much theater as restaurant, for exotic dishes eaten with the fingers while lounging on cushions. Plan to spend the evening. *Moroccan. Open 7 days. Dinner only. $$$. 7651 Sunset Blvd. 876-7651*

33 Mischa's. Borscht, stuffed cabbage, over 100 distinctive wines, and soulful Russian music in this cabaret restaurant which is still going strong with Russian emigres after midnight on weekends. *Russian/Continental. Dinner daily. $$$. 7561 Sunset Blvd. 874-3467*

34 La Toque. ☆ ☆ ☆ Chef-owner Ken Frank maintains a high level of inventive cuisine. The service and little-French-restaurant atmosphere are impeccable. Very French, very expensive, very good. Superb wine list. The patio is a lovely spot on summer evenings. The fixed price suggestion is an excellent choice. *French. Closed Su. Dinner only. $$$$. 8171 Sunset Blvd. 656-7516*

34 Schwab's Drug Store. Legend has it that Lana Turner was discovered at the counter. Usually full of out-of-work actors and actresses hoping for the same luck, especially over bagels at breakfast. *American-deli. Breakfast and lunch daily. $/$$. 8024 Sunset Blvd. 273-5111*

34 Chateau Marmont Hotel. A French Norman castle perched on a hill above Sunset Strip. A favorite of music and movie industry personalities, all luxury suites of the 1927 hotel have a balcony and a view. *8221 Sunset Blvd. 656-1010*

35 Oscar's Wine Bar. An authentically tacky pub favored by the English rock stars who stay at the Chateau Marmont across the street. Pitchers of Pimm's Cup, steak and kidney pie, and cut crystal bowls of trifle. *English. Dinner M-Sa. $$/$$$. 8210 Sunset Blvd. 654-3457*

35 Carlos 'n Charlie's. One of a chain of flashy restaurants that extends south to Acapulco, this lively spot's attraction is the singles scene more than the barbequed chicken and ribs. Even better action upstairs at the private *El Privado. American. Lunch M-F; dinner daily. $$$/$$$$. 8240 Sunset Blvd. 656-8830*

35 Imperial Gardens. You'll find record company execs at the sushi bar, Japanese businessmen in the tatami rooms, and live music in the lounge. Surprisingly authentic food for such a show biz favorite. *Japanese. Dinner daily. $$$/$$$$. 8225 Sunset Blvd. 656-1750*

36 The Comedy Store. The most important showcase for comedians in the area. The Main Room presents established comics; the Original Room offers continuous shows of rising new comedians; the Belly Room presents female talent. *8433 Sunset Blvd. 656-6225*

36 Roy's. Chinese food with a Jewish touch in a Hollywood music setting. Dishes are printed on giant playing cards—you show your hand to order. *Chinese. Dinner M-Sa. $$$/$$$$. 8430 Sunset Blvd. 656-1675*

37 Cock 'n Bull. ☆ Where Burton hangs out when he's in town. Some of the waitresses and customers go back 30 years. Bar is busy all afternoon. Welsh rarebit and a groaning board of hearty English fare for dinner. *English. Lunch M-F; dinner daily. Su brunch. $$$. 9170 Sunset Blvd. 273-0081*

38 Le Dome. ☆ ☆ Elegant informality with a great view. One of the most dramatic interiors in the city with one of the most interesting menus. A favorite with the music industry. *French. Closed Su. Open late. $$$$. 8720 Sunset Blvd. 650-6919*

38 Old World. A front patio for people watching. Salads are excellent, as are the Belgian waffles. *Healthy Continental. Open daily. Breakfast served. $/$$. 8782 Sunset Blvd. 652-2520*

Restaurants red
Architecture blue

Spago. ☆ ☆ ☆ Chef-*wunderkind* Wolfgang Puck gave up on *buerre blanc* at Ma Maison and opened his own pizza and pasta parlor, California-style—which means it is modern, extremely noisy, (an *Entertainment Tonite* with calories) and offers the likes of grilled squab with apple. *California/Italian/French. Dinner daily. $$/$$$/$$$$. 1114 Horn St. 652-4025*

Tower Records. Bills itself as the largest record store in the known world. Classical records are located in the annex across the street. *Open until midnight. 8801 Sunset Blvd.*

La Petite Maison. ☆ Once the gourmet-health food *Aware Inn*, La Petite Maison has retained its cozy-room ambience and reasonable prices, along with some of the original organic dishes. French specialties have been added along with a fresh coat of paint. *Health food/French. Lunch M-F; dinner daily. $$$/$$$$. 8828 Sunset Blvd. 652-2555*

Whiskey A Go Go. Live rock is the specialty here, with a floor up front by the stage for dancing. This has been one of the most popular clubs on the Strip since its opening in 1964. *8901 Sunset Blvd. 652-4202*

Scandia. ☆ ☆ During the '50s, this clubby restaurant with a view was one of the top 5 dining spots in LA. Today, though the food is uneven, it still offers an exemplary wine cellar, excellent *gravlaax*, and homemade Danish pastries during Sunday brunch. *Scandinavian/Continental. Closed M. $$$$. 9040 Sunset Blvd. 278-3555*

The Roxy. The foremost nightclub in town, decorated in art deco style. Rock and jazz performers, already famous or on the right path, are the headliners here. The club is frequently booked by the local music industry to showcase hot new talent. Two shows nightly. Limited food menu. *9009 Sunset Blvd. 878-2222*

Gazzarri's. The oldest rock club on the Strip boasts two stages and dance floors. Tuesday and Thursday are showcase nights; Friday through Sunday, local bands play. *9030 Sunset Blvd. 273-6606*

Rex's Fishmarket. ☆ Cousin of a Honolulu eatery, Rex's flies in fresh mahi mahi and opakapaka and has the only sushi bar/disco in town. Go for great Hawaiian fish, great service, or, after ten, the singles' scene. *Seafood. Lunch M-F; dinner daily. $$$$. 9229 Sunset Blvd. 550-1541*

WEST HOLLYWOOD: Geographically an extension of Hollywood, West Hollywood is spiritually and economically vastly different. While Hollywood has thrived by not looking too closely at the details and immortalizing the past, West Hollywood has prospered through minute attention to detail and tapping the pulse of the newest style. This is the area of the deocrator, the designer, and the art dealer, where the home furnishings, clothing, and accessories seen in the glossiest national magazines can be purchased. European in feeling through intimacy of scale and architectural diversity, streets are lined with well-kept stucco houses and storefronts, and chic restaurants abound.

Shopping. Treasured remnants from the past and the finest in contemporary design, Melrose Avenue offers all this and more. This area is on the cutting edge of fashion, full of invention, lively and unpredictable. Boutiques housed in modest storefronts attract through imaginative window display rather than architectural grandeur. Furniture, antiques, art deco accessories, and clothing ranging from second hand to the newest trends are found in the

section of the street from La Brea Avenue to La Cienega Boulevard. The area from La Cienega to San Vicente Boulevard is glossier; many of the shops here cater to the decorator trade and may not be open to the public. For fashionable, up-to-the-minute-clothing, try: Fred Segal, 8100 Melrose; Savage Space, 7623 Melrose; Hardware, 8620 Melrose. For vintage clothing: Repeat Performance, 7261 Melrose; Cowboys and Poodles, 6907 Melrose; Aaardvarks, 7579 Melrose. Art deco furniture and accessories: Harvey's, 7955-57 Melrose; Jazz, 8113 Melrose; Sheh-Sheh, 8172 Melrose. Fine antiques: Antiquarian Trader, 8483 Melrose; Lightfoot House, 8529 Melrose; Belgravia II, 8650 Melrose. Contemporary furnishings: Vermillion, 553 N. San Vicente Blvd.; Donghia, 8715 Melrose. Books: George Sand, 9011 Melrose; Bennett and Marshall, 8214 Melrose; Pettler and Lieberman, 8119 Melrose.

45 City Cafe. Country French milieu features intimate atmosphere, changing menu—*food as good as Ma Maison at half the price.* Chef from 3-star restaurant in southern France. Best espresso in LA. After hours for pastry, pastas and cool salads. *M-Th 9AM-midnight. F-Sa 9AM-1AM. Closed Su. $$. 7407½ Melrose Ave. 658-7495*

46 Via Fettucini. Trying to do for Italian food what Moustache Cafe has done for French: 46 different kinds of pasta in an unpretentious setting. *Lunch M-F; dinner M-Sa. $$/$$$. 7111 Melrose Ave. 936-5924.*

47 Nucleus Nuance. ☆ Follow a narrow hallway lined with vintage Hollywood photos, and you're back in the '30's. Art Deco, wine bar, and live music, along with pretty good—and healthy—continental food. *Lunch M-F; dinner M-Sa. $$/$$$. 7267 Melrose Ave. 939-8666*

48 Groundlings Theatre. A resident company does sleight-of-mouth improvisation, using suggestions from the audience. *7307 Melrose Ave. 934-9700*

49 Ristorante Chianti. ☆ ☆ One of the *grande dames* of Italian cuisine in Los Angeles. Etched glass and dark wood booths. Where the tradition began of amaretto cookie wrappers turned into *flying saucers. Italian. $$$$. 7383 Melrose Ave. 653-8333*

50 Antonio's. A stand-out for their unusual dishes in a city full of good Mexican food. The decor is colorful; mariachis make the rounds. Try the molé sauce, an unlikely sounding combination of bitter chocolate, nuts, and chilis. *Mexican. Closed M. $$$. 7472 Melrose Ave. 655-0480*

51 Moustache Cafe. Hearty bistro fare, served outside under a latticed patio or inside in traditional cafe decor. A fine place for a casual meal before a visit to the local little theaters. *French. Open daily. $$. 8155 Melrose Ave. 651-2111*

52 Improvisation. On Thursday, Friday, and Saturday, comedians, sometimes well-known, sometimes deserving, have the stage. Sunday through Wednesday, music is featured and Wednesday night is songwriter's showcase. *8162 Melrose Ave. 651-2583*

53 Guiseppe! ☆ Owned by Hollywood agents and producers, and designed by the firm that did *Bijan*, Guiseppe! is gorgeous and full of gorgeous people. The northern Italian cuisine is good; but it is the clublike feeling that is the hook here. Ask for the special rack veal and angel hair al Pomodoro. *Lunch M-F; dinner M-Sa. $$$$. 8256 Beverly Blvd. (Easy to miss; no sign.) 653-8025*

54 Ma Maison. ☆ ☆ ☆ Patrick Terrail's inventive marriage of uncompromising French cuisine and casual California atmosphere. (In the early days *chef extraordinaire* Wolfgang Puck—now owner-chef at *Spago*—cooked here.) New chef Claude Segal has introduced French country cooking, time-tested fundamentals applied to the best of the new cuisine. His menu offers one classic dish nightly. Bernard Erpicum deserves mention as the sommelier, appreciated because he doesn't snub California labels. All this still brings the celebrities and their Rolls' out to dine. Please note the telephone number, it's unlisted. *Closed Su. $$$$. 8368 Melrose Ave. 655-1991*

55 Studio Grill. ☆ ☆ A special restaurant, with personalized care and attention by owner Ardison Phillips reflected in everything from his paintings on the walls to the inventive dishes on the menu and the superb wine list including many of his own labels. Ask for seating in the Wine Room. This is a favorite with the creative community. *Continental. Open daily. No lunch Sa-Su. $$$. 7321 Santa Monica Blvd. 874-9202*

56 Gardenia. ☆ When the former chef of Studio Grill opened his own restaurant, he brought along some of the same dishes but chose a more modern, peach Deco decor designed to make all the ladies look beautiful. *Continental/ Italian. Lunch M-F; dinner M-Sa. Live entertainment weekends. $$$/$$$$. 7066 Santa Monica Blvd. 467-7444*

57 China Club. Chinese food garnished California-style with fresh fruits and vegetables. The food's a hit-and-miss affair, but the decor is the main attraction: From a concept by owner Sy Chen, interior designer Sampee Abe did the decor, graphic designer April Grieman created signage, graphics and artwork on tables and china. Grieman's bar mirror is already famous, as is the 30-foot mural by New York air brush artist Pater Sato. This is a prototype in America's digestion of Tokyo-modern, and will probably be remembered 20 years from now with as much affection as we currently view the Coconut Grove or Copa Cabana. *Dinner M-Sa. $$/$$$. 8338 W. Third St. 658-6406*

55 Plummer Park. A portion of Rancho La Brea, Plummer Ranch was operated as a truck farm and dairy from 1877 to 1943. The three-acre park now contains recreational facilities and the original Plummer home, currently headquarters to the Los Angeles Audubon Society. *Audobon House open M-Sa, 10AM-3PM. 7377 Santa Monica Blvd. 867-0202*

58 Villa d'este Apartments. A lush courtyard apartment built in 1928. Decorative wood garages face on to the street and the brick paved driveways lead into the central court with a fountain. The Spanish Revival units all have round arched windows and doors, fireplaces, high-beamed ceilings, and their own patios and terraces. *Private residence. 1355 Laurel Ave.*

59 Havenhurst Drive Apartments. From the same era and in a similar quaint Spanish courtyard style. These apartments are mementos of a romantic way of living from an earlier Hollywood era and they are cherished for their charm and design quality. *Private residence. 1400-14 and 1471-75 Havenhurst Drive.*

60 The Globe Theatre. A charming replica of the London theater where Shakespeare presented his work. Fittingly, the fare is Shakespeare, ranging through all the plays and including dramatic presentations of the sonnets. *Schedule varies; call ahead. 1107 N. Kings Rd. 654-5623*

61 Schindler House. In 1926, the innovative architect Rudolph Schindler built himself a double house, to be shared with his engineer, Clyde Chase. Schindler experimented with using tilt-up slab walls of concrete and opening up the house with courtyards and open-air sleeping lofts, a technique and spatial treatment which were novel at that time. The house is accessible behind the dense front foliage, and it is maintained by the Friends of the Schindler House. *833 N. Kings Rd.*

62 Matoi. Dependable, attractive sushi reataurant. *Lunch M-F; dinner M-Sa. $$. 8400 Santa Monica Blvd. 654-0945*

62 Hugo's. ☆ *The* white eastern veal specialty butcher shop has gone gourmet deli. Incredible (and not cheap) pasta and marinated salads to eat at red-checked tablecloth-covered tables, or to-go. *Italian Deli. M-Sa 9AM-9PM; Su 11AM-7PM. $$/$$$. 8401 Santa Monica Blvd. 654-3993*

62 Barney's Beanery. Immortalized by sculptor Ed Kienholz in the '60s, Barney's still offers breakfast, lunch, and dinner, a zillion labels of beer, and a friendly game of pool. *American. Open daily. $/$$. 8447 Santa Monica Blvd. 656-0433*

La Cienega Boulevard, from Melrose to Santa Monica Boulevard, is lined with shops full of beautiful antiques, art, rugs, and decorative items.

Two of the finest special-interest bookstores in Los Angeles are: **63 Zeitlin and Ver Brugge.** Early science and medicine; graphic arts. *815 N. La Cienega Blvd. 655-7581*

63 Heritage Book Shop. First editions. *847 N. La Cienega Blvd. 659-3674*

64 L'Orangerie. ☆ ☆ ☆ The grandest, most formal, of the French restaurants in LA, and one of the best. Prices reflect the fact that they fly in their fresh seafood and foie gras from France. But the prix fixe menu offered M, Tu, & W offers much the same food—and identical ambience—at reasonable prices. *Dinner daily. $$$$. 903 N. La Cienega Blvd. 652-9770*

65 L'Ermitage. ☆ ☆ ☆ The late restaurateur Jean Bertranou set the standard for elegant French dining in LA. Today, his restaurant continues the tradition of inspired haute cuisine in sumptuous surroundings. *French. Dinner M-Sa. $$$$. 730 N. La Cienega Blvd. 652-5840*

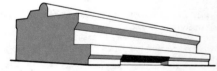

66 Pacific Design Center. Swelling above its small-scale surroundings, looking like a behemoth in a toy shop, the unmistakable silhouette of the blue-glass Pacific Design Center dominates the neighborhood. Designed by Cesar Pelli in 1975, this wholesale and retail mall for the interior design trade is nicknamed the *Blue Whale.* At night, fluorescent and neon lights glow through the skin of the building, making it look like a space station. *8687 Melrose. 657-0800*

Jean Lois Vignes tended some of California's first wine vineyards in the 1820's, and by the middle of that century the LA area sported over 90 different vineyards, the original heart of California wine country.

La Cage Aux Folles. If you loved the movie, you may enjoy this restaurant/night club. Your evening comes complete with pink feathers, quasi-French food, and a classy (if such a thing can be regarded as classy) drag-queen show. *French Cabaret. Dinner M-Sa. Shows 9PM & 11:30PM. $$$/$$$$. 643 N. La Cienega. 657-1091*

Chili Stop. Stop at the only take-out specializing in New (as in Albuquerque) Mexican food: Chili without beans that is hot, hot, hot; deep-fried *sopapilla* pastries drenched with honey; and on Fridays, blue-corn tortillas. *New Mexican. Tu-Sa 10AM-7PM. $/$$. 359 N. La Cienega Blvd. 657-4762*

Moghul. Authentic tandoori ovens produce succulent spicy chicken, kebabs, and puffy Indian breads. A daily lunch buffet offers curries as well. *Indian. Lunch and dinner daily. $$/$$$. 163 N. La Cienega. 652-7065*

Fat Burger. The hamburgers here are appropriately juicy, greasy, and fresh off the grill. Their popularity keeps the restaurant's doors open 24 hours a day. *American. $. 450 N. La Cienega Blvd. 652-8489. Also in Westwood.*

Pasta, Pasta, Pasta. ☆ Fresh pasta take-outs have been springing up all over town, but this is the original; basil-laced and spinach fettucini made daily, as well as lasagne for fifty on special order. You'll never settle for store-bought pasta again. *Italian. Tu-F 10AM-7PM, Sa 10AM-6PM, closed Su-M. $$/$$$. 8161 W. Third St. 653-2051*

Michel Richard. ☆ This master *patissier* turns desserts into art. Delicate mousse and meringue-filled cakes you could never bake at home. Tables for *petit dejeuner*, or salad and quiche lunches. Now also in Studio City, it is one of the few places to get fresh croissants on Sunday. *French. W. Hollywood shop M-Sa 9AM-7PM, closed Su. 310 N. Robertson Blvd. 275-5707. Studio City shop Tu-Sa 9AM-7:30PM, Su 8:30AM-4PM, closed M. 12321 Ventura Blvd. 508-9977*

Joe Allen. Like the original in New York's theater district, Joe Allen serves gargantuan salads and simple grilled food. Used brick and out-of-work actors in the bar. Heaters make the patio pleasant year-round. *American/Continental. Open daily 7AM-12:45AM. $$/$$$. 8706 W. Third St. 274-7144*

Ivy & LA Desserts. ☆ Everything here, from the Champs Elysee park chairs on the ivy-covered patio to the antique English platters over the fireplace inside, is charming and for sale. But your eye will still find its way to the plain white deli case. Therein lie the best chocolate fudge and marjolaine cakes in town. Pasta salads at lunch live up to the reputation established by LA Desserts. *Bakery/Continental. Breakfast & lunch M-Sa. $$. 113 N. Robertson Blvd. 273-5537*

Entourage. ☆ An interesting hand in the kitchen, creating such delights as duck roasted in almond liqueur. The atmosphere is chic. *French. Open 7 days. No lunch, Sa-Su. $$$. 8450 Third St. 653-1079*

Kathy Gallagher. ☆ A former model who mastered the restaurant ropes on the Upper East Side has brought a New York bar and grill to West Hollywood. Blond woods and lots of glass. If you don't go for the steaks and chops, you can make a meal of such exotic appetizers as Moroccan *b'stilla*, or brioche stuffed with brie. *American/Continental. Lunch & dinner daily. $$$. 8722 W. Third St. 271-9930*

72 Tail-O-the-Pup. We don't know whether to call this LA landmark art or architecture. In any case, go see it if you're in the neighborhood. It is a highly visible and cherished example of the Los Angeles tendency to turn advertising into a monument, designed by Milton Black in 1938. *$. 311 N. La Cienega Blvd. 652-4517*

73 Le Cou Cou. On the site of an old local favorite, this trendy new eatery offers immaculate appointments and fine service. The menu is noteworthy; try any of the first course salads and you won't go wrong. *Lunch 12-3PM, dinner 6PM-midnight. $$$. 829 N. La Cienega Blvd. 854-0088*

74 Doug Weston's Troubadour. Since the 1960s, this simple hall has heard some of pop music's greatest talent including Joan Baez, Bob Dylan, and Linda Ronstadt. The club is often the last stop before nationwide fame, and those who blaze ahead have been known to come back to play a set for nostalgia's sake. The bar is a favorite hangout for local musicians. Limited food menu. *9081 Santa Monica Blvd. 276-6168*

75 Cafe Figaro. Namesake of the New York coffeehouse, a dark and crowded place that is good for late night snacks and long discussions about the meaning of life. *American/Continental. Open 7 days. Open until 12:30AM. No lunch Su. $/$$. 9010 Melrose Ave. 274-7664*

75 Morton's. ☆ ☆ Honest enough to put the kitchen in front, straightforward enough to type the menu, and handsome enough, with pink tablecloths and palms, to attract the trend setters. *American. Closed Su. Dinner only. $$$/$$$$. 8801 Melrose. 276-5205 (unlisted)*

75 Trumps. ☆ ☆ A dramatic-sexy-trend-setter. Decor as stark as a modern mansion in Taos, important LA art on the walls, and food—mostly grilled—that combines French, California, and mother's home cooking (potato pancakes with goat cheese, for example). Find a seat on the overstuffed raffia banquettes in the bar well past midnight. *French/California. Lunch, LA's best afternoon tea, and dinner M-Sa. $$$$. 8764 Melrose Ave. 855-1480*

76 Studio One Backlot. An intimate cabaret featuring singers and comedians. Well-known personalities often appear. Dinner and full bar offered. *652 N. La Peer. 659-0472*

76 Rose Tatoo. Located behind Studio One disco, this pretty restaurant attracts a gay and straight crowd. Reasonable—and usually excellent—prix fixe dinners start with an overflowing basket of *crudites* and silken sauces for dipping. *Continental. Lunch M-F, dinner daily, Su brunch. $$$. 665 N. Robertson Blvd. 854-4455*

77 Los Angeles Palm. ☆ ☆ The best steak and lobster in town—also the most expensive. The room is always jammed, the waiters speedy. In other words, the same harried ambience as in the New York original. *American. Lunch M-F, dinner daily. $$$$. 9001 Santa Monica Blvd. 550-8811*

78 Chasen's. ☆ ☆ President Reagan's favorite restaurant featuring the world's most expensive chili, as well as a score of American and continental—often pedestrian—dishes. Fifties red leather booth-and-knotty-pine decor. It helps to be a star to get good service. No credit cards; a lot of the Old Hollywood customers have long had house accounts. *Continental/American. Dinner only daily. $$$$. 9039 Beverly Blvd. 271-2168*

Narrative/Museums/Shops black
Gardens/Parks/Piers green
Restaurants red
Architecture blue

79 Beverly Center. Hovering like a giant toadstool over Restaurant Row, this shopping center has raised cries of *traffic snarler* and *Beaubourg West*. Its four levels provide incredible choices for shopping, dining and entertainment. In addition to *The Broadway* and *Bullock's* department stores, there are such boutiques as *Rodier Paris, Judy's, Phillipe Salvet, Williams-Sonoma* and the very special *By Design*. The ground floor features the *Irvine Ranch Farmer's Market*, offering fresh meat and produce, and among the 25 restaurants schedules are the *Hard Rock Cafe, Tea Room St. Petersburg* and *Jerry's Famous Deli*. Visitors will be able to choose from 16 movies run in the Cineplex theater complex on the top floor.

79 Hard Rock Cafe. A 1950s roadside diner with loud music, pinball machines and hamburgers, ribs and fish cooked over mesquite fire. Great American desserts, an excellent value for the money. Opened by the owner of the original London Hard Rock Cafe and LA's Mortons. *Daily 11:30AM-midnight. $$. In The Beverly Center. 652-2690*

79 Food for Thought. A general bookstore/cappucino cafe in The Beverly Center that also serves beer, wine and deli foods. *#128 in The Beverly Center. 854-4475*

79 Tea Room St. Petersburg. Authentic Russian menu and entertainment in a very gaudy cabaret atmosphere atop The Beverly Center. Lots of caviar, standard stroganoff, and unusual specialties like grilled sturgeon and Siberian pelmeny. *M-W, 11:30AM-10:30PM; Th-Su, 11:30AM-2PM. $$$/$$$$. Entertainment Tu-Su after 9PM (cover charge). 8th Floor. 657-8830*

A number of the finest contemporary art galleries in Los Angeles are located in the West Hollywood area. Most are open 11AM-5PM, Tuesday-Saturday.

80 Newspace. *5241 Melrose Ave.*

81 Janus Gallery. *8000 Melrose Ave.*

82 Gemini G.E.L. Publishers of fine art prints by outstanding and internationally known contemporary artists. *8365 Melrose Ave.*

83 Space Gallery. *6015 Santa Monica Blvd.*

45 Asher/Faure. *8221 Santa Monica Blvd.*

45 James Corcoran. *8223 Santa Monica Blvd.*

45 Baum/Silverman. The front of the gallery exhibits fine ethnic artifacts; the rear, contemporary art. *8225 Santa Monica Blvd.*

45 Meghan Williams. *8225½ Santa Monica Blvd.*

45 Art Catalogues. Art books and catalogs. *8227 Santa Monica Blvd.*

65 Margo Leavin. *812 N. Robertson Blvd.*

65 Adam Meckler. *651 N. La Cienega Blvd.*

65 Rosamund Felsen. *699 N. La Cienega Blvd.*

65 Molly Barnes. *750 N. La Cienega Blvd.*

65 Stephen White Gallery of Photography. *835 N. La Cienega Blvd.*

Restaurants red
Architecture blue
Narrative/Museums/Shops black
Gardens/Parks/Piers green

---

6 BEVERLY HILLS

Beverly Hills is an affluent residential city of palatial homes surrounded by parklike lawns and gardens, swimming pools, and tennis courts. The 5-square-mile city has some of the highest property values in the world (houses worth over $1 million are almost common), and its shops, those on Rodeo Drive in particular, are premier in the world of fashion and luxury.

Commercial activities are restricted and geared toward service to the wealthy; most industrial activity is forbidden within city boundaries. Various municipal ordinances regulate many public activities. Laws dictate the size of real-estate signs and prohibit residents and visitors from parking overnight on the streets in front of homes. Affluence is also felt in professional presence: Beverly Hills has more doctors and psychiatrists than any other area its size—there is one doctor for every 52 residents.

Those adrift of the law in Beverly Hills can comfort themselves with the knowledge that they will share each of the city's lawyers with only 46 other people; while shade-seekers will be happy to know that the city has more than 23,000 trees.

The city was not always so magnificent. The first Westerners who traveled along what later became Wilshire Boulevard were part of the footsore Portola expedition of 1769. Later, the first resident of the area was Maria Rita Valdez, a soldier's widow, who used her inheritance as granddaughter of one of the pueblo's original founders to establish a 4500-acre ranch around 1810. Her simple house stood on the corner where Sunset Boulevard and Alpine Drive now intersect.

The area survived various booms and busts in sheepherding, farming, and oil drilling, but it wts not until 1906 that the neighborhood came close to becoming a city. At that time Burton Green bought the land for speculation and entered the name *Beverly Farms* as the title for his subdivision at the recorder's office. According to local folklore, Green picked the name while President Taft was vacationing in Beverly Farms, Massachusetts. The first home was built by Henry C. Clarke on Crescent Drive in 1907. By 1912, the bean field north of town was cleared to make way for the Beverly Hills Hotel. In 1914, the town population of 500 voted to incorporate the city.

The city's development accelerated when the movie colony arrived. First to settle inside the city limits was Douglas Fairbanks who bought land in the hills and developed it into Pickfair, the home he shared with Mary Pickford. Soon others came to build estates in what quickly became the social center of the movie industry. Today the city reigns as a hub of those who have been blessed by fortune, and a goal for those who aspire to the finer things in life.

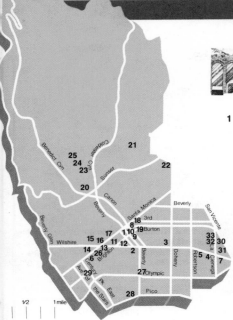

The three primary activities in Beverly Hills are shopping, eating, and watching. It is possible to do all three at once—buy an ice cream cone and window shop at the low end, or sit in the bar at Giorgio's and sip and spend simultaneously at the high end. It seems incredible that a city could become so famous on the strength of only three pastimes, but spectacle and indolence have great charm and few places on earth manage to accommodate luxury with the silken assurance of Beverly Hills.

The main shopping area is within the triangle created by Wilshire Boulevard, *little* Santa Monica Boulevard (so called to distinguish it from *big* Santa Monica Boulevard, the major thoroughfare that it parallels between Robertson and the San Diego Freeway), and Doheny Drive. Rodeo Drive is the most famous shopping street, justly compared to Madison Avenue in New York, Via Condotti in Rome, Bond Street in London, and the Faubourg Saint Honore in Paris. One reason for the comparison is that branches of luxury mercantiles are found on all these streets: *Gucci, Elizabeth Arden, Van Cleef and Arpels, Hermes,* and *Jaeger,* among others. Yet these establishments escape the disdain usually directed at chain stores; like princesses, each one is different. Rodeo Drive differs from its international peers in the freshly peeled newness which shines from every facade; it has emerged as the queen of shopping districts within the last ten years. Among the fabulous stores lining the Drive are: Jewels-*Van Cleef and Arpels, Omega, Fred Joaillier, Inamori.*
Leather-*Gucci, Bally, Celine, Hermes, Bottega Veneta.*
Beauty-*Vidal Sassoon, Elizabeth Arden, Georgette Klinger, Alan Edwards.*
Menswear-*Jerry Magnin, Bijan, Carroll and Co., Mr. Guy, Battaglia, Theodore Man.*
Womenswear-*St. Laurent/rive gauche, Courreges, Giorgio, Lina Lee, Ted Lapidus, Amelia Grey.*

California "sports wear" becomes major industry.
1949

1 Rodeo Collection. An array of penultimately expensive shops, boutiques and restaurants, this European galleria was conceived by architect Olivier Vidal and is housed in a bronze, glass and brick townhouse emporium that is a monument to opulence. Four levels featuring the best in international shopping for the truly discriminating surround an open-air plaza and central garden: *Ungaro, Ricci, Versace,* and *Bijan* fashions for women; *Yves St. Laurent* for men, *Vuitton* luggage, leather goods by *Fendi* and *Testoni,* and linens by *Pratesi. Personal Shoppers,* kiosks offering fresh flowers and international newspapers, underground valet parking remind you that you are shopping on one of the most famous and elite streets in the world with perhaps the highest commercial rents in the United States. *Shops closed Su. 421 Rodeo Dr.*

1 Excelsior Restaurant. ☆☆ Occupying the entire penthouse level of the Rodeo Collection is this extravagant restaurant offering cuisine which is, per owner Mario Casarini, "exquisitely French, with a touch of Italian coloratura" and served on Richard Ginori china in an elaborate beige and salmon Art Nouveau decor. There is also a piano bar/lounge *open 11:30AM-2AM with music nightly 8PM-2AM. Lunch 11:30AM-3PM daily, dinner 6PM-11PM daily. Reservations. $$$$. 275-5100*

1 Beverly Rodeo Hotel. A luxury hotel with an intimate, European flavor. *360 N. Rodeo Dr. 273-0300*

1 Cafe Rodeo. The front is open for people-watching on Rodeo Drive. Delicious salads are the specialty. *Continental. Open daily. Breakfast served. $$. 360 N. Rodeo Dr. 273-0330*

1 Cafe Swiss. A garden, an escape, good food, reliably prepared. *Swiss. Closed Su. $$/$$$. 450 N. Rodeo Dr. 274-2820*

1 Anderton Court. This is one of Frank Lloyd Wright's late works, built in 1953-54. Angles predominate and ramps make their way up each side. The whole building, topped by a jagged turquoise tower, appears very active and *coming-apart-at-the-seams. 328 N. Rodeo Dr.*

1 The Ginger Man. A noisy New York-style bar and restaurant where the daily specials are often above-and-beyond the call of duty. Actor Carroll O'Connor is part-owner and sometime piano player. *American/Continental. Lunch & dinner M-Sa. $$$. 369 N. Bedford Dr. 273-7585*

Wilshire Boulevard between Crescent Drive and Roxbury Drive is the home of the great department stores: *Saks Fifth Avenue, I. Magnin, Bonwit Teller, Neiman-Marcus.* Clustered around them are fine specialty stores, such as *Abercrombie & Fitch, Joseph's Salon Shoes,* and *Tiffany.* Lined by slick glass towers and lofty palm trees, the wide boulevard has a spacious and noble air.

"The most American of all American cities."
Hamilton Basso
1950

Restaurants red
Architecture blue
Narrative/Museums/Shops black
Gardens/Parks/Piers green

2 Hernando Courtright's Beverly Wilshire Hotel. The original structure was designed by Walker and Eisen and opened in 1928. Host to the famous and the royal, the symmetrical building is ornamented with Baroque decoration. The Beverly Wilshire has often been listed as one of the most prestigious hotels in the world. The new Beverly Wing, with marble facade and wrought iron balconies, was designed by Welton Becket and opened in 1971. The Beverly Wing lobby recalls the great eras of Europe with crystal chandeliers, marble arches, and silk draperies. El Camino Real, a private street separating the two wings, is lined with cobblestones and gas lights imported from Edinburgh Castle. *9500 Wilshire Blvd. 275-4282*

Within the hotel you may dine at:

2 LaBella Fontana. ☆ ☆ A formal dining room featuring service, cuisine, and wine cellar to meet the most discerning standards, plus velvet walls with Belgian lace curtains and piano music. *Continental. Closed Su, no lunch Sa. $$$$*

2 El Padrino Rotisserie-Bar. Relaxed dining in an early California atmosphere. Piano music, cocktails, dinner, and late supper. *Continental. Open daily. $$$.*

2 Don Hernando's Hideaway. Colorful Mexican decor, intimate. *Mexican/Continental. Dancing during dinner and late supper. Open 7AM-2AM, closed Su. $$$.*

2 Zindabad Pub serves drinks in an exotic, East Indian atmosphere.

2 Brentano's. A wonderfully comprehensive bookseller, emphasizing art books and recent fiction. There is a small gallery section for graphics and posters. Non-printed items such as Russian boxes and art glass are also sold. *9500 Wilshire Blvd. (Beverly Wilshire Hotel)*

3 Fowler Museum. A small museum specializing in European and American decorative arts. Notable collections are 15th-18th century silver, paperweights, carved ivories, and Russian porcelains. *Admission free. Open M-Sa, 1-5PM. Closed Su. 9215 Wilshire Blvd. 278-8010*

Other nearby restaurants are:

3 Brooklyn's Famous Pizza. New York-style thin-crusted pizza that tastes great plain (sauce and cheese) and even better with toppings. *Open M-Th, 11AM-12midnight; F-Sa, 11AM-1AM; Su, 4PM-12midnight. 9383 Wilshire Blvd. 858-1303*

4 Chrystie's Bar & Grill. Sleek and authentic Art Deco, like the adjoining Wilshire Theatre, Chrystie's has the atmosphere and menu of a simple grill in New York's theater district, and is hopping before and after the show next door. *American. Lunch & dinner daily; late supper. $$$. 8442 Wilshire Blvd. 655-3216*

5 Bagatelle. The chef-owner creates unique and unforgettable dishes. Lapin a la Piron, Napoleons, and seafood are recommended. *French. Closed Su. $$$$. 8690 Wilshire Blvd. 659-0782*

5 Chambord. A flattering decor of rose-colored walls and fresh flowers. The chef is particularly inventive with veal and fish. *French. Closed Su. No lunch Sa. $$$. 8689 Wilshire Blvd. 652-6590*

Restaurants red
Architecture blue
Narrative/Museums/Shops black
Gardens/Parks/Piers green

5 Andre's of Beverly Hills. One of the best values in town for soup-to-dessert dinners. *Italian/Continental. Closed M. No lunch Sa-Su. $$. 8635 Wilshire Blvd. 657-2446*

5 Homer and Edy's Bistro. ☆ The only restaurant in LA with authentic Creole cooking: gumbo and catfish and sinfully rich pecan pie. Homer and Edy want folks to feel like it's Mardi Gras all year round and the live New Orleans jazz played on weekends helps. *Creole. Lunch M-F; dinner Tu-Su. $$$. 2839 S. Robertson Blvd. 559-5102*

6 Jimmy's. ☆ ☆ A dazzling setting for the glamorous, who dine on dishes that match the beauty of the surroundings. *French. $$$$. Closed Su. No lunch Sa. 201 Moreno Dr. 879-2394*

7 Wilshire Theatre. A legitimate stage, recently restored to up-beat Art Deco glory, which presents musicals and plays. *8440 Wilshire Blvd. 852-1900*

Little Santa Monica Boulevard, between Cañon and Wilshire, has a homey charm, lined with one and two-story stucco shops adorned with New England or Mediterranean details.
You might look at:

8 The Price of His Toys (the difference between a man and a boy is...) An amusing shop for grown-ups. *9550 Santa Monica Blvd.*

8 Standard Cutlery and Supply Co. The world's largest selection of cutting implements. *9509 Santa Monica Blvd.*

8 Camp Beverly Hills. A collection of old and new casual clothing. *9509 Santa Monica Blvd.*

8 The Great American Sweatshirt and Happiness Company. You can prove that you were here when you get back there with a Beverly Hills T-shirt. *9640 Santa Monica Blvd.*

8 Rangoon Racquet Club. Kipling would have felt right at home among the palms and rattan. The menu mixes English with Indian-just like the Empire. *English. Closed Su. No lunch Sa. $/$$$. 9474 Santa Monica Blvd. 274-8926*

8 La Famiglia. ☆ No hanging Chianti bottle-decor here. A smart, modern look in an intimate, friendly Italian restaurant specializing in red and green pasta, and low-cal *nucova cucina. Italian. Lunch, M-F; dinner M-Sa. $$$/$$$$. 435 N. Cañon Dr. 276-6208*

9 Romeo and Juliet. ☆ ☆ The venerable Washington D.C. restaurant comes to Beverly Hills with the same refined Eastern decor and rich Italian menu. Expect to forget about the prices—and your diet. *Italian. Lunch, M-F; dinner M-Sa. $$$$. 435 N. Beverly Dr. 273-2292*

9 The Cheese Store. Notable for an extensive selection of imported cheeses. *419 N. Beverly Dr.*

9 Jurgensen's Gourmet Grocery. For fine wines and gift baskets. *409 N. Beverly Dr.*

9 Chess and Games Unlimited. Specialists in backgammon boards. *336 N. Beverly Dr.*

10 Jacopo's Pizzeria. Everything about theirs is particularly good. *M, 12noon-10PM; Tu-Sa, 12noon-12midnight; Su, 1PM-10PM. $$. 490 N. Beverly Dr. 858-6446*

12 Englander's Wine Bar. A high-tech wine bar that is jammed at lunch, more leisurely at dinner. Food is simple, yet as high-style as the decor. Great for good conversation, distinctive wines-by-the-glass, and jazz piano late at night. *Wine Bar/Continental. Lunch & dinner M-Sa. $$/$$$. 340 N. Camden Dr. 274-0248*

Santa Monica Boulevard

P		P
Boulmiche		Nili Design Jewelry

Little Santa Monica Boulevard

Camden Drive side		Rodeo Drive		Beverly Drive side
Hunter's Books	463	466		Carroll and Co. Men
Lina Lee				Carroll and Co. Women
Bottega Veneta				Eres
Allen Edwards Salon				Cafe Swiss
Theodore				P
Theodore Man				Williams Sonoma
Frette				Pierre Deux
Courreges				Elizabeth Arden
Caritta				Bijan
Bally of Switzerland				Amelia Gray
Vidal Sassoon				Edwards-Lowell
				Johnson & Murphy
Fred Joaillier	401	400		First Beverly Bank

Brighton Way

Mr. Guy	369	372		Cartier
P				Merle Norman Cosmetics
				Andrea Carrano
P				Lanvin Paris
				Beverly Rodeo Hotel
Gucci				Cafe Rodeo
Hermes				Cecil Gee of London
Wally Findlay Galleries				Gilda Antique Jewelry
Omega				Bally of Switzerland
Celine				St. Laurent/rive gauche
				Richard Bertine
Ted Lapidus	329	332		Kazanjian Jewelers
Jerry Magnin/Polo				Riazee
Polo by Ralph Lauren				Polin Salon de Beaute
Inamori				Daisy
Gunn Trigere Ltd.				Mille Chemises
Right Bank Clothing & Tea Room				David Orgell
Matthews				Nazareno Gabrielli
Jax				Georgette Klinger
Jewels by Edwar				Francis Klein Antique Jewelry
Yves St. Tropez				Milka Harp Hari Stylist
				Battaglia
Right Bank Shoe Co.	301	300		Van Cleef & Arpels

Dayton Way

Giorgio	273	272		Davante Galleries
				Petersen Galleries
Frank Hoffer				P
Brown Derby				American Savings

9525	9537	9535	9475

Wilshire Boulevard

9500

Beverly Wilshire Hotel

Not to scale

12 Mr. Chow. ☆ Glossy black and white interior hung with fine contemporary art. Tame, expensive Chinese food that often looks better than it tastes. The chef comes out from the kitchen for a nightly *noodle show*. *Chinese. Dinner daily; lunch M-F. $$$/$$$$. 344 N. Camden Dr. 278-9911*

12 Konditori Scandinavian. Jewellike open-faced sandwiches and smorgasbord. Wake up your appetite first with the icy-cold liquid rye bread called Aquavit. *Scandinavian. Closed Su. $$. 362 N. Camden Dr. 550-9950*

12 Mandarin. ☆ ☆ Among the most opulent Chinese restaurants in town. Amusingly, the specialty of this palace is Beggar's Chicken. *Chinese. Open daily. No lunch Su. $$$. 430 N. Camden Dr. 272-0267*

12 The Bistro. ☆ ☆ A stellar spot for seeing and being seen, the location of many of the parties noted in the local papers' society columns. The food does not take a back seat and is as enticing as the surroundings. *French/ Continental. Closed Su. $$$$. 246 N. Canon Dr. 273-5633*

12 The Bistro Garden. ☆ ☆ Summer suppers outdoors in the garden are incomparable. *French/Continental. Closed Su. $$$$. 176 N. Canon. 550-3900*

9 Nate 'n' Al. Of course there's a deli in Beverly Hills. Big-name stars often come in on weekends to read their Sunday newspapers and talk with friends. *Jewish. Open daily. Breakfast served. $/$$. 414 N. Beverly Dr. 274-0101*

10 R.J.s, The Rib Joint. Ribs, steaks, chicken—all of the highest quality, hickory broiled, and served in huge portions. The salad bar is really a salad block—40 feet long and filled with extraordinary things. *American. Open daily. No lunch Su. $$. 252 N. Beverly Dr. 278-9044*

6 La Scala. ☆ ☆ One of the finest restaurants in LA. This personal creation of Jean Leon proffers exquisite pasta and veal, chicken cacciatore that puts all others to shame, and a superb wine cellar, and pastries that God sends out for. The famous dine here often and tend to get the best service. *Italian. Closed Su. $$$$. 9455 Santa Monica Blvd. 275-0579*

13 Perpetual Savings Bank. Set back from the street, creating an impressive forecourt with a fountain. The arched windows are overgrown with ivy, creating hanging gardens. Edward Durrell Stone designed the bank in 1962. *9720 Wilshire Blvd.*

11 Cafe Casino. Fast-food French. The pate and coq au vin may not be the best, but they beat McDonald's. Where to teach the kids that there is more to food than a Big Mac. Sidewalk dining. *French. Open daily. 9595 Wilshire Blvd. 274-0201. Also in Santa Monica: 1299 Ocean Ave. 394-3717*

11 Cafe Beverly Hills. Home-style cooking 24 hours a day. *American. Open daily. $/$$. 9725 Wilshire Blvd. 273-6397*

14 Beverly Hilton. The jewel of the Hilton chain; balconied rooms encircle the swimming pool. *9876 Wilshire Blvd. 274-7772*

14 Trader Vic's. ☆ One in an international chain of Polynesian restaurants, with a South Seas decor that is exotic, and equally exotic rum drinks. Beware the mai tais—more than one, and you won't taste the Indonesian lamb. *Polynesian. Dinner daily. $$$. 9876 Wilshire Blvd. (in Beverly Hilton). 274-7777*

14 L'Escoffier. ☆ In the *olde worlde* tradition of velvet draperies and crystal chandeliers. The only restaurant in Los Angeles with haute cuisine, dancing, and a great view. *French. Dinner M-Sa. $$$$. 9876 Wilshire Blvd. (in Beverly Hilton). 278-4220*

14 Mr. H. A groaning board buffet. The Sunday brunch will leave you helpless for the remainder of the day. *American. Open daily. $$/$$$*

15 Spadina House. Hansel and Gretel would have lived here if they'd hit it big with their screenplay. The thatched-roof residence is an architectural fantasy from the Beverly Hills movie era, originally designed by Henry Oliver as a movie set in 1921. *516 Walden Dr.*

16 Beverly Hills Electric Fountain. The Electric Fountain began operating in 1931. Ralph Flewelling, architect of the Beverly Hills Post Office, designed the fountain and Merrel Gage sculpted the figure of the kneeling prospector on the column and the narrative relief of California's history on the base. *Wilshire Blvd. and Santa Monica Blvd.*

17 Cactus Garden. An attractive outdoor planting containing specimen cacti and succulents from several continents. *Admission free. North side of big Santa Monica Blvd. between Camden Dr. and Bedford Dr.*

18 U.S. Post Office. Terra-cotta and brick combine with classically framed windows and doors to create a noble structure in the Italian Renaissance style, designed by Ralph C. Flewelling in 1933. *9300 Santa Monica Blvd.*

18 Beverly Hills City Hall. The ornate Spanish Baroque City Hall was designed by architect William Gage in 1932. It is decorated with scroll ornament around the doors and a colorful tile dome. *450 N. Crescent Dr.*

19 Music Corporation of America (now Litton Industries). Period revival architect Paul Williams designed these two-story buildings in 1940 giving them Greek portico facades. They are fine examples of the classical style simplified and purified into what is called the Regency Moderne style. *360 N. Crescent Dr.*

18 Union 76 Gas Station. A 1950s American modern structure with a swooping concrete canopy held up by few supports. *Rexford Dr. and little Santa Monica Blvd.*

18 L'Ermitage Hotel. Luxury in the grand manner. *9291 Burton Way. 278-3344*

19 Cafe Monet. This unassuming French cafe has two unique features: fruit tarts made by chef/waiter/owner Roger Bourbon, and *Russian Night* on Saturdays after 10PM, when Russian emigres gather to eat chicken Kiev, down vodka, and dance. *French/Russian. Lunch, M-F; dinner, M-Sa. $$/$$$. 9045 Burton Way. 858-7779*

19 En Brochette. Everything you ever wanted on a skewer, plus quiches made by the exclusive Mrs. Tish's. Lovely patio for brunch or lunch. *American. Lunch daily; dinner Tu-Sa. $$/$$$. 9018 Burton Way. 276-9990*

Beverly Hills Hotel. This hotel has become the unofficial symbol of the Beverly Hills lifestyle and has been the backdrop to many Hollywood films. Much of the original 1912 building by Elmer Grey is lost to additions and remodeling. A major addition, the Crescent wing, was completed in 1949. The four-story, Mission Style hotel sits amid 12 acres of lush sub-tropical landscaping. Beyond the main building are 20 luxurious bungalows.

Two popular eating spots within the hotel are:

The Polo Lounge. Meetings are *taken* over breakfast and lunch here; deals made on phones at the tables. It is still star-studded—but easier to get into—after nine, when there is late supper and piano favorites. *Continental. Open daily. $$$. 9641 Sunset Blvd. 276-2251*

Coterie. A plush, Baroque room in the elegant hotel dining tradition, with cuisine that reflects the management's desire to keep hotel guests from fleeing the premises for dinner. *French. Dinner daily. $$$$. 9641 Sunset Blvd.*

Greystone Park (Doheny Mansion). Oilman Edward L. Doheny built this extravagant 55-room family home at the height of the movie star dream home era. The English Tudor mansion was designed by Gordon Kaufmann in 1923 and gets its name from its grey slate roof. The 16 landscaped acres feature balustraded terraces, fountains, and ponds. Although the stables, tennis courts, kennels, and lake have been covered for parking, what remains of the once baronial estate offers a breathtaking view of the West Side of Los Angeles. *The interior of the main building is closed to the public. Grounds open free to the public, 10AM-6PM. Guided tour reservations and summer concert series tickets: 550-4864. 905 Loma Vista Dr.*

Lloyd Wright House. Lloyd Wright built this concrete-block house in 1924 on a tiny corner lot. The side patio encloses a spreading tree and the design features a dramatic two-story living room. *Private residence. 858 N. Doheny Dr.*

Goldwyn House. The home of filmmaker and prominent producer Samuel Goldwyn is located high in Beverly Hills off Laurel Way. A large entrance court displays the Regency-Moderne house designed in 1935. *Private residence. 1200 Laurel Ln.*

Pickfair. In 1919, screen stars Douglas Fairbanks and Mary Pickford purchased this site and brought a wave of movie stars into the community. Architect Wallace Neff remodeled an existing hunting lodge to create this best-known film-star home. The white Colonial manor house was the scene of many celebrations during Hollywood's golden era of the 1920s and '30s. *Private residence. 1143 Summit Dr.*

Selznick House. Film producer David O. Selznick's home was designed by Pasadena architect Roland Coate, Sr. in 1930. The low-scaled Colonial house has a refined pedimented entrance and a beautiful wooded setting. *Private residence. 1400 Tower Grove Drive.*

Beverly Crest Hotel. To the south of Beverly Hills is this moderately-priced, full-service hotel offering good value. *125 S. Spaulding Dr. 274-6801*

Monument to the Stars. In 1923, severe water shortages threatened Beverly Hills with annexation by the City of Los Angeles. Film personalities rallied to preserve the independence of Beverly Hills; the Monument to the Stars was erected to immortalize their victory, a bronze spiral of film with a bas-relief base showing stars who fought the annexation: Will Rogers, Mary Pickford, Douglas Fairbanks, Rudolph Valentino, Harold Lloyd, and Tom Mix. *Beverly Dr. and Olympic Blvd.*

Ronald Reagan
U.S. President from Los Angeles
1981

---

28 Stellini's. ☆ This sort of junior version of the Palm has the added attraction of Cantonese specials in addition to excellent steaks and chops. The chef is from the recently-razed Luau as is owner Joe Stellini. Most of his customers have known him since the good old days of rum drinks and rumaki—both of which are fine here. *American/Chinese. Dinner Tu-Sa. $$$/$$$$. 9184 W. Pico Blvd. 274-7225*

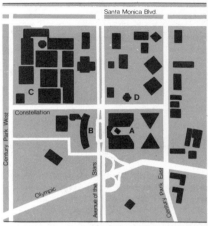

29 CENTURY CITY. A development built on what was originally the backlot for 20th Century-Fox Pictures. During the 1950s, the movie studios, and Fox in particular, found set construction to be prohibitively expensive and began to shoot on location. A decision was made to develop the prime property between Beverly Hills and Westwood. Alcoa Corporation arranged for and planned the city, which contains the Century City Shopping Center, the ABC Entertainment Center, and high-rise office buildings and condominiums. The bridge spanning Avenue of the Stars became famous in a scene in the movie *Planet of the Apes.*

A The ABC Entertainment Center and Century Plaza Towers. The handsome triangular towers were designed by Minoru Yamasaki. In the center are ramps and escalators leading down to an underground passageway beneath the street. During the summer this central area is used for dance and theatrical performances. The street, plaza, and concourse levels of the center feature a number of dining, shopping, and amusement amenities:

A Plitt Century Plaza Theaters. Two first-run movie theaters, the largest of which has perhaps the most comfortable seats in town. *553-4291*

A Plaza Four. A steak and seafood restaurant which offers Las Vegas-type entertainment. *Open daily. $$/$$$. 556-2111*

A The Avenue Saloon. A New York-style bar with an excellent view. *553-1855*

A The Hollywood Experience. A 55-minute, multi-screen show about the golden days of Hollywood. *Shown daily except Monday on the hour from 11AM-10PM. Admission charge. 553-0626*

A The Road Show. Legendary princes of the road like Stutz, Clenet, Auburn, Sceptre, Maserati, and Lamborghini are on display. Looking is free and consolation prizes such as keyrings and T-shirts are available. *553-1900*

Restaurants red
Architecture blue
Narrative/Museums/Shops black
Gardens/Parks/Piers green

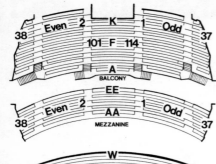

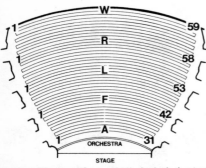

A Shubert Theatre. (Seats 1829). A plush theater for plays and musicals. *2020 Avenue of the Stars. 553-9000*

A Harry's Bar and American Grill. Maintains spiritual affinities with its continental cousin by sponsoring an annual Hemingway write-alike contest. Delicious food and the decor luxuriously comfortable. *Italian. Open daily. No lunch Su. $$$. 277-2333*

A Sports Deli. Three 25-inch televisions for the sports fans, aquaria of salt water fish for others. *Jewish. Open daily. Breakfast served. $$. 553-5800*

A Jade West. Sleek interior, Mandarin food. *Open daily. No lunch Su. $$. 556-3388*

B Century Plaza Hotel. Go under the street via a passageway to the Century Plaza Hotel. Architect Minoru Yamasaki designed this luxury hotel in the Late International style in 1966. The building curves around the circular entrance drive. A delicate fretwork of balconies covers the facade and lights up at night. *2000 Avenue of the Stars. 277-2000*

Within the hotel:

B The Vineyard. *Cuisine nouvelle* and a marvelous wine list in this vineyard-decor dining room. *M-Sa, lunch 11:30AM-2:30PM; dinner 6:00-10:30PM. Closed Su. $$$/$$$$. 2025 Avenue of the Stars. 277-2000*

B Garden Restaurant. A lovely setting outside on the courtyard for a casual meal. *American. Open daily. Breakfast served. $/$$*

B Yamato. Afraid of Japanese food? Yamato is the best introduction. Serene rooms, gracious service, tatami rooms available. *Open daily. No lunch Sa-Su. $$/$$$. 277-2840*

C Century City Shopping Center. One of the earliest of the grand shopping malls in LA, and still one of the best. Over 80 shops occupy an 18-acre site. Ample free parking is located underneath the concourse. The department store anchors are *Bullock's* and *The Broadway*.
Among the other appealing shops are:

C *The Pottery Barn.* The finest in domestics, specializing in a design-conscious contemporary
C style. *Bijoux.* Amusing gifts and nostalgia items.
C *Newsstand.* Papers and magazines from all
C over the world. *Jon Merten.* Luxury menswear.
C *La Nouvelle.* Designer womenswear. *Country*
C *Club Fashions.* California casual chic.
C *Heaven.* Glitzy plastic kitsch; funny and especially popular with teenagers. *Most stores in the complex are open until 9PM, Monday through Saturday. Sunday, 12-5PM. 10250 Santa Monica Blvd.*

30 Restaurant Row. La Cienega Blvd. between San Vicente and Wilshire is lined with eateries. This short stretch is a United Nations of the palate, offering Chinese food at **Su Ling,** *170 N. La Cienega, 652-4188;* Mexican food at the **Acapulco,** *134 N. La Cienega, 652-5344;* and Japanese teppan grill with a flourish at
31 Benihana of Tokyo, *38 N. La Cienega, 655-7311.* Two restaurants have been here long enough to have become LA institutions.
32 Lawry's Prime Rib. There is one dish on the menu—prime rib of such superb quality that people wait for a table. *$$/$$$. Open daily. Dinner only. 55 N. La Cienega. 652-2827.*
33 Tail O'The Cock. Fine steaks, roast beef, and other American specialties in a room polished by over 40 years of service. *$$/$$$. Open daily. No lunch Sa. Sun brunch. 477 S. La Cienega. 273-1200*

In Los Angeles, status means privacy, greenery, and space, and the Westside has all three. The higher the elevation, the higher the property values, and this predominantly hillside area is one of the city's choicest, with million-dollar homes abounding.

Behind tall hedges and thickets of plants are splendid homes often equipped with tennis courts and pools. Upper-class amenities are further assured by the neighborhood's five major country clubs: the Los Angeles, Brentwood, Bel Air, Hillcrest, and Riviera. Some say that there are more luxury automobiles here than anywhere else; whether or not it is true, Rolls-Royce sightseeing on the Westside is certainly easier than in London. Each of the neighborhoods has its own personality, but all are affluent, well-maintained, and glamorous.

WESTWOOD. Originally part of the 1843 land grant of Rancho San Jose de Buenos Ayres, the property changed hands many times, becoming the John Wolfskill ranch after 1884. Wolfskill sold the land to subdividers for a short-lived development known as *Sunset*, but the speculation plan failed and Wolfskill ended up with the property again in 1887. In 1919, Arthur Letts, founder of *The Broadway* and *Bullock's* department stores, bought the farmland and turned a neat profit by selling it to the Janss Investment Corporation shortly

Restaurants red
Architecture blue

Narrative/Museums/Shops black
Gardens/Parks/Piers green

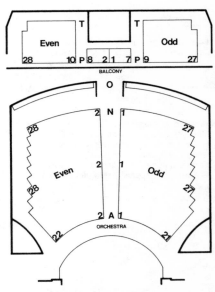

15

Stone
Canyon
Res

Beverly Glen

14

13

Frwy 405

Sunset

5
UCLA

Santa Monica Blvd

21

19

20

2 3
16
1
4

Wilshire

22 Sunset

23

Bundy

18 17

7 12

Westwood

Olympic

San Vicente

10

Pico

24

9

27

Berrington

11

8

25

Temescal

Pacific Coast Hwy

Cliffwood

7th

Montana

26

28

Acari

Sunset

National

Frwy 10

Robertson

0   1/2   1 mile

---

thereafter. In 1922 the Wolfskill ranchhouse was still the only home in the area. But by 1929 there were over 2,000 homes, and a bustling master-planned, Mediterranean shopping village was successfully developed by the Janss Company. UCLA opened classes on the Westwood campus the same year and the Westside began to flourish as a collegiate village and residential area. In 1926 Westwood was annexed to Los Angeles in a civic enlargement that included a large portion of the Santa Monica Mountains, the Pacific Palisades, and Brentwood. The shopping area was designed for promenades, not cruising, and by the 1960s traffic problems began to plague Westwood. The Intersection of Wilshire and Westwood Boulevards is now the busiest in Los Angeles. Beginning in the early 1970s, Westwood Village became the movie-going capital of Los Angeles, with the most intense concentration of first-run theaters in the world. It is a popular spot for nighttime strolling, and on summer evenings crowds fill the streets. *To avoid traffic and parking problems on Friday and Saturday nights, a special courtesy minibus leaves the Federal Building parking lot for a loop route every 10-15 minutes between 7PM and 2AM Friday and 11AM-6AM Saturday. The Federal Building is at 11000 Wilshire Boulevard at the corner of Veteran. All major theaters are on the minibus route.*

Mann Village Theatre. A prototype of the Westwood Spanish colonial is this theater designed by P.O. Lewis in 1931. *961 Broxton Ave.*

Mann Bruin Theatre. Across the street is this Moderne-style departure from the prevailing Spanish mode. Designed by S. Charles Lee in 1937. *925 Broxton Ave.*

Contempo Center. Restored and refurbished in the 1960s by A. Quincy Jones, and named for the fine Danish furniture store which occupies the center, this is a pleasant compound of shopping, dining, and theater all together. The original Mission/Craftsman-style building was by Stiles and Clements in 1929. *10800 Le Conte Ave.*

Mario's. They never miss: the pizzas here are consistently yummy and toppings diverse. Real bleu-cheese salad dressing. *Italian. M-F, 11:30AM-11:30PM; Sa-Su, 4PM-midnight. $$. 1001 Broxton Ave. 208-7077*

Even

Odd

28   10 P 8 2 1 7 P 9   27

BALCONY

O

N

2 1

28

27

Even

2   1

Odd

28

27

2 1

A

ORCHESTRA

22

27

---

1 Westwood Playhouse. (Seats 498). A small theater for reviews and musicals with good sightlines to the thrust proscenium stage. *10886 Le Conte Ave. (Contempo Center). 201-5454*

---

1 Stratton's. Dine under a canopy of wisteria in the lovely tile and stone patio or indoors in the old English-style dining room. *Continental. Closed M. $$$. 10886 Le Conte Ave. (Contempo Center). 208-8880 or 208-8886*

Bookstores. Westwood has one of the largest concentrations of bookstores in the city and most are open late. **Hunter's Books,** *1002 Westwood Blvd.* **B. Dalton Bookseller,** *904 Westwood Blvd.* **Westwood Bookstore,** *1201 Broxton Ave.*

1 Shopping. Westwood is crammed with interesting shops for every pocketbook. Clothing stores range from *Bullock's* to the chic *Alandale's.* The athletic crowd can choose from a variety of sporting stores such as *Champs* and *Nike.*

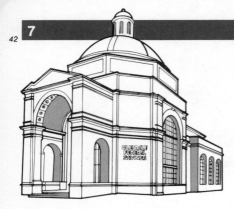

1 Glendale Federal Savings. A distinctive landmark with its colorful tile dome and central location, this 1929 building by Allison and Allison was the first business structure in Westwood. It housed the headquarters of the Janss Investment Corporation, creators of Westwood. It is a prime example of the Spanish colonial style planned for the original shopping village. *1099 Westwood Blvd.*

1 English Pantry. Freshly baked scones with lemon curd and a pot of English tea at mid morning or late in the afternoon. Light meals too, in the *very* English tea room or the more California patio. *English. Breakfast & lunch daily; dinner F-Su. $$. 1121 Glendon Ave. 208-2002*

1 Flax Art Supplies. An eyecatching red sculpture by local artist Franco Assetto wraps the front of this shop. *10852 Lindbrook Ave.*

1 Paul Bhalla's Cuisine of India. A luxurious introduction to the intricacy of Indian food. The emphasis is on lightly-spiced dishes. *Closed M. Dinner only. $$$. 10853 Lindbrook Dr. 208-8535*

2 Westworld Electronic Amusement Center. Many years ago, the world's first *Park-a-Tot* was opened at Gayley and Lindbrook in Westwood, with actress Jane Withers officiating. Today, harried parents can park older *tots* at Westworld, a sophisticated pinball arcade, while they shop. *10965 Weyburn.*

3 International Student Center. A multilingual restaurant, operated by UCLA. *1023 Hilgard.*

1 Yesterday's. When the day's shopping has you beat, their fresh-fruit daiquiris are heaven-sent. *1056A Westwood Blvd.*

2 Carl Anderson's Chatham. Danish dishes and open-faced sandwiches. A good value. *Closed Su. $$. 10930 Weyburn Ave. 208-4321*

1 The Good Earth. One in a chain of health-food restaurants, the Good Earth offers comfort and quality at reasonable prices. So popular, they opened an annex around the corner where you can buy whole wheat bread and giant cookies baked on the premises. *Organic. Breakfast, lunch & dinner daily. $$. 1002 Westwood Blvd. 208-8215*

1 Moustache Cafe. A casual, bistro-style spot. *French. Open daily. $/$$. 1071 Glendon. 651-2111*

1 Monty's Steak House. Mellow entertainment and a great view. *Open daily. 1100 Glendon Ave. 208-6633*

2 Dillon's Restaurant and Bistro. Perhaps the liveliest place in the Village. *1081 Gayley Ave. 208-5088*

4 La Barbera's. Consistently tasty pizza; and they serve divine pies. *Open daily, 11AM-1:30AM. $$. 11813 Wilshire Blvd. 478-0123*

Restaurants red
Architecture blue

3 Westwood Marquis. A central location in the village. A friendly and intimate luxury hotel. The dining room offers a wonderful Sunday brunch. *930 Hilgard. 208-8765*

4 Westwood Inn Motor Hotel. Convenient and budget-priced. *10820 Wilshire Blvd. 474-1573*

4 Holiday Inn Westwood. Offering a restaurant, bar, and pool at moderate prices. *10740 Wilshire Blvd. 475-8711*

4 Del Capri Hotel. Most units in this moderate/luxury hotel have kitchens; a continental breakfast is offered every morning. *10587 Wilshire Blvd. 474-3511*

5 UNIVERSITY OF CALIFORNIA AT LOS ANGELES. This world famous university grew out of a small state normal school established in 1881. The Regents of the University of California acquired the hilly Westwood site for their growing southern branch in 1925. The campus opened in 1929 with four main buildings laid out in a rectangular pattern, all built of brick and designed in an Italian Romanesque style. Now, there are over 85 buildings in a variety of styles ranging from meat-and-potatoes utilitarian to high-art modern. The 411-acre campus is beautifully landscaped with many unusual exotic plants and provides numerous spots for walking, jogging, or quiet reverie. Among the major schools are: medicine, geology, botany, engineering, geography, and management. The graduate schools are renowned in interdisciplinary areas, such as neurophysiology. Library holdings are among the world's largest. Access to the campus is primarily by walking or bicycling. Traffic is limited to a few through roads, and parking is difficult during the week. Campus minibuses circulate from Westwood to the center of campus during school hours. *Main information telephone: 825-4321*

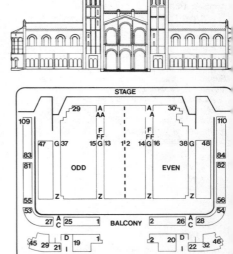

5 Josiah Royce Hall. (Seats 1850). One of the buildings of the original 1929 quadrangle, with classrooms, offices, and a public auditorium that presents a concert series featuring world-famous performers during the school year. The hall was designed by Allison and Allison. *UCLA Central Cultural Events Box Office: 825-9261*

Narrative/Museums/Shops black
Gardens/Parks/Piers green

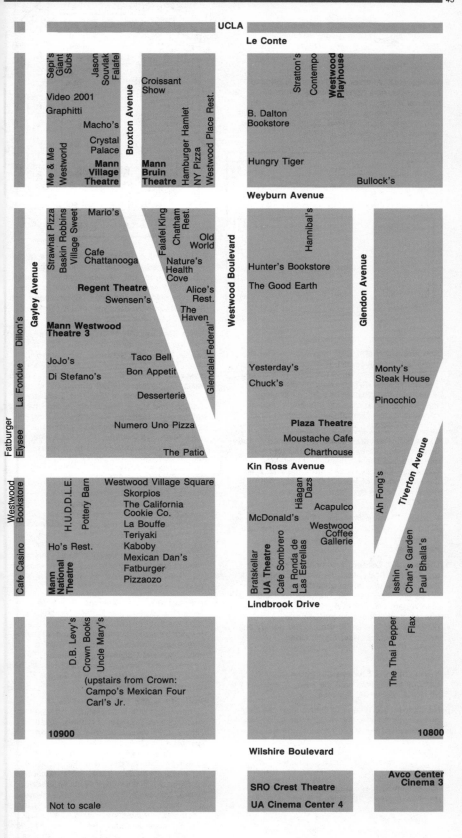

UCLA

Le Conte

Sepi's Giant Subs
Jason Souvlak Falafel
Broxton Avenue
Croissant Show
Stratton's
Contempo
Westwood Playhouse

Video 2001
Graphitti
Macho's
Crystal Palace
Me & Me
Westworld
Mann Village Theatre
Mann Bruin Theatre
Hamburger Hamlet
NY Pizza
Westwood Place Rest.

B. Dalton Bookstore

Hungry Tiger

Bullock's

Weyburn Avenue

Strawhat Pizza
Baskin Robbins
Village Sweet
Mario's
Cafe Chattanooga
Regent Theatre
Swensen's
Mann Westwood Theatre 3
JoJo's
Di Stefano's
Falafel King
Chatham Rest.
Old World
Nature's Health Cove
Alice's Rest.
The Haven

Taco Bell
Bon Appetit
Desserterie
Numero Uno Pizza
The Patio

"Glendale Federal"

Westwood Boulevard

Hannibal's

Hunter's Bookstore

The Good Earth

Yesterday's

Chuck's

Plaza Theatre
Moustache Cafe
Charthouse

Kin Ross Avenue

Glendon Avenue

Monty's Steak House

Pinocchio

Fatburger
Elysee
La Fondue
Dillon's
Gayley Avenue

Westwood Bookstore
Cafe Casino

H.U.D.D.L.E.
Pottery Barn
Ho's Rest.
Mann National Theatre
Westwood Village Square
Skorpios
The California Cookie Co.
La Bouffe
Teriyaki
Kaboby
Mexican Dan's
Fatburger
Pizzaozo

McDonald's
Bratskellar
UA Theatre
Cafe Sombrero
La Ronda de Las Estrellas
Häagen Dazs
Acapulco
Westwood Coffee Gallerie

Ah Fong's
Isshin
Chan's Garden
Paul Bhalla's
Tiverton Avenue

Lindbrook Drive

D.B. Levy's
Crown Books
Uncle Mary's

(upstairs from Crown:
Campo's Mexican Four
Carl's Jr.

10900

The Thai Pepper
Flax

10800

Wilshire Boulevard

Not to scale

SRO Crest Theatre

UA Cinema Center 4

Avco Center Cinema 3

5 College Library. Originally the main library of the campus, this brick Romanesque-style building now houses the undergraduate collection. The rotunda and grand staircase are notable. *Reference desk: 825-1938*

5 Haines Hall. Another building of the original quadrangle; now housing the Museum of Cultural History. The Gallery of the Museum features changing exhibitions of anthropological and archeological material. *Open M-F, 12-5PM. Admission free. Gallery: 825-4361*

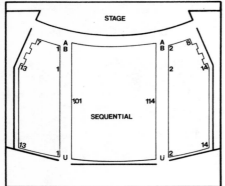

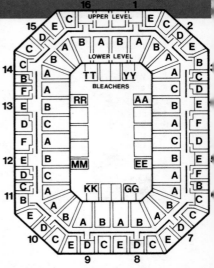

5 Schoenberg Hall. (Seats 550). Named for the composer who lived in Los Angeles between 1933 and 1951 and taught at USC and UCLA. The modern building houses the School of Music and the Institute of Ethnomusicology, as well as a small auditorium that hosts unusual concerts. *UCLA Central Cultural Events Box Office: 825-9261*

5 University Research Library. Designed in 1964 by A. Quincy Jones, this library, surrounded by trees, houses the main graduate research collection. Exhibitions of literary material from the Department of Special Collections are displayed on the first floor. *Reference desk: 825-4731*

5 Franklin Murphy Sculpture Gardens. A 4½-acre area displaying outstanding sculpture by such 20th-century masters as Noguchi and Matisse.

5 Dickson Art Center. A complex of classrooms, art studios, library, and the Grunwald Center for the Graphic Arts, which collects prints, drawings, and illustrated books. Also the site of the Frederick S. Wight Art Gallery featuring changing exhibitions of contemporary and historical art. The small shop in the gallery sells art books, posters, and crafts. *Open Tu-F, 11AM-5PM; Sa-Su, 1-5PM. Admission free. Gallery: 825-1461*

5 North Campus Student Center. A popular campus dining spot with the same low prices as all UCLA restaurant facilities.

5 Kerckhoff Hall. The only Gothic-style building on campus houses the student activity offices. It was designed in 1930 by Allison and Allison. The Student Coffee House inside has a sophisticated and exotic menu including chantilly crepes and cappucino, all for moderate prices.

5 Ackerman Student Union. In the center of campus, housing the student stores and the **Tree House Restaurant.** Actually four restaurants in one, the Tree House has fresh fruits and salads, quiches, and a full-meal section serving such entrees as Fettucine Alfredo, all at very low prices. The student store sells books and a full range of UCLA-imprinted wares.

5 Pauley Pavilion. (Seats 12,545). Home of the UCLA Bruins basketball team. Concerts, cultural events, and volleyball games are also held in the arena. Designed by Welton Becket and Associates in 1965, the construction eliminates interior columns. *UCLA Central Sports Ticket Box Office: 825-2101*

5 Drake Stadium. An 11,000-seat track and field stadium. *Event information: 825-4546*

5 Center for Health Sciences. The entire southern end of the campus, from Tiverton to Westwood fronting on Le Conte, is occupied by one of the largest medical complexes in the nation. The Schools of Medicine, Dentistry, Nursing, and Public Health are located here, as well as eight research institutes including the world-famous Neuropsychiatric Institute and the Jules Stein Eye Institute. The UCLA Hospital and Clinics, also located in the complex, operate a 24-hour emergency room, which is reached via an entrance at Tiverton and Le Conte. *Emergency: 825-2111*

5 Mathias Botanical Gardens. An 8½-acre shaded canyon, on the southeast end of campus off Hilgard and Le Conte, which has been artfully planted to create a natural-looking, woodsy environment. A number of the mature specimens are of unusual size and their majestic presence contributes to the peaceful atmosphere. No restroom facilities. *Admission free. Open M-Sa, 8AM-5PM; Su, 10AM-4PM. Garden information: 825-3620*

6 Wally's Liquor and Gourmet Foods. A California redwood and high-tech store that offers the best in food and wine. Boutique vineyard labels unavailable elsewhere, plus a cheese department that includes Buffalo mozzarella and California goat cheese. Ever-present owner Steve Wallace knows *everything* about California wines. *Open M-Sa. 2107 Westwood Blvd. 475-0606*

7 South of Wilshire on Westwood Boulevard is a concentration of fine bookshops, all small and specialized. **A Change of Hobbit.** Science Fiction. *1371 Westwood Blvd.* **Krown and Spellman Booksellers.** Classic, medieval, and Renaissance. *1945 Westwood Blvd.* **Sam Johnson's Bookshop.** *1947 Westwood Blvd.* **Technical Book Company.** Professional and scientific. *2056 Westwood Blvd.* **Vagabond Books.** Modern fiction, cinema, and theater. *2076 Westwood Blvd.* **Barry R. Levin.** Science fiction and fantasy literature. *2253 Westwood Blvd.* **Kenneth Karmiole Bookseller.** Rare and first editions. *2255 Westwood Blvd.* **George Houle Rare Books.** *2277 Westwood Blvd.* **La Cite des Livres.** French literature and magazines. *2306 Westwood Blvd.* **Needham Book Finders.** *2317 Westwood Blvd.* **Victor Lamkin Bookstore.** Russian books. *2320 Westwood Blvd.* **The Spanish Book Store.** Spanish and Latin American. *2326 Westwood Blvd.* **A Likely Story.** Children's books. *2355 Westwood Blvd.* **Howard Karno Books.** Latin American. *2367 Westwood Blvd.* **Hennessey & Ingalls, Inc.** Art and architecture. The best of its kind in LA. *10814 Pico Blvd.*

At the end of bookseller's row are several restaurants, and to the west, two nightclubs.

Matteo's. A celebrity hangout. The Neapolitan food is good, but the clientele is stellar. *Italian. Closed M. Dinner only. $$$/$$$$. 2321 Westwood Blvd.* 475-4521

Hymie's Fish Market. ☆ Perhaps the best seafood in this part of the city. Hymie's contrasts its simple surroundings with a high concentration of top showbiz clients. Excellent lobster bouillabaisse, clams, oysters, etc. *Seafood. Open M-Sa 6PM-late. Reservations. $$. 9228 W. Pico Blvd.* 550-0377

Mangia. ☆☆ This casual-chic modern Italian spot offers northern Italian cuisine with a light touch, to eat in or to-go. Try *ravioli nudi,* the delicate filling minus the pasta, or duck lasagne. Lovely patio. *Italian. Open Tu-Sa. $$$. 10543 W. Pico Blvd.* 470-1952

The Apple Pan. At all hours of the day or night, the counter is filled with a potpourri of LA society, lined up for one of the best hamburgers in town. *American. $. 10801 W. Pico Blvd.* 474-9344

O-Sho Sushi. A sushi bar and terrific teriyaki specials. The menu has pictures to help you make your choice. *Japanese. Open daily. No lunch Sa-Su. $/$$. 10941 Pico Blvd.* 475-3226

Anna's. Sicilian-style thick-crusted or crispy thin-crusted pizza, the sauce is good and the cheese plentiful. Light on toppings. *Lunch M-F, 11:30AM-2:30PM; dinner daily, 2:30PM-11PM. $$. 10929 W. Pico Blvd.* 474-0102

Club 88. Popular local punk rock nightclub. *11784 W. Pico Blvd.* 479-6923

Chung King. This ever-popular hole-in-the-wall serves spicy Szechuan food that can one night be good enough to claim the *Best in LA* title, and enough another night to cause indigestion. *Chinese. Lunch, M-F; dinner daily. $$. 11538 W. Pico Blvd.* 477-4917

Bo-Jay's Pizzeria. Try the house special, thick or thin crust. *Su-Th, 11AM-10PM; F-Sa, 11AM-midnight. $$. 12309 W. Pico Blvd.* 820-8791

It helps to have a sense of humor to appreciate **Pico Boulevard.** It is a nondescript series of stucco buildings, all close to the wide, heavily trafficked street. One of our favorite *only in LA* spots is: **Rent-a-Wreck.** The place to go if you've always wanted to cruise LA in a '58 Chevy. Any would-be motorist can walk in and rent the *bad* car of your choice, from a lemony cast of dozens. *12333 W. Pico Blvd.* 478-0676; 478-4393

Sawtelle Boulevard. Once the name of a small town that encompassed the area, Sawtelle is a thriving community of small businesses, most related to the gardening trade. A capsule piece of LA demography, it is a mix of Japanese and Mexican culture.

Yamaguchi Bonsai Nursery. You can buy a 100-year-old miniature tree, lotus stock, or leave your bonsai here while you vacation. *1905 Sawtelle Blvd.*

Papa Bach's. A bookstore specializing in poetry and new fiction. *11317 Santa Monica Blvd.*

2 Toledo. A pretty, intimate restaurant serving Castilian cuisine that tries for authenticity and mostly achieves it. One of the few places to go for *real* paella. *Spanish. Lunch, Tu-F; dinner, Tu-Su. $$$. 11613 Santa Monica Blvd.* 477-2400

11 Odyssey Theatre. A small avant-garde theater offering plays and performances. *12111 Ohio Ave. (near Bundy).* 826-1626

12 Mormon Temple. The 257-foot tower crowned with a 15-foot gold-leaf statue of the angel Moroni makes this a familiar landmark in the LA skyline. This is the largest temple of the Church of Jesus Christ of Latter Day Saints outside of Salt Lake City. Designed by architect Edward Anderson, the temple is open only to Church members. *Visitors may tour the grounds or visit the Visitor Information Center, open 7AM-5PM daily. 10777 Santa Monica Blvd.*

BEL-AIR: A posh hillside community, developed by Alphonzo E. Bell in the early 1920s. The name is a loose translation of the French for *lovely locale.* Along the winding roads with French and Italian names are hundreds of exclusive mansions carefully hidden from the street. Bel-Air's highest reaches are the homesites for film stars and international celebrities, perhaps living out Bell's wish to make his development a place for joyous living.

13 Bel-Air Hotel. Retreat from the city into a land of purple bougainvillea and gliding swans. This luxury hotel has a dining room that has long been a favorite for romantic meals, be they breakfast, lunch, or dinner. *Open daily. Sunday brunch. $$$. 701 Stone Canyon Rd.* 472-1211

14 Cafe Four Oaks. ☆ An old house, charmingly converted into an inventive, personal restaurant. Beef in bourbon is the specialty. *Continental. Closed M. Dinner only. Sunday brunch. $$$. 2181 N. Beverly Glen Blvd.* 474-9317

15 Adriano's Restaurant. ☆ The food, the hilltop, the personal attention will combine to make you feel transported to Italy. Don't be fooled by the shopping-center locale; this elegant spot specializes in unusual dishes. *Italian. Closed M. $$$$. 2930 Beverly Glen Circle.* 475-9807

15 Santo Pietro's Pizza. Casual sidewalk cafe and espresso bar with daily Italian specialties as well as pizza spun in the air by a champion frisbee thrower. *Italian. Lunch & dinner daily. $$. 2954 Beverly Glen Circle.* 474-4349

BRENTWOOD: Across the freeway and west of Bel-Air, Brentwood is chicly rustic, casual, and countrified. The Brentwood *flats,* densely built up with condominiums and apartments, are a popular area for the unmarried and upwardly mobile. The hills have twisting country roads lined with large specimen trees, huge estates, and breathtaking views. One of the prettiest streets is San Vicente Boulevard, between the VA hospital and Palisades Park, a popular spot for Westside joggers.

16 Sawtelle Veteran's Chapel. A quaint and delicate white wooden chapel built for the original veteran's center. Built in 1900 and designed by J. Lee Burton, it is a Victorian mixture of Gothic Revival elements. *11000 Wilshire Blvd.*

17 Gatsby's. The stars who eat here are as much of an attraction as the simple, well-prepared food. *Open daily. No lunch Sa-Su. $$$/$$$$. 11500 San Vicente Blvd.* 820-1476

Los Angeles' first orange grove was planted not by a farmer but by a fur trapper. Kentuckian William Wolfskill came to LA in the early 1830s and planted the area's first grove.

---

18 Several places nearby are popular spots for after-work eating and drinking. They include: **Bergin's West,** *11600 San Vicente Blvd.;* **Hamburger Hamlet,** *11648 San Vicente Blvd.;* **Mark Twain's Notorious Jumping Frog Saloon and Restaurant,** *11777 San Vicente Blvd.;* and **Donatello's,** *11712 San Vicente Blvd.*

18 San Vicente has many fine small boutiques and specialty shops. Two of the best are galleries of contemporary and ethnic crafts: **Alison,** *11658 San Vicente Blvd.;* **Del Mano Gallery and Studio,** *11981 San Vicente Blvd.*

19 Bel-Air Sands Hotel. Stunningly remodelled and offering an excellent restaurant, the moderately priced guest rooms and suites are tucked discreetly into an exclusive residential neighborhood. *Caribbean Terrace. Breakfast, lunch, 7:30AM-2:30PM daily; dinner 5:30PM-10:30PM, Champagne brunch Sa-Su, 10:30AM-3PM. 11461 Sunset Blvd. 472-2513*

20 Peppone. ☆ ☆ A cloistered and romantic hideaway with some of the best Italian food in town. Specialties are *spaghetti al tonno* and unusual seafood preparations. *Closed M. No lunch Sa-Su. $$$/$$$$. 11628 Barrington Ct. 476-7379*

20 Fine Affair. Elegant, intimate, and breathtakingly appointed with handpainted china, fine crystal, and silver, long stemmed roses. A varied menu of fresh fish, special lamb and veal dishes, chicken, soups and salads, homemade pastries baked fresh daily. Plants trailing across latticed ceiling create a lovely garden atmosphere. *French/Continental. Tu-F lunch, 11AM-2:30PM; dinner, 6PM-11PM. Sa dinner only, 6PM-11PM. Su brunch, 11AM-2:30PM; dinner, 6PM-11PM. Closed M. $$$. 666 N. Sepulveda Blvd. 476-2848*

20 Maria's Italian Kitchen. One of the best pizzas with a delightful crust and a variety of incredible toppings. Mostly takeout. *Open daily 10AM-10PM. $. 11725 Barrington Ct. 476-6112*

21 Mount Saint Mary's College. A small, private liberal arts college atop one of the most beautiful view sites in the city. *12001 Chalon Rd. 476-2237*

22 Temple House. Child actress Shirley Temple lived in this delightful small-scaled European farmhouse with her parents. It was designed in 1936 by John Byers and Edla Muir. Private residence. *231 N. Rockingham Rd.*

23 Cliff May Office. Cliff May is the architect famous for popularizing the California ranch house style. His own 1953 wood-paneled office can be seen here as well as works by May on a majority of the 13000 blocks of Riviera Ranch and Old Oak Streets. His low horizontal houses are immediately recognizable by their broad shingle roofs and stucco walls. *13151 Sunset Blvd.*

24 Will Rogers State Historic Park. This 187-acre park was the home of cowboy-humorist, writer, and performer Will Rogers between 1924 and 1935. Inside the house are possessions and memorabilia from his busy career. A nearby visitor center has a 10-minute film on Rogers's life, narrated by his friends and family, and sells Rogersiana. An avid polo player, Rogers's 900' x 300' polo field is the site of polo matches on *Saturdays during the summer at 2PM, no charge.* The extensive grounds have many spots for hiking through the chaparral-covered hills as well as picnicking. This is a fire hazard

Once bonfires were lit in the hills to signal ships approaching shore, giving Signal Hill its name.

area, so no fires are allowed. *Park open 8AM-7PM summer; 8AM-5PM winter; house open 10AM-5PM year 'round. No charge for admission. Parking fee. 14235 Sunset Blvd. 454-8212*

PACIFIC PALISADES. A community founded as a *new Chatauqua* in 1922 by the Southern Conference of the Methodist Episcopal Church. Made famous by its western border of ocean-front bluffs that frequently crumble down onto Pacific Coast Highway, the Palisades is an upper-class neighborhood with the highest median income of any area in the City of Los Angeles—twice that of most other areas. Many of the streets in the Palisades are named for bishops of the Methodist Church.

25 Self-Realization Fellowship Lake Shrine. An open-air temple dedicated to all religions, founded in 1950 by followers of Paramahansa Yogananda on what was once a movie set. Ponds, lakes, waterfalls, windmills, and gazebos make this a pleasant place for walking or meditation.

26 Case Study Houses. Some of the most important monuments of modern residential architecture in Los Angeles were initiated by one man: John Entenza, the editor of the influential and path-setting *Arts and Architecture Magazine,* recently revived. He founded the Case Study House Project to encourage Southern California architects to work with the latest in techniques and materials on actual homes. The results are:

26 Eames House. Designed by Charles Eames, this is a world-famous residence of pre-fabricated industrial parts fashioned in a composition resembling a Mondrian painting. Private residence. *203 Chautauqua Blvd.*

26 Case Study House. An International style low box designed by Charles Eames and Eero Saarinen in 1949. Private residence. *205 Chatauqua Blvd.*

26 Case Study House. An unusual 1948 work by Richard Neutra in redwood and brick. Private residence. *219 Chatauqua Blvd.*

27 Uplifters Club Cabins. In the early 1920s an offshoot group of the Los Angeles Athletic Club built cottages in the rustic hills of the Pacific Palisades. Many of the residences were log cabins. Private residences. *1, 3, and 18 Latimer Rd.; 31, 32, 34, and 38 Haldeman Rd.*

27 Rustic Canyon Recreation Center. A quiet sylvan glade for picnics and barbeques. *701 Latimer Rd., Rustic Canyon. 454-5734*

27 Kappe House. An expansively scaled concrete and wood home by and for architect Raymond Kappe, done in 1968. Private residence. *715 Brooktree Rd., Rustic Canyon*

28 Gladstones 4 Fish. There are more sophisticated restaurants that serve fresh seafood, but none with a better view. Perched over the beach, Gladstones is a great place to drink banana daiquiris at sunset, and take advantage of all-you-can-eat daily specials. *Seafood. Breakfast, lunch & dinner daily. $$/$$$. 17300 Pacific Coast Hwy. GL4-FISH (478-6738)*

Restaurants red
Architecture blue

The Yellow House. Simple favorites—crepes, omelettes, salads, sandwiches—in a sunny room. *American healthy. Open daily. Breakfast served. $. 147 W. Channel Rd., Santa Monica Canyon. 459-4401*

Restaurants red
Architecture blue
Narrative/Museums/Shops black
Gardens/Parks/Piers green

28 Les Anges. ☆ ☆ ☆ An intimate beach-white restaurant with Orrefors crystal, modern art, and *cuisine moderne,* which means the likes of sea urchin souffle in the spiny shell, and lobster with Pernod. Desserts are breathtaking (*creme brulee* with a crust carmelized by blow torch) and can be ordered, without coming for dinner, in the bar after 9PM. *French. Dinner, Tu-Su. $$$$. 14809 Pacific Coast Hwy. (enter on Entrada). 454-1331*

SANTA MONICA 8

Everyone wants to go to the beach! Sun, surf, and sand are a magnetic lure for millions of visitors to the unbroken line of broad public beaches running along the Los Angeles County coast from north of Malibu to Marina del Rey.

The wealth of things to do includes sunbathing, jogging, boating, fishing, and surfing. Ever present ocean breezes keep the temperature comfortable, while the water is usually warm, averaging around 70 degrees Farenheit in August.

Beach cities are the centers for easygoing lifestyles; the newest trends in youth culture often originate here: for example, the roller-skating craze started on the Venice boardwalk. The tolerant and harmonious melting pot mixes people of every social strata, ethnic background, and personal persuasion in an exciting melange of style and taste.

The beach has been a traditional summer destination for Southland residents for over 100 years. Pioneer Angelenos had to endure a bumpy stagecoach ride of as much as a day to get from downtown Los Angeles to Santa Monica. Now the same trip takes only 20-30 minutes via the freeway.

The area is popular—so much so that on a hot summer Sunday, beach goers can number over one million, and cars park bumper to bumper for over 40 miles up and down Pacific Coast Highway.

SANTA MONICA AREA. Santa Monica and its southern suburb of Ocean Park are a portion of the ranch land that Col. Robert Baker purchased and later subdivided in association with Senator John P. Jones in 1875. The town began as a simple seaside resort where vacationers could pitch tents under the shelter of trees in Santa Monica Canyon. Hotels and stores were built and soon the town had many year-round residents, voting to incorporate as an independent city in 1887. Santa Monica led a dual life as a quiet residential suburb which sheltered offshore gambling ships during the 1930s. Raymond Chandler immortalized the town as *Bay City* in his books. The slightly sleepy tempo of the town was permanently altered in 1966 by the opening of the Santa Monica Freeway. The northern sector of Santa Monica is wealthy and family-oriented. The central and southern parts of the city have attracted an influx of professionals and young singles drawn to the many apartments and condominiums, by the short commute downtown, the temperate weather, clean air, and abundant outdoor recreational facilities.

Narrative/Museums/Shops black
Gardens/Parks/Piers green

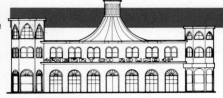

1 Santa Monica Pier. The smells of popcorn, cotton candy, and corn dogs, the soft resonance of the boardwalk underfoot, the calliope of the merry-go-round, and the metallic din of the penny arcade make the pier a spot for fun and nostalgia. Built between 1909 and 1921, the popular amusement space is lined with many restaurants and shops. Children will love the 70+-year-old carousel with its 56 prancing horses, familiar for its supporting role in *The Sting.* At night the long line of white lights strung along the pier's edge create a poetic landmark for those coming down the coast highway from the north. *Entrance at Colorado and Ocean Avenues.*

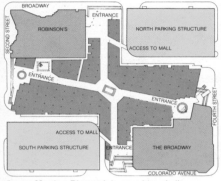

2 Santa Monica Place. A huge white skylit galleria shopping mall with three levels, it is the 1980 work of architects Frank Gehry and Associates. Tree-lined walkways lead you to over 150 stores including *Robinson's* and *The Broadway.* The picnic area has a separate section of restaurants open until 2AM. *315 Broadway, between Second and Fourth. 394-5451*

3 Bonnie & Clyde's. A fun stop after a day at the beach. Flavored popcorns served from a counter shaped like a '20s getaway car; sinfully-rich ice cream and brownies. *Ice cream parlor. Open Tu-Sa. $. 128 Broadway. 451-9755*

4 BelleVue French Restaurant. A cozy neighborhood spot renovated in a stylish version of country French. Try the marine salad or the Friday bouillabaisse. *Continental. Open daily. 101 Santa Monica Blvd. 393-2843*

4 Knoll's Black Forest Inn. One of the best German restaurants in town. The Black Forest cake is remarkable. *German. Closed Su-M. Dinner only. $$/$$$. 124 Santa Monica Blvd. 395-2212*

4 Mayfair Music Hall. A spirited cabaret theater, one of the many lively Santa Monica Bay spots catering to Anglophiles, offering revivals of English Music Hall entertainment. *Dinner served. Closed M-Tu. 214 Santa Monica Blvd. 451-0621*

3 Hotel Carmel. A well-kept economy hotel, close to the Santa Monica Mall and Santa Monica Place. *210 Broadway. 395-6195*

5 Palisades Park. The line of steep, lofty cliffs along the edge of the ocean is called the Palisades. A traditional spot for Angelenos to watch the sunset fade over the ocean, the park is one of the oldest and best maintained in the city. Its towering palms and semi-tropical trees form beautiful bowers for strolling or jogging. *Ocean Ave. from Colorado Blvd. to Adelaide Dr., Santa Monica*

6 Miramar Sheraton Hotel. A luxury resort hotel popular with Japanese and European tourists. The enormous Moreton Bay fig tree in the center courtyard was planted in the 19th century. *Ocean Ave. and Wilshire Blvd. 394-3731*

6 Camera Obscura. Near the Visitor Assistance Stand, a quiet upstairs room where startling projections of the outside world appear on a circular white surface. *Open by request at the Senior Recreation Center next door.*

6 Palisades Park Gates. Craftsman-style field stone gates, made in 1912 and decorated with tiles by Ernest Batchelder of Pasadena. *Ocean Ave. near Wilshire Blvd.*

6 Visitor Assistance Stand. The Santa Monica Chamber of Commerce gives free sightseeing maps and bus and tour information. *Open summer, daily 10AM-4PM, winter, Tu-Su, 11AM-3PM. Ocean Ave. near Arizona St. 393-7593*

7 Huntley House Hotel. A moderate to deluxe-priced high-rise hotel. Many rooms have ocean views. The restaurant upstairs has a panoramic view of the mountains and sea. *1111 Second St. 451-5971*

7 Michael's. ☆☆☆ A chef who knows how to play perfect simplicity against luxurious complexity in simply the most artful restaurant in town. Many consider this LA's very best eating experience. White umbrellas in an exquisite garden, masters on the walls. Michael's (soon to open in New York City) is expense account dining at its epogee. Details of decor and dining personally created and supervised by Michael himself. *French. Closed M. $$$$. 1147 Third St. 451-0843*

8 Wildflour Boston Pizza. The only pizzeria with a whole wheat crust as well as the traditional white. And a huge spinach salad loaded with avocado and artichoke hearts. *M-F, 11:30AM-10:30PM; Sa, 11:30-12midnight; Su, 4PM-12midnight. $$. 2222 Wilshire Blvd. 829-7829. Also on Main St. and Lincoln Blvd.*

8 Ma Facon. ☆☆ A Baroque setting, with purple velvet and silver-footed sugar bowl elegance, yet modern *cuisine nouvelle* prepared by a talented chef. *French. Lunch, Tu-F; dinner, Tu-Sa. $$$$. 1000 Wilshire Blvd. 394-2718*

8 Tampico Tilly's. A pleasant hybrid of old Mexico and young California. *Mexican. Open daily. Sunday brunch. 1025 Wilshire Blvd. 451-1769*

9 Warszawa. Hearty homemade Polish food in warm friendly surroundings. *Polish. Closed Tu. Dinner only. $$$. 1414 Lincoln Blvd. 393-8831*

10 Verdi. ☆☆ A doubly special evening at this *ristorante di musica,* where the serving of sophisticated Italian (Tuscan) food is lovingly and flowingly choreographed into performances from operas, operettas, and Broadway musicals sung by some of the finest young artists in Los Angeles. Designed by the architectural firm Morphosis, in a historic old building with its roots in the original Spanish land grants, the room is equally conducive to theater and restaurant. No cover charge. Call ahead for the program. Reservations imperative. *Italian. Tu-Su, beginning at 5:30PM. $$$. 1519 Wilshire Blvd. 393-0706*

10 Hiro Sushi. Greeted with friendly shouts as you enter, you may sit at the sushi bar to sample from Hiro's mastery, or eat at one of the tables in the dining area. *Japanese. $$. 1621½ Wilshire Blvd. 395-3570*

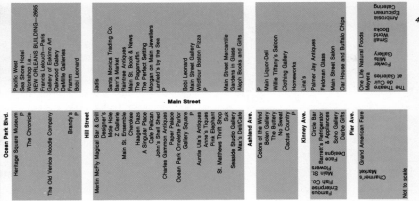

Main Street

Pacific West
Sea Shore Hotel
Workshop i.e...
NEW ORLEANS BUILDING—2665
Francis Lebouch—Paris
Gallery of Eskimo Art
Oakwood Gallery
DeMille Galleries
Framm
Bobi Leonard

Jadis
Santa Monica Trading Co.
Barr's Market
Raintree Antiques
Main St. Book & News
The Ragamuffin
The Perfect Setting
Morgan on Main Jewelers
Lanfield's by the Sea
P
Bobi Leonard
Main Street Gallery
Wildflour Boston Pizza
P
Main Street Mercantile
Gardens in Glass
Aleph Books and Gifts

P
Main Liquor-Deli
Willie Tiffany's Saloon
Clothing Gallery
Homeworks
Lina's
Palmer Jay Antiques
Feldman Glass
Main Street Salon
Oar House and Buffalo Chips

One Life Natural Foods
Meyera
The Theatre
de la Cuir
at Galeries
Fowler
Smith
Mills
Gallery
Small
World
Books
Ambrosia
Epicurean
Catering

Not to scale

Ocean Park Blvd.
P
Heritage Square Museum
The Chronicle
The Old Venice Noodle Company
Brandy's
P

Hill Street
Merlin McFly Magical Bar & Grill
Designer's
Mole Hole
Z Gallerie
Main St. Ensemble
Cherokee
Haagen Dazs
A Singular Place
Cafe Pelican
John's Shell Shed
Charles Gammon Antiques
Paper Palace
Ocean Park Omelette Parlor
Gallery Square
Auntie Ula's Antiques
Anne's Tiques
Pink Elephant
St. Matthews Thrift Shop
Suk
Seaside Studio Gallery
Max's Deli/Cafe

Ashland Ave.
Colors of the Wind
Bolen Gallery
The Buttery
No Sweat
Cactus Country
P

Kinney Ave.
Famous
Enterprise
Fish Co.
Main St.
Flowers
Face
Designs
Barrett's Refrigerator
& Appliances
Soho Gallery
Date Gifts
Circle Bar

Pier Ave.
Charmer's
Market
Mills
Market
Grand American Fare

Restaurant Italia. Fine northern Italian food in a gracious room. *Closed M. No lunch. $$/$$$. 1909 Wilshire Blvd. 394-9788*

Carlos & Pepe's. A favorite after-work meeting spot for the young of the Westside. The central bar serves great *nachos. Mexican. Open daily. $/$$. 2020 Wilshire Blvd. 828-8903*

Madame Wu's Garden. Familiar Chinese dishes served with style. *Chinese. Open daily. Lunch and dinner. $$. 2201 Wilshire Blvd. 828-5656*

Jack's at the Beach. Though it had more panache—and more celebrities—when it was perched over the surf on the long-gone Pacific Ocean Park pier, this historic restaurant continues its tradition of fine, fresh seafood, served formally. Though its prices were once high, they now fall into the mid-range by current LA standards. *Seafood. Lunch, M-F; dinner, M-Sa. $$$. 2700 Wilshire Blvd. 829-2846*

Bicycle Shop Cafe. A bistro-type cafe offering crepes, salads, and light dinners amid antique and modern cycling regalia. *Open daily, 11AM-2AM. $/$$. 12217 Wilshire Blvd. 826-7831*

La Mesa Drive. A beautifully landscaped street, under a canopy of huge Moreton Bay figs and lined with a number of fine Spanish-Colonial-style homes by John Byers, most done in the late 1920s. Examples are at *1923, 2102,* and *2153 La Mesa Drive.* Byer's own home at *1034 La Mesa* is a Monterey Colonial style variant with a second-story balcony. Private residences.

Le Marmiton. For the most elegant of picnics, or when you would love to eat in a fine French restaurant but can't afford it. *French. Take-out. Closed Su. $. 1327 Montana Ave. 393-7716*

Farther north is San Vicente Boulevard, one of the Southland's prettiest streets, its central grassy strip lined with large coral trees (*erythrina caffra*), the official tree of Los Angeles.

Brentwood Country Mart. A small, barn-red complex of 26 village shops including espresso bar, bookstore, fresh juice bar, deli, and grocery. Outdoor dining. *Closed Su. Corner of 26th St. and San Vicente Blvd.*

Le St. Michel Restaurant. Specializing in seafood and duck, prepared with the lightest of touches. The crisp duck skin and scallop salad is unique and memorable. *French. Closed M. Dinner only. $$$. 3218 Santa Monica Blvd. 829-3173*

7 Tortue Gallery. A small gallery showing contemporary art. *2917 Santa Monica Blvd. 828-8878*

Restaurants red
Architecture blue
Narrative/Museums/Shops black
Gardens/Parks/Piers green

---

17 Marquis West. Good, if not always exceptional Italian food in a comfortable, neighborhood restaurant setting. Some say the fried calamari are the best in 'LA. *Italian. Lunch, M-F; dinner M-Sa. $$$. 3110 Santa Monica Blvd. 828-4567*

18 Valentino. ☆ ☆ Some might bicker over which of the Italian restaurants is the very best, but few would ever exclude Valentino from the running. New and imaginative dishes constantly appear from Piero Selvaggio's kitchen. *Open daily. Dinner only. $$$$. 3115 W. Pico Blvd. 829-4313*

18 McCabe's Guitar Shop. An intimate cabaret featuring live performances of folk music and blues by well-known performers. *Open F-Sa; some Su. 3101 W. Pico Blvd. 838-4497*

2 Chez Jay. The steaks have been surpassed by those at newer LA restaurants, and the seafood is often frozen, but where else can you go for waterfront bar ambiance and hear Jay regale you with tales of hot-air ballooning? Jay's mom bakes the blueberry cheesecake and clears the tables, sweeping the peanut shells onto the floor. *American/Continental. Lunch & dinner daily. $$$. 1657 Ocean Ave. 395-1741*

2 Pacific Shores Hotel. Moderate to deluxe lodgings, with an ocean view. *1819 Ocean Ave. 451-8711*

Glossary of Sushi Terms

Maguro	Tuna
Toro	Toro
Hamachi	Yellow Tail
Shiromi	Halibut
	Sea Bass
Shake	Salmon
Saba	Mackerel
Aji	Spanish Mackerel
Ebi	Sweet Shrimp
Kani	King Crab
Tako	Octopus
Ika	Squid
Awabi	Abalone
Mirugai	Jumbo Clam
	Geoduck
Hashira	Scallop
Kaki	Oyster
Uni	Sea Urchin Paste
Ikura	Salmon Eggs
Masago	Smelt Eggs
Anago	Sea Eel (broiled)
Unagi	Fresh Water Eel (broiled)
Tamago	Egg
Tekka	Tuna Roll
Kappa	Cucumber Roll
Umeshiso	Plum Roll
Avocado	California Roll
Unakyu	Fresh Water Eel Cucumber Roll
Yakisakana	Broiled Fish
Nizakana	Cooked Fish

19 Gehry House. Both paradoxical and controversial, this sweet pink home from the 1920s has been transformed by owner-architect Frank Gehry, utilizing such industrial materials as corrugated galvanized metal and cyclone fencing to create a design statement that might have been concocted by the German Expressionists. A little bit of Dr. Caligari at Sunnybrook Farm. Private residence. *1002 22nd St.*

20 Santa Monica Civic Center. The complex includes the **Santa Monica Civic Auditorium** (seats 3,500), which presents big-name rock and jazz concerts, exhibits, and trade shows. *1855 Main St. (Box office, corner of Main and Pico).* 393-9961

20 MAIN STREET. Slightly south of Santa Monica proper is Ocean Park, once a seaside resort with thousands of tiny beach cottages and a large Coney Island-style amusement park. The neighborhood now includes a nostalgic shopping and dining area known as Main Street. It is a pleasant place for walking and browsing in unusual boutiques and fine antique shops. There is a high concentration of restaurants here, most of which have rear patios.

21 Pioneer Boulangerie and Restaurant. Hearty soups and fresh salads at the downstairs buffet, family-style Basque dinner upstairs, or a simple snack or continental breakfast on the outdoor patio. Built around a bakery, a glassed-in area allows you to see the cooks at work. *Open daily. Breakfast served. $/$$. 2102 Main St.* 399-1405

22 Heritage Square Museum. Santa Monica fought for years and finally succeeded gloriously in saving these two fine old 19th century homes. Both were moved and completely restored. Now the old *Roy Jones Home* (he was a son of one of the city's founders) has been redecorated, with each room reflecting one period of American life since the house was built. Local archives and artifacts are also stored here. The Jones house is noteworthy as a creation of famed architect Sumner P. Hunt. *Museum open Th-Sa, 11AM-4PM. 2612 Main St. 392-8537.* The Second home is now the pleasing Chronicle Restaurant.

22 The Chronicle. ☆ A restored 1906 home built for a former mayor of Santa Monica. The warm Victorian setting complements the fine food. *Continental. Lunch M-F, 11:30AM-3PM. Dinner M-Sa, 6AM-12 midnight. Su,5PM-11PM. $$$/$$$$. 2640 Main St.* 392-4956

22 Merlin McFly Magical Bar and Grill. The dazzling stained-glass windows are a treat in themselves, featuring giant glass portraits of masters of visual deception from bygone eras. Merlin's huge and intricate hand-carved mahogany bar lights up and belches smoke. In the evening magicians perform on the small stage. It is a little more than just a bar. *Open daily. 2702 Main St.* 392-8468

22 Jadis. Vintage clothing so well preserved and tastefully selected it seems as though none of our ancestors ever wore anything; they just packed it away in trunks, saving it for good. Also a wide selection of art deco furniture and collectibles of the choicest quality. *2701 Main St.*

8   SANTA MONICA

22 John's Shell Shed. Beautiful mollusks from the ocean floor. *2724 Main St.*

22 Paper Palace. Some of the most unusual postcards and memorabilia you'll ever find in Southern California. *2730 Main St.*

24 Main Street Gallery. Fine Oriental antiques. *2803 Main St.*

24 Colors of the Wind. Custom flags and banners by vexillographer Anders Holmquist are featured in this unusual store that sells brilliantly hued kites, clothes, and pennants with changing exhibitions. *M-F, 11AM-6PM; Sa-Su, 10AM-6PM. 2900 Main St.* 399-8044

24 The Buttery. Croissants and coffee, brioche, chocolate chip cookies, and pasta. *Tu-Sa, 7:30AM-9PM; Su, 7:20AM-5PM; closed M. 2906 Main St.* 399-3000

24 Homeworks. Novel gifts and housewares. *2913 Main St.*

24 Famous Enterprise Fish Company. Charcoal-broiling fresh fish over mesquite makes it taste like it was caught on a camping trip. One of the best fish restaurants in town. *Seafood. Open 7 days. $$. 174 Kinney St. (just off Main St.)* 392-8366

24 Charmer's Market. ☆ A former Bank of America branch is now selling fresh fruits and vegetables, cheeses, exotic vinegars and oils, magazines, and 25 different fine champagnes on ice; only in LA would there be a super-market with valet parking (and a small lot as well). With a restaurant in the center where the Venice *hip* wait an hour to eat French deli food. Where else but at *Rex* can you spend so much for so little that tastes so good. *Daily, 10AM-midnight. $$/$$$. 175 Marine St.* 399-9160

24 Meyera. Gourmet vegetarian cuisine with a French touch; homemade breads and pastries. *Vegetarian. Dinner daily. $$$. 3009 Main St.* 399-9993

25 The Rose Cafe and Market. Continental food served in the dining area, other foods available to go or cafeteria-style. The outdoor patio is good for an early morning continental breakfast. *Open daily. $/$$. 220 Rose Ave.* 399-0711

25 Via Dolce Confectioners. Set aside all your foregone conclusions about another chocolatier/ice cream shop. Owner/baker Robin Rose and her wonderful elves toil into the wee hours daily to bring you and the folks at *Macy's, Robinson's, Sakowitz* (in Texas) and *Buffum's* a truly special variation on that age-old cure for the sweet tooth. Using a unique blend of liqueurs whipped into rich dark chocolate, they make a selection of gourmet chocolate candies that give new dimension to the word *decadent*. Their Venetian ice creams are absolutely unparalleled. *Open daily. 11AM-12 midnight. 215 E. Rose Ave.* 399-1774

25 The Theatre at Galeries de Cuir. This newly opened 50-seat theater features changing original and Broadway productions, but it's the decor that gets the encore. The fresco Tiepelo-style murals, simulated Venetian inlaid marble floor, Louis XVI style French-Italian stage curtain all transport you to the Italian Renaissance. *Th-Su, 8:30PM. 208 Pier Ave.* 393-1601

"Nonconformity in our city is no feat; it's hard to find any standards to rebel against."
David Clark
1972

Narrative/Museums/Shops black
Gardens/Parks/Piers green

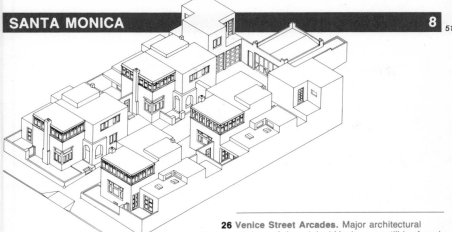

Horatio West Court. Located one block off Ocean Park Boulevard near Neilson Avenue, these impressively modern two-story apartments were built in 1919 by Irving Gill in a style far ahead of their time. Private residences. *140 Hollister Ave.*

VENICE AREA: Built on the swampy marsh of the La Ballona Rancho by tobacco magnate Abbot Kinney. He envisioned a model community fashioned after Venice, Italy, that would spur Americans to create their own cultural renaissance. He built a series of buildings styled after the Italian originals. The grand opening celebration started on July 4, 1905, lasted for three days, and drew a crowd of over 40,000. Visitors were ferried by festooned gondolas through a 16-mile system of canals and paraded down the street on camelback. But Kinney's dream was plagued by bad engineering, fires, storm waves, and political problems. By 1929, the city filled in and paved over all but three of the original 16 miles of canals. Even after its annexation by the City of Los Angeles, Venice's fun-zone amusement concessions, thrill rides, gambling houses, night clubs, and town-lot oil drilling gave it a reputation for extraordinary civic laissez-faire. By the '60s Venice was the last bastion of the anything-goes counterculture and a haven for the elderly. Almost all that is left of the excesses that so endeared Venice to reporters and sociologists is the weekend circus on Ocean Front Walk, in which physical culturists, executives, panhandlers, hipsters, families, pretty girls, and a crazy quilt of humanity promenade or roll along the boardwalk on every imaginable wheeled device from rollerskates to skateboards, bicycles, unicycles, rickshaws, tandems, wheelchairs, and small plastic tricycles. This small area is a favorite visiting spot for foreign tourists eager to see a more colorful realm of American culture.

The Traffic Circle. Once the Grand Lagoon, it is now a paved drive. *Windward and Main Sts.*

Main Post Office. Inside is a mural depicting the history of Venice by artist Edward Biberman. *Southwest corner of Main St. and Windward Ave.*

Ace Gallery. Changing exhibits of works by contemporary artists of international stature. *Northwest corner of Windward Ave. and Main St.*

Caplin House. Contrasting pink stucco and a light blue roof in an unusual and sophisticated 1979 design by Fred Fisher. Private residence. *229 San Juan Ave.*

Sidewalk Cafe. A bustling spot for seeing and being seen. *1401 Ocean Front Walk. 399-5547*

26 Venice Street Arcades. Major architectural portions of the original Venice can still be found at the corner of Windward Street and Pacific Avenue, where only the arcades of the St. Marks Hotel remain.

26 Venice Mural. Behind the Sidewalk Cafe is a large mural startling in its illusion by contemporary artist Terry Schoonhoven. *Between Market St. and Windward Ave.*

28 West Beach Cafe. A sleek white skylit box of a restaurant, serving impeccable food in *nouvelle California* style. *Open daily, 10AM-1AM. Closed M. $$/$$$. 60 N. Venice Blvd. 399-9246*

28 L.A. Louver Gallery. Works by contemporary artists. *55 N. Venice Blvd. 396-6633*

28 Hama Sushi. Every neighborhood has its favorite sushi bar. Hama, at the moment, is Venice's. *Sushi. Dinner daily. $$/$$$. 213 Windward Ave. 396-8783*

29 Robert's. A small local hangout for film and music people. *Continental. Closed M. Dinner only. Brunch Sa-Su. $$/$$$. 1921 Ocean Front Walk. 392-4891*

26 Spiller House. The angular tower of corrugated steel and unpainted wood rising three stories is actually a double house by Frank Gehry, built in 1980. Private residences. *39 Horizon Ave.*

27 La Grange Aux Crepes. Crepes of every imaginable type. *French. Open daily. $. 1025 W. Washington Blvd. 396-6005*

27 Chez Helene. A French country-style restaurant. *Closed M. Lunch Tu-Sa, 12-3PM. Dinner Tu-Su, 6:30-10PM. $$. 1029 W. Washington Blvd. 392-6833*

27 Comeback Inn. A neighborhood jazz club specializing in Latin American jazz. *1633 W. Washington Blvd. 7255*

30 Banjo Cafe. Live bluegrass music nightly. *Closed Su. 2906 Lincoln Blvd. 392-5716*

31 Bruno's Ristorante. You may think you missed a turn and ended up on a sound stage at nearby MGM: a Renaissance interior and usually good Italian food, plus an extraordinary collection of fine wines at bargain prices. A great place for introducing kids to Italian cooking beyond spaghetti and meatballs. *Italian. Open daily. $$/$$$. 3838 Centinela Ave. 397-5703*

MARINA DEL REY AREA: Built in 1960, the Marina has over 10,000 private pleasure craft, making it the largest man-made small boat harbor in the world.

32 Baja Cantina. Popular and intimate, a Mexican restaurant with a little romance. *Mexican. Open daily. Su brunch. $/$$. 311 Washington Blvd. 821-2250*

32 Jamaica Bay Inn. A moderately-priced hotel with its own beach. The beach is a good place to watch wind surfers. *4175 Admiralty Way. 823-5333*

32 Marina International Hotel. A fine luxury hotel. *4232 Admiralty Way. 822-1010*

32 Marina City Towers. Made distinctive by their rounded shapes that resemble enormous horseshoe magnets tugging at each other, the towers were designed by Anthony Lumsden for Daniel Mendenhall Johnson and Mann. *4333 Admiralty Way.*

32 Bird Sanctuary. Perhaps the only natural retreat remaining of the miles of duck marshes once covering the area. It is a sylvan haven, hemmed in by concrete roads on both sides. *Between Washington Blvd. and Admiralty Way*

33 Fiasco. One of the best of the sleek Marina restaurants and a favorite with the boating crowd. *American/Continental. Open daily. Sa-Su brunch. 4451 Admiralty Way. 823-6395*

34 Burton Chace Park. Perfect for yacht watching, fishing, kite flying, or moon gazing from the watch tower. Picnic facilities and comfort stations make this a good place for a family outing. *End of Mindanao Way past Admiralty Way.*

35 Fisherman's Village. Quaint restaurants and shops with a good view of the Marina Channel. *13755 Fiji Way. 823-5411*

35 Fun Fleet and Marina Belle. A 45-foot replica of a Mississippi River boat, the Marina Belle plies the waters of the Marina Harbor on a regular schedule. On summer nights a cocktail cruise is added. *Summer: on the hour, M-F, 11AM-5PM; Sa-Su, 10AM-5PM, on the hour. Cocktail cruises, on the hour beginning at 5PM, Tu-Sa, 12-5PM. Winter, Tu-Sa, 12-5PM. Boat House, south part of Fisherman's Village. 13727 Fiji Way. 822-1151*

35 Marina del Rey Sportfishing. Charter fishing boats go offshore for ¾- and ½-day cruises. Dock fishing, boat and tackle also available. *13717 Fiji Way. 822-3625*

36 Cafe Parisien. Casual French dining. *Closed M. Brunch daily. $$. 3100 Washington Blvd. 822-2020*

37 Marriott Inn, Marina del Rey. A luxury hotel. *Lincoln Blvd. and the Marina Freeway. 822-8555*

38 Gulliver's. Prime rib impeccably prepared, served by wenches in a setting taken from Elizabethan England. *Open daily. No lunch, Sa-Su. 13181 Mindanao Way. 821-8866*

Restaurants red
Architecture blue

39 Loyola Marymount University. The successor of St. Vincent's, the first college in Los Angeles, founded in 1865. Now a coeducational private Catholic University. *Loyola Blvd. at W. 80th St. 642-2700*

40 AMFAC Hotel. A luxury hotel. *8601 Lincoln Blvd. 670-8111*

41 Marriott Hotel. A luxury hotel. *5855 W. Century Blvd. 641-5700*

42 Quality Inn. A moderately-priced hotel. *5249 W. Century Blvd. 645-2200*

42 Hyatt Hotel. A deluxe hotel. *6225 W. Century Blvd. 670-9000*

42 Sheraton Plaza La Reina Hotel. This new hotel is conveniently located near airport and beaches. Every expected convenience plus extras like transportation to Disneyland, Universal Studios and Knott's Berry Farm. In-house restaurants and disco. Handicapped accommodations. *6101 W. Century Blvd. 642-1111*

Within the hotel is:
Le Gourmet. ☆ ☆ Without a doubt the best restaurant within striking distance of LAX—in fact, one of the best *nouvelle cuisine* restaurants in town. Dine in modern elegance on wonderful food, and then hop the shuttle bus to catch your flight. *French. Dinner only, after 6PM. $$$$. 6101 W. Century Blvd. 642-4840, 642-1111*

43 LOS ANGELES INTERNATIONAL AIRPORT. The third busiest air-travel center in the world, Los Angeles International is the hub of the Los Angeles Regional Airport system. In 1979, there were 542,976 landings and take-offs, with peak traffic periods handling as many as 100 aircraft per hour on the five east-west runways of the 3,500-acre airport site.

Once a neighborhood of private homes fronting on a small airport known as Mines Field, expansion of LAX began in 1960 and continues today as Los Angeles readies itself for 1984 and the Olympics.

New building development in the airport's central section will top $750 million and include a huge international terminal for the influx of Olympic athletes, dignitaries and tourists. Designed by Pereira, Dworsky, Sinclair and Williams, it will lie at the west end of the central terminal complex.

A second level of roadway, scheduled for 1983 completion, is being added at the terminal to ease conjestion and separate drop-off and pick-up traffic.

With airport traffic expected to double by 1990, LAX management is struggling admirably to keep pace. But until construction is finished, travel near and within the airport will be a headache of detours and closed lanes. Allow plenty of time for heavy construction traffic. Near the airport, tune in AM 530 on your radio dial for hourly traffic updates.

Organization. Most international airlines are on the north side of the airport, or to the right as you enter from Century Boulevard to World Way. The small commuter airlines are located at the west end, and the national and domestic carriers are on the south.

Connections. Transportation between terminals is provided by the blue, green, and white buses labeled *Airline Connections*. These buses stop at the island in front of each ticketing building. Other buses will take you to parking lots A, C, and VSP, and to the West Imperial Terminal. *There is no charge.*

Handicapped Connections. A special minibus has extra-wide doors and a ramp lift for wheelchairs. *Call 646-8021. There is no charge.*

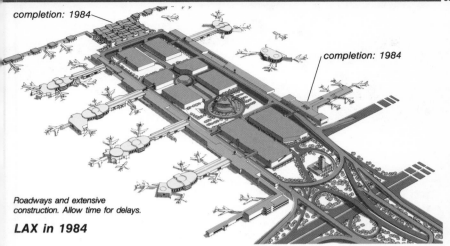

completion: 1984

completion: 1984

Roadways and extensive construction. Allow time for delays.

LAX in 1984

Parking. Despite the availability of over 20,000 parking spaces, parking may be a problem. There are four types of lots available, listed by descending price:
Central Terminal. Lots 1-7. Convenient, but very expensive if used long-term. Best for under two hours. May be full during peak periods.
Lot A. Corner of 96th Street and World Way. A tram connects this to the terminals, or it is a brief downhill walk to the cental area. Good for under 24 hours.
Lot C. Corner of Sepulveda and 96th Street. Has a free connecting tram. Best for under 24 hours. *No charge for first 3 hours.*
VSP Lot. Corner of 111th and La Cienega Blvd. Has a free connecting tram. Best for 24 hours and over. *No charge for first 3 hours.*

Getting to and from the airport. Your vacation or trip will begin sooner if you take the bus rather than private car. Parking is unnecessary and buses let you off in front of every terminal at the airport. Remember that buses not only pick you up from the airport, they take you there from many locations.

Airport Service Bus, Los Angeles County:
1. **Downtown Area Stops:** Greyhound-RTD Terminal; Hotels—Bonaventure; Hilton; Figueroa; Hyatt Regency; Biltmore; Mayflower; New Otani.
2. **Wilshire District Stops:** Hotels— Hyatt-Wilshire; Ambassador; Sheraton Town House.
3. **Beverly Hills-Century City stops:** Hotels— Century Plaza; Beverly Hilton; Beverly Wilshire.
4. **Hollywood-Universal City Stops:** Hotels— Hollywood-Roosevelt; Holiday Inn; Sheraton-Universal.
5. **Westside and San Fernando Valley Stops:** Hotels— Westwood Holiday Inn; Valley Hilton.
6. **Pasadena Stops:** Hotels—Pasadena Hilton; Huntington Sheraton.
7. **San Gabriel Valley Stops:** El Monte RTD Station; Hotels—El Dorado Inn, West Covina; Howard Johnson, Pomona; Holiday Motor Lodge, Montclair; Ontario International Airport. *Phone for information: 646-4761*
8. **Orange County:** Buses go to hotels and sites in Buena Park, Disneyland, Santa Ana, Laguna Hills, Seal Beach, Long Beach Airport, Orange County John Wayne Airport. *For information: (714) 776-9210*

9. **Eastern San Fernando Valley:** FlyAway bus service to the Van Nuys Airport Terminal at 7610 Woodley, corner of Saticoy. At the airport, board buses in the center island outside of the baggage claim area. *For information: 994-5554 or 781-5554*

10. **Santa Monica Area:** Santa Monica Flight Line's Yellow and White Vans service the Miramar, Huntley House, Holiday Inn, Pacific Shore, and Ocean Village Hotels hourly, 6AM-9PM during the week. Weekends longer interval. Board buses at the airport at the center island outside of the baggage claim area. *Information: 393-9231*
11. **Glendale-Burbank Area:** Brown vans from Crown Commuter go to Glendale and the Hollywood-Burbank Airport. *Information: 750-5439*
12. **Western San Fernando Valley and Ventura Area:** The Great American Stage Lines brown and gold big buses go regularly to and from Woodland Hills, Thousand Oaks, Oxnard, and Ventura. *Information: (805) 499-1995*

Theme Building. Rising 135 feet above the terminal area, the theme building houses a Host International Restaurant, an 80-foot observation deck, and a branch of the Bank of America. The restaurant is a fine place to watch planes take off and land, and an inexpensive way to feel like you're going somewhere when you can't afford a vacation. *Restaurant: American. Lunch 11AM-5PM daily; brunch Sa-Su, 10AM-3PM; dinner M-Sa, 6PM-11PM. $/$$. 646-5471*

RTD Airport Transfer Terminal. All airport-bound bus lines run to and from a point just outside LAX at Vicksburg and 98th Street. Operating daily, a minibus (line 206), picks up passengers and takes them to terminals within the airport complex. Line 206 operates all day and night, except in the early morning between 1AM and 5AM. Frequency is 6 to 8 minutes throughout the day and every 12 minutes in the late evening. Ask for a *FREE* transfer from any RTD line to Route 206. RTD regional lines serving LA International Airport are lines: 88, 607, 834, 869, 871, 873, and 877.

West Imperial Terminal. A separate terminal just south of the main airport handles charter flights and supplemental carriers. A free blue and green bus marked *West Imperial Terminal* (WIT) connects you with the main terminal every half hour, 7:30AM-11:30PM. Take the bus from the center island in front of each baggage claim area. *6661 W. Imperial Highway*

Information. *Inside the airport, yellow telephones are available to reach the Airport Information Aides. The aides are on duty from 7AM-11:30PM daily. Multilingual information and assistance is available by calling visitor information: 488-9100. Information on buses, limousines, and parking is available by dialing A-I-R-P-O-R-T.*

A crescent of mountains encloses Los Angeles on the north and east. Formed of the Santa Monica and San Gabriel ranges, this natural barrier functions as both physical and psychological boundary, enhancing the sense of civic isolation, offering refuge from the complexities of twentieth-century life and giving the city an intriguing topological complexity.

MALIBU: Conjuring up visions of lissome blondes and perfect suntanned bodies, Malibu is as advertised and more. The first perfect bodies here were the deer, for whom the Chumash Indians named the area. The Humaliwo Indians were the first human settlers. In 1805, the Topanga-Malibu-Sequit rancho, an expanse that included over 22 miles of pristine Pacific oceanfront, was granted to Jose Tapia. In 1887, Frederic H. Rindge, a wealthy easterner, bought the intact rancho and began lifetime efforts to keep outsiders away. A loophole in the law enabled the Rindges to exclude the Southern Pacific Railroad from their property by constructing their own small gauge railroad.

Later, the widowed Mrs. Rindge foiled state attempts to build a highway by planting alfalfa along the proposed route. When this ruse failed to stop the state, she resorted to dynamite. Her protests were carried as far as the State Supreme Court, but the family financial reserves were depleted by the feud and in the end the government won. In 1929, the Pacific Coast Highway (then called the Roosevelt Highway) was officially opened and the Rindge Corporation declared bankrupt. The Malibu rancho was soon broken up and development came to the ocean.

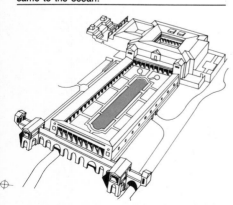

1 J. Paul Getty Museum. A detailed replica of a Roman seaside villa that faces a spectacular ocean view and creates the feeling of life as it might have been at the time of the Caesars, sans togas. Oil billionaire J. Paul Getty had the museum built on the plan of the Villa dei Papyri in Herculaneum, once reputedly the home of Julius Ceasar's father-in-law. The original villa, buried in the eruption of Vesuvius in 79 AD, was reoccupied and remodeled over several centuries. The design of the Getty Museum is an amalgam of plans from a 300-year period from 200 BC to 79 AD. Colonnaded walkways, mosaics, frescoes, and Roman-style landscaping have been used to recreate the Mediterranean setting. The crisp and idyllic period piece houses a collection of superb Greek and Roman antiquities on the ground floor. Small galleries face an atrium courtyard, creating viewing areas appropriately scaled for the pieces on display. Upstairs are European paintings from the Renaissance through Baroque periods and a collection of French decorative arts housed in period rooms. A tearoom serves light meals in the terraced garden. Books on the museum, the collection, and related subjects are available in the bookstore. Architects Langdon and Wilson and consultant Norman Neuerburg designed the museum, which opened in 1974. *Open mid-June to mid-September, M-F, 10AM-5PM; mid-September to mid-June, Tu-Sa, 10AM-5PM. Parking reservations recommended for guaranteed admission. Admission free. 17985 Pacific Coast Highway. 454-6541*

2 Las Tunas Beach. Located nearby. The name does not refer to canned fish, but is Spanish for the fruit of the prickly pear cactus.

MALIBU BEACH AREA:

3 Malibu Art and Design. A contemporary general store of domestic and personal items coupled with an art gallery that shows leading local artists. *Open M-Sa, 10AM-6PM; Su 12PM-5PM. 3900 Cross Creek Rd. 456-1776*

3 Pasquale's. A lively jazz club with a beautiful beach front location. Famous artists and studio musicians of lesser reputation but equal talent are featured. *22724 W. Pacific Coast Hwy. 456-2007*

3 Tidepool Gallery, One of the area's finest seashell stores also sells art inspired by the ocean. *22762 W. Pacific Coast Hwy.*

3 Wine Cellar Malibu. A front patio for people-watching, a side garden for more secluded dining. The menu ranges from sandwiches to sophisticated entrees. *Continental. Open daily. No dinner M. Su brunch. $/$$. 22853 Pacific Coast Hwy. 456-2953*

4 Malibu Pier. Built in 1903 by Frederick Rindge as a landing point for ranch supplies and for his private railroad, the pier was reconstructed in 1946 and is now owned by the state. Fishing is permitted. *23000 Pacific Coast Hwy.*

4 Alice's Restaurant. *Organic American. Open daily. Su brunch. $$. 23000 Pacific Coast Hwy. 456-6646*

Malibu Sport Fishing Landing. Located on the pier, has boats that make regular day and half-day surface fishing cruises. The bait and tackle shop rents equipment for pier or boat use. Fishing licenses are sold for boat fishing; no license is necessary for pier fishing. *Open daily, 6AM-5PM. 23000 Pacific Coast Hwy. 456-8030*

Malibu Surfrider State Beach. Affectionately known as *the Bu* by surfers, it has a world-famous right reef point break. The surfing here is best in August and September when south swells are in evidence. A good location to watch surfers in action is from the adjacent Malibu pier.

Malibu Beach Colony. At last, a listing about where the movie stars *do* live. An exclusive and very private beach for the famous and wealthy since 1926, when silent movie queen Anna Q. Nillson moved here. Many of the *beach cottages* have bedrooms sufficient to sleep the staff of the Johnny Carson Show and hot tubs big enough to soak the Olympic swim team. The drives and beach here are private, but the dramatic Stevens House by John Lautner can be seen from Pacific Coast Highway as a double-height concrete quarter-circle rising into the sky. Private residences.

Moonshadows. Bountiful salads, steaks, and piped-in sounds of surf, plus the view of the breakers. *American. Dinner daily. $$$. 20356 Pacific Coast Hwy. 456-3010*

Whale Watch. Seafood and sushi in this tacky but *in* spot with those who live in the Malibu Colony nearby. You may not spot a whale on the horizon, but you'll undoubtedly see some Hollywood celebs around you. *Seafood. Dinner except Tu. $$/$$$. 6800 Westward Beach Rd. 457-5571*

La Scala Malibu. ☆ Outside, a patio full of flowers; inside, an intimate dining room. *Italian. Open daily. $$$$. 3835 Cross Creek Road, in the Malibu Country Mart. 456-1979*

Pepperdine University. Established in 1937 by founder of Western Auto Supply Stores George Pepperdine, this nondenominational four-year college moved to its present hilltop location overlooking the ocean in 1973. William Pereira designed the new facilities on the 819-acre Malibu campus, home of Seaver College which offers a comprehensive liberal arts curriculum for bachelor's/master's degrees in 50 major subject areas. The University also has a School of Law with coursework leading to the juris doctor. There are 3 satellite centers in Southern California and undergraduates can participate in a year-in-Europe program at the picturesque Heidelburg University, Germany campus. *24255 W. Pacific Coast Hwy. 456-4000*

Holiday House. A long-time favorite for elegant dining with an ocean view. There is an outside patio. The inside dining room features art deco decor. *Continental. Closed M. Lunch Sa-Su only. Sa-Su brunch. $$$. 27400 Pacific Coast Hwy., north of Latigo Canyon. 457-3641*

Paradise Cove. A private beach, full of nooks and crannies for walking and exploring. Admission fee.

Sandcastle Restaurant. A Cape Cod-style restaurant that prides itself on the romantic sea-front location and superb seafood. Try scalone, a mixture of scallops and abalone. *Continental. Open daily. Breakfast served from 6AM. $$/$$$. 28128 W. Pacific Coast Hwy., in Paradise Cove. 275-2503*

Narrative/Museums/Shops black
Gardens/Parks/Piers green

7 Point Dume. Named in 1782 by George Vancouver, the English explorer, for Father Dumetz, a Jesuit at the Ventura Mission. A residential area with a hard-to-get-to beach. Until the 20th century, the point was high and peaked, but the top has been shaved off for a housing development.

8 Leo Carrillo State Beach. A broad and clean sandy beach named for the Los Angeles-born actor, Leo Carrillo (1880-1961). Descendant of one of California's oldest families and son of the first mayor of Santa Monica, Carrillo became famous as Pancho, the sidekick to TV's Cisco Kid. There is surfing at the northern end of the beach.

8 Point Mugu State Park. A secluded and idyllic park with 70 miles of trails, a tall-grass prairie preserve, beautiful sycamores and lovely canyons. Excellent for day hikes and picnics. Camping hook-ups are provided. *Advance camping reservations required. Pacific Coast Hwy., across from Leo Carrillo State Beach. 457-5538*

SANTA MONICA MOUNTAINS: One of the most intriguing aspects of Los Angeles is its relationship to its mountain ranges. Unlike other cities, where nature is hours away, Los Angeles has two nearby mountain systems: the Santa Monica Mountains, a semi-wild and rugged chain of canyons and peaks running right through the center of the city; and the San Gabriel Mountains, a nearby section of the large Angeles National Forest.

The Santa Monicas offer numerous breathtaking views of the Los Angeles Basin and the San Fernando Valley from their summits, while retaining a wild environment within their ridges and valleys. The visible mountains are part of a chain which rises from the floor of the Pacific, forming the Channel Islands, the beach plateau, and the series of peaks that extend into the city center at heights averaging between 1,000 to 2,000 feet. They are a place to discover both what the city is and what it once was. Slopes are covered with a collection of evergreen shrubs and scrubby trees known as chaparral. This plant life includes chamise and sage on the lower, drier hills, and a denser cover of scrub oak, sumac, wild lilac, and manzanita along stream beds. The *wild* plants seen everywhere, oats and mustard, were actually introduced only 200 years ago by the Franciscan padres. Fire hazard is a major consideration in this region. Plant life is bone dry in the summer and the smallest spark or flame can ignite a raging brush fire that will quickly spread over thousands of acres.

Mulholland Drive, a narrow, winding country road, snakes aross the crest of the Santa Monicas. It was named for the Welsh engineer who was responsible for the first major aqueduct in the city, bringing water and subsequent rapid development. Development has constantly threatened the wild areas of the Santa Monicas. This threat is somewhat abated by a recent federal law that will create one of the largest urban parks in the country of much of the mountain territory. Great tracts still remain in private hands, however, and it is likely that many of them will soon be built up with view homes. Until then, from Oxnard to downtown Los Angeles, the Santa Monicas are a natural preserve, displaying the way the city looked before the arrival of Europeans.

9 Malibu Creek State Park. Four thousand acres, which include Malibu Creek, 2-acre Century Lake, ageless oaks, chapparal, and volcanic rock. There is excellent day hiking on almost 15 miles of trails. Local movie companies sometimes film on location in this secluded park. *Open daily. No camping. Admission free, parking charge. 28754 Mulholland Dr., Agoura. May be entered from Malibu Canyon. 991-1827*

10 Topanga Canyon. This rustic community prides itself on the kind of wholesomeness that would make the *Whole Earth Catalog* envious. Before anyone ever hand-painted a VW bus, before anyone other than a Mexican national wore huaraches, before the dome became a residential noun rather than a part of St. Peter's, Topanga was an alternate community. Its bucolic homes are sheltered on the hillsides under large groves of sycamores, or scattered along the creek running through the base of the canyon. Indian settlements in the area have been dated to at least 5,000 years ago. The name Topanga means mountains that run into the sea.

10 Topanga State Park. Nine thousand untouched acres to explore and enjoy. The high peaks offer superb views of the ocean and San Fernando Valley. A self-guided trail explains the ecology. Grassy meadows and woodlands are perfect for picnics. Water and sanitary facilities are available. *No overnight camping. Open daily. Admission free. 20825 Entrada Rd. (Entrada Rd. leads off Topanga Canyon Rd. There are no park signs on Topanga Canyon Rd., so watch carefully.) 455-2465*

11 Topanga Corral. Music—country, rock n' roll, rhythm and blues—and eats. The rough-sawn decor complements the foot-stomping atmosphere. *American. Open daily. Dinner only. $$. 2034 S. Topanga Canyon Blvd. 455-9045*

13 Paolo's. Only three freeway exits away from Magic Mountain is a small delight. Homemade pasta, subtly sauced veal, and solicitous service. *Italian. Closed M. Dinner only. $$. 24523 Newhall Ave., Newhall. (805) 259-5418*

13 Le Crocadile Bistro. At last there is a decent French bistro in the outermost reaches of the San Fernando Valley. Convenient to Cal Arts and Magic Mountain. *French. Lunch & dinner daily except Tu. $$/$$$. 24246 Lyons Ave. Newhall. 362-6341*

13 California Institute of the Arts. Founded with an endowment from Walt Disney in 1970, this small, four-year college has schools of film, dance, theatre, art, and music. The buildings were designed by Ladd and Kelsey. *McBean Parkway and the Golden State Freeway, 27400 McBean Parkway, Valencia. (805) 255-1050*

"The variety of the great masses of tar, the movement which one sees in all of them at once, the pitchy smell, the sight of that great lake of strange matter, and these phenomena, present an astonishing and frightful aspect, reminding one of the pictures painted of the infernal caverns ... In hot weather animals have been seen to sink in it and when they tried to escape they were unable to do so, because their feet were stuck, and the lake swallowed them..."

José Longinos Martínez
1792

All-time recorded high temperature: **110°**
September 1, 1955.

14 The Cascades. Water being aerated on the last step of its 233-mile journey from the Owens River Valley creates an aquatic sculpture. In 1913, engineer William Mulholland ushered the life-giving flow into LA with the words, "There it is. Take it" thus enriching the annals of speechmaking with the shortest public remarks on record. *Golden State Freeway (Interstate 5) past Balboa Blvd.*

15 William S. Hart Park. "While I was making pictures, the people gave me their nickels, dimes and quarters. When I am gone, I want them to have my home." With this testament, silent film cowboy star William S. Hart bequeathed his 253-acre ranch for use as a public park. One hundred ten acres have been preserved as a wilderness area. The developed portion of the property includes an animal compound stocked with domestic beasts and a herd of buffalo, picnic sites, and Hart's ranch-style home, called La Loma de los Vientos, which contains a number of paintings and sculptures by Charles M. Russell. *Open daily, 10AM-7:30PM; home tours, Tu-Sa, 10AM-5PM every half-hour. Admission free. Junction of Newhall Ave. and San Fernando Rd., 24151 Newhall Ave., Newhall. (805) 259-0855*

16 Placerita Canyon Park and Nature Trail. A 314-acre native chaparral park, located in a picturesque canyon amid stands of California live oak. There is a nature center and self-guided tour designed to illustrate the relationships of the plants and animals in the area. *Nature Center open daily, 9AM-5PM. Admission free. 19152 Placerita Canyon Rd., Newhall. (805) 259-7721*

SAN GABRIEL MOUNTAINS. True wilderness is found in the San Gabriel Mountains, which form a natural barrier protecting the northeast side of Los Angeles with steep peaks and remote forested areas. In contrast to the urban availability of the Santa Monicas, the San Gabriels were rigidly inaccessible for many years to anyone but a seasoned outdoorsman. This changed in 1935 when the Angeles Crest Highway (State 2) was opened, providing the first of an interlacing network of mountain highways that easily bring travelers to secluded destinations. Route 2 begins in La Canada and provides access to most of the 691,000 acres of the Angeles National Forest, of which the San Gabriels are only a portion.

Some of the more remote sections of the region have colorful histories. The discovery of placer gold deposits triggered a small gold rush as early as 1843 near the east and west forks of the San Gabriel River. At the end of the decade a town named Eldoradoville sprang up and soon rivaled northern Gold Rush towns as a den of iniquity. The town was later destroyed by heavy floods. Gold fever was resuscitated during the Depression, when jobless Southern Californians improvised a camp and panned for hardscrabble gold with kitchen utensils. During the boom of the 1880s, Angelenos made the horse trail up Mt. Wilson a favorite vacation spot. Professor T.S.C. Lowe opened up the Mt. Lowe Railroad in 1893 to bring delighted tourists 3000 feet up the steep incline to the mock-alpine hamlet near Echo Mountain's peak. The railway was destroyed by fire, but another **17** famous landmark, the **Mt. Wilson Observatory**, still stands near the peak of 5,710-foot Mt. Wilson.

All-time record low temperature: **27.9°**
January 4th, 1949.

The San Gabriels are popular for many forms of outdoor recreation—hiking, bicycling, fishing, birdwatching, and in winter, a variety of snow sports. The quiet trails are seldom crowded—the only groups you might see are Boy Scout troops. There are great contrasts in vegetation and terrain; water makes all the difference. One moment you can be walking in a fern dell and the next in an arid chaparral landscape. Wildflowers abound, including poppies, Indian paintbrush, lupines, and wild tiger lilies. Skunk cabbage grows near springs, and at altitudes over 5000 feet, pine trees flourish. Three levels of ranges add variety to hiking pleasure. The front slopes near Altadena are good for day hikes, with well-maintained trails leading through waterfalls and pools and near cliffs and ravines. Vegetation here is primarily alders, oaks, and cedars. In places such as Bear Canyon, the middle ranges take you to the last reserves of mountain lions and bighorn sheep in Southern California. At the top of the range, many of the slopes are stark and are a rugged rock climber's paradise. One of the most challenging of the higher areas is Mt. San Antonio, or Old Baldy, at 10,080 feet the county's highest peak. Sightseeing drives will provide only a sample of the wealth that the San Gabriels contain. Getting out and walking around is the best way to understand this area. Much is virgin territory, and the thrill of trailblazing is still available.

It is recommended that visitors stop at the Red Box Ranger Station for trail and road information, brochures, and books. *Station, open daily during the spring and summer, weekends during the fall and winter, located on Route 2 at the Mt. Wilson junction. To telephone ahead, call the "O" operator and ask for Red Box #2 station.*

Headed north toward the San Gabriel Mountains, you will find a spectacular family amusement park.

SIX FLAGS MAGIC MOUNTAIN. If the kids want thrills and fun, but you want a day in the country, the 75 rides and attractions of Magic Mountain are the answer. The amusement park is set into 200 beautifully landscaped acres atop the rolling hills of Valencia, with grassy knolls, trees, and shrubbery creating a spacious and sylvan feeling quite different from the crowded hurly-burly of the conventional amusement park.

Rides at Magic Mountain are guaranteed to be fast and scary. There are five roller coasters to test your mettle. The **Colossus** is boasted to be the largest, fastest, highest, and steepest wooden roller coaster ever built. After 9,200 feet at speeds up to 65 miles per hour, who could argue? The **Revolution** offers a 360-degree vertical loop at 60 miles per hour, while the **Gold Rusher** is a theme roller coaster on which you become a passenger aboard a runaway mine train. The unusual **Mountain Express** offers a ride in single cars rather than in attached caravans. Even little tykes can practice for the big time on the kiddie roller coaster in **Children's World**.

Magic Mountain has two memorable rides for those who like to get soaking wet as part of the fun. Similar in concept and course, the rides differ in modes of conveyance: the **Log Jammer** features hollowed-out logs; the **Jet Stream**, speed boats. These vehicles are not attached to any track under the water chutes they follow, so the degree of damp encountered depends on how much the passengers rock and whether the rider in front ducks.

The **Electric Rainbow** and the **Enterprise** provide lessons in basic physics as passengers are held against the sides of revolving drums by centrifugal force. For panoramic views of the surrounding territory, try the **Eagle's Flight Tramway**, a 40-degree inclined funicular railroad to the top of Magic Mountain, or the **Sky Tower**, a ride to the observation deck of a 384-foot *space needle* structure.

Fast fun on the level is featured at **Sand Blasters**, where dunebuggies are powered by electric motors, or Standard Oil's **Grand Prix**, where visitors can play at being Mario Andretti. The newest ride in the park is the **Buccaneer**, a swinging pirate ship where half the fun is watching your mateys on the other side of the boat as they make a precipitous drop from a 70-degree arc.

The past is not forgotten at Magic Mountain. Visit the gently rolling countryside, populated with buffalo, long-horned cattle, and elk, aboard the **Grand Centennial Trainride**, a replica of a turn-of-the-century steam train. The **Grand Carousel** is an exquisitely restored 1912 merry-go-round. At **Spillikin Corners** such traditional American crafts as glassblowing and blacksmithing are demonstrated and goods are sold in quaint shops.

Four theaters offer entertainment: **Greenwillow Theatre** near Spillikin Corners has shows on the hour from 2 to 9PM. The **Rockin' Country Jamboree** features up to 15 performers in an high-energy hoe-down. **Magic Moments Marionette Theatre** is air-conditioned, dark—and while this alone could recommend it to some—features a spectacular marionette revue called **Hooray for Hollywood**. Dolphins and high divers alternate their amazing skills at the new **Aqua Theatre**, a 110,000-gallon salt water tank in a 1500-seat amphitheater. Shows are presented from 1 to 9PM. The largest theater is the **Toyota Showcase**, where every evening the **Great Rock and Roll Time Machine** takes spectators through the history of rock music from Chuck Berry to the Beatles via slides, film, and recorded and live music. Famous performers such as Loretta Lynn occasionally appear in this theater.

Youngsters aren't ignored. **Children's World** has gentle rides, an **Animal Farm** full of pettables, and **Wizard's Village** where they can clamber and climb. Look for the trolls who are the park mascots.

A newly created 24-acre expansion includes **Roaring Rapids**, a 1200-foot-long artificial white-water rapids featuring raft rides that end in a 25-foot waterfall.

Food is plentiful at the park, although a half-hour wait after meals before hitting the larger rides is recommended. The **Four Winds**, at the summit of Magic Mountain, offers a delicious salad buffet at lunchtime and hot meals in the evening. The **Timber Mill** serves hearty American-style food. The specialties at **La Cantina** are Mexican. Other spots are the **Valencia Terrace** for farm-style breakfasts, and the **Deli** for sandwiches and juices. Naturally, hot dogs, soda pop, etc. are abundant everywhere.

One admission fee at Magic Mountain conveniently covers all rides and attractions. No worries about who has the ticket book—once you're in, all doors are open. Height and weight restrictions on some rides. *Summer: open daily 10AM-midnight. Spring, fall, winter: open weekends and school holidays only, 10AM-6PM. Magic Mountain Parkway off Interstate 5, Valencia. (805) 255-4100*

10   SOUTH BAY/HARBOR

One of the world's largest man-made harbors was only two feet deep 125 years ago.

Since its beginnings as a rustic port for the hide and tallow trade, the LA Harbor has become the nation's largest canning and fishing port. Over 125,000 tons of cargo move across the wharves daily. Ship arrivals in 1979 totaled 3,950; close to 100 large ships can dock simultaneously, and there are anchorage berths for thousands of small craft along the 28 miles of waterfront. The original port consisted of a small landing constructed in 1835 by Juan and Jose Sepulveda. August Timm bought the landing from the Sepulvedas and was soon after the lucky recipient of a shipwreck in his front yard. Timm utilized the stranded ship as a dock by extending planks out to it, thus expanding the harbor. At this time, the bay was so shallow that ships had to anchor offshore and unload cargo into smaller boats.

Modernization of the port occurred largely through the work of one man: Phineas Banning, a free-wheeling entrepreneur who made a fortune in shipping, stage and telegraph lines, and real estate. With a crude dredge he deepened the harbor to 16 feet, started a small breakwater, and developed a new town just south of San Pedro, which he named Wilmington after his home in Delaware. By 1868, he had built a railroad connecting downtown LA to Wilmington, and later to San Pedro. Wilmington was incorporated as a city in 1872; San Pedro followed in 1883.

The two new cities faced expansionist pressure from the landlocked city of Los Angeles. In 1876, the Southern Pacific completed its Transcontinental Railroad link, thus providing the overland connection, but the emerging metropolis still needed access to the sea. Despite its shallow, unprotected harbor, San Pedro outmaneuvered Santa Monica for federal funding and became the main port-of-entry for the City of Los Angeles. Work began in 1899 on a new breakwater and a major port expansion.

In 1909, Los Angeles annexed San Pedro and Wilmington, creating the famous *shoestring strip*, a stretch of city land, at places only a half-mile wide, from downtown to the harbor which provided for a seaport and transportation route entirely within city limits. The city made several improvements in the port, dredging from 35 feet to the present 51 feet. The harbor is the foremost port-of-call in Southern California for passenger vessels. Also within the region are several oil refineries and aircraft-construction facilities.

LOS ANGELES HARBOR: In the center of Los Angeles Harbor is Terminal Island, once linked to San Pedro only by ferry, now linked by the Vincent Thomas Bridge and to Long Beach by the Gerald Desmond Bridge.

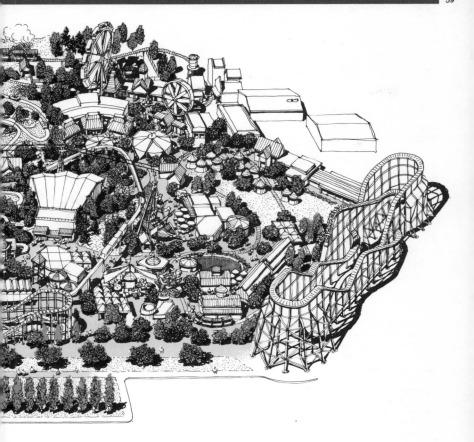

Maritime Museum. A museum of nautical history located in a remodeled ferry building in the Port of Los Angeles. The office of Pulliam and Matthews designed the refurbishment. Much of the old ferry gear remains in the two-story structure, giving visitors a sense of imminent departure. There is a fine view of harbor operations from the promenade deck. Next to the museum, the bow section of the US Navy cruiser *Los Angeles* offers a chance to explore. Museum collections include a number of ship models; perhaps the most fascinating is a 16-foot scale model of the *Titanic*, built from cardboard and match sticks by a 14-year-old boy. The Naval Deck is replete with Navy memorabilia, including the bridge deck of the cruiser *Los Angeles*. A timeline history of the harbor beginning in 1840 gives a graphic summary of the dredging and construction. *Open 7 days. M-F, 9AM-4PM; Sa-Su, 12:30-4PM. Admission free. Berth 84, San Pedro. 548-7618*

Fisherman's Dock and Fish Harbor. On the western side of the main channel and on the southern side of Terminal Island, respectively. Centers for the commercial fishing industry.

Ports O'Call Village and Whaler's Wharf. At the harbor's edge is a replica of other times and other places. Nineteenth-century New England, a Mediterranean fishing village, and early California live again in this shopping and eating complex. The Village Boat House, located in Ports O'Call Village, offers daily cruises of the harbor area where visitors can

see the inner harbor, yacht harbor, freighter operations, scrapping yards, and the Coast Guard base. *Tour hours vary with the season; for information call 831-0996. Ports O'Call. Berth 77, San Pedro*

4 **Princess Louise Restaurant.** Launched in 1921 to cruise between British Columbia and Alaska, the *Princess Louise* is enjoying a busy dotage as a theme restaurant. The harbor view from the port side is fascinating. A number of the cabins have been restored and may be visited before or after dining. One room contains replicas of the crown jewels of England. *Continental. Open daily. $$. Berth 94, San Pedro. 831-2351*

5 **North of Ports O'Call.** On the western side of the main channel are the container terminals, piled high with steel freight containers, and the passenger liner terminals. The terminal for the *Catalina Steamer* and the Catalina helicopter is located just north of this point.

6 **Vincent Thomas Bridge.** Spanning the main channel between San Pedro and Terminal Island. Clearing the water by 185 feet so that military planes can fly under it, the 6,500-foot-long turquoise suspension bridge is the most visible landmark in the harbor. Freighters are berthed on the northern side of Terminal Island. Drydocks are located across the back channel in the Long Beach side of the harbor and in the Naval Shipyard on the southeastern end of Terminal Island.

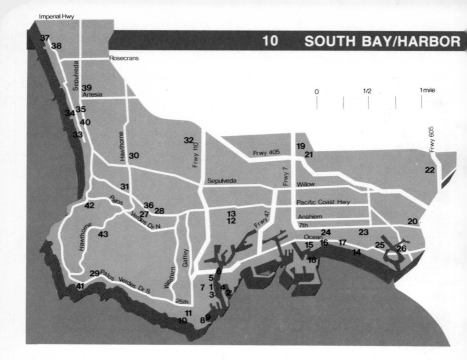

Naval Shipyard. Visitors are sometimes allowed to board Navy ships in dock. *The schedule is erratic, so call to check first. Visitors welcome on weekends from 1-4PM. 547-6721*

SAN PEDRO AREA: The streets of downtown San Pedro (pronounced by natives as San Pee-dro) retain much of the flavor of their colorful past as a seaman's port town. The region's commercial fishing fleet is a major part of the area economy, employing many mariners of Portuguese, Greek, and Yugoslav descent. Strong ethnic traditions make shopping in the multitude of small ethnic grocers a delightful experience.

7 Papadakis Taverna. A lively restaurant serving Greek food. If the mood is right, the waiters dance. *Very popular, reservations essential. Greek. Closed M. $$. 301 W. Sixth St., San Pedro. 548-1186*

8 Cabrillo Beach Fishing Pier. A 1,500-foot publicly owned fishing pier. Shop sells equipment and live bait; no rentals. No license or fee required. *Open daily, 7AM-11PM. End of Stephen M. White Dr., San Pedro. 833-1510*

9 Cabrillo Beach Marine Museum. Children will love the exhibition areas of the Cabrillo Marine Museum. Architect Frank O. Gehry has built a succession of small stucco, galvanized steel, and wood-beam buildings to house saltwater aquaria, lively exhibits, and marine laboratories. The message of the playground-like structure is that learning about the environment, particulary the marine world, is fun. Museum volunteers are always on hand for tours and workshops. The museum's former quarters, in the renovated 1928 Cabrillo Beach Boathouse, houses more exhibits including dioramas, fossils, and over 15,000 seashells. *Open daily 9AM-5PM. Admission free. 3720 Stephen White Dr. 548-7562*

10 The Point Fermin Marine Life Refuge. A tidepool community next to the museum. Brochures for a self-guided exploration of tidepool biology are available at the museum.

10 Point Fermin Park. Thirty-seven landscaped acres on the palisades overlooking the Pacific and Los Angeles Harbor. The lookout point has coin-operated telescopes; the whale-watching station offers information on the California grey whale regarding its annual winter migration to the Gulf of California. The Victorian Eastlake-style lighthouse, constructed in 1874 from bricks and lumber brought around Cape Horn by sailing ship, is not open to the public. The lighthouse originally used oil lamps approximating 2,100 candlepower until 1925 when electric power was installed. This park is a popular place to watch hang-gliders. *Gaffey St. and Paseo del Mar*

11 Fort McArthur Military Reservation and Angel's Gate Park. Currently headquarters for the Army 47th Artillery Brigade, the fort has been under government jurisdiction since 1888. The lower reservation was used during World War II as a training center and was one of the primary West Coast defense fortifications. Angel's Gate Park, named after the gap in the breakwater that protects the Port of Los Angeles, surrounds a pagoda which houses the *Friendship Bell*, given by the Republic of Korea in 1976 to commemorate the US Bicentennial. The 20-acre park offers a spectacular view of the Pacific and Point Fermin. *Ft. McArthur: Western Ave. and Paseo del Mar. 831-7211. Park is open daily, 8AM-6PM; admission free. 548-7710*

12 Drum Barracks. The last remaining building of Camp Drum, a 7,000 soldier Union Army outpost. Although California sympathized with the Confederacy during the Civil War, this large Union Military presence kept the state in the blue ranks. The Barracks have been refurbished as a museum of Civil War memorabilia. *Hours vary: call for schedule. 1053-55 Cary Ave., Wilmington. 518-1955*

Phineas Banning buys Rattlesnake Island (now Terminal Island) and 2400 acres of estuary from the Dominguez family for $20,000 and begins developing new wharf and town.
1857

Worst ever smog attack: harbor and airport closed.
1954

Narrative/Museums/Shops black
Gardens/Parks/Piers green
Restaurants red
Architecture blue

3 Gen. Phineas Banning Residence Museum. In 1864 Phineas Banning, father of the Los Angeles harbor, built this Greek Revival clapboard home of lumber from the Mendocino coast, Belgian marble, and European colored glass. The house is now decorated with period furnishings. Tours through the building include the restored kitchen, where food is cooked using Katherine Banning's recipes, as well as family and public rooms of the mansion. The museum is located in 20-acre Banning Park, which offers picnic facilities and playground equipment. *Access to the house by tour only; tours given W, Sa & Su at 1, 2, 3, and 4PM. Admission free. 401 E. M St., Wilmington. 548-7777*

South of the harbor is the City of Long Beach, since 1940 a major port and site of Signal Hill, an oil field which once led the world in production. In 1921, a wildcat well was sunk on the hill, with gushing success. Quickly incorporated as a 2¼-square-mile city consisting only of oil wells, it brought riches to all who drilled the hill. The name derives from a signal marker erected by the US Coast Survey at the peak of the hill around 1890. As with many of Los Angeles' oil fields, Signal Hill reserves have been depleted by overdrilling. From the sandy strand south of Long Beach, you can see the tropical camouflage created to conceal the almost 600 still-producing offshore oil wells; each palm-clad fake island covers ten acres of sound-proofed oil wells. The Long Beach harbor is new, constructed since 1940. It is a major port for automobile imports and Alaskan crude oil, and a major West Coast port-of-entry.

14 Belmont Pier. 1,300-foot municipal pier. The bait shop also rents equipment. *Snack bar available. End of 39th Pl., Long Beach. 434-6781 (bait shop)*

15 Long Beach Convention and Entertainment Center. A variety of entertainment—rodeos to rock concerts, symphony to ballet. *Year round. 1300 E. Ocean Blvd., Long Beach. Ticket information: 436-3661. 24-hour recorded event information: 436-3673*

16 Villa Riviera Apartments. A prominent, 16-story French chateau-style apartment house with a central spire, picturesque pitched roof balconies, and stained-glass windows. Private residence. *800 E. Ocean Blvd., Long Beach*

17 Long Beach Museum of Art. Located in a 1912 Craftsman-style home, the museum sponsors changing exhibitions that emphasize contemporary Southern California art. The archives of artists' videotapes are the largest on the West Coast. The permanent collection includes work by the Laguna Canyon School of the 1920s and 1930s and regional WPA-sponsored pieces. The carriage house has a bookstore and exhibition gallery. Sculpture by prominent contemporary artists is displayed around the beautifully landscaped site. *Open W-Su, 1-5PM. Admission free. 2300 E. Ocean Blvd. 439-2119*

18 The Spruce Goose. The largest wooden aircraft ever built, boasting a 320-foot wingspan, a 219-foot length, and an 80-foot tail height. It was conceived in 1942 by Howard Hughes as a prototype for a fleet of air cargo transports. Technical difficulties delayed completion until November 2, 1947, when the one and only flight of the *Hercules* took place. *Pier J (next to the Queen Mary) 435-7766*

18 Queen Mary. The majestic *Queen Mary*, the largest passenger ship ever built, is now permanently berthed in Long Beach Harbor. Launched in 1934, the 50,000-ton *Queen Mary* epitomized art deco luxury when she and her crew of 1,200 cruised the North Atlantic. In 1964, she was retired from service, purchased by the City of Long Beach, and converted into a tourist attraction and luxury hotel. Her upper decks have been refurbished, one of her four propellers encased in a steel room to make visible the portions of her anatomy formerly seen only by fish, and her main turbine revealed under glass. The third-class passenger cabins in the hull have been rebuilt to accommodate a museum housing the Jacques Cousteau *Living Sea* exhibit, while other areas display marine memorabilia and models. A tour guide uniformed as a bosun's mate escorts visitors to the bow and up to the bridge for a commanding view of Long Beach and the Los Angeles Harbor. The promenade deck offers liquid refreshment in the observation

18 lounge and food in the **Lord Nelson, Sir Winston,** and **Lady Hamilton restaurants**

18 The **Capstan** serves lighter, more moderately-

18 priced fare. Operating as the **Queen Mary Hotel** *(435-3511),* the original first-class cabins have been refitted as first-class hotel rooms, with many of the original appointments; prices depend on port or starboard position, Marysgate Shopping Village, designed to look like an Elizabethan Village, is located adjacent to the *Queen Mary* and offers 25 stores and cafes. *Open daily, 10AM-4:30PM for tours; restaurants and shops remain open later. Admission charge for tour and museum. Pier J, Long Beach. 435-4733*

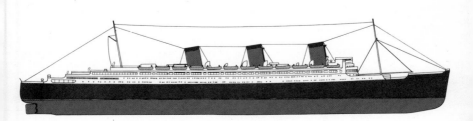

10 SOUTH BAY/HARBOR

19 Rancho Los Cerritos. The romance of the old rancho days is recalled at this restored 1844 Monterey-style adobe. The two-story residence was built by Don Juan Temple on part of the 1784 Nieto land grant. Subsequently enlarged, the house is furnished as it was between 1866 and 1881 when the Bixby family used it as headquarters for their ranching empire. Exhibitions include: the children's room, complete with dolls and toys, the weaving room, and the foreman's bedroom. The exhibit wing features material relating to social and economic aspects of rancho life and a research library of California materials. Some of the original walks and trees planted in the mid-19th century remain in the restored five-acre garden. *Open W-Su, 1-5PM. Admission free. 6400 Virginia Rd., Long Beach. 424-9423*

20 Rancho Los Alamitos. Another part of the original 1784 Nieto land grant. The adobe house has been enlarged four times since it was built in 1806. The interior is very much as it was when the Bixby family occupied it during the 1930-40s. The grounds contain a dairy and horse barns, a blacksmith's shop, and a five-acre native California garden planted with cactus and succulents, kitchen vegetables and herbs, and exquisite Chinese and Japanese wisteria. *Open W-Su, 1-5PM. Visitors must be accompanied by docents. Admission free. 6400 Bixby Hill Rd., Long Beach. 431-2511*

20 Filling Station. Quiche, soups and salads on a refreshing, ever-changing menu. *M-F, 7AM-2:30PM, Su, 8AM-2PM, closed Sa. 762 Pacific Ave., Long Beach. 437-3324*

21 Bixby House. One of the few remaining examples of English architect Ernest Coxhead's residential work, this is a shingle-style house built in 1895 for a member of the Bixby family. The wood-shingle Victorian house has Craftsman design elements. *Private residence. 11 La Linda Dr., Bixby Knoll, Long Beach*

22 El Dorado Park. An 800-acre recreational facility. El Dorado East Regional Park is an unstructured activity area containing meadows and several lakes where fishing is permitted. The largest lake rents paddle boats. There are over four miles of bicycle and roller-skate paths and an archery range. El Dorado West City Park offers an 18-hole golf course, night-lit tennis courts, tennis shop, roller-skate rental, six baseball diamonds, duck pond, children's playground, bandshell, a branch of the Long Beach Public Library, and a number of game courts. The El Dorado Nature Center, located in the east section, is an 80-acre bird sanctuary and native chaparral community. The small museum in the center of one of the two lakes exhibits material about the natural history of Southern California. *Maps for self-guided tours are available at the Museum; a guided tour of the Nature Center is offered every Sunday morning, 9AM. Hours: El Dorado Park East: daily, 7AM-sunset; vehicle admission fee charged. El Dorado Park West: daily, 6AM-10PM; admission to park free; charge for facility use. Nature Center: W-Su, 8AM-4PM; admission free. El Dorado Park East and Nature Center, 425-8569; El Dorado Park West, 425-4712; facility reservations, 432-5931. 7550 E. Spring St., Long Beach*

23 Fourth Street. At the less expensive end of the shopping spectrum, Fourth Street has a number of little shops ranging from chic to modest that carry antiques, art deco accessories, crafts, and clothes. *Between Redondo and Lucille Avenues.*

Narrative/Museums/Shops black
Gardens/Parks/Piers green

24 Acapulco y Los Arcos. A chain operation that consistently serves innovative and delicious Mexican food. *Mexican. Open daily. $. 733 E. Broadway, Long Beach. 435-2487*

25 NAPLES AREA. Always a Latin-lover, Los Angeles has embraced not only old Mexico but Italy as well. Naples, like Venice to the north, is a 20th-century attempt to re-create a romantic spot equal to the European original. Work on the development was begun in 1903 when a section of Alamitos Bay was dredged to make a small cove with an island, formed from the excavated mud in the center. Picturesque cottages were built on curving streets, canals were dug and spanned by quaint footbridges; by the end of the 1920s, the one-half mile square community was complete. Today, Naples seems more Midwestern than Italian, with well-maintained shingled homes and carefully tended gardens. The perimeter of the island is bordered by walkways that overlook Alamitos Bay and a small beach. In the center, Colonnade Park is encircled by the Rivo Alto Canal. Although the island is accessible by car, its true charm is seen only by the pedestrian. This is a wonderful place for an afternoon of strolling, picnicking, and boat-watching. *Second St. off Marina Dr., Long Beach*

25 South Long Beach restaurants: A Tout Va Bien. Pleasant, popular and casual. *French. Closed M-Tu. $$. 5730 E. Second St., Naples.*

26 439-9888. Bogart's. If you like *Casablanca*, try Bogart's. Wicker, ceiling fans, potted palms, and the ever-present piano player singing *As Time Goes By. Su brunch, 10AM-3PM. Marina Pacifica Center, Second St. and Pacific Coast Hwy. 594-8976*

PALOS VERDES PENINSULA AREA. To the north of the harbor are the Palos Verdes Hills—literally *green sticks*—but, understandably translated as *green trees.* Palos Verdes is an exclusive residential community with an outdoors lifestyle, western ranch homes, Spanish haciendas, horse trails, and countless lovely hiking paths leading through the forests of eucalyptus. The hills are a succession of 13 marine uplift terraces created by Palos Verdes' slow rise from the ocean floor.

27 South Coast Botanic Gardens. A model experiment in land reclamation. Until 1956 the site was a diatomaceous earth mine. When mining activity ceased, the trash dumping began–3,500,000 tons were poured in. Starting in 1960, the Los Angeles Department of Arboreta and Botanic Gardens initiated a planting program. Beautifully landscaped, the 87-acre gardens now contain mature specimens from all continents except Antarctica. Plants are grouped according to botanical family. The gardens also offer horticultural and botanical displays, a gift shop, gardening demonstrations every Sunday at 2PM and a picnic area. *Open daily, 9AM-5PM. Admission fee. Tram tours M-Th, 11AM, 1, 2, and 3PM; Sa-Su, 11AM, 1, 2, 3, and 4PM; fee for tram. 26300 S. Crenshaw Blvd., Rancho Palos Verdes. 377-0468*

28 Lomita Railroad Museum. Housed in a replica of the 19th-century Greenwood Station in Wakefield, Mass., the museum displays memorabilia from the steam era of railroading. The station is flanked by an impeccably restored 1902 steam locomotive and a 1910 wooden caboose, both of which may be boarded. The annex across the street has picnic benches, a fountain, and a 1913 boxcar. Souvenir corner sells gifts. *Closed M-Tu; open W-Su, 10AM-5PM. Admission fee. 250th St. and Woodward Ave., Lomita. 326-6255*

9 Wayfarer's Chapel. Occupying a prominent hillside location overlooking the ocean, this chapel is the national monument to Emmanuel Swedenborg, Swedish theologian and mystic. It was designed by Lloyd Wright in 1946. The architect wanted to create a *natural church* that fused with its environment. The glass structure, supported by a redwood frame, is transparent and blends with the surrounding redwood grove. *5755 Palos Verdes Drive S., Rancho Palos Verdes*

0 Del Amo Fashion Center. Three hundred fifty-five stores in 2.4 million square feet of space—the largest center of its kind. The main department stores are *The Broadway, Sears, J.C. Penney, Robinson's, Bullock's, I. Magnin, Ohrbach's,* and *Wards.* Also found in this world of merchandising are a number of independent fashion stores, 30 restaurants, and dramatic interior spaces defined by bronzed glass and unique architectural features. *3525 Carson, between Hawthorne and Madrona, Torrance*

0 Magic Pan. In a provincial setting, crepes are perfectly cooked on a revolving apparatus at the end of the dining room and then rolled around savory sweet fillings. *Open daily. 21444 Hawthorne Blvd., Del Amo Fashion Plaza, Torrance. 542-7757*

1 Marengo. Chicken Marengo, seved by waiters in Napoleonic costume, is the specialty of the house. *French. Closed Su and Lunch Sa. $$/$$$. 24594 Hawthorne Blvd., Torrance. 387-1174*

2 Alpine Village Inn. Twenty-two shops offer an array of goods in a replica of a German Alpine Village. The inn serves enormous portions of German food; you can quaff a stein while listening to the band in the beer garden. Children may pet domestic animals in the farm or take a ride in the amusement park. *German-Swiss. Open daily. $$. 833 Torrance Blvd., Torrance*

BEACH CITIES OF REDONDO, HERMOSA, MANHATTAN, AND EL SEGUNDO. A jumble of pastel cottages squeezed along a stretch of beachfront mark a series of former summer resorts prospering as permanent communities. At the south end is Redondo, a mixture of affluent new and slightly seedy old, with an interesting and well-kept pier and marina complex. Next is Hermosa, the prototype beach town with its concentration of T-shirted surfers, T-shirted families, and T-shirted elderly retirees. Just to the north is Manhattan Beach which, despite a hardy contingent of stable families, remains the singles capital of the beach party circuit, favored by the suntan-seeking, fun-loving, white-collar workers of the South Bay area. North of Manhattan is El Segundo, a sedate neighborhood bordered by the airport on the north and an oil refinery to the south.

33 Monstad Pier. 200-foot privately owned pier. Tackle shop rents and sells equipment and bait. *Restaurant available. Pier open daily, 24 hours a day. Admission fee. Tackle shop open daily, 5:30AM-9PM. Coral Way, Redondo Beach*

33 Fisherman's Wharf. Many unusual shops line the narrow path leading to the end of the pier, including places to buy and eat fresh fish and the ubiquitous souvenir shops. A popular place on summer nights when many restaurants are open late. *Redondo Beach*

33 Concerts by the Sea. One of the best jazz clubs in the Southland. Its performers read like a roster of who's who in jazz. *Closed M-W. 100 Fisherman's Wharf, Redondo Beach. 379-4998*

33 Redondo Sport Fishing. Choose from a short 45-minute harbor cruise (available all year), local offshore fishing, or deep-sea cruises to Catalina and Santa Barbara Islands. An exciting seasonal whale watch allows you to observe the migration of the California grey whale from breathtakingly close range. *24-hour reservations, 372-3566 or 772-2064*

33 Redondo Sportfishing Pier. 250-foot privately-owned pier. Tackle shop rents and sells equipment and bait. *Snack bar available. Pier open 24-hours daily; tackle shop open daily, 4:30AM-9PM in winter, 24 hours a day in summer. End of Harbor Drive and Portofino Way, Redondo Beach*

34 Hermosa Beach Fishing Pier. A 1,320-foot municipal pier. Shop rents equipment and sells bait. *Snack bar available. Pier open daily, 24 hours; bait shop open daily, 7AM-5PM. End of Pier Ave., Hermosa Beach. Bait Shop, 372-2124*

34 The Lighthouse. In the block next to the pier is one of the best and oldest jazz clubs in Los Angeles. Fine music and top-flight performers rather than fancy decor has kept the doors open since the 1950s. *Closed M. 30 Pier Ave., Hermosa Beach. 372-6911*

35 For an out-of-the-way book fix: **The Either/Or Bookstore.** Writer Thomas Pynchon used to come in here to pick up the latest in fiction when he lived nearby. *124 Pier Ave., Hermosa Beach. 374-2060*

35 Pedone's. A very good thin-crusted pizza. *M, 4PM-11PM; Tu-Su, Noon-11PM. $$. 1501 Hermosa Ave., Hermosa Beach. 374-9131*

36 Cafe Courtney. A cozy cafe with friendly service. The patio with a view is a lovely place for brunch. *French. Open daily. $$. 2701 Pacific Coast Hwy., Hermosa Beach. 376-2455*

37 Manhattan Beach State Pier. A 900-foot municipal facility, without tackle or snack shops. *Pier open daily, 24 hours a day.*

38 Cafe Pierre. Rustic and comfortable. *French. Open daily. No lunch on Sa. $/$$. 317 Manhattan Beach Blvd., Manhattan Beach. 545-5252*

39 The Silk Route. Lounge on cushions while you savor exotic tastes. A second room provides conventional seating. *Afghani and Iranian. Closed M-Tu. Dinner only. 124 N. Sepulveda Blvd., Manhattan Beach. 379-4849*

40 Sausalito South. A San Francisco look, with Tiffany lamps and hanging plants, a young crowd, pretty good fresh seafood and a friendly oyster bar. *Seafood. Lunch & dinner daily. $$$. 3280 Sepulveda Blvd., Manhattan Beach. 564-4507*

40 Saint Estephe. ☆ If this charming French restaurant were located in West LA, it would live up to the best of them, and probably charge a lot more. *French. Lunch, M-F; dinner Tu-Su. $$/$$$. 2640 N. Sepulveda, Manhattan Beach. 545-1334*

41 MARINELAND. A combination aquarium and marine circus situated on dramatic cliffs overlooking the Pacific. The Sky Tower rises to 344 feet above sea level for a panoramic view. Inside the park are several open-air amphitheaters where sea lions, dolphins, and killer whales perform amazing stunts and charming charades in large pools. Hanna-Barbera characters Yogi Bear, Huckleberry Hound, Snagglepuss and others roam the park posing for pictures as well as performing on a dry-land stage. *Passages Beneath the Sea*, a series of exhibits designed by Encyclopedia Britannica, is 30 aquaria full of an amazing assortment of marine creatures in settings that reproduce their native habitats. Elsewhere, you will find tanks full of whiskery walruses and enormous koi and fish that watch you watching them. The Marine Animal Care Center is a hospital behind glass, where you can question lab technicians about their patients via a two-way microphone.

Baja Reef is Marineland's newest attraction. You don mask, snorkel, wetsuit, and fins provided at an additional fee by the park to swim through a replica of the reefs of the Mexican coastline between Ensenada and Cabo San Lucas; schools of fish dazzle your eyes and tickle your toes. Height and Weight minimums.

A number of food stands around the park provide basic hot dog, hamburger, pizza sustenance. The palisades tend to get windy, so a scarf and sweater are in order. *Open daily, 10AM-7PM. Admission fee. 6600 Palos Verdes Drive S., Palos Verdes. 377-1571*

© 1980 Access Press Inc.

Malaga Cove Plaza. In their original 1922 plan for Palos Verdes, Charles H. Cheney and the Olmstead Brothers envisioned four area community centers. Malaga Cove Plaza, designed by Webber, Staunton and Spaulding in 1924, is the only one of the four constructed. It is a Spanish revival design of two-story shops in an arcade. The plaza has a picturesque brick bridge over Via Chico and a fountain inspired by the Fountain of Neptune in Bologna, Italy. *200 Palos Verdes Dr. between Via Corta and Via Chico.*

42 La Rive Gauche. Well-prepared food in a rustic and chic room. Their roasted quail with raspberries is unique and memorable. *French. Open daily. No lunch M. $$/$$$. 320 Tejon St., Palos Verdes. 378-0267*

43 Borrelli's. Lovely Mediterranean decor. The service is particularly solicitous. *Northern Italian. Closed M. No lunch on weekends. $$. 672 Silver Spur Rd., Rolling Hills Estates*

43 Hungry Tiger. Chain owned by Flying Tiger Airlines. Fish is flown in fresh every day. Simple dishes are best here; oysters and clams on the half shell are hard to beat, unless you choose lobster. *American-style seafood. Open daily. No lunch on weekends. $$. 27300 Hawthorne Blvd., Rolling Hills Estates. 541-2632*

Often compared to an Italian landscape, Silverlake/Los Feliz is an area of lovely private homes nestled on the eastern edge of the Hollywood Hills.

Built before the advent of *pad construction*, in which bulldozers cut huge swipes out of the hillsides to make flat tracts on top of the slopes, the homes here conform to the shape of the hills. The picturesque undulations of the land, fabulous views of the surrounding city, and lack of tract development have inspired much innovative residential architecture by some of Los Angeles' most famous modern and contemporary architects. Works by masters such as R.M. Schindler, Richard Neutra, Gregory Ain, and John Lautner can be found in abundance in this area. The Silverlake Reservoir, built in 1907, is a jewel in its Mediterranean setting. From atop the nearby hills, visitors can see a picture-postcard view of winding roads, tiled roofs, and homes perched intimately along the contours of the slopes, with the glistening lake in the center. It is a scene far removed from the everyday urban intensity of other parts of the city. The roadway surrounding the lake is used for biking, strolling, and jogging.

The neighborhood has been maintained since its original residential development in the 1920s, and both Silverlake and Los Feliz are among the few real neighborhoods left in Los Angeles. The gracious Spanish and contemporary homes are occupied by many professionals. It is a melting pot neighborhood representing every ethnic group and nationality. Residents find the hillside privacy, view homes, quiet streets, and tolerant lifestyle appealing.

Before the area became popular with the new settlers to the city, it was part of the local Indian trail system. The Cahuenga Indians used a portion of what is now Ferndell in Griffith Park for their Mococahuenga, or council grounds. The entire region was once a portion of the 6,600-acre Rancho Los Feliz, granted in 1841 to the widow of Antonio Feliz by the Mexican governor of California. The northern portion of the property now called Griffith Park was bought in 1882 by Col. Griffith J. Griffith. Griffith was embroiled in several scandals in his lifetime, and so it took him several attempts to donate what he saw as an ideal playground to the city.

In the early 1920s, Los Feliz was a popular area for film stars' homes.

1 GRIFFITH PARK: Located at the southern end of the Santa Monica Mountains, over 4,000 acres make Griffith Park the largest municipal park in the country. The park is divided into two main areas: the flatlands, containing structured recreation such as golf courses, scenic areas, pony and train rides, tennis courts, merry-go-round, the Zoo, Travel Town, the Observatory, and the Greek Theatre; and the mountainous central and western areas, which have been left undeveloped except for numerous hiking and horse trails. There are four main entrances to the park: Western Canyon Road, off Western Avenue north of Los Feliz Boulevard, leading to Ferndell; Vermont Avenue and Hillhurst Avenue, north of Los Feliz Boulevard, leading to the Greek Theatre and the Bird Sanctuary; Crystal Springs Drive, off Riverside Drive, leading to the Ranger Station, merry-go-round and golf courses; and the junction of the Golden State (Interstate 5) and Ventura (California 134) Freeways, leading to the Zoo and Travel Town. *The park opens at 5AM and closes at 10:30PM. Mountain roads close at dusk. For general information, contact the Visitors Center, 4730 Crystal Springs Rd. 655-5188*

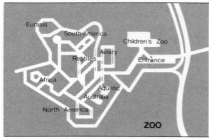

2 Zoo. The zoo opened in 1966 and has over 2,000 animals, grouped according to continent of origin, on 75 landscaped acres. Many of the animals are in environments that simulate their natural habitat with surrounding moats, thus allowing visitors to see them without bars. Children may mingle with gentle beasts in the Children's Zoo. The Animal Nursery proudly displays the newest arrivals. *Stroller and wheelchair rentals, picnic tables, snack bar, and tram tour are available. Open daily, 10AM-6PM in summer; 10AM-5PM in spring, fall, and winter. Admission charge. 5333 Zoo Dr. 666-4090*

3 Travel Town. The romance of the rails lives at this open-air museum of transportation, displaying many antique railroad and trolley cars, locomotives, planes, and automobiles. An enclosed structure houses several fire trucks and a circus animal wagon. A trolley ride circles the park and many of the exhibits are open for children to climb on board. Members of a model-train club work on an enormous train layout on Saturday. *Open daily, 9AM-5PM. Admission free. Zoo Dr. 662-5874*

3 Live Steamers. The Los Angeles Live Steamers Club bring their tiny steam locomotives to an area just northeast of Travel Town each Sunday. The trains run on tracks only seven inches apart, but they're authentic in every detail and powerful enough to pull several fully loaded cars. Children are given free rides and a chance to examine the charming miniatures. *Open Su only, noon-4PM. Northeast of Travel Town. Admission free*

4 Train Ride. Another tiny train, this one runs daily. Adults, as well as children, may ride. *Open daily, 10AM-4PM. Admission charge. Crystal Springs Dr. 665-6788*

4 Pony Rides. A safe, small track with ponies for children. *Open daily, 10AM-4PM. Crystal Springs Dr. Admission fee. 664-3266*

5 Tennis. Vermont Canyon. 12 day-use courts. City-registered players may make reservations; others will be allowed to play as courts become available. The shop sells clothes and rents equipment. Refreshments sold. *Courts, 7AM-7PM; shop, 8AM-6PM. Admission fee.*

6 *Vermont Ave. and Vista del Valle.* **Peppertree Lane.** Four day-use courts. No reservations taken. *Courts, 7AM-7PM. Admission fee. Griffith Park Dr.*

6 Soccer. A field is located at the Griffith Recreation Center, near the intersection of Riverside Drive and Los Feliz Boulevard.

7 Horseback Riding. The equestrian track near Riverside Drive functions as a practice area that leads to all trails. There are 43 miles of horse trails within the park. While the Department of Parks and Recreation does not maintain stables, several commercial stables on the outskirts of the park rent horses by the hour. All accept cash only and require a security deposit.

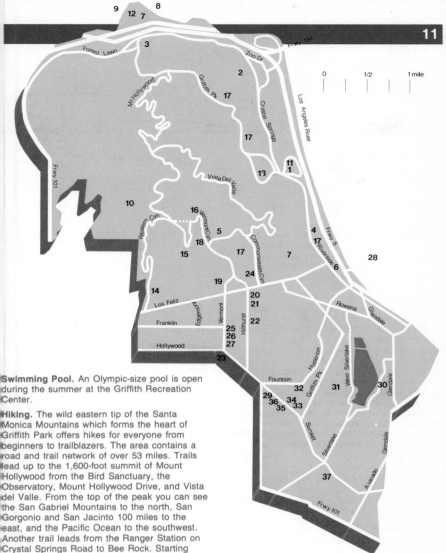

Swimming Pool. An Olympic-size pool is open during the summer at the Griffith Recreation Center.

Hiking. The wild eastern tip of the Santa Monica Mountains which forms the heart of Griffith Park offers hikes for everyone from beginners to trailblazers. The area contains a road and trail network of over 53 miles. Trails lead up to the 1,600-foot summit of Mount Hollywood from the Bird Sanctuary, the Observatory, Mount Hollywood Drive, and Vista del Valle. From the top of the peak you can see the San Gabriel Mountains to the north, San Gorgonio and San Jacinto 100 miles to the east, and the Pacific Ocean to the southwest. Another trail leads from the Ranger Station on Crystal Springs Road to Bee Rock. Starting across from the merry-go-round parking lot, a gentle trail leads into the Ferndell. Free trail maps are available at the ranger station, which is also the starting point for several guided hikes, including a monthly evening outing held during the full moon. *Call the rangers at 665-5188 for schedule.*

Biking. There are no specific bike paths, but regular paved roads are open to cyclists. Bikes are not permitted on the fire roads or horse trails.

Bar "S" Stables. *8AM-3:30PM weekdays; 7:30AM-3:30PM weekends. 850 Riverside Dr., Glendale. 242-8443*

Livingston Stables. *7:30AM-5PM daily. 910 S. Mariposa Blvd., Burbank. 843-9898*

Studio Stables. *7AM-5PM daily. 914 S. Mariposa Blvd., Burbank. 845-1440*

Sunset Ranch. *Half-day rates also offered. Night rides in summer during the full moon. 8AM-5PM daily. 3400 N. Beachwood Dr. 469-9612*

Baseball. A baseball diamond in the Crystal Springs Recreation Area is open by permit. It is used by city college teams for their league games.

Cricket. Two fields are located in the center of the equestrian track near Riverside Drive.

Restaurants red
Architecture blue

13 Merry-Go-Round. A well-preserved merry-go-round on the green, constructed in 1926 and moved to the park in 1936. *Open Sa-Su, 11AM-dusk; daily 11AM-5PM during school vacations. Admission charge. Park Center Picnic Area, off Griffith Park Dr. 665-3051*

Scenic Drives. The park is laced with roads, many of which offer scenic views of Los Angeles. Mount Hollywood Drive, on the western side of the park, offers spectacular views of the San Fernando Valley from between Griffith Park Drive and Vista del Valle. Vista del Valle, between Mount Hollywood Drive and Bee Rock, passes fine vistas of the Los Angeles Basin. Bee Rock is a monstrous lump of igneous stone, named for the bees that have set up housekeeping on its pitted surface. Fine southern views may also be enjoyed from Western Canyon Road, off Western Avenue. *A road map is available from the ranger station on Crystal Springs Dr.*

14 The Ferndell. A natural glade along a spring-fed stream, planted with native and exotic ferns. Paths and picnic tables make this an outstanding place to retreat from the world for an al fresco meal. *Fern Dell Dr. between Black Oak Dr. and Red Oak Dr., off Los Feliz Blvd. near Western Ave. 9AM-5PM daily.*

Narrative/Museums/Shops black
Gardens/Parks/Piers green

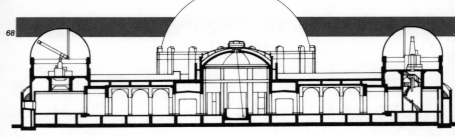

15 Observatory and Planetarium. The striking green copper-domed Moderne structure was designed in 1935 by John C. Austin and F.M. Ashley. The obelisk and bas-reliefs are by Archibald Garner; the interior murals by Hugo Ballin. Displays in the Hall of Science explain astronomy and physical sciences in participatory exhibits. The pendulum in the center of the rotunda hypnotizes visitors with its constant gentle swing. A fascinating show in the Planetarium Theatre re-creates eclipses, northern lights, and cycles of the stars through the use of a huge Zeiss projector. For sci-fi lovers, a show in the Laserium surrounds the audience with laser light, *laser rock* and *starship-sound. For more information on this popular show, call 997-3624; admission charge. Hall of Science open daily: summer, 1-10PM; spring, fall, winter, 2-10PM; admission free. Planetarium shows are given M-F, 3PM and 8PM; Sa-Su, 1:30, 3:00, 4:30, and 8:00PM; admission charge. Northern end of Vermont Ave.* 664-1191

16 Bird Sanctuary. A wooded canyon with ponds and a stream where birds are encouraged to nest. There are picnic tables. Rangers lead a 45-minute walking tour from the parking area on Vermont Canyon on Su at 1PM. *Open dawn till dusk. Vermont Canyon Rd., just north of the Greek Theatre*

17 Golf. There are five golf courses; two full-sized 18-hole courses. City-registered golfers may make reservations; others will be allowed on the green as space becomes available. *Call 485-5572 for information*

Picnic Areas. Eighteen picnic areas are located in the park. All have benches and tables; those in Ferndell and Vermont Canyon have barbecues and water. Park Center and Mineral Wells have some areas with cooking facilities. Visitors may also picnic on the grass.

19 Ennis House. Located at the top of a Hollywood hill, this Mayan-style house is perhaps the best example of Frank Lloyd Wright's concrete-block houses. Private residence. *2607 Glendower Ave.*

20 Los Feliz Inn. A hearthside English dining room serves food with more than a nod to French traditions. Fish is always good here; game sometimes turns up on the menu. One of the best in this part of town. *Continental. Gentlemen requested to wear jackets. $$$. 2138 Hillhurst Ave.* 663-8001

21 Villa Lasagna. A mix of professional and amateur opera, show tunes, and folk melodies, sung around the piano in a homey atmosphere. *$/$$. 2112 Hillhurst Ave.* 660-6694

22 Katsu. ☆ ☆ Possibly the most extraordinary presentation of any sushi bar in LA, often crowded with a trend-setting group of patrons. New wave Japanese in a neighborhood restaurant. Thousand dollar ceramic originals designed by Mineo Mizuno are the standard plates. Highly recommended. *Japanese. Lunch, M-F Noon-2PM; dinner, M-Sa 6PM-10PM. Closed Su. $$/$$$. 1972 Hillhurst Ave.* 665-1891

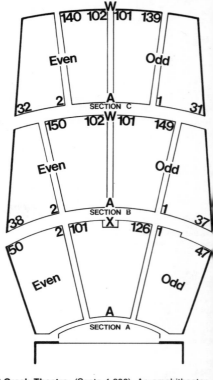

18 Greek Theatre. (Seats 4,600). An amphitheater nestled in the foothills of Griffith Park. The theater facade has Doric columns, making good the name. The season runs from June to the first week in October. Programs range from popular, rock, and folk music to classical ballet. The Greek Theatre is ringed by picnic tables; box lunches may be purchased from concessionaires inside. *Bring a sweater. Beer and wine available. Admission charge. 2700 N. Vermont Ave.* 660-8400

22 Palermo. Something they're serving (pizza) must be extraordinary as this eatery is as famous for its out-on-the-street lines as it is for its pizza. New location which will hopefully have the lines. *M-Su, 11AM-10:30PM. Closed Tu. $$. 1850 N. Hillhurst Ave. $$.* 663-1430

23 BARNSDALL PARK. Located at the top of a hill and ringed by a thick grove of olive trees, this shady oasis in the flatlands of eastern Hollywood offers a full spectrum of city park pleasures including picnic facilities. It is operated by the City of Los Angeles Department of Cultural Affairs. *4800 Hollywood Blvd.*

---

260 acres/day become housing tracts. Farming ceases as major industry.
1965

Restaurants red
Architecture blue
Narrative/Museums/Shops black
Gardens/Parks/Piers green

Ordinance is passed prohibiting the serenading of women without a license.
1838

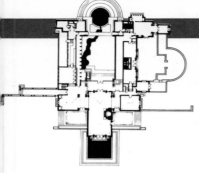

...ollyhock House. Located in the park is the ...rst house in Los Angeles designed by Frank ...oyd Wright. Built in 1921 on the site of an ...live grove purchased by oil heiress Aline ...arnsdall. She commissioned Wright to design ...cultural and residential complex of unique ...tructures. The central building is the Hollyhock ...ouse, named for its abstracted geometric motif ...ased on the flower. The city restored the home ...n the 1970s, refurbishing it with many of the ...riginal Wright furnishings. *An interesting ...uided tour is offered. Admission charge. Tours: ...u, Th on the hour, 10AM-1PM, and the first Sa ...nd Su of each month, on the hour, 12-3PM. ...eservations and information, 662-7272*

Municipal Art Gallery. The large, grey concrete ...uilding with a high portico entryway, a 1971 ...rthur Stevens design, is a gallery for regularly ...hanging exhibits of work by Southern ...California artists and craftsmen. Special exhibits ...t Christmas time are geared to delight the ...oung. The gallery offers an innovative program ...f tours for small groups. The Municipal Gallery ...heatre shows a lively and varied bill of films ...nd concerts. *Gallery admission charge. Hours, ...u-Su, 12:30PM-5PM. Closed M. Tours, 2PM. ...60-2200. Information on special and group ...ours, 662-8139*

Junior Arts Center. An extensive program of ...ophisticated and innovative studio arts classes ...or children and young people ages 4-18. The ...allery has changing shows designed for a ...oung audience emphasizing participation and ...ctivity. Free special events often make the ...ark a gala carnival. *Charge for classes, gallery ...ree. Open M-Sa, 9AM-5PM; Gallery, Tu-Sa, ...0AM-5PM; Su, noon-5PM. Closed M. 666-1093*

Arts and Crafts Center. Another Frank Lloyd ...Vright design from 1921, this center offers ...lasses in arts and crafts for adults and older ...eenagers. *Class charge. M-Th, noon-9PM; F-Sa, ...oon-5PM. 661-6369*

Lovell House. This is Los Angeles' finest ...example of International Style architecture. ...Designed by Richard Neutra in 1929, the free-...lowing plan and industrial materials were ...considered experimental. The steel-frame house ...s built on a steep hill with slabs and balconies ...supported by cables. The best view is from ...below on Aberdeen Avenue. Private residence. ...4616 Dundee Dr.

By the turn of the century, 100,000 people had crowded into LA, and 10,000 of them were *hooked up* to the telephone lines.

25 Tepparod Tea House and Tepparod Thai Restaurant. For a quieter experience. Spicy Thai food, a blend of Chinese, Indian, and French influences, served in serene rooms. The mint chicken is amazing; the refreshing coconut ice cream improbably contains nuggets of corn. *Thai. Closed M. $/$$. 4645 Melbourne Ave. 666-9919. 4649 Melbourne Ave. 666-9117*

26 Chatterton's Book Store. A high-ceilinged, airy white barrel brimming with books. Including one of the best selections of contemporary poetry and small-press literature in the city, as well as a staggering array of foreign and literary periodicals. Music plays and there are seats for reading. *Usually open late. 1818 N. Vermont Ave.*

27 Sarno's Cafe Del Opera. The piano in the front room is the center for opera and popular tunes by professionals and amateurs, some of whom have stage bravado that makes up for lack of vocal equipment. The action starts after 8PM. Bring your music and tell the pianist if you want to join the fun. *Closed M. $/$$. 1714 N. Vermont Ave. 662-3403*

28 La Strada. The attraction here is opera, sung tableside by professionals. The atmosphere sometimes gets zany, with singers singing, waiters serving, and patrons coming and going. *Closed M. Showtimes 8 and 10PM. F and Sa, midnight show. $. 3000 Los Feliz. 664-2955*

28 The Great Scot. A British inn, with beamed ceilings and fireplace. The beef is of high quality and the selection of imported beer and ale is one of the largest in town. *British. Open 7 days. No lunch Sa; Su brunch. $$. 2980 Los Feliz Blvd. 664-0228 (now* **Tam O'Shanter Inn***)*

29 L.A. Nicola Restaurant. ☆ Tailored by owner-chef Larry Nicola, this is a personal place that combines the architectural whimsy of Morphosis with a delicately eclectic menu. Highly recommended. *Continental. Lunch, M-F 11:30AM-3PM; dinner, M-Sa 5:30PM-10:30PM. Closed Su. $/$$. 4326 Sunset Blvd. 660-7217*

29 El Cid. The food in this Spanish colonial cabaret is only run-of-the-mill, but the Flamenco guitar and Flamenco dancing are remarkable. *Mexican/Spanish. Closed M. $$. 4212 Sunset Blvd. 668-0338*

30 Neutra House. In 1933, architect Richard Neautra built this home for himself of experimental modern materials. When it was destroyed by fire in 1963, the present house was built similarly using steel and glass. This International Style house is considered a landmark in modern architecture. Private residence. *2300 E. Silverlake Blvd.*

30 2200 Block of E. Silverlake Boulevard. A concentration of Richard Neutra houses. They are at numbers 2250, 2242, 2240, 2238, 2226, 2218, 2210, and 2200. All of the glass, steel, and stucco homes were built between 1948 and 1962 in the clean and elegant style which made the Austrian-born architect famous. Private residences.

31 *Silvertop* Residence. Hidden away at the top of a driveway is John Lautner's famous 1957 residence built over six lots. The cantilevered pool and tennis court may be partially seen at the rear of the house on Redcliff Street. This sculptural home is technically ingenious as well—with walls and ceilings that move at the touch of a button. Private residence. *2138 Micheltorena St.*

31 Oliver House. This house by Rudolph Schindler from 1933 combines International Style and traditional styles. Private residence. *2236 Micheltorena St.*

32 Casita del Campo. A refreshing outdoor patio. The menu is nicely handled. *Mexican. Open daily. $/$$. 1920 Hyperion Ave. 662-4255*

33 El Conquistador. Good Mexican food with dishes on the menu that are slightly off the beaten path. *Mexican. Open daily. $/$$. 3701 Sunset Blvd. 666-5136*

34 Mihitabel. Women's clothing and accessories. The style whimsical, the fibers natural. The jewelry section includes unusual antique and modern pieces. *3707 W. Sunset Blvd.*

35 Julian. Clothing and doo-dads. One of the specialities is way-out pillows. *3716 W. Sunset Blvd.*

35 The Soap Plant. A store that at times seems to transcend merchandising and become art. Goods include bath preparations from around the world, little toys, and decorative home and personal accessories. People have been known to drive for miles to keep current with its imaginative window displays. *3720 W. Sunset Blvd.*

36 Creative Handweavers. An extensive stock of yarns and threads for weaving plus ethnic clothing and accessories. *3824 W. Sunset Blvd.*

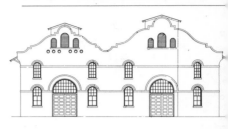

37 Olive Substation (now Jerde Partnership, Architects). The Olive Substation of the Los Angeles Pacific Railroad, built in 1907, was one of several Mission-style stations in the city taken over by the Pacific Electric Railway Company in 1911. The present owners have renovated it. Private office. *2798 Sunset Blvd.*

12   NORTH CENTRAL LA

Tucked into two pockets of steep hills and surrounded by the freeway system and the Los Angeles River is an islandlike region of great cultural and geographic variety.

The center of the area is an industrial lowland at the meeting place of the San Gabriel and San Fernando Valleys. Flanking the industrial sector is the sloping terrain of Echo Park-Elysian Park and Highland Park-Eagle Rock. Both areas are predominantly blue-collar Hispanic-American districts; the dialects of nearly every Latin American country can be overheard on the streets.

The small frame houses perched high on the tightly woven streets give the appearance of a rural setting and huge stands of eucalyptus trees run across the hillsides and into the canyons. Trails form a network through the overgrown wild areas across the slopes and ravines in Echo Park to Elysian Park and over the crest of Mount Washington in Highland Park. A mix of romance and economy makes this residential area attractive to creative young people.

The first residents of the neighborhood were the Yang-Na Indians, who camped in the Elysian Park Hills hunting for small game with bows and arrows. Several hillside springs fed by the Los Angeles River supplied the Indians with water. When the pueblo's first settlers arrived they continued to use these water sites and added a waterwheel and pipe system to bring the water down to the settlement from the hills. Around 1910, moviemakers came to the neighborhood, among them Mack Sennett, who built his first studio near Glendale Boulevard, and Laurel and Hardy who used the impressively steep stairways near Allesandro and Glendale Boulevards for several film gags.

1 ELYSIAN PARK. The second largest park in the Los Angeles area (over 600 acres), occupying several hills and valleys. The parkland was set aside for public use at the founding of the city in 1781. The main part of the park has been left in its natural state, the slopes covered with the shrubs and low trees known as chaparral. These areas are crisscrossed with hiking trails. **Chavez Ravine Arboretum**, the area on Stadium Way from Scott Avenue to Academy Road, was planted

with rare trees at the end of the 19th century; many mature and beautiful specimens remain. The center of the park along Stadium Way has picnic areas, some with cooking facilities. A scenic plaza with a small, man-made lake is located a quarter mile north of the end of Stadium Way. There is also a small children's play area.

2 Los Angeles Police Academy Rock Gardens. The training center for the Los Angeles Police Department is built on land leased from the city in Elysian Park. The rock garden was designed by Francois Scotti and constructed in 1937. It contains a series of cascades and pools, a small amphitheater, and outdoor dining area. *A small cafe is open to the public weekdays from 7AM-3:30PM, serving simple, reasonably priced meals. 1880 Academy Dr. 221-3101*

Restaurants red
Architecture blue
Narrative/Museums/Shops black
Gardens/Parks/Piers green

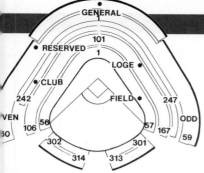

GENERAL

RESERVED

101

1

LOGE

CLUB

242

FIELD

247

VEN

106

56

57

167

ODD

60

302

301

59

314

313

odger Stadium. (Seats 56,000). Home of the
os Angeles Dodgers baseball team, Dodger
tadium is nestled in one of the world's largest
arking lots, which is in turn nestled in the
een slopes of Chavez Ravine. The unique
antilevered construction eliminates view-
ocking pillars within. Box, loge, general
dmission, and bleacher seats are available,
though boxes are usually in short supply
ecause they are generaly sold to season-ticket
olders. All levels of the stadium are well
upplied with food stands selling the famous
odger Dogs; you might ask for the
nadvertised spicy dog, a polish sausage on an
nion roll. Numerous kiosks sell such Dodger-
nprinted merchandise as T-shirts, baseball
quipment, stuffed animals, and team pennants.
giant color screen in the outfield flashes
stant replay, baseball quizzes, batting
verages, and the scores of other games
ound the country. The screen also acts as an
ectronic cheerleader, signaling when it is time
bellow the Dodger cheer, *Charge!* The screen
nnot be seen from the bleachers. *1000
ysian Park Ave. 224-1400*

kola's. Serving some of the best abalone in
wn for 46 years. The rest of the menu is
mple and hearty Yugoslavian. A fine place for
nner after the ballgame. *Yugoslavian. Closed
. $$. 1449 Sunset Blvd. 628-8005*

arragan Cafe. A neighborhood favorite for
exican food. Some unusual dishes on the
enu and old favorites honestly prepared.
ghtly entertainment in the bar. One of the
st in town. *Open daily. $/$$. 1538 W. Sunset
vd. 628-4580*

avelers Cafe. Good food in modest
rroundings. The fish dishes are especially
sty here. *Philippine. Open daily. 1651 W.
mple. 413-6008*

00 Block of Carroll Avenue. Carroll Avenue
part of Angelino Heights, one of the first
burban areas of the city. In the 1880s this
mote hilly location was sought after by
ofessionals as soon as public transportation to
e area became available. A number of the
ock's original elaborate Victorian homes have
en restored by their owners. The
ighborhood's well-preserved period feeling is
uch appreciated by filmmakers, and movie
oduction crews are frequently found on the
streets. The Carroll Avenue Foundation has
encouraged the preservation of the area and
offers annual tours of the homes. Some of the
architectural monuments include: 1316 Carroll
Ave., an Eastlake type of Victorian house,
recognizable by the rectilinear ornamented
panels and elaborate woodwork; 1330 Carroll
Ave., the **Sessions House**, designed by
Victorian architect, Joseph Cather Newsom,
displays fine spindlework; 1345 Carroll Ave. is a
typical Queen Anne Victorian house with fish-
scale shingles and wrought iron railings around
its upper widow's walk. Private residences.
624-5657

7 ECHO PARK. During the 1870s, Echo Park
Lake provided water for nearby farms. In 1891,
the land was donated to the city for use as a
public park; Joseph Henry Tomlinson designed
the layout utilizing the plan of a garden in
Derbyshire, England. The 26-acre park is
attractively landscaped with semitropical plants
and a handsome lotus pond. The lake has
paddle boats available for hourly rental. *Open
daily; no admission fee. Glendale Blvd. and
Park Ave.*

8 Angelus Temple. In the 1920s and 1930s,
Aimee Semple McPherson preached her
Foursquare Gospel within this circular structure.
The large, domed, classical building was based
on the design of the Mormon Tabernacle in Salt
Lake City. *1100 Glendale Blvd.*

8 Cocina Corina. A little take-out stand offering
wonderful burritos at low prices. *Mexican. Open
daily. $. In front of the Sunset East Car Wash,
southeast corner of Sunset and Alvarado Blvds.*

8 Burrito King. Another take-out stand, also
offering wonderful burritos at low prices.
*Mexican. Open daily. $. Northeast corner of
Sunset and Alvarado Blvds.*

8 Les Freres Taix. Like dining at your great
aunt's, if she happens to be French. An
excellent wine list and atttentive service. *Open
daily. $/$$. 1911 Sunset Blvd. 484-1265*

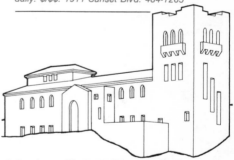

9 Southwest Museum. One of the finest
collections of western Indian artifacts in the
world is housed in a 1914 Mission-style building
designed by Sumner Hunt and Silas R. Burns.
The museum is best entered through the
250-foot-long tunnel entrance off Museum Drive.
The underground passage is lined with
dioramas of southwestern Indian life and leads
to an elevator up to the main tower. Among the
notable holdings are the Poole Collections of
American Indian basketry, Navajo blankets,
pottery, and a full-sized Blackfoot tepee. The
exhibition areas are: The Plains Hall, Hall of
Prehistory, Southwest Hall, California Hall,
Northwest Coast Hall, and the Basketry Wing.
There are changing exhibits in the bookstore
area and entrance hall. The noncirculating
library is open to the public for research only.
There is a gift shop and book shop. *Open Tu-
Su, 1-4:45PM. Closed mid-August through mid-
September and most holidays. Admission free.
234 Museum Dr. 221-2163*

10 Casa de Adobe. Theodore Eisen designed this historical re-creation of a Mexican adobe in 1917. The house is located in a portion of the Sycamore Grove Park owned by the Southwest Museum. *Open W, Sa, Su, 2-5PM. 4603 N. Figueroa St. 221-2163*

10 El Alisal. El Alisal (the Sycamores) is a unique owner-built residence conceived and executed by Charles Fletcher Lummis, founder of the Southwest Museum and the first city librarian. Constructed of granite boulders from the nearby arroyo, hand-hewn timbers and telephone poles, the structure is a romantic combination of styles. Most of the original furniture is gone, but the home and gardens remain as a monument to a most extraordinary man. *Open Su-F, 1-4PM. Closed Sa. Admission free. 200 E. Ave. 43. 222-0546*

11 San Encino Abbey. Called *Oldestone Abbey*, this private home is a hybrid of California Mission and European Gothic style. It was built from 1909 to 1925 by Clyde Brown. Brown imported parts of old European castles and monasteries to create his own medieval environment. *Private residence. 6211 Arroyo Glen, Highland Park*

12 Judson Studios. Since 1897 this studio has been well known for its stained-glass work. Tours once a week show you the workshop in action. The Moorish and Craftsman style building is owned by a fourth-generation Judson descendant. *Lobby and gallery open 9AM-5PM, M-F. Tours by appointment on Th. 200 S. Ave. 66. 255-0131*

13 Heritage Square. The home of a number of Victorian structures that have been saved from destruction. Some of the structures include: the Hale House, a Queen Anne-Eastlake house built circa 1888 of redwood, the interior is decorated with Victorian period furnishings; and the Valley Knudsen Garden Residence, a rare example of the Second Empire French style applied to an 1880s frame Victorian house. It's operated by the Cultural Heritage Board of Los Angeles. *Open second Su and third W of each month, 11AM-3PM. Admission: 50 cents. 3800 N. Homes St. 485-2433, 222-3150*

14 Eagle Rock. A massive sandstone rock, 150-feet high, imprinted with a natural formation resembling an eagle in flight on its southwest side. It was described by Dr. Carl Dentzel, the late director of the Southwest Museum, as "the most distinctive natural landmark in the city of Los Angeles." *Northern end of Figueroa St. Visible from the 134 Freeway traveling east from Glendale to Pasadena*

14 Eagle Rock Playground Clubhouse. A significant building by Richard Neutra built in 1953. The Clubhouse has a magnificent view. *1100 Eagle Vista Dr.*

15 Occidental College. A small liberal arts college founded in 1887, formerly affiliated with the Presbyterian Church. The campus core was designed by Myron Hunt after the college's move to the Eagle Rock area in 1914. *1600 Campus Rd. 259-2974*

16 Lawry's California Center. ☆ A vision of the California life-style—Mexican food served cafeteria-style in pavilions and patios surrounded by beautifully landscaped gardens of seasonal color. May to November the evening steak Fiesta Dinner offers barbecued New York steak, fresh swordfish or salmon, and hickory smoked chicken in an artful setting. Mariachi music. Culinary take-home offered in the excellent wine and gift shop. *Mexican/American. Open daily. No Fiesta Dinner on M. $$. 568 San Fernando Rd. 225-2491. Tours 11:30AM, 1:30PM, 2:30PM. Advance reservations for 10 or more. 224-6840*

> *"Los Angeles is a region not a city...but neither the size of the place nor the incoherence of its government accounts for the lunacy of the place and for which it is known above every other characteristic."*
>
> Westbrook Pegler
> 1938

13 PASADENA

Pasadena's international fame rests on a single day's activity, the annual New Year's Day Tournament of Roses Parade, and the post-parade Rose Bowl football game.

Parade festivities have been held yearly since 1890 when a *Battle of the Flowers* was first fought. Citizens draped garlands of fresh flowers over horse and buggy teams and carts in a celebration of the Southland's mild winter climate and climaxed the event with a gala Roman chariot race. The races were thought to be too dangerous and so a substitute event, the national football college championship game known as the Rose Bowl, has been held since 1916.

A hundred years ago Pasadena was known for its booming land values rather than its blossoms. The city was the best example of Southern California's most desirable attractions: fertile soil, fragrant citrus groves, shaded avenues, and the ever-present snow-capped mountain peaks. Pasadena was created by and epitomized the Los Angeles real-estate boom of the 1880s. In 1886, at the height of the boom and the year it officially became an independent city, Pasadena had 53 active real-estate agencies—this for a population of less than 4,500. Promoters arranged five daily trains to Los Angeles and a special theater express for downtown three nights a week.

Salesmen advertised the region's sunny and dry, healthful climate, hotels were quickly erected, and get-rich-quick schemes proliferated. The promotional madness was short lived. By the end of 1906 the boom collapsed, the population dwindled, and town lots, once clamored for, now grew weeds.

Pasadena's founders could not have foreseen such a stir. The colony of Midwest pioneers who formed a stockholding company to develop the northwestern part of the San Gabriel Valley wanted an easier life and prosperity as farmers. In 1873, a group of people from Indiana led by Dr. Thomas B. Elliott formed to locate a settlement in California. Elliott's colony (later known as the Indiana colony) chose land that had belonged to several owners between its early existence as Rancho San Pasqual and when they bought it from Dr. John Griffin and Benjamin Wilson, a Yankee trapper and first mayor of Los Angeles under American rule. The colony lasted until the Panic of 1873 wrecked the organization, but a few shareholders stayed on to form an orange-growing association that founded Pasadena in 1874. They chose the town's name from a Chippewa Indian phrase meaning *Crown of the Valley.*

The city became nationally known in the 1880s as a resort center with hotels such as the now-defunct Raymond which entertained 35,000 guests in the heyday boom year 1886-87. Only the still lavish Huntington-Sheraton and the diminished Hotel Green remain from Pasadena's high-resort area.

Pasadena's population increased through several small booms in the 1920s, and it was soon the most important suburb of Los Angeles, now numbering over 100,000 residents. Commuters from the suburb were brought to the LA mainstream with the construction of the first freeway in Los Angeles, the 1942 Arroyo Seco Parkway. The city continues to grow both on the cultural and scientific fronts. It has a culturally active resident population that enjoys a genteel and conservative lifestyle in aristocratic homes set amid lush, well-established gardens.

Narrative/Museums/Shops black
Gardens/Parks/Piers green

The city's scientific and intellectual life has been much enriched since Amos G. Throop endowed Throop University in 1891, a university dedicated to "the higher appreciation of the value and dignity of manual labor." This small technical school became the world-famous California Institute of Technology. Cal Tech's presence in the Pasadena area has spawned a plethora of high-technology firms and an associate organization, the Jet Propulsion Laboratory (JPL) in adjoining La Canada - Flintridge. When any US unmanned spacecraft ventures out to explore Mars or Jupiter, it is controlled from JPL's sophisticated headquarters in the Verdugo foothills.

1 Pasadena City Hall. At the junction of two broad avenues, the splendid City Hall dominates the Pasadena Civic Center. The domed Baroque structure was designed in 1925 by John Bakewell, Jr. and Arthur Brown, Jr. Planned in the old-world tradition of civic structures, the building has a fountain courtyard with formal gardens. *100 N. Garfield Ave.*

1 Pasadena Public Library. The Renaissance-styled public library sits at the north end of the Civic Center axis. Architects Hunt and Chambers designed the library in 1927. *285 East Walnut St.*

2 Pasadena Post Office. Federal architect Oscar Wenderoth designed the 1913 Italian Renaissance building. *1022 Colorado Blvd.*

3 Pacific-Asia Museum. In 1924, Grace Nicholson commissioned the firm of Mayberry, Marston and Van Pelt to design a traditional Northern Chinese building to house her extensive collection of Far Eastern art. The finished building is not purely Chinese but an imaginative amalgam of rare beauty and serenity. The museum features changing exhibits of art of the Far East and Pacific Basin. The second floor contains several gift shops that offer merchandise including kitchenware, clothing, and Oriental household objects. *Closed M and Tu. Open W-Su, 12-5PM. Donation requested. 46 N. Los Robles Ave. 449-2742*

4 Plaza Pasadena. Near the Civic Center on Green Street, the new shopping area is filled with a number of specialty shops and department stores. The 60-foot-high ceiling of the mall is completely covered with a mural by contemporary artist Terry Schoonhoven, creating two additional trompe l'oeil rooms. *Go up to the bridge level for the best view.*

4 Crown Bed & Breakfast Inn. Built in 1905 as a speculation by craftsman designer Louis B. Easton, this cozy, wood-panelled and beamed-ceiling house is on the National Registry of Historic Places. Five spacious bedrooms, each individually decorated in period antiques with personal attention to all lodging details, from fresh flowers in each to an escort to the Rose Parade. Within walking distance of the Pasadena Convention Center. *Continental breakfast. 530 S. Marengo Ave. 792-4031*

4 Miyako. The house specialty is sukiyaki, a mixture of meat and vegetables cooked in a seasoned sauce, prepared at your table by a kimono-clad waitress. Traditional Japanese decor enhances the meal. *M-F, 11:30AM-2PM; M-Sa, 5:30PM-10PM; Su, 4:30PM-9PM. $$. 139 S. Los Robles. 681-3086*

5 Stottlemeyer's. How many sandwich combinations can you imagine? Stottlemeyer's has compiled a list of 150 possibilities, each humorously named for a famous personality. Desserts are also excellent. *M-F, 11AM-10PM; Sa-Su, 11AM-7PM. $. 712 E. Colorado Blvd. 792-5351*

5 Beadle's Cafeteria. Plain American food, freshly prepared. The prime rib and leg of lamb are favorites with the regulars who line up daily. *Open daily, 11AM-7:45PM. $. 850 E. Colorado Blvd. 796-3618*

6 Pasadena City College. A two-year college, part of the Pasadena Area Community District. *1570 E. Colorado Blvd. 578-7123*

7 Applegate's Landing. Amusing architectural treasures, simple American meals. Especially popular with children who love to serve themselves from the salad bar at the back of the 1935 Ford pickup. *M-Sa, 11AM-10PM. Su, 10AM-9PM. $$. 1978 E. Colorado Blvd. 796-1900*

8 Brotherton's Farmhouse. A barely converted bungalow that serves Midwestern food of the type that helped generations to grow big and strong. Chicken pie is especially good. *Tu-Su, 11:30AM-8:30PM. $. 2239 E. Colorado Blvd. 796-5058*

9 Acapulco. A casual, family restaurant that offers imaginative interpretations of Mexican favorites. The crab enchilada is famous. *Su-Th, 11AM-10PM; F-Sa, 11AM-midnight. Su brunch, 10AM-3PM. $. 2936 E. Colorado Blvd., Pasadena. 795-4248*

10 Lake Street. From California to Colorado is one of the main shopping streets with numerous specialty shops clustered around *Bullock's* and *I. Magnin's*. **Del Mano Gallery,** *492 South Lake St.*, sells a variety of fine American crafts, as well as beautiful, handmade jewelry. **Street Skates,** in the rear of the same building, rents and sells roller skates.

11 Konditori. Open-faced Danish sandwiches are the specialty of the house. Breakfast until 11:30AM offers Swedish pancakes or smoked salmon and eggs. The umbrella-shaded patio is a lovely spot to relax with pastry and coffee. *M-Sa, 7:30AM-5:30PM. $. 230 S. Lake St. 792-8044*

11 Saw Mill. Good steaks, chicken, and seafood; a self-serve salad bar. The cocktail lounge has a comfortable living-room feeling with a fireplace and couches. Entertainment nightly from 7PM. *Lunch, M-Sa, 11AM-4PM. Dinner, Su-Th, 4-10:30PM; F-Sa, 4-11:30PM. $/$$. 340 S. Lake St. 796-8388*

10 Burger Continental. A self-serve counter that offers hamburgers in native or exotic dress. Middle Eastern specialities are a surprise on the menu. The rear patio is tree-shaded by day, lit with Christmas bulbs in the evening. *Su-Th, 7AM-10PM. F-Sa, 7AM-midnight. $. 535 S. Lake St. 792-6634*

One hundred years ago, when LA had boomed to 11,000 people, there were 92 telephones. The train station had the easiest number to remember: 1.

---

12 The Chronicle. ☆ A lovingly restored Victorian house reminiscent of San Francisco that serves beautifully prepared continental fare and seafood. The front room is lace-curtained; the back is draped in elegance. The wine list emphasizes California vintages and is one of the best in the city. *M-Sa, 11:30AM-2:30PM. M-Th, 5:30-10:30PM. F-Sa, 5:30-11:30PM. Su, 5-10PM. $$$/$$$$. 897 Granite Dr., just off South Lake St. 792-1179*

2 Marianne's. Gourmet French cooking in a proper dining room. A row of private booths with adjustable lighting and lace curtains for privacy is available by request. Mousse and quenelles of remarkable lightness. *Tu-F, 11:30AM-2PM. Tu-Sa, 5:30-9PM. $$/$$$. 45 S. Mentor Ave. 792-2335*

13 Maldonado's. Well-prepared and handsomely presented food accompanied by song, opera, or harp. One of the most successful combinations of food and entertainment in the city. Chicken Marengo is recommended. *M-F, 11AM-3PM; dinner seatings seven days a week at 6 and 9PM. $$/$$$. 1202 E. Green St.*

14 California Institute of Technology. One of the finest schools of science in the country. Famous for its engineering, physics, and astronomy departments, it has produced over 14 Nobel laureates and a well-known faculty, which included Albert Einstein. Architect Bertram Goodhue laid out the plan of the institute in 1930, inspired by a medieval scholastic cloister. Other buildings on the original campus were designed by Gordon Kauffman. *1201 E. California Blvd. 795-6811*

Nearby, facing onto Sierra Bonita Street, is Kauffman's Spanish Renaissance Atheneum Faculty Club.

15 Hotel Green, Green Hotel Apartments and Castle Green Apartments. One of the two remaining examples of Pasadena's grand hotel era. Architect Frederick Roehrig's grand Moorish and Spanish Colonial design is an immense extension to the older Hotel Green structure, originally known as the Webster Hotel, and built in 1890 for promoter E.C. Webster and patent medicine manufacturer Colonel G.G. Green. In the 1920s, Roehrig more than tripled the hotel's size with elaborate bridged and arched additions that include the domed and turreted Castle Green Apartments built in 1897 across the street at *99 S. Raymond*, and the Green Hotel Apartments (1903) at *50 E. Green St.*, newly renovated and modernized as a senior citizen's home.

16 Wrigley House. The broad Mission-style home is surrounded by a rolling lawn and well-kept gardens. It is an example of the grand mansions found on the boulevard in the first decades of the century. This is now the headquarters of the Tournament of Roses Association. *391 S. Orange Grove Blvd.*

17 Pasadena Historical Museum (Fenyes Mansion). The 1905 neoclassical residence, designed by Robert Farquhar and formerly the home of the Finnish Consul, is now occupied by the Pasadena Historical Society Museum. The main floor retains its original furnishings, including antiques and paintings. The basement houses a display of Pasadena history, including memorabilia, paintings, and photographs. The adjacent library is open to researchers only. The four-acre grounds are beautifully landscaped and contain a wandering stream with several pools as well as Sauna House, a replica of a 16th-century Finnish farmhouse with a display of Finnish folk art. *Open Tu, Th, and the last Sunday of every month from 1-4PM. Admission free. 470 W. Walnut St. (corner of Walnut and Orange Grove Blvds.) 577-1660*

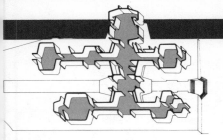

Norton Simon Museum. One of the finest collections of art in the United States is housed in this striking building, designed by Ladd and Kelsey. The spacious galleries are hung with works according to school or century, spanning over 2,000 years. Among the notable holdings are: Indian and Southeast Asian sculpture; Old Master paintings and drawings, including works by Rembrandt, Reubens, Tiepolo, Raphael, Breughel, and Hals; Goya etchings; tapestries; 17th-century botanical watercolors; impressionist painting and sculpture, including works by Cezanne, Toulouse-Lautrec, Renoir, and Van Gogh; a large selection of work by Degas, including an exquisite series of small bronze dancers; Picasso; Maillol; and work by the German Expressionists. The museum shop has one of the finest selections of art books in the city and also offers prints and cards. *Open Th-Su, noon-6PM. Admission charge. 411 W. Colorado Blvd. (northwest corner of Colorado and Orange Grove Blvds.) 449-6840*

Westmoreland Place and Arroyo Terrace/Greene and Greene Houses. Gamble House. This is the best known of the Craftsman-style bungalow houses built by Charles and Henry Greene. Built in 1908 as a vacation home for the Gamble family, it is now a public house/museum where docents lead you through, explaining the Japanese influences on the home's deep overhanging roofs and crafted woodwork. The house is furnished with tables, chairs, and Tiffany glass works designed by the brothers Greene. (Next door is the Cole House at 2 Westmoreland Place. This 1906 Greene and Greene house is now part of the Neighborhood Church.) *Gamble House is open for tours Tu and Th, 10AM-3PM and the first Su of each month and Sa preceding, noon-3PM. Closed the month of May. Admission charge. Westmoreland Place. 793-3334*

Located on Arroyo Terrace are a colony of Greene and Greene bungalows. All are worth noting, although some are in better condition than others. They are: Charles Sumner Greene House (1906) at #368; White Sisters House (1913) at #370, home of Charles Greene's sisters-in-law; Van Rossen-Neill House (1903, 1906) at #400 has a wall of burnt *clinker* brick and Arroyo boulders; Hawkes House (1906) at #408, resembles a Swiss chalet; Willet House (1905) at #424 is a remodeled bungalow; and at #440 is the Ranney House (1907). *Private residences.*

Prospect Boulevard and Prospect Crescent. The stone entrance gates at Orange Grove and Prospect Boulevards were designed by Charles and Henry Greene in the 1910s. Along this boulevard lined with camphor trees is the Greenes' 1906 Bentz House at 657 Prospect Blvd. At 781 Prospect Blvd. is Alfred and Arthur Heineman's Hindry House, half hidden behind shrubbery. A narrow street entered from the southwest side of the boulevard is Prospect Crescent Street. This leads to Frank Lloyd Wright's Millard House at 645 Prospect Crescent. The concrete-block house from 1923 resembles a small, pre-Columbian tower, giving it the name of *La Miniatura*. (The studio house near the pond was designed by Wright's son, Lloyd Wright, in 1926.) The house is set in a ravine, and there's a better view from below on Rosemont Street. *Private residences. Prospect Blvd. between Orange Grove Blvd. and Seco St.*

21 **Ambassador College.** A four-year, liberal arts institution emphasizing theology. The campus also houses the headquarters of the Worldwide Church of God. Formerly part of *millionaires row*, the college contains four fully-restored mansions, as well as several newer buildings. *300 W. Green St. 577-5111*

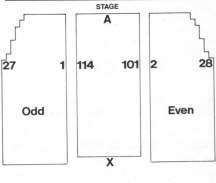

21 **The Ambassador Auditorium.** (Seats 1,262). A well-appointed concert hall featuring world renowned performers. *Ticket information, 300 W. Green St. 577-5511*

Old Town. An area bounded roughly by Delacey Avenue on the west, Holly Street on the north, Arroyo Parkway on the east and Green on the south. There are a number of interesting gift and antique shops. **Four**
22 **Quarters**, *34 S. Raymond*, specializes in gifts
22 from around the world. **Aarnun Gallery**, *99 E. Colorado*, exhibits reasonably priced work by local artists as well as fine graphics. Both sides of Colorado Boulevard are lined with small shops. Along Holly are a number of shops selling antiques and memorabilia.

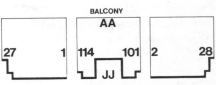

Los Angeles Wins in the Rose Bowl		
1923	USC over Penn State	14-3
1932	USC over Tulane	21-12
1933	USC over Pittsburgh	35-0
1939	USC over Duke	7-3
1940	USC over Tennessee	14-0
1944	USC over Washington	29-0
1945	USC over Tennessee	25-0
1953	USC over Wisconsin	7-0
1963	USC over Wisconsin	42-37
1966	UCLA over Michigan	14-12
1968	USC over Indiana	14-3
1970	USC over Michigan	10-3
1973	USC over Ohio State	42-17
1975	USC over Ohio State	18-17
1976	UCLA over Ohio State	23-10
1977	USC over Michigan	14-6
1979	USC over Michigan	17-10
1980	USC over Ohio State	17-16

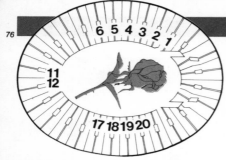

23 The Rose Bowl. (Seats 104,700). Since 1902, the Midwest has met the West here in the most famous college football match of all. The Rose Bowl is also home to the Los Angeles Aztecs, one of the first professional soccer teams in America. *Events regularly scheduled; open weekdays, 8AM-4PM. Admission free. 991 Rosemont Blvd. 793-7193*

23 Rose Bowl Flea Market. Held on the second Sunday of each month at the Rose Bowl. This bargain-pickers' paradise offers everything from junk to antiques. *Admission charge*

24 Art Center College of Design. A nationally famous college of design. Established in 1930, the college moved into a striking Craig Ellwood designed building on a 175-acre campus in 1976. Courses of study offered are: illustration, communication design, photography, industrial design, film, and fine arts. *1700 Lida St. 577-1700*

2 New Ice House. A friendly night spot featuring a wide variety of music, comedy, and magic acts. *24 N. Mentor Ave. 449-4053*

10 Huntington-Sheraton Hotel. This rambling building is the only resort hotel still operating in Pasadena. The designers of this gracious Mission Revival hotel desired that each room have sunlight pour in at least one time during the day. No wonder the first owner closed the hotel after one unusually rainy season! Railroad magnate Henry Huntington reopened the hotel in 1914. The luxurious inn is now operated by the Sheraton Hotels. *1401 S. Oak Knoll Ave. 792-0266*

25 Eaton Canyon Nature Center. Just east of central Pasadena. 184 acres of native California plants. The small museum contains displays on the ecology of the area and gives leaflets for self-guided tours through the canyon. *Open daily, dawn to dusk. Admission free. 1750 N. Altadena Dr. 794-1866*

25 Domenico's. A family-run pizzeria for more than 20 years. Consistently good pizza and delicious toppings. *$$. 2411 E. Washington Blvd. 797-6459*

> *"...I should think there is more opportunity for nature-study within the city boundaries of Los Angeles than in any other urban district in the world, and the rabbit shooting must be superb."*
> R. G. Macdonell
> 1935

14   SAN GABRIEL VALLEY

San Gabriel and the San Gabriel Valley are examples of parents eclipsed by their offspring. The first settlement of the Los Angeles region was made here in 1771, when two priests, 14 soldiers, and four mule drivers chose a spot near the banks of the San Gabriel and Rio Hondo rivers to found the Mission San Gabriel Archangel.

The Mission was the fourth in a line of Franciscan outposts running up the coast from San Diego to north of San Francisco; it consisted of a small stockade and simple dwellings fashioned from willow branches and mud. Ten years later, a small party of 44 set forth from the mission compound traveling eight miles to the southwest to establish a satellite settlement they called El Pueblo de Nuestra Senora la Reina de Los Angeles de Porciuncula, or, as it is known today, Los Angeles. For many years the mission and its provincial garrison maintained a close but testy relationship. The parent mission dominated all aspects of Southern California's political and economic life in a way in which some townspeople felt was restricting and to the sole benefit of the mission. The friars at the San Gabriel mission became land barons on a vast scale; over a million and a half acres of land were devoted to extensive vineyards, olive groves, and a thriving cattle ranch of over 40,000 head of cattle. Work was invariably performed by the extensive labor force of local Indians, either converted or conscripted.

While life at San Gabriel was relatively peaceful, in Mexico revolution was brewing. Colonials in California and Mexico resented Spain's civil and economic restrictions, and the revolt of 1821 successfully created a new government. Church and state were hastily split asunder when Mexican authorities declared a secularization of the mission regime. Interpreted as a total dismantling of property, nearly all of

the mission cattle were slaughtered, dropping in number from 16,500 in 1834 to only 72 in 1843. The Indians who were to have shared in ownership of mission properties lost out to counter claims by settlers of European descent. Mexico divided the San Gabriel Valley lands into several ranchos; the largest, Rancho Santa Anita, was granted to Hugo Reid and William Workman. Reid, a Scottish emigre who became a Mexican citizen, married the daughter of an Indian chieftain and wrote a pioneer work of anthropology on the Gabrieleno Indians. Workman was a Yankee pioneer who had arrived via the Overland Trail. The Santa Anita Rancho became a large and successful cattle ranch. Other portions of the countryside were cultivated as farm land, and a succession of owners including William Dalton and William Wolfskill, the originator of the citrus industry in Southern California, developed the fertile abundance which had been only potential in the San Gabriel farmlands.

By the time California became part of the Union, the San Gabriel Valley area was a well-known stopping place on the traveler's route into Los Angeles. The Valley maintained a rural profile while LA began its exponential growth pattern. Several small towns popped up in the San Gabriel region as the ranchos began to be broken up into small farm tracts. One of the first was El Monte, started as a trading post for Americans arriving overland from the East. For many years thereafter, El Monte was the source of most of the bacon seen on Los Angeles tables, as the region's hog ranching center. The site of Alhambra is part of the former San Pascual Rancho and was later acquired by J.D. Short and Benjamin D. Wilson. Short and Wilson laid out a subdivision in 1874 and named it Alhambra because one of their relatives saw a resemblance between Washington Irving's *stern melancholy country* and the landscape around the tract.

The next big spurt of development in this eastern Valley came in 1903 when Arcadia and San Marino were founded. The two wealthiest men of the times each created a land development of his own. E.J. *Lucky* Baldwin named his subdivision Arcadia after the district in Greece whose poetic name meant a place of rural simplicity, while Henry E. Huntington named his palatial estate after the Republic of San Marino, and created a small independent city of extremely luxurious homes.

In the 1920s and 1930s, the San Gabriel Valley was a near paradise of dense orange, lemon, and walnut groves stretching out on both sides of the main boulevards. Small ranches raised poultry and rabbits or specialized in such exotica as the Lion Farm (200 lions available for view or rental to motion picture studios, zoos, amusement parks, or circuses), ostrich, or reptile farms. In more recent years, the small communities of the Valley, nearly all independent cities, have spread undefinably one into another, creating a large suburban region of small stucco homes extending some 30 miles over the valley floor.

3 Mission San Gabriel Archangel. Founded in September 1771 by Fathers Pedro Cambon and Angel Somera. The present Mission Church consists of the remains and renovation of the one built by Indian workers from 1791 to 1805. Constructed of stone, mortar, and brick, it has an unusual design because the side northwall is the major facade. Its capped buttresses and narrow windows were influenced by the style of the Cathedral of Cordova, Spain. The church originally had a vaulted roof but it was replaced by a flat one when it was damaged in the earthquake of 1803. In 1812 the church tower on the facade was toppled by another earthquake. When the church was completely restored in 1828, a new bell tower was constructed on the northside wall of the altar end. The bell-tower wall with its three rows of arched openings creates the characteristic image of the Mission. (Also see the Mission's winery, oldest and largest in California, now a museum.) *Open daily: 9:30AM-4PM. Admission charge. 537 W. Mission Dr., San Gabriel. 282-5191*

Panchito's. Everything from the salsa to the building itself has been made by the owner—and the personal involvement shows. The 18-ingredient secret family-recipe marinade soaks flavor into steaks and seafood. The grapevine that shelters the patio comes from rootstock at the San Gabriel Mission. *Mexican. Closed M. No lunch Sa-Su. $$. 261 S. Mission Dr., San Gabriel. 289-9201*

Ortega-Vigare Adobe. (Now Blessed Hope Church of San Gabriel). Begun approximately in 1795, this is one of the oldest adobes in Southern California. It was built by Don Juan Ortega and purchased by Don Juan Vigare in 1859. Only half of the original structure remains; a former hallway is now the front porch. *616 S. Ramona St., San Gabriel*

The first orange seed planted in California was sown in 1920 on the site of the Misson San Gabriel.

City government closes year with surplus in goods equivalent to $3.00.
1838

4 San Gabriel Civic Auditorium/The Mission Playhouse. This immense auditorium was designed especially for John Steven Groarty's Mission Play, a favorite tourist attraction during the 1920s. The authentic Mission style building was created by Arthur Benton who modeled the playhouse after the Mission San Antonio de Padua in Monterey County. Heraldic shields of the Spanish provinces, donated by Spanish King Alfonso on the playhouse's opening in 1927, adorn the interior. *320 S. Mission Dr.*

5 Tokyo Lobby. Decorated with folk art; a Japanese restaurant that appeals to Americans. *Japanese. Open daily. No lunch Sa-Su. $/$$. 927 Las Tunas Dr., San Gabriel. 286-9945*

Television sets in Los Angeles	
1946	400
1947	5,000
1948	79,640
1949	354,000
1950	415,600
1951	831,232

Restaurants red
Architecture blue
Narrative/Museums/Shops black
Gardens/Parks/Piers green

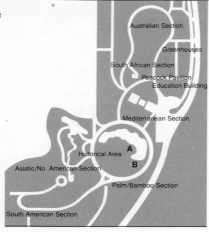

Australian Section

Greenhouses

South African Section

Peacock Pavilion
Education Building

Mediterranean Section

Historical Area

A
B

Asiatic/No. American Section

Palm/Bamboo Section

South American Section

6 Los Angeles State and County Arboretum.
No need to go to Africa or Brazil to visit a jungle—a visit to the Arboretum and the lake where Humphrey Bogart once pulled the *African Queen* through the slimy muck, leeches and all, is certainly more economical. Located on a 127-acre portion of the former Rancho Santa Anita, the Arboretum houses plant specimens from all over the world, arranged by continent of origin. The lake in the middle of the property is spring fed, a result of natural waters seeping up along the Raymond fault which runs across the property. The Gabrieleno Indians used this as a water source for hundreds of years before E.J. *Lucky* Baldwin bought the rancho in 1875. The Baldwin Ranch was not only a working ranch but one of the earliest botanical collections in the Southland. Witness several exceedingly tall *Washingtonia robusta* palm trees; at 121 feet they might set a world record. Peacocks and guinea fowl roam among the lush plantings, delighting with their vivid promenades, and startling with their raucous cries. Demonstration gardens show California domestic horticulture at its best. A snack bar offers refreshment; a gift shop sells books and gifts. *Open daily, 9AM-4:30PM. Admission charge. 301 N. Baldwin Ave., Arcadia. 446-8251*

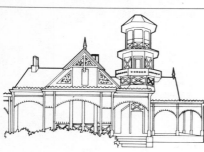

A *Lucky* **Baldwin Queen Anne Guest Cottage.**
Baldwin, a high-living and often outrageous silver-mining magnate, owned the Rancho between 1875 and 1909. The gay red and white gingerbread Queen Anne style building was created as a lavish guest house for visitors to the estate. The cottage and its delicately scrolled woodwork were designed by architect A.A. Bennett.

B **Hugh Reid Adobe.** A reconstruction of Reid's original 1839 structure, and built of more than 15,000 hand-made adobe blocks. Reid owned the 13,319-acre Rancho Santa Anita between 1841 and 1847.

66% of population born out of state. Significant minority from New England, well-to-do families.
1900

7 Santa Anita Race Track. Thoroughbred horses race against the backdrop of the San Gabriel mountains on one of the most beautiful racetracks in the country. The park features a lushly landscaped infield, children's playground, and numerous eating places that run the gamut from hot dogs to haute cuisine. Weekdays, the public is invited to watch morning workouts (a continental breakfast is served at Clocker's Corner); on Saturday and Sunday, a free tram tour of the grounds is offered. The action in the saddling enclosure and walking ring may be viewed immediately prior to post time. In addition to the regular season, the Oak Tree racing Association sponsors thoroughbred racing in October. *Season: December 26-early April. Morning workouts: weekdays 7:30-9:30AM. Free tram tours: Sa-Su, 8:30AM. Post time: 12:30-1:00PM. Admission charge. 285 W. Huntington Dr., Arcadia. 547-7223*

8 Talk of the Town. A club-like steakhouse serving large, well-prepared portions. The bar is decorated with horse-racing memorabilia (the owner is a former jockey) and, during the season at Santa Anita, is quite a hang-out for the racing crowd. *American. Closed Su. $$. 3730 E. Foothill Blvd., Pasadena. 793-6926*

9 Alex's. Good pizza, good lasagna, good value. *Italian. Closed M. Dinner only. $$$. 140 Las Tunas Rd., Arcadia. 445-0544*

10 Edward's Steak House. Nicely grilled steaks and chops, a surprise or two (like lamb shanks), and at least one fresh fish each day. The sawdust-on-the-floor informality makes this a good place for kids. *American. Open daily. No lunch Sa-Sun. $$. 9600 E. Flair Dr., El Monte. 442-2400*

11 La Parisienne. A tiny, unpretentious spot which pays serious attention to the cooking. Bouillabaisse is rich with saffron; pastries win raves. *French. Closed M. Dinner only. $$/$$$. 1101 East Huntington Dr., Monrovia. 357-3559*

12 Do-Nut Hole. You can drive through the two donuts of this donut place at any hour of the day or night. The monument to the *raised glazed* was built in 1958. *Elliott and Amar near intersection with Hacienda, north of the freeway*

"I am a foresighted man, I believe that Los Angeles is destined to become the most important city in this country, if not in the world, It can extend in any direction as far as you like; its front door opens on the Pacific, the ocean of the future. The Atlantic is the ocean of the past. Europe can supply her own wants; we shall supply the wants of Asia. There is nothing that cannot be made and few things that will not grow in Southern California. It has the finest climate in the world: extremes of heat and cold are unknown. These are the reasons for its growth."

Henry E. Huntington
1912

13 Huntington Library, Art Galleries, and Botanical Gardens. A 207-acre estate, formerly the home of Henry E. Huntington (1850-1927), pioneer railroad tycoon and philanthropist, now one of the greatest attractions in Southern California.
The Huntington residence, designed by Myron Hunt and Elmer Grey in 1910, now houses the art gallery. The collection emphasizes English and French painting of the 18th century; among the famous works displayed are Gainsborough's *Blue Boy*, Lawrence's *Pinkie*, Reynold's *Sarah Siddons as the Tragic Muse*, and Romney's *Lady Hamilton*. The gallery also exhibits an impressive collection of English and French porcelains, tapestries, graphics, drawings, and

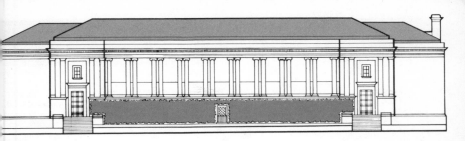

furniture. The Library, desgined by Myron Hunt and H.C. Chambers in 1925, houses extensive holdings of English and American first editions, manuscripts, maps, letters, and incunabula. Displayed are a number of the most famous objects in the collection, including a Gutenberg Bible, a first folio of Shakespeare plays, and Benjamin Franklin's autobiography in manuscript. The Library also contains a small number of Italian Renaissance paintings. The gardens were designed and developed by William Hertreich beginning in 1904. In addition to expansive lawns and formal-planting arrangements which incorporate 17th-century Italian sculpture, they contain extensive rose and camellia gardens, a Shakespearean garden of plants mentioned by the Bard, and a number of annual beds. The Japanese garden is entered through a moon gate over an arched bridge spanning a koi pond. It features an authentically-furnished 16th-century teahouse, specimens of bonsai, and a Zen rock garden. The astonishing 12-acre desert garden has the largest and most unique variety of cacti and succulents in the world. *Open Tu-Su, 1-4:30PM. Sunday visitors must make reservations. Admission free. 449-3901*

Chez Sateau. ☆ An award-winning young Japanese chef practised in the art of French cooking opened his own restaurant near Santa Anita. The cuisine is complex (grapefruit consomme) and most often works, even though the decor leaves something to be desired. *French. Lunch, M-F; dinner daily. Su brunch. $$/$$$. 850 S. Baldwin Ave., Arcadia. 446-8806*

Le Biarritz. Too many dinner houses in the area serve food out of a microwave. Not Le Biarritz. Simple fish and more sophisticated beef and veal specialties with a French touch. *French/Continental. Lunch, M-F; dinner M-Sa. $$. 2655 E. Valley Blvd., West Covina. 964-8813*

Golden Shark. This heavily-Chinese community boasts some of LA's best—but least known— Chinese restaurants. Golden Shark, run by Hong Kong film star Michale Cheung, resembles a grand Hong Kong eatery, with banquet specialties like bird's nest soup on the regular menu. *Chinese. Open daily. $$. 404 S. Atlantic Ave., Monterrey Park. 289-9401*

> *"The onward march of progress brings many changes and an old resident of the city would be bewildered at the metropolitan appearance of Los Angeles."*
> LA Star
> May 4th, 1879

15 GLENDALE/BURBANK

They seem like the Siamese twins of the eastern San Fernando Valley, but the two stubbornly independent cities of Glendale and Burbank are as unlike each other as bordermates can be.

Although they share a common boundary at the base of the Verdugo Mountains, Glendale is a quiet conservative bedroom community, while Burbank is a land of papier-mache bricks, styrofoam trees, rubber boulders, and break-away walls.

Both cities were origanally part of Mission San Fernando and were deeded in 1794 to Jose Maria Verdugo, the captain of the guards at the San Gabriel Mission. The 433-square-mile Rancho San Rafael remained in the Verdugo family until a financial crisis forced foreclosure in 1869. By 1883, thirteen Americans had arrived and were working farm plots in a townsite the Americans chose to call Glendale, the name coming from the title of a painting one of the group had seen. In 1887, five speculators filed plans for the town of Glendale.

In the year, a small town was founded nearby by real estate promoters on the site of the Rancho La Providencia, which had been owned by a physician-sheep rancher, Dr. David Burbank. The two cities grew slowly until the 1904 extension of the Pacific Electric Railway brought hundreds of new citizens. In 1906, Glendale incorporated, followed by Burbank in 1911. Tropico, a competing city, sprang up south of Glendale in 1911. The site of photographer Edward Weston's first studio, the town's main economic activity was strawberry farming. Glendale annexed Tropico in 1918. Many of Glendale's homes date from the 1920s when it flourished as a suburban haven for transplanted Midwesterners. Glendale still retains a *Main Street USA* image on some of the older downtown streets. The intersection of Adams and Palmer Streets was the site of the first Baskin-Robbins ice cream store in 1948.

The southern portion of Glendale is predominantly commercial while the northern has the original residential array of small, pastel-colored stucco homes. A series of newer, more affluent subdivisions have recently been constructed on the steep hillsides of the Verdugo Mountains.

Much of Burbank's growth is attributable to the opening in 1928 of a small airplane manufacturing site near the Burbank airfield. Alan Loughead's (he later changed the spelling to Lockheed) prototype industrial plant spawned a huge aerospace and electronics industry employing thousands, centering around the Hollywood-Burbank airport.

To the tourist, Burbank's fame and fortune is not in fuselages. The small city is the television and movie production capital of the world. At least four major television and film studios (NBC, Universal, Burbank, and Disney) have their working facilities here, and, with the exception of the closed Disney lot, guided tours are available to show you what the stars do when they go to work.

1 Descanso Gardens. The 165-acre gardens are famous for their collection of camellias, with over 100,000 plants representing 600 varieties. The landscaping also includes extensive displays of azaleas, roses, deciduous trees and shrubs, and bulb flowers, all located in a mature California live-oak grove. The variety of plants insures that something is almost always blooming. The camellias perform from late December through early March. The serene teahouse is nestled in a Japanese-style garden that features a flowing stream forming waterfalls and pools. Tea and cookies are served from 11AM-4PM. Hospitality House sells books and gifts and offers exhibits of flower arrangements and art. *Open daily, 9AM-4:30PM. Admission charge. Tram tours on the half hour; F and Sa, 1-4PM; Su, noon-4PM. 1418 Descanso Dr., La Canada/Flintridge. 790-5571*

2 Jet Propulsion Laboratory. Affiliated with California Institute of Technology, although it is not an educational facility. This center for advanced research and engineering is the NASA contractor for unmanned exploration of the solar system and the Department of Energy contractor for research into energy-related fields. The 175-acre complex contains 200 buildings and employs 5,000 people. *Open house last Sunday of each month, 1-5PM. 4800 Oak Grove Dr., La Canada/Flintridge. 354-4321*

3 Catalina Verdugo Adobe. The Catalina Verdugo Adobe was built for Jose Maria Verdugo's blind daughter, Dona Catalina, in 1875 on part of the original Rancho San Rafael. The single-story adobe is now a private residence in excellent condition. *2211 Bonita Dr., Glendale*

4 Casa Adobe de San Rafael. Tomas A. Sanchez, one-time sheriff of Los Angeles County, also lived on Rancho San Rafael. His one-story hacienda is surrounded by huge eucalyptus trees planted by Phineas Banning, founder of the Los Angeles Harbor. The historic house was restored in 1932 by the city of Glendale. *Open Su, W, 1-4PM. 1330 Dorothy Dr., Glendale*

Restaurants red
Architecture blue

Narrative/Museums/Shops black
Gardens/Parks/Piers green

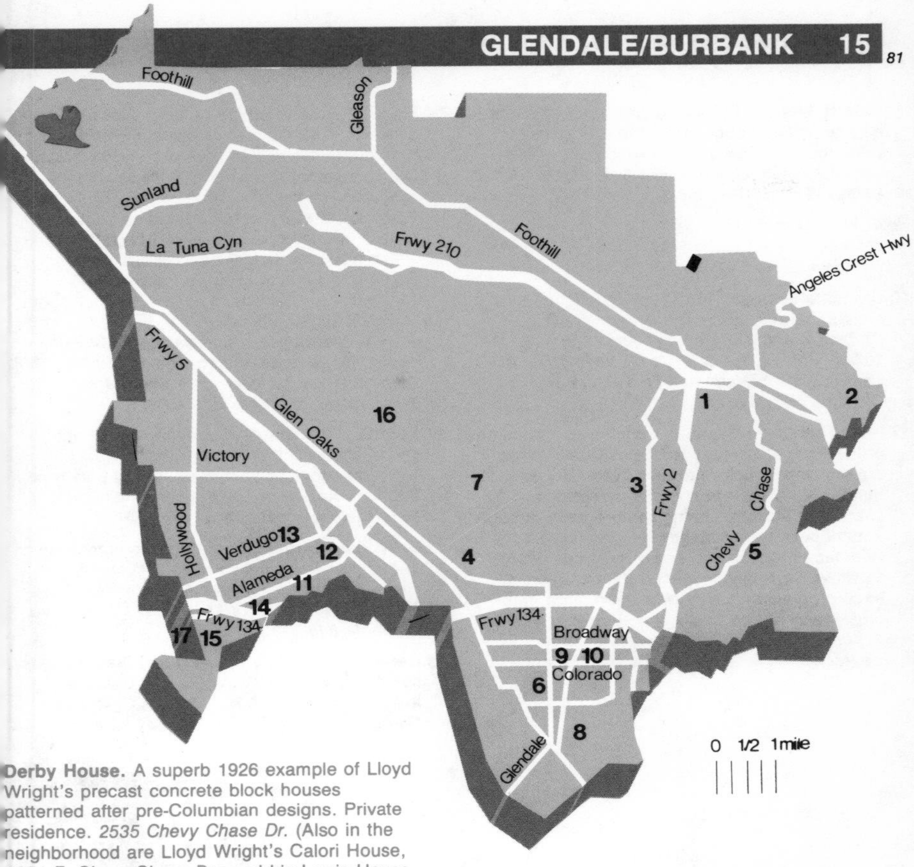

Map labels: Foothill, Gleason, Sunland, La Tuna Cyn, Frwy 210, Foothill, Angeles Crest Hwy, Frwy 5, Glen Oaks, 16, Victory, Hollywood, Verdugo 13, 12, Alameda, 14, 11, Frwy 134, 17 15, 7, 4, 6, Frwy 134, Broadway, 9 10, Colorado, 8, Glendale, 1, Frwy 2, 3, 2, Chevy, Chase, 5

0   1/2   1mile

Derby House. A superb 1926 example of Lloyd Wright's precast concrete block houses patterned after pre-Columbian designs. Private residence. *2535 Chevy Chase Dr.* (Also in the neighborhood are Lloyd Wright's Calori House, *3021 E. Chevy Chase Dr.,* and his Lewis House, *2948 Graceland Way*). Private residences

Seafood Broiler. The decor is slightly fast-food, but the fish is fresh, quickly cooked over charcoal. A good value. *American. Open daily. $/$$. 919 S. Central Ave., Glendale. 243-1195*

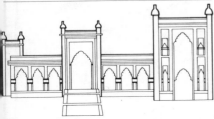

Brand Library. The exotic *El Miradero* was inspired by the East Indian Pavilion at the 1893 Chicago World's Fair. The white domed *Seracenic* style home with minarets was built in 1904 for Leslie C. Brand who donated it to the city of Glendale with the stipulation that the property be used as a public library and park. In 1956, it was opened as an art library. The 1969 addition houses an art gallery that exhibits contemporary Southern California art, a lecture and concert auditorium and arts and crafts studios. The extensive, beautifully landscaped grounds are lovely for picnicking. *Open Tu-Sa, noon-6PM; Tu and Th nights until 9PM. Closed Su and M. Admission free. 1601 W. Mountain St., Glendale. 956-2051*

Forest Lawn. Perhaps the best known resting place, next to Valhalla or the Elysian Fields. Founder Hubert Eaton envisioned "the greenest, most enchanting park that you ever saw in your life...vistas of sparkling lawns, with shaded arborways, and garden retreats, and beautiful, noble statuary." Forest Lawn contains reproductions of three European churches: The Church of the Recessional, modeled after a 10th-century English church; Wee Kirk O'the Heather, a copy of a 14th-century kirk in Glencairn, Scotland; and the Little Church of the Flowers, inspired by the English church in Thomas Gray's *Elegy in a Country Churchyard.* All three may be visited when they are not being used for services. In addition to their nostalgic architecture, each contains a room of historical memorabilia. The Memorial Court of Honor in the Great Mausoleum contains a stained-glass interpretation of da Vinci's *The Last Supper,* as well as reproductions of famous Italian statuary. The world's largest religious painting, entitled *The Crucifixion,* by Jan Styka, measuring 195 feet by 45 feet, is displayed every hour on the hour in the Hall of Crucifixion-Resurrection. A companion behemoth, *The Resurrection,* by Robert Clark, is revealed every hour on the half hour in the same hall. The Court of Freedom displays objects from American history, as well as a 20 foot by 30 foot mosaic copy of Turnbull's *The Signing of the Declaration of Independence.* Additional attractions are the collection of originals of every coin mentioned in the Bible, the Court of David, containing a reproduction of Michelangelo's famous work, and the chance to pay your respects to the earthly remains of a number of Hollywood luminaries, such as Clark Gable, W.C. Fields, Nat King Cole, and Jean Harlow. The exact whereabouts of graves is never disclosed by the Forest Lawn staff. *Open daily, 10AM-5PM. Admission free. 1712 S. Glendale Ave., Glendale. 254-3131*

6 Mauro's. ☆ Rome comes to Glendale. A truly elegant restaurant, the bar copied from the Grand Hotel in the Eternal City, the large dining room broken into intimate spaces by columns. The pasta is divine. *Italian. Open Tu-Su, dinner only. Closed Su. $$$$. 514 S. Brand Blvd., Glendale. 247-5541*

6 Churchill's. Typical high-quality English prime rib haven. *Lunch, M-Sa 11AM-3PM; dinner, M-Th 5-10PM, F-Sa 4PM-10PM. Closed Su. $$. 209 N. Glendale Ave. 247-3130*

6 Cafe le Monde. French, Spanish, and Filipino cuisine and the best lemon mousse crunch cake south of Blums, San Francisco. *French/Filipino. Lunch, T-F; dinner Tu-Su. $$/$$$. 915 N. Glendale Ave.* 240-1621

9 Aoba. Excellent food served in a simple setting. *Japanese. Open daily. $/$$. 201 W. Harvard St., Glendale.* 242-7676

10 Glendale Galleria. 160 shops, boutiques and restaurants, including *The Broadway, Buffum's, Ohrbach's* and *J.C. Penney.* Ample parking. *M-F 10AM-9PM, Sa 10AM-6PM, Su Noon-5PM. At Central and Colorado just off Ventura and Glendale freeways*

11 NBC Television Studios. Famous as the home of the *Tonight Show,* NBC Television Studios are the largest color facilities in the United States. A 1½-hour tour of the complex is offered for visitors. During the progress through a number of sound stages, guides explain the videotape process and use of communication satellites for transcontinental transmission. A huge prop warehouse stores everything from break-away chairs to silicone cobwebs. Studio 1, home of the *Tonight Show,* is open for inspection, as is the wardrobe department.

Tickets to attend taping of NBC shows are available. The number of seats is somewhat limited and all seats are on a stand-by basis. Out of state visitors should write to: *Tickets, NBC Television, 3000 W. Alameda, Burbank, California 91523.* No tickets will be sent out of state, but a letter of priority will be returned which gives the holder first chance at the Burbank ticket line. Because of frequent changes in availability, it is recommended that would-be taping attendees call the studio for current information. *Open daily 10AM-5PM; during the summer, the studios open at 8:30AM. Admission fee for tour; show tickets free. 3000 W. Alameda, Burbank.* 845-7000

11 Robbie's Rib Cage. Essentially a take-out place, although there are a few tables. Incredibly good ribs, chicken, sweet potato pie. *Southern American. Closed M. No lunch Su. $. 2711 Olive Ave., Burbank.* 845-7897

12 Szechuan Garden. Unpretentious surroundings and a chef who's worth traveling for. Try General Chang's chicken. *Chinese. Open daily. No lunch weekends. $/$$. 128 S. Victory Blvd., Burbank.* 843-8787

13 Genio's. An upbeat Italian menu that changes constantly but achieves consistent quality. *Italian. Closed Su. $/$$. 1420 W. Olive Ave., Burbank.* 848-0079

Chadney's. A friendly, hospitable steak house that is a favorite hang-out for people from across the street at NBC. *American. Closed M. $$. 3000 W. Olive Ave., Burbank. 843-5333*

Smoke House. A good, long-established steak house that takes care with the thing that really matters—meat. They age their own and grill it over hickory. *American. Open daily. $$. 4420 Lakeside Dr., Burbank. 845-3731*

Castaways. Go for drinks and a truly spectacular night view of the LA Basin. *Polynesian. Open daily. $$. 1250 Harvard Blvd., Burbank. 848-6691*

Yugoslavian Village. A hearty repast that owes a little to the East and a little to the West. A nice adjunct to a visit to Universal Studios or the Hollywood Bowl. *Yugoslavian. Closed M. Dinner only. $$. 3365 Barham Blvd., Universal City. 876-9292*

UNIVERSAL STUDIOS. Was it a real shark? Could the space ship actually have been that large? How did they make the sea part? If he's not dead, where is he? Universal Studios Tour was designed to answer these and more questions about the wonderful world of trickery known as movies. The tour takes in a good portion of the 420-acre Universal Studios lot. It is divided into two parts: a 2½ hour guided tour of the studio environs and then another couple of hours in the Visitors' Entertainment Center. For the first portion, visitors are conveyed in comfortable Glamortrams with explanations and running commentary provided by humorous guides. Visitors are taken on a survey of architecture, most of which will seem familiar as it has been used in innumerable movies and television shows. An artificially aged European town, the nationality of which changes with the signage; a colonial village that can serve for the 18th or the 20th century depending on what's parked at the curbs; a New York patrolled over the years by Baretta, Kojak, and Columbo; and an eerie Victorian mansion are all part of this carpenter's smorgasbord.

Next, the small but hearty trams endure a collapsed railroad bridge, attempted ingestion by the star of *Jaws*, the parting of the Red Sea, a flash flood, a runaway train, an alpine avalanche, and a laser war with aliens. This portion of the tour not only gives insights into the suave ways in which Holywood produces instant disaster, but also helps to explain why the starlets never get their hair mussed.

The tour pauses at Prop Plaza for an examination of enormous props that turn regular-sized folks into wee folk by comparison. A western jail and mobile forest are among the other creations of the prop makers' art displayed here. A snack bar and picnic area offer a chance for refreshment and a leisurely gaze over the San Fernando Valley.

The Entertainment Center is the final and longest stop of the day. Visitors may wander at will and take in the fascinating show. In one theater, stuntmen prove that cats aren't the only ones with nine lives. A visit to Castle Dracula will introduce you to some of Universal's most frightening monsters. In the Screen Test Theatre visitors may find themselves on camera as actors in scenes which are immediately cut into already-released films via the magic of videotape. Animal stars will astonish you with their tricks in another theater. There is even an opportunity to go in and watch some movies.

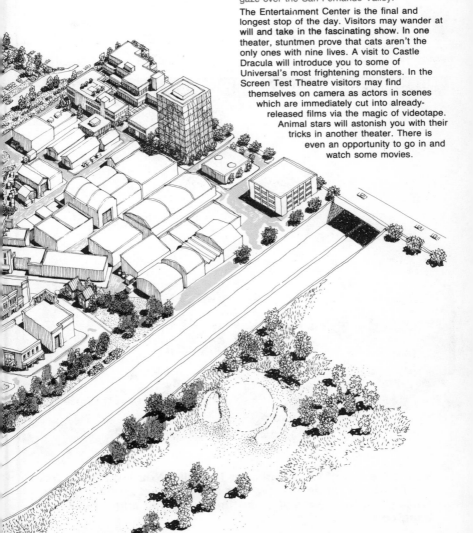

Naturally, food stands and gift shops abound. Make sure that no one misses the opportunity to take a picture of the Hulk who roams the Entertainment Center. *Admission fee. Summer: month of June open daily 9:30AM-4PM. July and August open daily 8AM-6PM. Spring, fall, winter: M-F, 10AM-3:30PM. Sa-Su, 9:30AM-4PM. 100 Universal City Plaza, Universal City.* 877-2121

17 Fung Lum. ☆ This 5 million dollar Chinese restaurant with a view looks like the set of a Universal movie, yet everything—the gilt teak ceilings, golden dragon statues, silk-covered rosewood chairs—were made in Taiwan. Obviously for tourists, but with quite good Cantonese food. *Chinese. Open daily lunch & dinner. $$/$$$. 222 Universal Terrace Pkwy.* 760-4603

17 Universal Amphitheatre. The theater presents a full range of entertainment year round. 980-9421

17 Womphopper's Wagon Works Restaurant is an 1800s-style wagon factory allegedly inspired by C.L. Womphopper, America's first wheeler-dealer used-wagon salesman. This new restaurant, located immediately adjacent to Universal Studios, features an enormous selection of burgers, chicken, steak, ribs, salads, fish, sandwiches, chili, and a special menu for children. Womphopper's also features live country-western entertainment nightly as well as exhibition cooking in the main dining room. *American. Open daily, 11AM-2AM. $/$$. Lankershim atop the hill at Universal Studios Tour.* 508-3939

17 Victoria Station. Continue your Universal City-induced fantasy mood at a re-creation of London's famous train station. This family-oriented steak house has a funicular railroad from the parking lot to the restaurant. *American. Open 7 days. Sa-Su brunch. $$/$$$. 3850 Lankershim Blvd.* 760-0714

17 Campo de Cahuenga. The treaty ending the war between Mexico and America was signed here on January 13, 1847 by Lt. Col. John C. Fremont and Gen. Andreas Pico. The historic meeting opened the way for California's entry into the Union. The declaration was known as the Treaty of Cahuenga, after this building constructed by Thomas Feliz in 1845. The existing structure is a 1923 replica of the original, which was demolished in 1900. *Open M-F, 8AM-4PM. Admission free. 3919 Lankershim Blvd.* 769-8853

14 Burbank Studios. Once solely occupied by Warner Brothers Picture Company, the lot was turned into a shared venture in 1972 with the arrival of Columbia Pictures Company. Both companies now produce television shows and feature films in comfortable cohabitation. A fascinating walk-through, called the VIP Tour, is available. Advance reservations must be made; no visitors are allowed without them. The tours are limited to 12 adults per group and involve a lot of walking—wear comfortable, casual clothes. Unlike the Universal Stuios Tour, the Burbank tours are designed as an introduction to the actual, behind the scenes, technical workings of the motion picture crafts. At the end of the tour, guests who have made additional reservations may dine in the Blue Room, the studio commissary, where a number of actors and technicians take their meals. There is an extra charge for eating in the Blue Room. *Open by reservation only. Admission fee. Additional reservations must be made for the Blue Room. 4000 Warner Blvd., Burbank.* 843-6000

One-third of previous orange acreage now converted to tract home developments.
1956

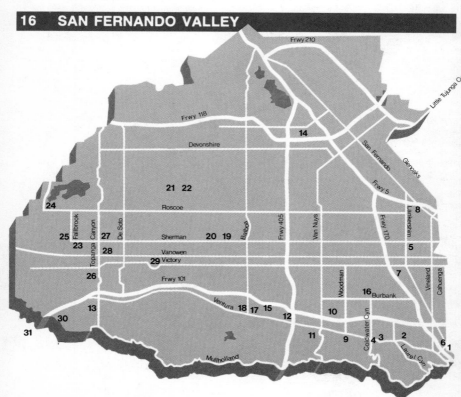

You drive out of LA Basin over the hills. You look down from the crest. As far as the eye can see is a vast sprawling city, surpassing in scale and extent anything you might have imagined.

At night it's spectacular: colorful and glittering with millions of lights in every direction, its mountain-ringed boundaries disappearing into the sky. It is a *doppelganger* metropolis added to the urban original on the flip side of the Santa Monicas. It is the San Fernando Valley. Even though is is separated from the city proper by a full-blown mountain range, most of the San Fernando Valley (known to residents as *The Valley*) is part and parcel of the city of Los Angeles. Some things distinguish it, however, and they are:

Space—a lot of it, predominantly flat.
Heat—more of it, the Valley is usually 10-20 degrees warmer than the LA Basin.
People—over one million, a third of the population of the city of Los Angeles and nearly as many as the city of Denver.
Streets and cars—an extended grid of seemingly endless boulevards and streets crosses the length and breadth of the Valley, reinforcing its dominant car culture. The uneven service of public transit makes an automobile a necessity here. For anyone accustomed to eastern American or European city scale, the Valley is unimaginable—the portion within LA city alone now consists of over 140 million acres. When on May 22, 1915, the City of Los Angeles originally annexed the San Fernando Valley, it effected a land grab which more than doubled its size; overnight it added 177.19 square miles to its 107.62 square miles.

Until 1913, land use in the Valley was limited to ranching and non-irrigated agriculture. The first settlement was the San Fernando Mission in 1797, soon followed by four Spanish Ranchos: El Encino, El Escorpion, San Rafael, and La Providencia.

Between 1847 and 1869, the isolation of the ranching region was broken by two stage lines crossing the Valley to connect Los Angeles with San Francisco. In the early 1870s the area passed into Yankee ownership and was used for large-scale farming. By 1874, the Southern Pacific Railroad extended service from Los Angeles to San Fernando, and within ten years, thousands of Easterners, lured by promotions, came to the Valley to invest in land. A party atmosphere of free lunches, band concerts, and frantic, free-wheeling auctions took over the region. Townships sprang up, property changed hands, and cities changed names faster than in some cases, could be recorded. In the late 1880s, the great land boom development hoopla collapsed. For several years after, the land had little value. Two syndicates of investors became aware both of plans for the construction of a giant aqueduct to bring water from the Owens Valley and of the extension of the Pacific Electric Railroad into the area. They quietly bought up thousands of acres of Valley property in the hopes of huge speculative profits, once again consolidating property into a few hands.

The Owens River Aqueduct brought the water to the City of Los Angeles in 1913; property values boomed, and one group of investors profited on their investment at a ratio of about eight to one. When word of the syndicate's activities got out, it created a public furor, but the job had been done. Valley ranchers were barred from using the water because they were outside city territory. They quickly voted to join the municipality of Los Angeles. By 1930, the assurances of water and city services spawned another land boom in the Valley and its residential population exploded. Hundreds of thousands moved into the Valley encouraged by jobs in nearby aviation, electronics, and entertainment industries. Several decades of accelerated development made the area famous for rapid-start tract-house neighborhoods and

instant shopping centers. The vast spaces were quickly filled up due to a low density development pattern: only 7.2 people per acre here compared to the Wilshire District's 38.9 persons per acre. The Valley is predominantly residential and almost 80% white, remarkably homogeneous for such a large population group. The west and south sides are more affluent than the east, and heavy industry is almost exclusively concentrated in the northern area around San Fernando, Sylmar, and Pacoima. With these few exceptions, it is basically all of one fabric, very middle class and extremely mobile. Until recently, single-family ranch-style homes outnumbered multiple dwellings two-to-one, leaving it a place where it is still possible to maintain a semblance of the American dream: to own one's own home, with a spacious yard and a filled two-car garage.

1 Maneeya Thai. A slick, reliable Thai eatery. The usual Thai egg rolls and *mee krob*, plus deep-fried squid and sauteed baby clams. *Thai Lunch, M-F; dinner M-Sa. $$. 3737 Cahuenga Blvd. W. 760-9691*

1 The Baked Potato. Lots of jazz and baked potatoes stuffed with such goodies as shrimp and cheese. *Open daily. $$. 3787 Cahuenga Blvd. 980-1615*

2 Wine Bistro. Wine bar and pretty good bistro fare in a woodsy, warm setting. *French. Lunch & dinner, M-Sa. $$. 11915 Ventura Blvd. 766-6233*

2 Teru Sushi. ☆ ☆ Great sushi bar, great service, and Japanese specialties. Highly recommended. *11940 Ventura Blvd. 763-6201*

3 Le Pavillon. French cafe food with an organic bent: crepes, omelettes, and more than generous salads. Recommended. *French. Lunch & dinner M-Sa. $$. 12161 Ventura Blvd. 980-0225*

3 Art's Deli. A full-service deli that is a favorite with Valley tennis players. Pastrami is a house specialty. *Jewish. Closed M. Breakfast served; early dinner. $$. 12224 Ventura Blvd., Studio City. 769-9808*

3 Sportsmen's Lodge and **Sportsmen's Lodge Restaurant.** A moderately-priced hotel in a verdant setting. Inside, the glass-walled dining room looks out onto ponds, a stream, and a waterfall. All this beauty and the food is good too. *Continental/American. Open daily for dinner only. Sunday brunch. $$/$$$. 12388 Ventura Blvd. Restaurant, 984-0202. Hotel, 769-4700*

3 Bla-Bla Cafe. Entertainment ranging from comedy and cabaret singing through Sunday afternoon amateurs. *Limited food available. Open daily. $$. 12446 Ventura Blvd. 769-7874*

4 Harry's Open Pit Barbecue. Good, messy, long-smoked ribs. The beef, ham, and chicken are also fine. *$. Coldwater Canyon & Ventura Blvd. 789-3880*

4 La Serre. ☆ ☆ Exquisite haute cuisine in an elegant greenhouse. Considered by some to be the best restaurant in the Valley. Limousine service available by arrangement. *French. Closed Su. No lunch Sa. $$$/$$$$. 12969 Ventura Blvd. 900-0500*

4 Camille's. Reasonably priced yet innovative French food, some dishes with a *nouvelle* touch. Romantic setting of white trellised booths. *French. Lunch, Tu-F; dinner Tu-Sa. $$$. 13573 Ventura Blvd. 995-1660*

Restaurants red
Architecture blue
Narrative/Museums/Shops black
Gardens/Parks/Piers green

4 Mulberry Street. Tuesday night home of George Segal and his Beverly Hills Unlisted Jazz Band, this place serves good pizzas and has great atmosphere. *Tu-Sa, 6PM-1AM. Closed Su-M. $$. 12067 Ventura Blvd.* 980-8405

5 Palomino Club. The primo country-western club in the city, featuring top singers and bands. The long tables and rustic decor add atmosphere. Steak-house style is served. *American. Open daily. No lunch. $$. 6907 Lankershim Blvd.* 764-4010

6 Donte's Jazz Supper Club. One of the best jazz clubs around, featuring exemplary performers in a particularly civilized atmosphere close to Universal Studios. The food is recommended. *Italian. Closed Su. No lunch. $$. 4269 Lankershim Blvd.* 877-8347

7 Yellowtail. Well-prepared seafood and an excellent California wine list. The bouillabaisse has passionate fans. *French. Closed M. Dinner only. $$. 6221 Laurel Canyon Blvd.* 766-5269

8 Theodore Payne Foundation. An organization devoted to the preservation and propagation of native California flora, named for the pioneer California botanist. The foundation maintains a nature trail up the hillside and a nursery where seeds and plants are sold at very reasonable prices. *Open M-Sa, 8:30AM-5PM. Closed Su. Admission free. 10459 Tuxford St., Sun Valley.* 768-1802

9 Albion's. ☆ Well-prepared and tastefully garnished *nouvelle cuisine* served in a lovely Belle Epoque atmosphere. *French. Closed M. Tu-Su, dinner only. $$$$. 13422 Ventura Blvd. Sherman Oaks.* 981-6650

10 Sunkist Headquarters Building. Architects A.C. Martin and Associates built this head-quarters for the industry that is synonomous with Southern California: orange growing. Sunkist is the trademark of the citrus-growing collective of ranches all over the Southland. *14130 Riverside Dr., Sherman Oaks*

10 Fashion Square. Located in Sherman Oaks between Woodman and Hazeltine on Riverside Drive. One of the first large shopping plazas in the area. Anchored by *Bullock's* at one end and *The Broadway* at the other, the brick-paved outdoor promenades are lined with good quality shops.

11 Le Cafe. A stunningly modern restaurant. The Room Upstairs features top-flight jazz talent on Thursday, Friday, and Saturday. *French/Continental. Open daily. $$/$$$. 14633 Ventura Blvd., Sherman Oaks.* 986-2662

11 L'Express. Unfortunately the view from the sidewalk cafe is of Ventura Blvd., but nevertheless, L'Express tries to be a lively *fin de siecle* French bistro. Steak and *pommes frites* and pate with conichons in the Valley. *French. Open daily, 11AM-1AM. $$/$$$. 14910 Ventura Blvd.* 990-8683

11 Lannathai. A Thai restaurant more elegant than most: diners sit around what was once a swimming pool in a swimming pool showroom, now full of koi. With 86 specialties on the menu, a good place to begin an education in Thai food. *Thai. Lunch M-F; dinner daily. $$. 4457 Van Nuys Blvd., Sherman Oaks.* 995-0808

12 Aux Delices. Classic French cuisine. The chef has a particularly fine hand with fish. *French. Closed M. Tu-Su, dinner only. $$$$. 15466 Ventura Blvd., Sherman Oaks.* 783-3007

Music, dancing, singing, slaughtering cattle, and gambling are the usual pastimes of the inhabitants.
John Frost, 1850

13 Le Frite. The Valley bistro—crepes, omelettes, quiche—all nicely prepared and served 'til late. *Cafe French. $$. Two locations: 15013 Ventura Blvd., Sherman Oaks; closed Su; 990-1791. 22616 Ventura Blvd., Woodland Hills; closed M.* 347-6711

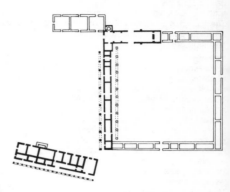

14 Mission San Fernando Rey de Espana. Founded in 1797 by Friar Fermin Lasuen. Until the dissolution of the missions in the mid-1830s, San Fernando was an essential part of the economic life of Los Angeles, supplying a great portion of the foodstuffs for the fledgling community. The original buildings were completed in 1806, but were subsequently destroyed by earthquake and were replaced in 1818. History repeated itself in the 1971 Sylmar/San Fernando earthquake when the church again sustained damage so grave that had to be reconstructed in 1974. The adobe construction of the early period had a simple yet monumental quality which achieved richness through the repetition of structural elements. This quality is best observed in the 243-foot-long convento, where 19 semicircular arches supported by massive square pillars form a loggia over time-hollowed tiles. Tours of the mission include working, sleeping, and reception areas, giving visitors a sense of day-to-day life during the early days of the complex. *Open 7 days, 9AM-5PM. Admission fee. 15151 San Fernando Mission Rd.* 361-0186

14 Andreas Pico Adobe. This is the second oldest home in Los Angeles, built by Mission San Fernando Indians circa 1834. Andreas Pico, brother of the one-time governor, bought it in 1853, and with his son Romulo added a second story in 1873. By the early 1900s it had fallen into disuse, but in 1930 the curator of the Southwest Museum purchased and restored it. It was bought by the City of Los Angeles in 1967, and the San Fernando Historical Society has its headquarters here. *Open Sa-Su, 1-4PM, weekdays by appointment. 10900 Brand Blvd., Mission Hills.* 365-7810

15 94th Aero Squadron Headquarters Restaurant. A 1973 version of a French provincial farmhouse complete with bales of hay in the front yard. A fun place to take the kids. Located near the Van Nuys Airport. *American. Open daily for lunch and dinner. Sunday brunch. $$. 16320 Raymer St.* 994-7437

Restaurants red
Architecture blue
Narrative/Museums/Shops black
Gardens/Parks/Piers green

Tujunga Wash Mural. The longest mural in the world is an ongoing project on the walls of the Los Angeles County Flood Control District Channel, which parallels Coldwater Canyon Boulevard between Burbank Boulevard and Oxnard Street. The mural is a production of the Social and Public Art Resources Center, an organization that supports community art programs in Los Angeles. It depicts the history of California, ancient to modern, and includes sections on the dinosaurs, Indian and mission life, the building of the railroads, and discovery of gold.

Rancho de los Encinos State Historical Park. Just north of Ventura Boulevard, step back to the time when the only news coming into the Valley came by stagecoach and dusty travelers stopped off here to refresh themselves. Among the five acres of expansive lawns, duck ponds, and tall eucalyptus are a nine-room adobe built in 1849 by Don Vicente de la Osa and a two-story limestone French-style home designed in 1870 by Eugene Garnier. *Home tour: W-Su, 8AM-5PM. Admission fee. Grounds open W-Su, 8AM-5PM. 16756 Moorpark St., Encino. 784-4849*

Benihana of Tokyo. The teppan-grill tradition of Japan, raised to the level of theatre by a chef trained to handle a knife like a samurai. *Theatrical Japanese. Open daily. No lunch, Sa-Su. $$$. 16226 Ventura Blvd., Encino. 788-7121*

Monteleone's. Fine Italian food. *Closed M. $$/$$$. 16911 Ventura Blvd., Encino. 986-2245*

Town and Country Shopping Center and **Plaza de Oro.** Unusual for the absence of large department stores. Both plazas are open, rambling complexes, with different levels and handsome landscaping. Shopping here has a relaxed almost village-like quality. *17200 Ventura Blvd., Encino*

Oak Tree. An astonishing oak tree, estimated to be over 1,000 years old. The branches spread 150 feet and the trunk is over 8 feet in diameter. *Louise Ave., 210 feet south of Ventura Blvd., Encino*

Adam's. Ribs broiled over oak and mesquite, a 55-foot salad bar, an authentic soda fountain, an extensive historical photo collection of the San Fernando Valley, and 350 potted plants. One of the most popular and lively places in the Valley. *$$/$$$. 17500 Ventura Blvd., Encino. 829-9971*

Weinstube. A marvelous German restaurant—homey, with a menu that goes way beyond. *German. Closed M and Tu. Dinner only. $$. 17739 Sherman Way., Reseda. 345-1994*

The Country Club. 1000-seat nightclub. Live music most nights, ranging from country-western to rock, new wave, R&B, etc. Full restaurant and bar. *Free parking. Closed M. Dinner only. $$. 18415 Sherman Way, Reseda. 881-9800*

Chicago Pizzaworks. The specialty is pizza, thick-crusted Chicago-style. Even people who hate pizza go for the *chocolate thing. Open daily. $. 18706 Ventura Blvd., Tarzana. 996-4840*

20 Epicurean Express. Owner-chef Joe Donohue doesn't charge for overhead—there is none. With only a dozen seats, and everything available for take-out, Epicurean Express is able to dish up elegant fare for less than it would cost in a white tablecloth restaurant. Call for daily specials and forget about cooking tonight. *Continental. Tu-Su, 11AM-9PM. 19014 Ventura Blvd. 996-7977*

21 The Greek Market. An exceptional deli/market, serving sandwiches, salads, and Greek specialties, selling imported groceries. *Greek. Closed Su. $. 9034 Tampa Ave. Northridge. 349-9689*

22 California State University at Northridge. A branch of the California State University system, offering both undergraduate and graduate courses in a number of liberal arts and science disciplines. Richard Neutra was made architect of the campus in 1960 but designed only the 1961 Fine Arts Building. *1810 Nordhoff St., Northridge. 885-2000*

23 Shadow Ranch. A restored 1870 ranch house built by LA pioneer Albert Workman and located on nine acres that were at one time part of a 60,000-acre wheat ranch. The stands of eucalyptus on the property, planted in the late 19th century, are purported to be the parent stand of the trees which are now one of the most prominent features of Southern California botany. The ranch is presently used as a community center. *Open M-Sa, 9AM-5PM. Sun, 2-5PM. House tours by appointment. Admission free. 22633 Vanowen St. 347-9126*

24 Orcutt Ranch Horticultural Center. Originally part of a 200-acre estate belonging to William and Mary Orcutt, the home was designed by C.G. Knipe in 1920. The extensive gardens, lush landscaping, and venerable trees accented by statuary are relaxing and lovely. There are spots for picnics, walking trails, and horticultural demonstrations. *Open daily 7AM-5PM. House tours given the last Sunday of each month from 2-5PM. Admission free. 23600 Roscoe Blvd., Canoga Park. 883-6641*

25 Canoga Mission Gallery. Early film star Francis Lederer designed and built this as a mission-style stable in 1934-36. Later Mrs. Lederer remodeled it for use as a gallery and gift shop of Californian and Mexican arts. *Open W-Su, 11AM-5PM. 23130 Sherman Way, Canoga Park. 883-1085*

28 Dugout Pizzeria. A step back into the '50s: long dark bar, leather booths, pinball machines. *Tu-Sa, 11:30AM-11PM. Su, 4PM-11PM. Closed M. $$. 20039 Vanowen St. 883-5100*

26 Woodland Hills Promenade. One of the most posh of the indoor malls. Centered almost *Saks Fifth Avenue* and *Bullocks Wilshire*, the tiled corridors are lined with luxury mercantiles. Lighting, fountains, and indoor landscaping add to the cool elegance of the place. *Between Oxnard and Erwin Sts. on Topanga Canyon Blvd., Woodland Hills*

26 The Pizza Cookery. An exposed kitchen lets you watch the cooks as they hoist yours in the air. Very cheesy and very good. *M-Th, 11AM-11PM; F-Sa, 11AM-1AM; Su, 4PM-10PM. $$. 6209 Topanga Canyon Blvd. 887-4770*

Restaurants red
Architecture blue
Narrative/Museums/Shops black
Gardens/Parks/Piers green

Southern California boasts more than 20% of all American swimming pools.
1960

Name "Sunkist" adopted by newly formed Southern California fruit growers exchange.
1893

27 Antique Row. Over 28 shops specializing in Americana. The range is memorabilia (Grandma's Antiques) to publications, with an emphasis on golden-oak Victorian furniture, bric-a-brac and collectibles. *Sherman Way between Canoga Ave. and Topanga Canyon Blvd., Canoga Park*

27 Michael's Canoga Inn. An intimate and friendly neighborhood inn which serves some unusual Belgian specialties. *Belgian/Continental. Open daily. No lunch Sa-Su. $$. 21129 Sherman Way, Canoga Park. 340-6446*

29 Los Angeles Pierce College. A branch of the Los Angeles Community College System specializing in agriculture, horticulture, landscape architecture, and animal husbandry. *6201 Winnetka Ave., Woodland Hills. 374-0551*

29 Farm Tour. The Animal Husbandry Department at Pierce College offers a free guided tour of one of the last working farms in the city. It's all here: cows milking, hens laying, goats bleating, pigs wallowing. Children will love the close look at farm life, while adults appreciate the picturesque bucolic setting. Reservations must be made one week in advance for the tours, held only during the school year. *M-F, 3:30-5:30PM. 6201 Winnetka Ave. 884-4455*

30 Leonis Adobe. The home-improvement tendencies of the San Fernando Valley may be traced back to 1879 when Miguel Leonis decided to upgrade a one-story 1844 adobe which he owned. A second level and balcony in the modish style of Monterey, the then state capital, were added to the simple rectangular structure, thus making it the first chic home in the area. *Open W, Sa, Su, 1-4PM. Admission free. 23537 Calabasas Rd., Calabasas. 346-3683*

30 Agostino's. Even with fancy decor, it can't get away from feeling like a restaurant next to Ralph's. Still, it is the best Italian this far out in the Valley, with homemade pastas and a bountiful luncheon buffet. *Italian. Lunch & dinner daily. $$/$$$. 23683 Calabasas Rd., Calabasas. 716-7001*

30 Boccaccio's. This mostly reliable continental restaurant may be in the midst of a housing development, but it offers some degree of sophisticated service and a truly marvelous oak tree and lakeside view. *Continental. Lunch & dinner M-Sa. $$$. 32123 W. Lindero Canyon Rd., Westlake Village. 889-8300*

30 Calabasas Inn. An expansive garden setting, popular for dinner and drinks at sundown. *American. Closed M. No lunch, Sa-Su. Su brunch. $$$. 23500 Park Sorrento, Calabasas. 888-8870*

31 Renaissance Pleasure Faire. An authentically re-created 16th-century country fair that annually offers 200,000 visitors to the Paramount Ranch in Agoura a step backward in time. Harps, bagpipes, and brass consort to fill the air with music from dawn to dusk for six weekends in May and June as peasants and royalty, tradespeople and craftsmen perform and hawk their woven cloths, gold and silver, candles and baskets. *From Los Angeles, take the Ventura Freeway west to the Chesebro Road exit and follow the signs. Tour and shuttle buses available. Admission fee. For information, 851-7354*

Restaurants red
Architecture blue
Narrative/Museums/Shops black
Gardens/Parks/Piers green

A key to the names of a few of the San Fernando Valley communities:

Calabasas: From *Canada de Calabasas*, meaning canyon of the wild gourds.

Canoga Park: Originally named Owensmouth for the reservoir terminus of the Owens River Aqueduct, changed to a deviant form of the Indian word for water, *canoea*, referring to a stone Indian water fount once built on the site.

Chatsworth: Named after Chatsworth Park in Devonshire, England.

Encino: From the Spanish word for *live oak*.

North Hollywood: Originally *Toluca*, later changed to *Lankershim*, named for Col. James B. Lankershim, son of Valley pioneer Isaac Lankershim, later changed to North Hollywood.

Northridge: Formerly known as *Zelzah*, a Biblical name meaning an oasis, changed to the simpler *North Los Angeles*, then called *Northridge Village* to avoid confusion with LA, later abbreviated to Northridge.

Pacoima: A local Indian word for *running water*.

Reseda: Once a truck farming community known as *Marian*, later changed to the name of a flower.

San Fernando: Named for Ferdinand III of Castile, a 13th-century saint.

Sepulveda: Named for the prominent early Southern California family who owned vast tracts of rancho lands from San Bernardino to Palos Verdes.

Sherman Oaks: Named for its developer, General M.H. Sherman, co-builder of the city's interurban electric system.

Simi: Probably from the Chumash Indian word for *place* or *village*.

Studio City: Originally known as *Laurelwood Laurel-Grove*, and *Maxwell Laurel Terrace*. It began to be called Studio City after the Keystone Kops used it as a location site. Later the area became Mack Sennett Studios, then Republic Studios, and still later CBS Studios.

Sylmar: Meaning a sea of trees, referring to the miles of olive groves planted there in 1893.

Tarzana: Named by Valley resident Edgar Rice Burroughs for his fictional character. It was formerly known as *Runnymeade*.

Tujunga: Probably from the Gabrieleno Indian word for *mountain range*.

Van Nuys: Named for Isaac Newton Van Nuys, pioneer Valley land developer.

Warner Center: Named for movie pioneer Harry Warner's thoroughbred horse ranch formerly occupying the site.

Woodland Hills: Beginning in 1923, it was known as Girard after its founder Victor Girard. He planted thousands of trees in a subdivision that in 1941 became formally known as Woodland Hills.

"Los A. is silly—much motoring, me rather tired and vague with it. California is a queer place—in a way, it has turned its back on the world and looks into the void Pacific. It is absolutely selfish, very empty, but not false, and at least, not full of false effort. I don't want to live here, but a stay rather amuses me. It's a sort of crazy-sensible."

D.H. Lawrence
1923

All city streets renamed from Spanish (Calle Principal) to English (Main Street). Place names unchanged.
1897

This is the true Los Angeles Basin—edged by mountains and water, scored by railroad tracks, freeways, and rivers.

Industry provides the economic base of the area; the flat expanse offers no obstacles to construction of factories and roads. The development of this region was largely dependent on the Southern Pacific Railroad and the Pacific Electric Interurban Railroad. Buying up huge tracts of land as they built their lines, the transportation giants later subdivided their holdings into a series of communities for workers and their families.

The flat expanses, right-angled streets, and unimpeded vistas seemed familiar to newcomers from the Midwest and South who had responded to the boosterism and land fever of the 1880s and post-World War I period by arriving in large numbers, eager to join the labor force of the city of the sun. Many of these communities have remained unincorporated;

like the jigsaw patterns of the other parts of Los Angeles County, the boundaries between city and county hop and skip around each other.

East Los Angeles and South-Central Los Angeles, the two major communities in Area 17, are of great ethnic importance. Approximately 90% of the people living in East Los Angeles are Hispanic and form the largest concentration of Latinos in the country. The community extends from the view homesites of Boyle Heights through the flatlands to the ranch homes of the Whittier Hills. South-Central Los Angeles is home to the city and county's largest concentration of black residents. It extends through the Baldwin Hills to the plains area that includes Watts, Willowbrook, and Compton.

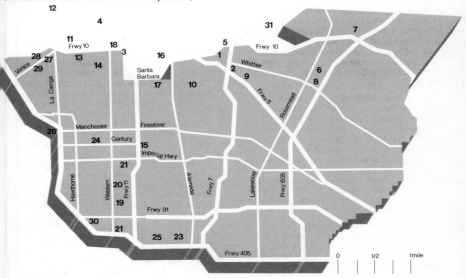

Lincoln Park. One of the oldest parks in the city, the 46 acres were purchased in 1874. Over 300 varieties of trees grace the grounds, a number of them are rare and enormous, dating back to the beginning of the park.

Plaza de la Raza. Fronting on the park's small lake, it is a complex of theater, classroom, and office space serving as a cultural and educational center. It is the main forum for activities of interest to LA's Spanish-speaking community. Activities include musical performances, dance, drama, and seasonal festivals based on themes related to Mexican holidays and family life. *Small admission charge. 3540 N. Mission Rd. 223-2475*

Los Angeles County General Hospital. The highly visible, 20-story Moderne structure, completed in 1934, covers 89 acres and is the largest general acute hospital in the country. *1200 N. State St. 226-2622*

Hollenbeck Park. A 21-acre park donated to the city in 1892. There are a number of old trees, including a lovely stand of jacaranda. The clubhouse sponsors recreation programs. *415 S. St. Louis St.*

3 Veracruz. An introduction to the delight of Mexican fish dishes, like *huachinango relleno con mariscos*, red snapper stuffed with seafood, baked in sauce, and topped with melted cheese, olives, and hard-boiled eggs. *Mexican. Closed M. $/$$. 2306 Union Ave. 265-9096*

4 El Mercado. For Mexican flavor without leaving LA County, try El Mercado, a bustling combination of food market, shops, and restaurants moving to the music of mariachis on the mezzanine, Latin records in the basement. The main floor is a market, full of stalls selling the ingredients for Mexican cooking; along the walls on this level are a tortillaria, a bakery snack bars with food to go, and delicatessens. The mezzanine has a series of cafeteria-style restaurants where a large variety of dishes are available. Mariachis play from around noon until midnight on this level; they'll take special requests for a small donation. In the basement are shops selling everything from furniture to Mexican crafts to utilitarian domestic goods. *Open daily; shops, 10AM-8PM; restaurants, 12PM-12AM. 3425 E. First St.*

Restaurants red
Architecture blue
Narrative/Museums/Shops black
Gardens/Parks/Piers green

William Wolfskill, credited with planting Los Angeles' first Orange Grove, also is said to have spread eucalyptus throughout the area, starting with a seed sent from Australia.

4 La Paleta. Michoacan-style ice cream and frozen ice bars, delicious enough to upset your meal plans and make you dine on them alone. Try avocado ice cream or mango ice. *Open daily. 3532 E. First St.*

5 California State University, Los Angeles. A branch of the California State University system. *San Bernardino Freeway at Eastern Ave. 224-3271*

6 Whittier Narrows Nature Center. A 127-acre sanctuary for an enormous variety of birds, plants, and animals, located along the San Gabriel River. The small museum has exhibitions that describe the aquatic environment. *Open daily, 9AM-5PM. Admission free. 1000 N. Durfee Ave., South El Monte. 444-1872*

7 El Monte Historical Museum. Located in a 1936 WPA building, the museum contains three main sections; archives of pioneer diaries, books, maps, photographs, and other printed material; a reproduction of the interior of an El Monte home circa 1870-1890; and a depiction of the town (known as Lexington until 1868) circa 1855, including general store, barber shop, police department, and school. *Open Tu-F, 10:30AM-4PM. 3100 Tyler Ave., El Monte. 444-3813*

8 Pio Pico State Historic Park/Casa de Pio Pico. Don Pio Pico, former governor of California, built this hacienda on his 9,000 acre *El Ranchito* in 1850. The U-shaped house is a 13-room, two-story adobe mansion with two-to-three-foot-thick walls. Covered porches link the side wings to the central portion of the house; a well is located in the courtyard. Restored by the State of California, it now appears much as it did in 1870. *Open: casa, W-Su, 1-4PM; park, W-Su, 10AM-5PM. Admission charge. 6003 Pioneer Blvd., Whittier. 695-1217*

9 Uniroyal Tire Company Building. A fine example of Los Angeles' unique history of exotic revival styles. Morgan, Walls and Clements designed the now-closed tire factory as Samson Tyre and Rubber Company's fortress, basing it on the design of an ancient Assyrian Palace. *5675 Telegraph Rd., City of Commerce*

10 Farmer John's Pig Mural/Clougherty Meat Packing. Little pigs romp and play in a painted, life-size farm landscape that becomes a part of the real building. Real trees become inseparable from painted ones and pigs peer in windows, real and painted. The murals, begun in 1957, were the ingenious work of Les Grimes, a scenic artist who usually worked for movie studios. Grimes gave his life to the project, falling to his death from a scaffold in 1968. *3049 E. Vernon Ave., Vernon*

11 Parisian Room. One of the best jazz clubs in the city, featuring internationally known performers. The small restaurant in the same building serves mouth-watering home-style barbecue. *Closed M. La Brea and Washington Blvds. 936-8704*

12 Rosalind's West African. Liberian-born Rosalind, and her Peace Corps-vet husband, offer an adventurous selection of West African dishes, like ground-nut stew, yam balls, and plantains with ginger and cayenne. *African. Dinner Tu-Su. $$. 1941 S. La Cienega Blvd. 559-8816*

13 William Grant Still Community Arts Center. A community arts center named for the famous late black composer and long-time resident of LA. Offers exhibitions, festivals, and workshops. *Admission free. 2520 W. View St. 734-1164*

15 Watts Towers. A dream made real, one of the great works of folk art in the world. Simon Rodia created these masterpieces, working alone from 1921 to 1954, framing them from salvaged steel rods, dismantled pipe structures, bed frames, and cement. "How could I have help?" asked Rodia, "I couldn't tell anyone what to do...most of the time I didn't know what to do myself." Building without conscious plan, as if listening to some siren in his unconscious, scaling the heights of his work using a window washer's belt and bucket, Rodia's glistening fretwork grew slowly over the years until the central tower topped out at 107 feet. Glass bottle fragments, ceramic tiles, china plates, and over 70,000 seashells embellish his creation, encrusting the surface so thickly that they seem to be the primary building material, forming a skin that has the calcified delicacy of coral. When the towers were completed in 1954, Simon Rodia deeded his property to a neighbor and left Los Angeles forever. He died in 1965 in Martinez, California, unwilling to the end to talk about his life work in Watts. Vandals disfigured the spires, the house was condemned for demolition. Citizens rallied and saved the art treasures. Extensive renovation work commenced in 1978 and is on-going; although there is currently no public access, the structures are easily seen from all sides and through windows in the surrounding fence. The complex is administered by the Department of Cultural Affairs of the City of Los Angeles. *1765 E. 107th St.*

15 The Watts Towers Art Center. A community art center that hosts exhibitions, art classes, and special programs of music, dance, and poetry reading. *1727 E. 107th St. 569-8181*

14 Clark Memorial Library. In 1924, William Andrews Clark, Jr. commissioned this beautiful library. A decade later it was bequeathed to UCLA as a memorial to Clark's father. The most notable features of the site are the formal gardens that lie atop the underground library vaults. The building, an Italian baroque design by Allyn Cox, is a genteel set piece furnished with antiques recalling the 18th century. *Tours of this UCLA research facility must be scheduled in advance. Open by appointment only. 2520 Cimarron St. 731-8529*

16 Second Baptist Church. Internationally known Period Revival architect Paul Williams built this Lombardian Romanesque church in 1925. The church is a center for black community activities. *2412 Griffith Ave.*

17 Dunbar Hotel. The first hotel in America built specifically for blacks. Dr. John Alexander Somerville had the three-story structure built in 1928 because prejudice made it impossible for blacks to find adequate lodging while traveling. During its heyday in the 1930s, almost every prominent black who visited Los Angeles stayed at the Dunbar. The Museum in Black, a community organization, is presently converting the hotel into an historic cultural center. *4225 S. Central Ave.*

GARDENA: As befits a solid Japanese community, Gardena boasts a number of excellent Japanese restaurants. Among them:

Kanpachi. An exceptional sushi bar. *Closed Su. Dinner only; open late. $$. 14813 S. Western Ave. 515-1391*

Kawafuku. An elegant dining room, private tatami rooms, and a teppan grill. The beef teriyaki is savory. *Open daily. $$/$$$. 1636 W. Redondo Beach Blvd. 770-3637*

Tsuruya Japanese Cafeteria. A great place to introduce the family to Japanese food at a moderate price. *Closed Su. Breakfast served; closes early. $. 1630 W. Redondo Beach Blvd. 323-6841*

Gardena and Bell are the only cities in Los Angeles County to allow legalized gambling. The following clubs have 24-hour-a-day pan and poker games. Players are charged a half-hourly *rental* on their seats; the house takes no cut of the betting action. All clubs offer around-the-clock food service.

The Normandie. *14808 S. Western Ave., Gardena. 323-2424*

Rainbow Club. 13915 S. Vermont Ave., Gardena. 323-8150

The Monterrey. *13927 S. Vermont Ave., Gardena. 329-7524*

El Dorado. *14511 S. Vermont Ave., Gardena. 323-2800*

Horseshoe Club. *14305 S. Vermont Ave., Gardena. 323-7520*

Gardena Club. *15446 S. Western Ave., Gardena. 323-7301*

Ascot Speedway. Escape the frustrations of speed limits, fuel shortages, and pollution consciousness with a visit to the Valhalla of heavy horsepower. See sprint cars do the half-mile in less than 20 seconds; motocross motorcycles leave the ground in daredevil leaps. Dirt-track racing is presented Wednesday through Sunday nights. *Admission charge. 18300 S. Vermont, Gardena. 323-1142 or 321-1101*

Dominguez Ranch Adobe. The story of the Dominguez family's Rancho San Pedro goes back to the Spanish settlement of California. Juan Jose Dominguez traveled as a soldier with Father Serra's original expedition from Mexico to found the California missions. In 1782, he was rewarded for his long record of military service with a land grant from the Spanish crown. It was the first such land concession in Southern California and covered all the harbor area south of the Pueblo de Los Angeles, over 75,000 acres. Juan Jose's nephew, Don Manuel, inherited the rancho and built a home on it in 1826. The distinguised family has been active and influential in South Bay politics; Don Manuel was alcalde (mayor) and then judge under both the Mexican and United States governments, and his six daughters lent their names to many parts of the Southland (Del Amo, Victoria, Carson, Watson). A visit to the well-preserved adobe is an easy step into the gracious rancho lifestyle. Although many structural changes have been made in the original building and the 1826 configuration has been abandoned, the interior has been restored as an historical museum, displaying many of the original furnishings. The adobe is now part of the Dominguez Memorial Seminary, operated by the Claretian Order. *Open the the public Tu-W, 1PM-4PM, and the 2nd and 3rd Su of each month, 1PM-4PM. Groups over 10 must make advance reservations. No admission charge. 18127 S. Alameda St., Compton. 631-5981 or 636-6030*

24 Hollywood Park. This lovely racetrack sponsors thoroughbred racing April through July, harness racing August through December. The track is beautifully landscaped with lagoons and tropical trees. A computer-operated screen offers patrons a view of the back stretch, as well as stop-action replays of photo finishes and racing statistics. Food possibilities range from the elegant Turf Club Terrace to the International Food Fair, to the Wine and Cheese Cellar and the Carnation Ice Cream Parlor. The children's play area has a giant, four-way slide and other modern playground equipment, as well as Gameland, an electronic game area. *Post times are 2PM and 7:30PM. Admission charge. 1050 S. Prairie Ave., Inglewood. 419-1500*

Tracton's. Good old American cooking that has been giving customers their money's worth for over 20 years. Two-pound slabs of prime rib and giant stone crabs in a club-like setting. *American. Lunch M-F; dinner daily. $$$. 3560 S. La Cienega Blvd. 931-1581. Also in Encino: 16705 Ventura Blvd. 783-1320*

25 California State University, Dominguez Hills. A part of the California State University system. *100 E. Victoria St., Carson. 515-3300*

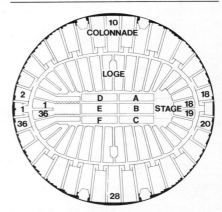

24 The Forum. Encircled by white pillars that make it look slightly like its namesake, the 17,000-seat Forum hosts concerts, ice hockey, basketball, tennis, boxing, and other sports and public events. From October through April, it is home to the Los Angeles Lakers basketball team and the Los Angeles Kings hockey team. *Admission charge varies with event. Manchester and Prairie Aves., Inglewood. 673-1300*

Centinela Ranch House/La Casa de La Centinela Adobe/Ignacio Machado Adobe. Built before 1836 for Ignacio Machado, this is the main house on Rancho Aguaje de Centinela. The well-preserved house is made of adobe with a wood-shingle roof, and is furnished with 19th-century antiques. Some of the original planting is maintained. *Open W and Su, 2-4PM. 7634 Midfield Ave. 649-6274*

CULVER CITY was home to three major motion picture studios: Metro-Goldwyn-Mayer, Selznick International Studios, and Hal Roach Studios. At one time this small town outstripped Hollywood to become the producer of one half of the films made in the United States. The sole surviving studio, MGM, is much reduced in scope since the advent of location shooting.

27 Virgilio's. Fine Italian food, with care reflected in the quality of ingredients and service. *Italian/Continental. Open daily. No lunch Sa-Su. $$$. 2611 S. La Cienega Blvd. 559-8532*

28 The Antique Guild. A block-long Moderne building designed in 1930 by E.L. Bruner, formerly the home of Helms Bakeries. This is now an enormous store specializing in antiques and period reproductions. A small tearoom is located among the departments devoted to furniture, jewelry, books, plants, and gifts. *8800 Venice Blvd.*

29 Metro-Goldwyn-Mayer Studios. This classical colonnaded building is the original 1916 administrative offices of Triangle Motion Pictures. Metro-Goldwyn-Mayer took over the studios in 1924 and the monumental Moderne style Thalberg Building erected in 1938-39 is the most distinctive building in the complex. It is on Grant Avenue and can be seen from Washington Boulevard beyond the north parking lot. *10202 Washington Blvd. MGM is not open to the public.*

30 Fox Hills Mall. One of the largest and most popular shopping malls. There are three floors with 131 merchants selling everything from fresh roasted nuts to bolts of cloth as well as clothing for all ages. The electronic game center is a popular spot with youngsters. *May Company* and *J.C. Penney* are the department store anchors. *Sepulveda and Slauson Blvd., Fox Hills. 390-7833*

East Los Angeles Murals. A large number of outdoor wall murals have been executed in East Los Angeles, Boyle Heights and City Terrace under sponsorship of city summer youth programs, the City-Wide Mural Project and private business. Utilizing the skills of professional artists and community youths and children, these colorful paintings depict pre-Columbian and Chicano subjects, as well as other topics relating to Hispanic culture. Notable examples are found at: *The Estrada Courts Housing Project, Olympic Blvd and Grande Vista Ave.; Brooklyn Ave. at N. Soto St., N. Gage Ave., and Gifford Ave.; First St. between Lorena St. and Indiana St.; Whittier Blvd. between S. Soto St. and Atlantic Blvd.; and the Ramona Gardens Housing Project, Alcazar St. between Marchison St. and Indiana St.*

Goodyear Blimp. The *Columbia*, queen of the air, lives in Carson. She is a blimp, and is probably the best known and loved corporate symbol in the United States. Her measurements are awesome: 192-feet long, 59-feet high, 50-feet in diameter, with a volume of 202,700 cubic feet. Deflated, she weighs 12,000 pounds; filled with helium, an inert, lighter-than-air gas, her weight drops to 150 pounds. The bag of the dirigible is dacron-coated with neoprene rubber; there is no structure within the bag and the form is due to the shape of the bag itself held up by gas pressure. Cruising speed is 35 miles per hour; top speed is 53 miles per hour. The normal cruising altitude of 1,000-1,500 feet gives the blimp and its logo maximum recognition from the ground. The blimp is used for a number of purposes besides advertising: it acts as a camera platform for TV coverage of sports and public events; it assists the American Cetacean society with the annual count of the California grey whales during their winter migration; and it has carried instruments aloft for a number of scientific experiments. The blimp has even been a movie star, making appearances in *Nashville, Help,* and *Black Sunday.* The *Columbia* travels six months out of the year, so there is a good chance that she will be away when you pass. You are most likely to see her on the ground in the early morning or at twilight. The hangar area is closed to the public and rides on the airship are not available. The hangar of the Goodyear blimp is located off Main Street in Carson, just north of the Dominguez Channel. It is clearly visible from the intersection of the Harbor and San Diego Freeways.

31 East Los Angeles College. Free, public 2-year community college with undergraduate courses and occupational programs. One of the first colleges to offer free, non-credit courses to anyone in the community. *1301 Brooklyn Ave., 1 block west of Atlantic and Riggin. 265-8650*

...It struck me as an odd thing that here, alone of all the cities in America, there was no plausible answer to the question, "Why did a town spring up here and why has it grown so big?"
Morris Markey, 1932

---

18   ORANGE COUNTY NORTH

If Orange County seems fresh off the drawing board, that's because it is. Before Walt Disney opened his Anaheim amusement park in 1955, Orange County was a long sweeping plain of orange trees covering the area between the Santa Ana Mountains and the Pacific Ocean.

The ranchos of the Spanish and Mexican periods became the farms and orchards of the Yankees in the middle of the 19th century. In 1857, a cooperative agriculture colony was established by fifty Germans, who named their community Anaheim, combining the name of the local river, the Santa Ana, and the German word for home, heim.

Originally part of Los Angeles County, autonomy of the area was mandated by the California legislature in 1889. The region proved to have fertile soil and beneficial weather for growing; by the end of the 19th century, large-scale citrus cultivation had begun. For the first fifty years of the 20th century, Orange County seemed a vision of the Biblical land of milk and

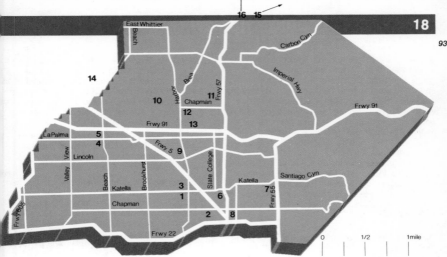

money. Well-tended groves of Valencia orange trees stretched as far as the eye could see, perfuming the air with the fragrance of their blossoms. In the 1950s, land values began to skyrocket, fueled by a post-war generation eager for a suburban lifestyle. As land became more valuable for homes and developments, the groves began to disappear. By the next century, the trees will be just a memory, immortalized in the names of streets and condominium tracts.

Public transportation both to and within Orange County comes in many forms. To find Disneyland and other attractions you might try the brief (about 35 minutes) and delightful Amtrak local to Fullerton from Union Station. From the Fullerton train station, walk about 1½ blocks to Commonwealth and Harbor. From here you can board an Orange County Transit District bus #41/43 to get to the Disneyland Hotel.)

The Orange County Transit District has extensive service throughout the county. *The OCTD telephone is (714) 636-RIDE. OCTD also has a Dial-a-Ride curb-to-curb service within limited areas; reservations, (714) 540-0412.*

The Southern California Rapid Transit District has service from its main terminal at Sixth and Los Angeles Streets in Los Angeles to major locations in Orange County. Greyhound Bus has no local service between Los Angeles and Orange County north of San Clemente, but Trailways can take you from downtown Los Angeles to Laguna Beach or Santa Ana. From the Westside of Los Angeles, a convenient way to get to Orange County is the regularly scheduled Airport Coach Service from Los Angeles International Airport. The coaches take you directly to the major hotels, to Disneyland, and to the Orange County Airport. *Airport Coach information: 646-2760.*

A reliable and easy shuttle service runs between the major amusement parks and hotels in the Anaheim-Buena Park area, South Coast Plaza and Newport Beach. Called the Funbus, it circulates about every 35 minutes; its hours approximating the hours the parks are open. *Funbus information: (714) 635-1390*

For more information about transportation, special events, sightseeing services or accommodations, the Anaheim Area Visitors and Convention Bureau has an office at the Anaheim Convention Center, *800 W. Katella Avenue. Phone (714) 635-8900*

Orange County Taxis: American Cab, *1102 W. 17th St., Santa Ana (714) 558-8522;* Anaheim Yellow Cab, *1619 E. Lincoln, Anaheim (714) 535-2211;* Checker Cab, *511 E. Third St., Santa Ana (714) 542-6776*

1 Anaheim Convention Center. Just down the street from Disneyland. It has a 9,100-seat arena, two 100,000-square-foot exhibition halls, and 27 meeting rooms set in attractively landscaped grounds. The center is used for events ranging from concerts to conventions. *800 W. Katella, Anaheim. (714) 999-8950*

1 Inn at the Park. Adjacent to the Convention Center. *1855 S. Harbor Blvd., Anaheim (714) 750-1811*

1 Hansa House. A Scandinavian, all-you-can-eat smorgasbord. The groaning boards feature some unusual dishes, like corn fritters and herring plate, as well as a full range of beautiful entrees and unusually good salads. Recommended for families. *Scandinavian/ American. Open daily. $/$. 1840 S. Harbor Blvd., Anaheim. (714) 750-2421*

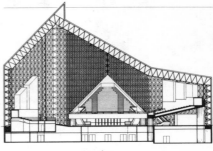

2 Garden Grove Community Churches (including the Crystal Cathedral). Only a few blocks away from Disneyland is the new all-glass Crystal Cathedral of the Garden Grove Community Church, which rivals the Matterhorn in visibility. The enormous cathedral is 415 feet long, 207 feet wide, and 128 feet high. Made of white steel trusses and tempered silver glass, it is a shimmering extravaganza seating 2,862

Restaurants red
Architecture blue

Narrative/Museums/Shops black
Gardens/Parks/Piers green

people. The landmark church, designed by architects Philip Johnson and John Burgee, opened in 1980. Dr. Robert Schuller, the church's leader, began his ministry in a drive-in theater in 1955. His idea for accessible religion via drive-in churches and television services has proven successful. The church's previous center was designed by architect Richard Neutra in 1961. It is an International style steel and glass church where services were made visible to passengers inside 1,400 automobiles, assembled for drive-in services. Neutra's son Dion designed the adjacent 15-story Tower of Hope for the expanding church administration in 1967. *12141 Lewis St. and 4201 Chapman, Garden Grove. (714)971-4000*

3 DISNEYLAND: The kingdom where fantasy and magic are around the next turnstile and dreams are as advertised. The complex covers 76 acres and has cost over $200 million to build. New attractions are added almost every year. You can expect to spend at least eight hours in Disneyland. A good beginning for your day (or two or three) is to ride the Monorail or the Disneyland Railroad around the perimeter of the park. This orientation journey will give you an overview of the layout of the enormous grounds and perhaps an idea of which part of the park most appeals to you.

This Magic Kingdom is divided into seven areas: Main Street, Adventureland, New Orleans Square, Bear Country, Frontierland, Fantasyland, and Tomorrowland.

A Main Street. Close to the entrance to the park is Main Street, USA, an American town circa 1900, full of horseless carriages, horse-drawn wagons, nickelodeons, ice cream parlors, and the corner Market House. This re-creation of small-town America at the turn of the century is charming in its delicacy of scale and perfection of detail. Small shops with wooden floors that resound under your feet and glass display cases at precisely the right height for children's noses sell a variety of nostalgic merchandise. Nearby is one of Disney's most astonishing

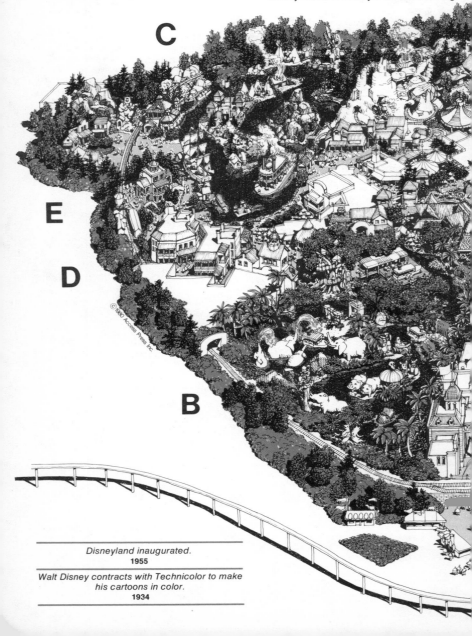

Disneyland inaugurated.
1955

Walt Disney contracts with Technicolor to make his cartoons in color.
1934

echnological feats, the Great Moments with Mr.
Lincoln show at the Opera House. Our 16th
president is brought to life via audio-
animatronics in an impressive display.

The Plaza, hub of the park, is located at the
end of Main Street. From this point, the other
park areas spread out and you may enter the
land of your choice via its unique theme gate.

Adventureland. Built around the jungle river
ride. The Nile, Congo, and Amazon are toured
in canvas-topped, flat-bottomed boats:
elephants bathe, crocodiles guard a ruined
temple, hippos attack the boat but are driven
off by a shot from the brave guide leading the
safari. The Swiss Family Robinson house
perches in the outspread limbs of an enormous
tree overhanging the Jungle Cruise. More
audio-animatronic magic is at work in the
Enchanted Tiki Room, where exotic birds come
to life in an amusing show.

C Frontierland. Next to Adventureland. Replete
with cowboys, Indians, and settlers. There are
battles, a blazing fort, and the Horseshoe
Revue Saloon where you can enter through the
swinging doors of an authentic western saloon
and see the entertainment of can-can girls. The
Rivers of America run along the shore of
Frontierland, and they are plied by an amazing
assortment of vessels: the *Columbia*, a fully
rigged sailing ship; the *Mark Twain*, a
Mississippi stern-wheeler; and even log rafts
that are poled across the river to Tom Sawyer's
Island, for an expedition to Fort Wilderness and
Castle Rock. The newest attraction in
Frontierland is Big Thunder Mountain Railroad,
an exciting ride through a deserted mine during
which riders confront floods, rockslides, swarms
of bats, and fierce animals, and live to tell the
tale.

D New Orleans Square. Also on the Rivers of
America. Filigreed balconies overlook winding
streets ablaze with flowers and lined with quaint
shops. Every day is Mardi Gras with Dixieland
music heralding the parades. For an exciting

adventure, take a ride with the Pirates of the Caribbean on flat-bottomed boats that explore a haunted grotto hung with Spanish moss and glide into a seaport for pillage and plunder. Ghosts inhabit the Haunted Mansion, which uses holography to bring many of the 999 residents of the Mansion to wonderfully disembodied life.

E Bear Country. An audio-animatronic Jamboree of mechanical bears will set your toes a'tapping. Davy Crockett's Explorer Canoes let you paddle along the Rivers of America between graceful pines.

F Fantasyland. Sleeping Beauty's Castle is the entrance to this magical land. Over drawbridge and through the stone halls is the world of storybook characters familiar since childhood. The Casey Jr. Circus Train chugs past Cinderella's castle, Pinocchio's village, and the homes of the Three Little Pigs. Take a flivver on Mr. Toad's Wild Ride, flying through 19th-century England. The whirling teacups of Mad Tea Party will leave your head a'spin, or you can ride elegantly on one of the 72 hand-carved horses of King Arthur's Carousel. Boats glide through It's a Small World with scenes of children of many lands all singing the same tune in their own native tongue.

The most popular ride in Fantasyland is the Matterhorn, a 14-story replica of the Swiss mountain built for white-knuckle fun. You are hoisted aloft in tandem bobsleds for a plunge through ice caverns and hairpin curves that ends with a splashy finale.

G Tomorrowland. The future is predicted—in some cases with great accuracy as rides such as the Monorail and People Mover are only now being realized in the *real* world after their Disneyland debut over 25 years ago. The prognostications of McDonnell Douglas Mission to Mars and the Rocket Jet may prove equally accurate. The Adventure Through Inner Space takes you on a journey into microscopic reality. The aquatic world is equally accessible via the Submarine Voyage. The perils of outer space will thrill you in Space Mountain, a $20-million high-speed journey to the stars. Visitors enter the ride through a simulated NASA control center and board rockets which travel aloft through a fascinating series of optical effects. The downward plummet is equally spectacular, with showers of meteors illuminating the ride home.

Summer nights in Disneyland offer a series of special events amd musicals entertainment. The Electric Light Parade is held every evening at 8:50 and 11; fabulous floats and Disney characters move down Main Street illuminated by 100,000 sparkling lights. The parade is capped by a spectacular fireworks display. Music fills the air in almost every corner of the park. The Plaza Garden features big band music and dancing. The Space Stage in

Tomorrowland has twice-nightly shows featuring famous pop and folk music performers. Tomorrowland Terrace has rock concerts and dancing. Continuous Dixieland jazz on the French Market Stage enlivens the atmosphere in New Orleans Square.

In addition to formally scheduled concerts, Disneyland is full of roving minstrels, troubadours, and musicians. Food, ranging from nonalcoholic drinks and light snacks to multi-course dinners, is widely available in the more than 25 restaurants and snack centers. The menu in each place is keyed to complement the neighboring attractions.

Admission to Disneyland is by general admission charge or a ticket book that includes ride coupons and general admission. Ticket books are a good value, offering a substantial discount over the cost of admission and individually purchased ride tickets. The park offers numerous services, such as pet kennels, package lockers, stroller rentals, baby changing station, and first-aid dispensary. Some rides

have height and weight minimums. *Guided tours are available for first-time visitors; a small fee is charged for this service. Harbor Blvd. Exit off the Santa Ana Freeway and follow the signs to Disneyland in Anaheim. (714) 533-4456 or (213) 626-8605. Fall, winter, spring: W-F, 10AM-6PM; Sa-Su, 9AM-7PM. Closed M-Tu. Summer (mid-June to mid-September): 9AM-Midnight daily.*

4 KNOTT'S BERRY FARM: The oldest theme amusement park in the world had its start in 1934 when Mrs. Cordelia Knott began selling homemade chicken dinners to supplement income from the family's berry farm. Mrs. Knott's chicken kitchen not only survived the Depression, it spawned a 150-acre entertainment facility which emphasizes the wholesome aspects of an idealized and simpler America. The farm is divided into three areas: the Old West Ghost Town, Fiesta Village, and the Roaring '20s Airfield.

Old West Ghost Town. A replica of an 1849 mining town. Walk along the broad sidewalks as the sheriff shoots it out with a couple of gunslingers who always come back for more. In the Birdcage Theatre, old-time melodramas are presented, offering the audience a chance to hiss the villain and cheer the hero to the accompaniment of a tinkling piano. The

Butterfield Stagecoach tours the countryside, making riders bless the day that shock absorbers were invented. Plan on getting wet if you choose to take a ride at Timber Mountain, where your log boat twists and turns as it floats through old sawmill and logging camps before splashing 42 feet in its final descent.

Fiesta Village. A tribute to California's Latino heritage. Parades, pinatas, parrots, mariachis, and mercados are found within a lushly landscaped and tiled plaza. There is a dance area which features Latin and rock music. The Marionette Theatre is particularly artful and very appealing to children. Fiesta Village also offers a selection of rides. The most popular attraction is Montezuma's Revenge, a roller coaster with cars that spin through a 360-degree loop at 55 miles per hour and then shoot backward. Up to 1,500 people an hour line up voluntarily to have this done to them. Also located in this area is Dragon Boat, a Viking ship dangling from a huge A-frame, thrilling riders by swinging back and forth until it achieves a 70-degree arc.

Roaring '20s Airfield. Evokes some of the aspects of a Prohibition era carnival, with shooting galleries and carnival rides. The 20-story Sky Jump is a simulated parachute jump that drops riders toward the ground at free fall speeds.

4 Knott's Good Time Theatre. The 2,100-seat theater presents extravaganza ice shows at 3:30, 5:30, and 8:30PM every day except Wednesday. Champion figures skaters perform stunning production numbers that re-enact American amusements and pastimes of the last fifty years.

Knott's Berry Farm started as an eatery. The original restaurant, in an expanded format, still survives as Mrs. Knott's Chicken Dinner Restaurant. The other major restaurant is the Steak House. The Airfield Eatery is a replica of a 1920s plane hangar where full meals are served at the Garden Room Buffet and the Cable Car Kitchen. In Fiesta Village, La Concinita offers Mexican-style dinners and a number of smaller stands supply quick snacks.

Height and weight restrictions on some rides. *Spring, fall, winter: open daily, 10AM-6PM (open till 10PM, F-Sa). Summer: open daily, 9AM-midnight. 8039 Beach Blvd., Buena Park. (714) 952-9400*

---

5 Movieland Wax Museum and Palace of Living Art. A museum of over 200 movie and TV stars cloned as exquisitely detailed, life-sized wax figures arranged in scenes from their most famous films. Many are dressed in clothes worn where the scenes were made. Among the celebrities are stars from the early days of film: Mary Pickford, Charlie Chaplin, Laurel and Hardy, the Keystone Kops, William S. Hart, and Tom Mix; also stars from the middle years: Jean Harlow, Edward G. Robinson, Shirley Temple, John Wayne, Gary Cooper, Clark Gable, Vivian Leigh; and current heart throbs like Barbra Streisand, Christopher Reeves, Burt Reynolds, and Henry Winkler. Some tableaus invite the visitor to enter: you can stand on a porch beside John Wayne or walk the yellow brick road to Oz.

5 California Plaza Restaurant. The Wax Museum includes this pleasant dining spot. It is housed in an early California-style building, where imported tile, extensive landscaping, and fountains create a relaxing atmosphere for a light meal of soup, salad, or a sandwich. Beer and wine are served. There is also a cafeteria within the museum.

5 Ming's Family Restaurant. Where the Orange County Chinese hold their banquets. Seafood specialties such as crispy shrimp in baked salt, plus Hong Kong noodles. *Chinese. Lunch & dinner daily. $$. 7880 Beach Blvd., Buena Park. (714) 522-8355*

5 Palace of Living Art. Adjacent to the Hollywood Wax Museum and included in the price of admission. Contains imitations of famous sculpture and three-dimensional wax reproductions of famous paintings. *Open daily, 9AM-10PM (F-Sa till 11PM). 7711 Beach Blvd., Buena Park. (714) 522-1154*

5 Haunted House. Across the street is a rickety Victorian mansion full of scary spirits.

5 California Alligator Farm. Reptile zoos have been tourist attractions in Southern California for more than a century. Several years ago, the Los Angeles region had many alligators and ostrich farms, but the California Alligator Farm is the last of its breed. Among the inhabitants are alligators, crocodiles, lizards, snakes, all housed in glass-fronted cages or pens. Regularly scheduled shows are educational. Visitors are offered the chance to pet a snake. A small shop sells souvenirs. *Open daily, 10:30AM-6PM (summer evenings till 8PM). 7671 La Palma Ave., Buena Park. (714) 522-2615*

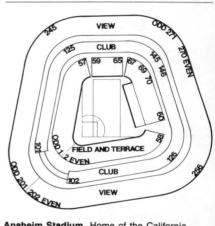

6 Anaheim Stadium. Home of the California Angels baseball team, the California Surf Soccer team, and the Rams football team. The 70,000-seat stadium features chair-type seats and good visibility. *2000 S. State College Blvd., Anaheim. For times and ticket information: (714) 634-1002*

Within the area are several excellent and luxurious restaurants:

7 Bessie Wall's Fine Food and Spirits. Just when you think you are never going to find it, you're there. This is a hideaway restaurant in a revamped Spanish-style home. Warm hospitality and attention to detail make the extra drive worthwhile. *Mexican/Continental. Open daily. No lunch Sa-Su. Su brunch. $$/$$$. 1074 N. Tustin Ave., Anaheim. (714) 630-2812*

8 La Brasserie Restaurant. An intimate and relaxed bistro specializing in home-style soups, well-prepared fish, and delicious veal. The library dining room is very appealing. *French. Closed Su. No lunch Sa. $$$. 202 S. Main St., Orange. (714) 978-6161*

8 Chez Cary. Red velvet, crystal chandeliers, footstools for the ladies. The wine cellar is extensive, the menu luxurious. *Continental. Open 7 days. Dinner only. $$$/$$$$. 571 S. Main St., Orange. (714) 542-3595*

Hansen House (Mother Colony House). Built in 1857, this white clapboard house with a narrow front porch is in the Greek Revival style. This was the first house in Anaheim, built by George Hansen, founder of the *Mother Colony*, a group of Germans who left San Francisco to grow grapes in Southern California. Inside the restored home is an exhibit on Anaheim's history. *Open W, 3-5PM, Su, 1:30-4PM. 414 N. West St., Anaheim.*

FULLERTON: Muckenthaler Cultural Center. The cultural center is located in a lovely Spanish Baroque house that overlooks the valley. The 1923 house was given to the city of Fullerton by the Muckenthaler family in 1963 and is used for art exhibits, classes, receptions, and cabaret theater. *Admission free. Closed M. Tu-Sa, 12-5PM. 1201 W. Malvern Ave., Fullerton, just east of Buena Park. (714) 738-6595*

California State University at Fullerton. A branch of the California State University system. *800 N. State College Blvd., Fullterton. (714) 773-2011*

The Cellar. In the cellar of the Villa del Sol. A menu of sophistication and imagination, influenced by *nouvelle cuisine*. The restaurant has an atmosphere of carefully considered elegance. One of the most rewarding in town. *French. Closed Su. M. dinner only. $$$/$$$$. 305 N. Harbor Blvd., Fullerton. (714) 525-5682*

13 Ruby Begonia's. A comfortable spot to ease the cares of the day. The intimate disco is a favorite with locals. *American/Continental. Open daily. Sa., 5:30PM-2AM, Su., 9:30AM-2PM, 1500 S. Raymond, Fullerton. (714) 635-9000*

14 LA MIRADA. La Mirada Civic theater. Musicals, drama, and ballet in a new stage/theater. *Just north of Buena Park. 14900 La Mirada Blvd., (714) 994-6310 or (714) 994-6150*

16 San Dimas Mansion. ☆ Maine lobster, Grand Marnier souffles, and sumptuous Sunday brunches in an elegant 1887 Victorian mansion. *Continental. Lunch & dinner W-Su. $$$. 121 N. San Dimas Ave., San Dimas. (714) 599-9391*

15 Sycamore Inn. Built on the site of an historic stage coach stop, the restaurant continues a tradition of warm hospitality. Prime rib on the buffet, huge stone fireplace and wingback chairs. *American. Lunch & dinner daily. $$$. 8318 Foothill Blvd., Cucamonga. (714) 982-1104*

> *"...We find ourselves suddenly threatened by hordes of Yankee emigrants, who have already begun to flock into our country, and whose progress we cannot arrest."*
>
> Governor Pio Pico
> 1846

The California Gold Coast is an earthly paradise of temperate climate, a shoreline of alternating smooth sandy beaches with majestic rocky promontories, green canyons, rolling hills, and a feeling of suspended time.

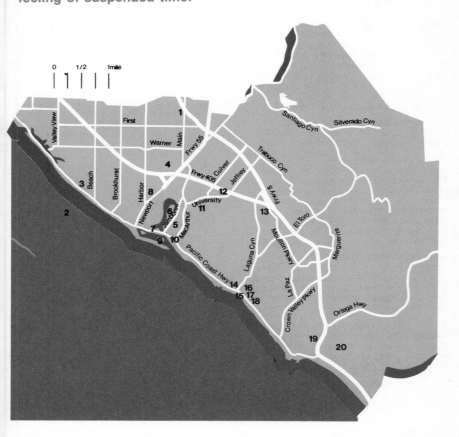

Along the coast, boating, golf, tennis, and other recreation are the major businesses, while the interior hills are devoted to the quiet murmur of intensely technical industry and education.

The beaches have a series of distinct identities: Huntington Beach is a surfer's paradise; Newport and Balboa are havens for the yachting crowd; Corona del Mar is a quiet beachside community; Laguna Beach is an art colony as intimate and colorful as any seaside resort on the French Riviera; Dana Point is newly developed wth a large marina; and San Juan Capistrano and San Clemente are gracious residential areas.

Developed as planned communities of the 1960s, thousands of tract homes cover the hilly acreage formerly devoted to farming and orange groves on the Irvine Ranch. The new town of Irvine surrounds the Irvine campus of the University of California.

Businesses in south Orange County are usually housed in one-story, tilt-up slab concrete buildings, the best examples of which are seen in the Irvine Industrial Park. The area is a mecca for high-technology expertise, electronics and computers forming the most important sector of the economy.

1 **SANTA ANA AREA: Charles W. Bowers Museum.** A picturesque Spanish Colonial Revival building housing a collection of permanent and changing history and art exhibits. The whale exhibit and the collection of Orange County historical objects will delight children. The central courtyard of the 1932 Frank Lansdown museum has a luxuriously planted garden. *Closed M. Open Tu-Sa, 9AM-5PM; Su 1-5PM. Admission free. 2002 N. Main St. (714) 972-1900*

2 **HUNTINGTON BEACH AREA: Surfing:** It was imported from Hawaii in 1907 to encourage passenger traffic on the Pacific Electric Railway. The replacement of traditional, heavy mahogany boards by lightweight fiberglass and foam core ones and the invention of the neoprene rubber wet suit made surfing an all-season sport. The first surfing contests were held at Huntington Beach and it remains a worldwide haven for surfers, who congregate at the Huntington Pier to enjoy unusual wave conditions created by the agglomeration of pilings; this is the best place to watch the year-round action.

3 **The Golden Bear.** A popular nightclub featuring top jazz, rock, and folk artists. *306 Pacific Coast Hwy. (714) 536-9600*

4 **COSTA MESA AREA: South Coast Plaza.** This is buyer's heaven, the location of choice for connoisseurs of shopping centers. Over 176 stores, including all the usual department stores and the best of the luxury emporiums, such as *Jaeger, Courreges, Kron Chocolatier,* etc. It is the busiest mall in the United States, with more than 20 million visitors annually. *3333 Bristol St. (off #405, San Diego Freeway). (714) 546-6683*

4 **Rizzoli's International Bookstore.** The most elegant, literate, and beautiful bookstore chain now has a nearby LA address. Worth a detour at South Coast Plaza. *M-F, 10AM-9PM; Sa, 10AM-6PM; Su, 12PM-5PM. 3333 Bristol, Costa Mesa (in South Coast Plaza.)*

4 **Pronto.** Elegant northern Italian dining, with luscious buffets during *Happy Hour* and for Sunday brunch. *Italian. Lunch & dinner daily. $$$. 3333 Bristol St. (714) 540-8038*

4 **La Cuisine.** ☆☆ Orange County's answer to L'Ermitage. Elegant yet comfortable surroundings, the finest table appointments, and the most exquisite—and innovative—French food south of Los Angeles. *French. Lunch Tu-F; dinner Tu-Su. Su brunch. $$$$. 24312 Del Prado, Dana Point (714) 661-6801. Also in Costa Mesa: 1400 S. Bristol St. (714) 751-4252*

4 **South Coast Repertory Theatre.** Two small legitimate theaters. *655 Town Center Dr. (next to the South Coast Plaza Hotel). (714) 957-4033*

4 **South Coast Plaza Hotel.** A luxury hotel; the Weekend Specials are a good value. *6600 Anton Blvd. (714) 540-2500*

5 **NEWPORT BEACH AREA: Newport Harbor Art Museum.** Changing exhibits of contemporary art and a permanent collection of 20th-century art emphasizing works by Southern California artists are presented in this internationally famous museum. The Sculpture Garden Cafe has light meals and snacks; the gift shop sells catalogs and books. *Closed M. Open Tu-Su, 11AM-5PM; F, 11AM-5PM and 6-9PM. Donation requested. 850 San Clemente Dr. (714) 759-1122*

6 **Newport Harbor.** There are 10 yacht clubs and 10,000 boats in this aquatic playground. The exclusive residential area has been a prestige summer resort for many years. The bay includes: Lido Isle, Linda Isle, Harbor Island, Bay Isle, and Balboa Island.

6 **Newport Dunes Aquatic Park.** A 15-acre lagoon with sail and paddle boat rentals. There are picnic facilities, campgrounds, dressing rooms, and launching ramp. *Admission charge. Pacific Coast Hwy. near Jamboree Rd. (714) 644-0510*

6 **Upper Newport Bay.** A remarkable and idyllic 741-acre preserve for ducks, geese, and other avian users of the Pacific Flyway, surrounded by the bluffs of Newport Bay. Paths along the far reaches of the estuary are wonderful for quiet early morning walks. *Backbay Dr. off Jamboree Blvd.*

7 **Whale Watching.** Noted marine naturalist Doug Thompson rents his schooner *Kelpie* for whale-watching curises. March features hour tours. Reservations recommended. *3416 Via Oporto #7, Newport Beach. California Pacific Tours (714) 661-5174*

7 **Marrakesh.** Hollywood-Arab decor of tiled fountains and pillows on the floor. A sumptuous setting for elaborate Moroccan dinners that include pigeon pie, cous cous, and baklava. *Moroccan. M-F 6PM-10PM; F-Su 5:30PM-11PM. $$$. 1100 W. Pacific Coast Hwy., Newport Beach. (714) 645-8384. Also in Studio City: Su-Th 5PM-10PM, F-Sa 5PM-11PM. 3003 Ventura Blvd. 788-6354*

7 **Ambrosia.** Among Orange County's most formal restaurants, serving haute cuisine in an atmosphere of cut-velvet luxury. Gentlemen must wear ties. *French. Open 7 days. Dinner only. $$$$. 501 30th St. (714)673-0200*

8 **Crab Cooker.** Well-loved and always crowded. They do not accept reservations, even, as one story has it, from a President of the United States who wanted to circumvent the line. Mesquite-broiled seafood. *Open 7 days. No lunch Su. $$/$$$. 2200 Newport Blvd. (714) 673-0100*

9 **Balboa Island.** Actually three islands connected by bridges. They are, in descending size, *the big island, the little island,* and *Collins Island.* A favorite island pastime is an evening stroll among the luxury homes.

9 **Balboa Ferry.** Three tiny ferries take you between the Balboa Peninsula and Balboa Island. *Palm Street on the Balboa Peninsula or Agate Avenue on Balboa Island.*

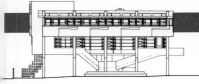

Lovell Beach House. A monument of modern architecture, this beach home was designed by Rudolph Schindler in 1926, a fine example of his early constructivist style combining grace, lightness, and strength in a style far ahead of its time. Private residence. *East corner of 13th St. and Beach Walk, Balboa*

Balboa Pavilion. Built in 1905, this historical landmark is in the heart of the town. It now houses a restaurant, gift shop, and ocean view bar, and is the Newport Terminal for Catalina Island tours, whale-watching expeditions, and harbor cruises aboard the *Pavilion Queen*, which last 45 or 90 minutes and show you the Newport Harbor. *400 Main St., Balboa. (714) 673-5245*

Sherman Foundation Center. A jewel of a botanical garden and library specializing in the horticulture of the Pacific Southwest. The well-maintained grounds are lush with unusual seasonal flowers and famous hanging baskets. The tea garden serves pastries and coffee. A gift shop sells a variety of horticultural items. *Open daily, 10:30AM-4PM. Admission charge. 2647 E. Pacific Coast Hwy., Corona del Mar. (714) 673-2261*

University of California at Irvine. Founded in 1965 on 1,000 acres donated by the Irvine Company. Twenty-five buildings house five major schools and a number of inter-disciplinary and graduate departments. Full-time enrollment is 10,000. The campus was laid out as an arboretum; over 11,000 trees from all over the world form a green grove in the center of the tan hills of the Irvine Ranch. A self-guided tree tour brochure is available at the Administration Building. The Fine Art Gallery sponsors exhibitions of 20th-century art and is open free of charge Tuesday through Saturday from 10AM to 5PM. Theatrical performances are held in the Fine Arts Village Theatre, the Concert Hall, and Crawford Hall. *San Diego Freeway (#405) to Jamboree Rd. west to Campus Dr. South. General information: (714) 833-6922*

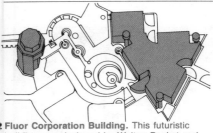

Fluor Corporation Building. This futuristic building was designed by Welton Becket and Associates in 1976. The imposing podlike structures on the roof are enclosures for air conditioning equipment. It is best viewed from the San Diego Freeway (#405). *3333 Michelson Dr., Irvine*

Lion Country Safari. Free roaming wild animals walk right up to your car and nuzzle the windows in this drive-through 500-acre preserve. A petting village, animal nursery, and a Zambezi River cruise add to the fun. No convertibles are allowed (car exchanges available). Admission fee. *Intersection of Irvine Center Dr. and the San Diego Freeway (#405), Irvine (714) 837-1200*

Hugging the coast midway between Los Angeles and San Diego, the town of Laguna Beach is primarily an artist's colony and vacation spot known for its cultural attractions, particularly the celebrated *Pageant of Masters.*

A Mediterranean climate, beautiful 3½-mile beach and artsy atmosphere have made Laguna Beach a popular resort for years. John Steinbeck lived here while writing *Tortilla Flat*, and Bette Davis made her home here during the 1940s. An exciting moment for younger locals came when ex-Beatle George Harrison began inquiries into the area, but the outcome is secret.

Most of the 20,000 year-round residents commute to industrial areas outside of Laguna Beach; the community supports a primarily *cottage industry*—small shops, arts and crafts galleries and tourist services.

14 Hortense Miller Garden. 2½ acres of spectacular native fauna, birds. Advance reservations required. *Tu-F & Sa AM. 22511 Allview Terrace. 497-3311*

14 Festival of Arts/Pageant of the Masters. An impressive blend of art, entertainment, and technical wizardry wherein great works of art are re-created with live models. Using acrylic paints to deflect stage lighting, artists paint backgrounds and create shadows and creases for the wardrobes of models who must hold the pose completely immobile for a minute and a half in sculpture and painting tableaux. For seven weeks each year, some four hundred volunteers and a small staff of professionals present a magical event to well over 100,000 wide-eyed audience members at a performance where stage lighting is so critical to the *living pictures* that a matinee performance would be unthinkable. Consistently sold out months in advance. *650 Laguna Canyon Rd. (714) 494-1147*

15 All American Bagel Co. Fresh New York-style bagels with deli toppings, pizza, sandwiches, cheesecake. *Open daily from 6AM. $. 238 Laguna Ave. (714) 497-5110*

16 Forest Avenue Mall. Three tiers of fascinating shops. Galleries, boutiques, gourmet food and restaurants, gemstones, and tennis specialties, all in a rustic, cozy mall just blocks from the ocean and Festival of Arts. *332 Forest Ave.*

16 Lumberyard Plaza. An old lumberyard is now the unique home of 27 shops, boutiques, galleries, and restaurants. Open-air mall makes walking and shopping convenient and fun. Next door to beach. Walk to Festival of Arts site. *384 Forest Ave.*

17 Poor Richard's Kitchen. Steaks and seafood served on a patio overlooking the ocean. Very good soup and salad bar. *Open daily 8AM-9PM. $$. In Village Fair Mall, 1198 S. Coast Hwy. 497-1667*

17 Vacation Village. Resort sits on private beach. Pools, whirlpool, recreation, and restaurants. Rooms, suites, and studios all reasonably priced. *647 S. Coast Hwy., PO Box 66, Laguna Beach 92651. (714)494-8566*

17 The Village Fair. Shopping mall with 40 shops, galleries and restaurants covering a block. Free parking. *Open daily; many shops open till 9PM. 1100 S. Coast Hwy.*

18 Ron's in Laguna. Sumptuous dinners of prime rib, leg of lamb, chicken canelloni, etc., served with soup or salad, potato or rice, vegetables and rolls. *Open daily, lunch 11:30AM-4PM; dinner 4PM-10PM. Su brunch 11AM-3PM. Call for weekly specials. $$/$$$. 1464 S. Coast Hwy. (714) 497-4871*

18 Surf & Sand Hotel. Modern rooms with ocean view. Two restaurants, entertainment in hotel. Excellent service. Highly recommended. *1555 S. Coast Hwy. (714) 497-4477*

18 The Towers. For elegant dinners in the hotel with the best view in town. *Open daily, breakfast 7AM-11AM; lunch 11AM-2:30PM; dinner 5:30-11PM. Su brunch 8AM-3PM. $/$$. 1555 S. Coast Hwy. (714) 497-4477*

18 Sherman Library & Gardens. Lush garden, exhibit rooms, and library on historic estate. Just 10 minutes up coast in Corona del Mar. *Open daily, 10:30AM-4PM. Small fee. 2647 E. Coast Hwy. (714) 673-2261*

18 Maison Giraud. True *haute cuisine* overlooking the Pacific. Choose quail, pheasant, squab, salmon, scallops, oysters, shrimp, veal, lamb. Notable wine list. *Open daily except M. Lunch 11AM-2PM; dinner 5PM-10PM. Su dinner 5PM-8PM. In Village Fair Mall, 1164 S. Coast Hwy. (714) 494-4668*

20 Capistrano Depot. ☆ Take Amtrak direct from Union Station to this refurbished train station, where lunches and dinners feature dishes from the best of the old railroad lines, and jazz accompanies drinks in the boxcar bar. *American. Open daily. $$/$$$. 26701 Verdugo St., Capistrano. (714) 496-8181*

"Local conditions are especially beneficial for pulmonary ailments, asthma, liver trouble, nervous disorders, and old age. The sunny skies, the delightful winter climate, and the beautiful walks all contribute to make Los Angeles a veritable sanitarium."

Ludwig Louis Salvator
1876

"The wet season is the season in which it can rain but may not; and the dry season is the season in which it cannot rain, but occasionally does."

Helen Hunt Jackson
1883

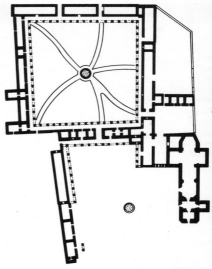

19 Mission San Juan Capistrano. Founded in 1776 by Father Junipero Serra, this simple adobe is considered one of the oldest churches in California. In 1796, Indian laborers under the charge of a Mexican stonemason began a grand stone church that was completed in 1806, only to be destroyed by earthquake six years later. Instead of rebuilding the momumental stone structure, services resumed in the older adobe church. In the 1890s, the Landmarks Club saved the adobe from destruction, and in the 1920s it underwent major restoration. The magnificent stone church is now under replication (completion due circa 1982). The famous swallows that return to Capistrano each March 19th, St. Joseph's Day, are *cliff swallows* that build their gourdlike nests in the broken arches of the ruins of the stone church. *Open 7 days, 7AM-5PM. Admission charge. Camino Capistrano and Ortega Hwy. (714) 493-1111*

20   CATALINA ISLAND

Visitors from eastern states concerned about California falling into the ocean may be startled to realize that part of Los Angeles County is already located 27 miles offshore.

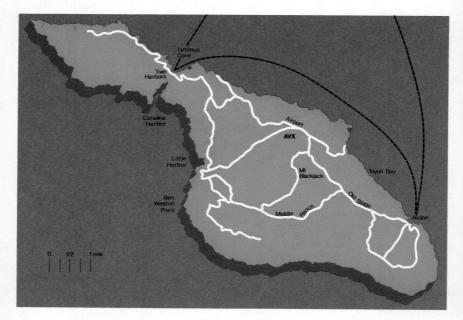

Catalina Island is a small (28 miles long and 8 miles wide) portion of the archipelago formed by the peaks of the Peninsular Range. The island was known as *mountain ranges that are in the sea* to its earlier inhabitants, a Shoshonean-speaking tribe of Gabrieleno Indians.

Catalina's attractions are fabled and true: mountains, canyons, inlets—all virtually unspoiled—a view of California as it was hundreds of years ago.

Herds of wild bison (left by a movie crew several decades ago), boars, and goats roam free over the back region of the island. A buffalo joyously rolling over on its back like a big puppy is a sight not quickly forgotten by back-country hikers.

Catalina is perfect for a vacation of a week or less. Even a half day is enough time to see Avalon, the island's only town, with small winding streets worthy of exploration, and abundant Mediterranean-style architecture giving it the ambience of an Italian seaside hill town. For a family vacation or a romantic weekend getaway, the island offers recreational possibilities for every interest.

Most of the island has been in private ownership since the resettlement of the native Indian population to the mainland in 1811. Avalon was named in 1888 by the sister of an early developer, George Shatto, after the island of Avalon in Tennyson's *Idylls of the King*, the island of blessed souls in Celtic mythology. William Banning, son of Phineas Banning, formed the Santa Catalina Island Company for the purpose of developing a pleasure resort around 1892. In 1919, William Wrigley, Jr., the chewing-gum scion, purchased controlling interest in the company and fulfilled Banning's dream by building a great casino in Avalon, promoting deep-sea fishing, and making the island the site of spring training for his basball team, the Chicago Cubs. While Avalon became a popular tourist spot during the 1930s, most of the interior of the island and much of the coastline remains undeveloped. A nonprofit foundation named the Santa Catalina Island Conservancy acquired title to about 86% of the island in 1975 and joined forces with the County of Los Angeles to administer this unique open space. *For information on the island's attractions, phone 510-1520*

AVALON AREA. Casino. Spanish-Moderne with Moorish elements, it is still the primary landmark. The circular structure designed by Sumner and Spaulding in 1929 occupies a point on the northwest end of Crescent Bay and houses an art gallery, museum, motion-picture theater, and, yes, a ballroom, where even now you can dance to the music of the big bands. You can even reserve it for a terrific private party.

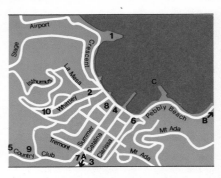

Other Avalon recreational possibilities are:

A Wrigley's Memorial Botanical Garden, fishing, swimming, window shopping, golf, tennis, and all sorts of sightseeing tours, such as the glass-bottom boat trip, flying-fish boat trip and scenic terrace drive. Tours range from 40 minutes to 4 hours. The 3-hour *Around the Island Tour* departs Avalon, noon. Rentals for everything are easy and available—bikes, horses, strollers, fishing tackle, etc. If you want to bring your bike along, contact your cross-channel carrier for details.

2 Catalina hotels: All are open all year. Many offer lower rates fall through spring.
Hotel Catalina. The charm of yesterday in a renovated Victorian hotel only a half-block from the beach. Movies for guests every afternoon. *Moderate prices. 129 Whittley. 510-0027*

3 Las Casitas. Moderately-priced bungalows and studios, all with kitchens. There are a pool and tennis courts. *400 Avalon Canyon Rd. 599-1010*

4 Pavilion Lodge. On the beach in the heart of town. Moderately-priced. *513 Crescent. 599-1010*

5 Paradise Island Inn. A unique tropical setting. Moderately-priced. *888 Las Lomas. 510-0325*

5 Mr. Gee's. Exotic and tropical. *Cantonese/Polynesian. Open daily. Dinner only. Su brunch. $$. 888 Las Lomas (in the Paradise Island Inn). 510-0327*

6 Cafe Prego. Old world warmth and charm. Try the homemade vegetable soup. *Italian. Open daily. Dinner only. $$. 603 Crescent. 510-1218*

7 The Sand Trap. A local favorite. The specialty is omelettes. *Open daily during summer only. Breakfast and lunch. $. Avalon Canyon Rd. on the way to Wrigley Botanical Garden, Avalon. 510-1349*

8 Chi-Chi Club. Year 'round live jazz and bluegrass. *Open daily, 8AM 'til 2AM. 107 Summer Ave. 510-9176*

9 Catalina Island Country Club Restaurant. Fresh local seafood in a casual atmosphere. *American. Summer only. Closed M-Tu. Dinner only. $$. On Country Club Rd. in the Catalina Island Country Club. 510-0960*

10 The Zane Grey Pueblo Hotel. Tahitian teak beams in an open-beam ceiling, hewn-plank door and log mantle, walls of mortar mixed with goats milk combine with blessed isolation and an extraordinary view of the ocean and the hills in this, the former Avalon home of the foremost writer of the American West. *199 Chimes Tower Rd. PO Box 216, Avalon. 510-0966, 510-1520*

Restaurants red
Architecture blue
Narrative/Museums/Shops black
Gardens/Parks/Piers green

20 CATALINA ISLAND

OUTSIDE AVALON. A visit to Catalina's interior or its rugged coastline is highly recommended. While Avalon's population swells from 2,000 to 10,000 on summer weekends, the remaining portion of the island is quiet.

Two Harbors. A boat trip to Two Harbors, at the Isthmus, is lovely. You can see this historic Banning house and adjoining barracks area. Bring a picnic as facilities here are sparse. *Halliday Bus Service will take you to the Isthmus from Avalon at 11AM daily. 510-0840*

The Interior. El Rancho Escondido may be visited on the Inland Motor Tour; it is home to some of America's finest Arabian horses. Native wildlife in Catalina's underdeveloped interior is extraordinary; more than 100 species of birds make Catalina their permanent or part-time home. There are 400 species of native plant life, including eight types found only on Catalina. They include the Catalina Ironwood, the Wild Tomato and the Dudleya Hassei, whose generic name means *live forever.*

Driving. Rental cars are not allowed in the interior. If you know a friend with a car on the island, you may obtain a temporary card key to drive outside of Avalon from Santa Catalina Island Conservancy for $7.00.

Hiking. Why not walk? Permits are required to hike into the interior and may be obtained free of charge at the Visitor's Information center in Avalon or at the Cove and Camp Agency at the Isthmus.

Camping. *Arrangements for camping at Black Jack or Little Harbor must be made through the County Department of Parks and Recreation, PO Box 1133, Avalon, CA 90704. 510-0688. A brochure describing the trails may also be obtained from the department. Arrangements for camping at Little Fisherman's Cove (Two Harbors) must be made through Catalina Cove and Camp Agency, PO Box 1566, Avalon, California 90704. 510-0303. All camping by permit only and advance reservations are required.*

How to get there:
Boat. Year-round service from the ports of Long Beach and San Pedro. Fast (less than 2 hours) big boats; refreshments. Mid-June thru mid-September: five trips daily from both ports. Mid-September thru mid-June: 3 trips daily. During peak months, service direct to Two Harbors/Isthmus area is available. Reservations for all sailings advisable. Call from Los Angeles: 775-6111; for the Harbor area: 832-4521; from Orange County: (714) 527-7111

B Airplane and Helicopter. ASAP (All Seasons Air Pacific) departs daily from Long Beach airport on Piper Chieftains. Ground transportation provided to Avalon from *Airport in the Sky* terminal. *420-1883.* Helitrans flies helicopters hourly from San Pedro for the 18-minute flight to either Pebbly Beach or Two Harbors. *548-1314 or 800-262-1472. Advance reservations necessary.*

C Getting to the terminals. To get to the Long Beach Terminal by bus, take RTD 36 from downtown LA. Grayline Tours to the Terminal area are available from Anaheim. To get to the San Pedro Terminal by bus, take Grayline Tours from LA. A summer-only service (May-October) connects to Newport Beach. *Contact Catalina Passenger Service, Balboa Pavilion, (714) 673-5245*

"It is the ambition of every citizen of L. A. to have a palm tree in his front yard and two citrus trees in his back yard. Add an atrocious glorified-barn structure called a house, stuccoed and whitewashed and weighted down by red or green tiles, and the "native son" is a happy child in a God-ordained, man-made paradise..."

Willard F. Motley
1939

---

21 DESERT AREAS

The Antelope Valley, the northernmost portion of Los Angeles County, is extremely arid high desert, sparsely populated and undeveloped, providing a nearby escape from urban claustrophobia.

Vasquez Rocks County Park. A surrealistic tumble of lacy sandstone rocks, some several hundred feet high that are great for climbing. The area is an outcropping of the San Andreas Fault. Named for the famous 19th-century bandit, Tiburcio Vasquez, it was used as one of his numerous hideouts. *Admission free. Escondido Canyon Road off California Highway 14*

1 Saddleback Butte State Park. Native chaparral on a sandstone bluff. There is a magnificent stand of Joshua trees, bizarre shaped plants that are improbable members of the lily family. *170th St. off California Highway 138*

2 Antelope Valley Indian Museum. Burrowed into the rock of Piute Butte, this architecturally unique museum, built in a sort of Swiss troglodyte style, houses artifacts of Native American culture. *15701 E. Avenue M. (805) 946-2554*

3 Devil's Punchbowl Regional Park. A 1310-acre county park located in the high desert area near Pearblossom. The rocky area is rich in native plants and includes a number of hiking trails. The Punchbowl is a natural depression in a slope of tumbled boulders. The park also includes a lovely stream, the size of which varies greatly with the season, ringed with willows and other water-loving plants. *Admission free. 2800 Devil's Punchbowl Rd., Pearblossom (805) 944-9151*

4 Valley Butte State Poppy Reserve. Two thousand acres set aside for the preservation of the golden poppy, the California state flower. During the spring, the reserve is carpeted with a solid blanket of flowers. *Open in spring only. Admission free. 17 miles west of Lancaster off California Highway 138*

Restaurants red
Architecture blue

Narrative/Museums/Shops black
Gardens/Parks/Piers green

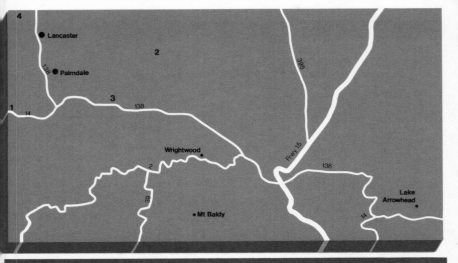

Marvelous terrain, year 'round sports and hedonistic pleasures are found in the Colorado Desert a little more than 100 miles from Los Angeles.

Palm Springs is a smartly casual resort, located at the base of Mt. San Jacinto. It is the golf capital of the world, sponsoring over 100 tournaments annually, as well as a mecca for tennis players, sunbathers, shoppers, and diners. Mineral hot springs have been an attraction here for millenia: the Agua Caliente Indians utilized these revitalizing natural spas for ritual and medicinal purposes. Soaking and sunning continue today as favorite Palm Springs pastimes, not only in the hot springs, but also in almost 7,000 swimming pools. Natural artesian springs in several nearby canyons enable the native Washingtonian Palm to grow in oasis cultures. The region is also known for its beneficial climate. The clean air has a light-as-a-feather quality at an average daytime temperature of 88 degrees, humidity is very low, and the yearly rainfall averages 5.39 inches.

The area surrounding Palm Spring appeals to the nature lover. Dramatic rock formations, stark mountain ranges, intricate canyons and varieties of plants unique to the region combine in a clearly etched landscape. Just a few of the numerous attractions of the nearby desert area:

1 **Anza Borrego Desert.** This 470,000 acre state park is a well-maintained desert preserve with an unusual number of flora and fauna varieties. The striking geological formations here resemble a miniature Grand Canyon. Carrizzo Gorge and Plain are particularly beautiful.

2 **Idyllwild.** A community nestled in mile-high mountain. There are tall stands of pines, tumbled rock formation for climbing, trails for hiking, skiing in winter.

3 **Indian Canyons.** Andreas, Murray, and Palm Canyons offer large and unusual rock formations, hiking trails and a stand of majestic Washingtonian Palms believed to be almost 2,000 years old.

4 **Joshua Tree National Monument.** 870 square miles of unearthly mountain and desert flora, including joshua trees, 50-foot-high members of the lily family.

5 **Lake Cahuilla.** Fishing, swimming, boating, and picnicking.

6 **Living Desert Reserve.** A 900-acre desert-interpretive center containing nature trails, a botanical garden, a visitors' center, and a giftshop/bookshop.

7 **Palm Spring Aerial Tramway.** A spectacular tramride, the largest single-span lift in the world, travels to an altitidue of 8,516 feet on Mt. San Jacinto for a view of the surroundings that is more than eagle's eye. At the top there is a bar, restaurant, shops, and 54 miles of hiking trails.

8 **Palm Springs Desert Museum.** A large cultural facility with permanent collections and changing exhibitions of contemporary and historical art. There is a fine collection of over 1,300 American Indian artifacts.

9 **Salton Sea.** A sea below sea level. Swimming, boating and water skiing are available at this 38-mile-long inland sea. A National Wildlife Refuge is located at the southern end. The Visitors' Center has history and wildlife exhibits

10 **Whitewater Canyon.** Interesting scenery and a trout farm. *Picnic facilities and grills for freshly caught fish. Rental tackle and bait available.*

The year 'round, semitropical sunshine of LA has attracted visitors to the southland since the 19th century.

The Los Angeles climate is similar to Nice, Athens, or other Mediterranean resort areas. However, unlike the Mediterranean, Los Angeles is seldom humid. The crisp aridity of the desert meeting the ocean makes the weather remarkably consistent throughout the year. The newcomer is often surprised by the seeming lack of seasons. Instead, great fluctuations in the weather occur from year to year, or in seven- to ten-year cycles of extreme drought alternating with torrential downpours. Angelenos have passed water rationing plans one year only to be deluged by rains and mudslides the next year. This variance in precipitation makes the total average rainfall of 14 inches per year a misleading statistic. In reality, some years may have 25 inches or more, while others feel sprinkles of only 7 inches or less. The temperature average of the Los Angeles Basin is more reliable. The mercury has seldom dropped below 40 degrees, and snow has fallen momentarily on only a handful of occasions.

Seasonal variations are subtle, and to the uninitiated, almost indistinguishable. In the fall, hot dry desert winds peculiar to the southland and known as Santa Anas or Santannas rake the basin, exposing the mountains with crystalline clarity. This is the fire season, when the summer-dried grasslands of the hills become perfect kindling in near-zero humidity.

Winters in Los Angeles are mild, with many bright sunny days and occasional rainstorms. The signal of the Southern California springtime is fog-shrouded coastlines, while inland areas enjoy mild temperatures and clean skies. Summers tend to have intense sunlight coupled with baking heat. Temperatures of 90 degrees plus are common in August and September. Smog tends to be the bane of the summer season. The overall climate of Los Angeles can be divided into several distinct subclimates. The greater the distance from the ocean, the greater the extreme in temperature. The inland San Fernando, San Gabriel and Antelope Valleys are both the hottest and coldest; summer temperatures here can reach over 100 degrees in the day and cool off to 60 in the evening. Frost warnings are occasionally issued in valley areas in the winter, a remnant of the era when these fertile flatlands were important citrus industry centers.

Mountains and foothills have temperatures below freezing in the winter, with many ski resorts in the San Gabriel and San Bernardino mountains enjoying snowfalls that can extend as low as 3,500 feet.

The beach areas are usually 10 to 20 degrees cooler than downtown LA, and experience less variation between day and night temperatures than does the central city.

No description of Los Angeles is complete without a mention of smog.

The term was coined to describe a combination of smoke and fog that was first noticed in Los Angeles in 1943. The city has more smog than most other areas, ironically, because of two of its greatest assets: the mountains, which hold the pollutants in place instead of allowing them to be dispersed, and the sunshine, which cooks the pollutants into a visible hazy layer. An atmospheric phenomenon known as an inversion layer holds automobile and industrial pollutants in a low, poorly ventilated layer, trapped by warm air currents from above. While artist-pundit Claes Oldenburg once suggested that a giant hole be drilled in the mountains in order to install an exhaust fan, more practical suggestions have aimed at diminishing auto traffic, believed to account for at least two-thirds of smog, by encouraging carpooling and use of public transport. Gasoline pump nozzles are fitted with unwieldy but effective vapor recovery gaskets. In addition, stringent controls on stationary pollution sources and industry have been enacted.

Los Angeles is situated on the western edge of a region of great contrasts.

Cut off from the desert by steep mountains on the north, south and east, and isolated by the Pacific Ocean on the west, writer Carey McWilliam's phrase for the region, "an island on the land," is particularly appropriate.

The County of Los Angeles covers an area nearly as large as the state of Connecticut: approximately 75 miles from north to south and 70 miles from east to west, rising from sea level at the coast to an elevation of a few hundred feet downtown. The county area includes mountain ranges, invisible major rivers, long beaches and wide alluvial plains, of which the major example is the Los Angeles Basin. Traversing the basin are three of Southern California's larger rivers: the San Gabriel, the Los Angeles and the Santa Ana. The major portion of their flow is underground; cement control channels have been constructed in the places where they normally surface in order to control the tendency toward seasonal flooding. The Los Angeles River has its source in the mountains near the San Fernando Valley, and is joined by numerous creeks before it empties into the sea at Long Beach.

A long string of beaches forms a diagonal where the plains of the basin end and meet the ocean. From Ventura southward to Orange County, the Los Angeles coastline offers almost seventy miles of continuous sandy beaches, nearly all free and accessible to the public. Surrounding the beaches and basin are a ring of rugged mountain ranges. There are three main chains: to the north, the Santa Monicas separate the main part of the City of Los Angeles from the more arid San Fernando Valley; to the northeast, the San Gabriel mountains separate Los Angeles from the Mojave Desert; to the southeast, the Santa Ana Mountains and the San Joaquin Hills are the transition to the mountains of Orange and San Diego Counties. The region's highest peak, the 10,064-ft. Mt. San Antonio, or Old Baldy, can be seen on clear days against the city's eastern skyline, in the midst of the San Gabriel Mountains.

In contrast with the rest of the United States, where the landscape has been formed over *hundreds* of millions of years, most of the geological processes which have created Los Angeles have taken place within the last *few* million years.

Consequently, the folding, warping, uplift and erosion which create the topography are more visible on the surface of the land than in other areas.

Most of the Los Angeles Basin was deposited from 12 million years ago (the Pliocene period) to 2 million years ago (the Pleistocene period), when thick beds of siltstone, sandstone, shale and conglomerate were laid down as ocean sediment. The terrestrial deposits were subsequently uplifted and deposited and uplifted over and over again. The uplifting process is continuing: the best example for the amateur geologist is the Palos Verdes Hill. This coastline terrace is composed of thirteen different beach shorelines, raised and etched and raised again over a period of 20 million years.

Los Angeles is within the boundaries of "earthquake country," but the dangers from earthquakes are far less than popular lore describes.

Earthquakes are the result of large continental and ocean-building processes taking place within the earth's mantle. The continents and oceans rest on enormous scale-like plates, which are constantly moving, subsiding and regenerating. The San Andreas fault marks the major boundary between the Pacific and North American plates, which are moving past each other at the rate of about 5 centimeters (2 inches) a year. The San Andreas Fault cuts through the desert near Palmdale, the most distant part of Los Angeles County. Earthquakes are created because the sides of each fault, like the San Andreas, generally remain stuck together until enough strain has accumulated to rupture the rock bond between the plates. The resulting release of energy is known as an earthquake.

Earthquakes are measured by two systems. The most commonly used is the Richter scale, developed by Dr. Charles Richter of Cal Tech in 1935, used to explain the earthquake's magnitude; it is expressed in whole numbers and their decimal fractions. The Richter scale is logarithmic; each whole number is ten times the preceding one. Thus the amplitude of an 8.6 magnitude earthquake is not twice as large as a shock of magnitude 4.3, but more than 10,000 times as large. A quake of 2 on the Richter scale is the smallest normally felt by humans. Shocks of 7 or more are considered to be major. The Richter scale is not used to estimate damage. Instead, the subjective Mercalli scale assesses damage in terms of a scaled index of Roman numerals.

While earthquakes occur constantly throughout California, only a few are strong enough to even be felt. Even fewer will cause damage and only one in thirty years in the entire State of California is expected to be serious. While the potential for damage is greater if an earthquake occurs in a heavily populated area, devastation is unlikely. Since the 1933 Long Beach quake, when unreinforced masonry buildings suffered the greatest damage, major building code revisions have mandated structural safeguards for modern buildings.

If you should happen to be caught in an earthquake:

- **Remain calm.**
- **Most earthquake danger is from falling debris.** If outdoors, stay outside and move away from buildings and utility wires. If indoors, get under a sturdy desk or table or stand in a doorway.
- **Keep away from windows** — glass tends to shatter.
- **Don't use candles, matches or open flames** — ruptured gas lines are hazardous.
- **If in a moving car, stop and remain inside until the shaking is over.**

Ethnic diversity has characterized Los Angeles since its earliest days.

The founders of the pueblo numbered 2 Spaniards, 2 Blacks, 11 Indians, and 29 mestizos (a mix of European, Indian, and Black ancestry) in their total headcount of 44. A native Gabrieleno Indian population of 30,000 welcomed the new settlers. The early arrivals in the wave of immigration that commenced in the 1850s included New England traders, followed by scions of old Atlantic families. During the 1870s, Europeans appeared, especially from Germany, France, and Great Britain, some to escape religious persecution and wars, others to enjoy the winter climate.

The railroads became great immigration brokers in the last half of the 19th century. Chinese, Japanese, Mexicans, and Blacks were brought in succeeding waves to break road and lay track. These people stayed to make homes, many becoming laborers in the fledgling agriculture and fishing industries. After the railroads were built, large chunks of unused right-of-way remained in the hands of the transportation giants. Much of this land was sold to homeseekers from the Midwest, enticed here by the combined promotions of the Chamber of Commerce and the railroads. Iowans in particular responded; by the 1920s, upwards of 150,000 showed up for the annual Hawkeye picnic in Long Beach. Increasing industrialization offered more job opportunities after 1920. The new arrivals were blue collar and farm workers: Anglos from the Dust Bowl States; Blacks from the South; and Mexicans joining the Hispanic community that had been here since the founding of the pueblo. Uncle Sam was the travel agent of World War II: between seven and eight million servicemen passed through California. Many liked what they saw and returned in the 1950s. Political unrest, wars, and changes in immigration laws brought Latin Americans, East Indians, Southeast Asians, Eastern Europeans, and Iranians to Los Angeles during the 1960s and 1970s.

The Bicentennial of the City of Los Angeles has been celebrated by a population that is approximately 49% Anglo, 25% Hispanic, 16% Black, and 10% Asian.

1781 Pueblo founded.
1782 Three founding families expelled.
1783 Water given first priority.
1784 Fathers of missions and pueblos dead.
1785 Donations for first chapel requested.
1786 Settlers assume legal title to land.
1787 Contraband traders steer clear of LA.
1788 First mayor for Los Angeles.
1789 King grants land titles.
1790 Pueblo population triples.
1791 30 adobes for the pueblo.
1792 First tourist extols attractions.
1793 Threadbare Angeleno begs clothing at Mission.
1794 English invasion feared imminent.
1795 Vancouver names coastal points.
1796 Grapes and olives planted.
1797 San Fernando Mission founded.
1798 Public grainery to guard against famine.
1799 Mission vs pueblo in water rights fight.

1800 Surplus wheat exported.
1801 Pueblo escapes massacre.
1802 Humboldt visits Southland.
1803 Joint American-Russian sea otter expedition.
1804 California divided in half.
1805 American ship promises new trade.
1806 Plague overruns Southland.
1807 Mysterious visitor believed a spy.
1808 Viceroy asks money and prayers for king.
1809 Civic unrest increases.
1810 Troops repell Indian attack.
1811 Hidalgo inspires Mexican revolution.
1812 Earthquake damages local buildings.
1813 Spain tries to oust mission power.
1814 Government outlaws foreign trade.
1815 First English-speaking settler.
1816 LA River floods—town center moved.
1817 LA children get first school.
1818 Pirates raid coast—two captured.
1819 Smallpox decimates pueblo.
1820 California otter population exterminated.
1821 Mexico gains independence from Spain.
1822 Plaza Church dedicated.
1823 Mexico declared a republic.
1824 Indians rebel against mission.
1825 Mexico reshuffles California government.
1826 Mission welcomes American fur trappers.
1827 Despite drought city finances healthy.
1828 Original Indian village razed.
1829 American settlers significant minority.
1830 Santa Fe traders reach LA.
1831 Revolt restores civil rights.
1832 Indian population declines by half.
1833 New school starts.
1834 Missions broken up—property divided.
1835 LA declared capital city.
1836 Urban jobs number 23% in first padrone.
1837 California Civil War.
1838 Mexico decrees amnesty for all.
1839 Governor orders all aliens out of California.
1840 Smallpox rages—countered by first vaccinations.
1841 US Navy charts coast as immigration increases.
1842 Luck uncovers Placerita Canyon gold.
1843 Yankees call land grab a mistake.
1844 Casualties light as state warfare ends.
1845 Great drought ravages Los Angeles.
1846 Gringos occupy LA—Angelenos revolt.
1847 Cahuenga Treaty seals peace.
1848 Sutter strike turns beef to gold.
1849 Land boom follows Ord's city survey.

1850 State joins Union—city incorporates.
1851 Sudden fabulous wealth engulfs LA.
1852 Fortunes change hands in horserace of the century.
1853 City celebrates greatest Fourth of July.
1854 Butterfield Stage ends civic isolation.
1855 Mayor quits to join lynch mob—instantly re-elected.
1856 Sisters of Charity open infirmary amid city crime wave.
1857 Vigilantes seek revenge for dead sheriff.
1858 Army pack camels arrive in LA.
1859 Silver strike at Fort Tejon.
1860 Bullfighting out—baseball in.
1861 Wife killer reaps mob vengeance.
1862 Armed city splits over Civil War loyalties.
1863 LA called "toughest town" in the nation.
1864 Land values plummet as ranching dies out.
1865 "Murder Capital" tries gun control law.
1866 City gets central park—mayor signs law.
1867 LA installs new gas lights.
1868 Hayward and Downey open first bank.
1869 Banning completes first city railroad.
1870 Mayor and council arrested.
1871 Chinese massacre shocks world.
1872 First woolen mill built as market crashes.
1873 Invalid influx strains city hospitality.
1874 Notorious bandito Vasquez caught.
1875 LA High School graduates first class.
1876 Lang Junction Golden Spike joins nation to LA.
1877 First trainload of oranges shipped east.
1878 Huntington buys Santa Monica—city fears stranglehold.
1879 Tax collector absconds with city funds.
1880 Temple block gets LA's first paved sidewalk.

1881 1st issue of *LA Times* celebrates city centennial.
1882 LA first city in country to be fully lit by electricity.
1883 Bicycles menace pedestrians—city enacts regulations.
1884 City paralyzed by first worker's strike.
1885 Santa Fe breaks Southern Pacific monopoly.
1886 RR rate war brings in immigrant flood.
1887 Land prices soar 500%.
1888 Ladybugs save orange harvest from blight.

1889 City bans gambling.
1890 Labor violence stuns city—wages drop.
1891 Mayor regains illegally held city land from RR.
1892 Doheny strikes oil downtown with a shovel.
1893 Financial panic—banks fail.
1894 Economic bondage fought by "Free-Harbor League."
1895 Sherman and Clark consolidate All-City RR.
1896 Port for Los Angeles saved by "Little Giant."
1897 First LA auto built by E. E. Erie.
1898 City opens country club.
1899 Work begins on port—President watches ceremonies.

1900 Pidgeons open mail service to Catalina.
1901 Angels Flight opens to cheers.
1902 City takes over water system.
1903 Motorists start self-help club.
1904 Kinney founds Venice-of-the-West.
1905 Voters ok $1.5 million for Owens water rights.

1906 LA rushes aid to northern city quake victims.
1907 Multimillion dollar aqueduct approved.
1908 LA shoots first movies.
1909 Mayor Harper out in nation's first recall.
1910 20 killed as unionists bomb LA Times.
1911 Women achieve full sufferage
1912 Hollywood becomes film center.
1913 30 thousand cheer as Owens Aqueduct opens.
1914 LA welcomes first Panama Canal vessel.
1915 Police mass for race riots at *Birth of a Nation* premier.
1916 Watts elects first California black assemblyman.
1917 America's sweetheart gets $1,000,000 contract.
1918 LA celebrates armistice at huge Hazard Pavilion fete.
1919 Philharmonic orchestra performs first concert.
1920 Temperance Union triumphs—Prohibition passes.
1921 First air passenger service to New York.
1922 Pacific fleet picks LA Harbor for home.
1923 80 thousand seats filled as LA Coliseum opens.
1924 Owens Aqueduct bombed by fighting farmers.
1925 Movies that talk thrill LA.
1926 Sister Aimee believed drowned— resurfaces in desert.
1927 Huntington's will leaves home and library to public.
1928 485 dead as dam fails—Mulholland takes blame.
1929 Graf Zeppelin docks at Mines Field.
1930 Mrs.Sterling granted wish—Olvera Street reclaimed.
1931 City leads nation in business failures.
1932 LA hosts tenth Olympic Games.
1933 Quake rocks Long Beach: 120 dead. $60 million damages.
1934 Republicans vow to blow up state if Sinclair elected.
1935 Hoover Dam completed.
1936 Police block migrants' entry into city.
1937 City declares bankruptcy.
1938 New mayor vows to set things right.
1939 Three day gala marks Union Station opening.
1940 West's first freeway opens.
1941 City mobilizes after Pearl Harbor attack.
1942 Government evacuates Japanese to camps.
1943 Zootsuit riots inflame city.
1944 World's celebrities find refuge in city.
1945 Unconditional victory but uneasy peace.
1946 Homeless crowds fuel tract home craze.
1947 City outlaws smog.
1948 Mad man Muntz revolutionizes modern merchandising.
1949 Television mania enthralls consumers.

1950 Bunche wins Nobel Peace Prize.
1951 Hollywood Ten indicted for contempt of Congress.
1952 City builds fall-out shelters—US tests first H-bombs.
1953 McIntyre named Cardinal.
1954 Killer smog attack closes down city.
1955 Disney opens Magic Kingdom.
1956 Signal Hill oil declared depleted.
1957 LA becomes third largest city in US.
1958 Skyline going up as height ban lifted.
1959 Communist boss barred from Magic Kingdom.
1960 LA convention picks JFK.

1961 Firestorm consumes Bel Air.
1962 First black on city council.
1963 Demonstrators strike schools for civil rights.
1964 City crowned with new Music Center.
1965 Watts ghetto explodes.
1966 Youth throng to Sunset Strip.
1967 Century City peace marchers arrested.
1968 Assassin kills Robert Kennedy.
1969 Tate-La Bianca murders traced to drug cult.
1970 Court orders LA to desegregate schools in one year.
1971 Quake jolts San Fernando—65 dead, $478 million damage.
1972 California coast saved—Proposition 20 passes.
1973 Gas lines raise tempers.
1974 SLA shootout—Patty Hearst missing.
1975 State Supreme Court upholds LA water rights.
1976 Mars touchdown for JPL's Viking I.
1977 Rationing looms in water shortage.
1978 Voter's revolt ok's Prop. 13 tax cut.
1979 Tempers flare as gas prices soar.
1980 City minorities regain majority.
1981 Dodgers win World Series
1982 Raiders footbal team move to Coliseum
1984 LA hosts XXIIIrd Olympiad

200/LA FIRSTS

1781 1st settlers found El Pueblo de La Reina de Los Angeles de Porciuncula.
1783 1st water system, la Zanja Madre, built.
1784 1st land grants: Governor Filipe de Neve awards grazing lands to army veterans, setting a tradition for subsequent land distribution.
1790 1st census records 30 families.
1797 1st vines and olives planted.
1798 1st Los Angeles jail.

1800 1st wheat export: 3400 bushels to San Blas mark economic self-sufficiency of pueblo.
1805 1st American, Capt. William Shaler of the "Lelia Byrd," arrives in San Pedro.
1817 1st school, 1st school teacher, 1st paid civil servant—$15/month—Maximo Pina.
1818 1st American settlers: Pirates Joseph Chapman (white) and Thomas Fisher (black) are captured and remain.
1824 1st Indian rebellion.
1826 1st American overland explorers: Jedediah Smith and party.
1829 1st vaccinations against smallpox, performed by James O. Pattie.
1833 1st regular city school classes.
1834 1st LA orange orchard planted by Vignes.
1836 1st vigilante committee, 1st lynching.
1836 1st revolution: Governor Alvarado declares California a republic.
1841 1st commercial orange grove started by William Wolfskill.
1842 1st California gold strike in Placerita Canyon under Oak of the Golden Dream by Francisco Lopez. Nuggets attached to roots of wild turnips. This triggers "Rush of the San Fernando Placers."
1843 1st commercial manufacture of champagne by Vignes and Pierre and Louis Sainsevain.
1844 1st bullring.
1847 1st Fourth of July celebration held on Fort Hill: Declaration of Independence read in English and Spanish.

1848 1st overland mail carried by Kit Carson.
1849 1st accurate maps of the city drawn by Lt. Edward Otho Cresap Ord.

1850 1st Protestant services conducted by Methodist minister J.W. Brier.
1850 1st Chinese in LA: Ah Fu and Alluce.
1850 1st US census.
1850 1st American baby (boy) born in LA.
1851 1st city police force.
1851 1st newspaper, the *Los Angeles* Star, publishes its 1st issue in Spanish and English.
1852 1st LA County Board of Supervisors.
1853 1st regular shipping connects world to LA.
1854 1st overland run from San Francisco to LA—the Butterfield Stage—comes through Fremont Pass, changing the isolated character of the city.
1854 1st attempt at water management: City appoints water commissioner, who is paid more than the mayor.
1854 1st Jewish services, conducted by Rabbi A.W. Edelman.
1854 1st book published: William Money's *Discovery of the Pacific Ocean.*
1855 1st college, St. Vincent's, opens in city plaza.
1856 1st power plant built by William H. Perry.
1856 1st ice cream sold.
1857 1st camels: Secretary of War Jefferson Davis imports 57 from Egypt to US Army Fort Tejon for desert transport—experiment fails.
1857 1st Wells Fargo office.
1858 1st pleasure resort: "The Garden of Paradise," opened by George Lehmann.
1858 1st city cemetery.
1858 1st hospital opened by Sisters of Mercy.
1858 1st fire insurance.
1859 1st foreign consulate—France.
1859 1st union local—Typographic.
1859 1st oil found in mountains above San Fernando by Philadelphia and California Oil Company.
1859 1st city annexation: 1.2 sq. mile southern extension.
.1860 1st commercial fishing conducted by Chinese who catch albacore and sardines.
1860 1st telegraph service links rest of US to Los Angeles.
1860 1st baseball club formed by girl's school as bull-fighting declared illegal.
1862 1st Board of Health.
1862 1st major land grading project: "Beale's Cut" through Tejon Pass.
1864 1st Protestant church: "St Luke's" built jointly by Presbyterians and Episcopalians.
1865 1st oil boom begins with pioneer oil strike.
1867 1st iron water mains deliver city water.
1868 1st iron safe permits opening of 1st bank, run by Downey and Hayward.
1868 1st real estate office opened by Robert Maclay Widney.
1869 1st railroad, promoted by P. Banning, is 22 miles long to San Pedro.
1869 1st locomotive, and 1st LA Railway Station.
1869 1st Japanese immigrants.
1870 1st medical society, the LA County Medical Association, opens with 7 members.
1870 1st LA River bridge.
1873 1st horse trolley established by R. M. Widney: Spring and 6th St. Railroad.
1873 1st synagogue: Congregation B'nai Brith dedicated.

1873 1st naval oranges imported from Brazil by Luther Tibbits.
1873 1st LA newspaper printed on a steam-driven press: *LA Herald.*
1873 1st LA city high school built on Poundcake Hill.
1873 1st major campaign to attract tourists to LA.
1874 1st art auction, art gallery, resident artist and art teacher.
1874 1st hillside reservoir allows construction of 1st hillside subdivision—Prudent Beaudry builds Bunker Hill.
1874 1st major housing shortage.
1875 1st eucalyptus trees.
1876 1st kindergarten.
1876 1st transcontinental passenger run between San Francisco and LA.
1876 1st Catholic Cathedral—St. Vibiana's.
1877 1st carload of oranges shipped to the East by Wolfskill Orchard in LA.
1878 1st public library.
1880 University of Southern California founded.
1880 1st shipment of raisins from LA County.

1881 1st issue of the *LA Times:* Gen. Harrison Gray Otis.
1822 1st telephone company service.
1882 1st electric street lights and power plant—T. H. Howland.
1883 1st bookman: C. C. Parker opens 1st major bookstore.
1883 Southern Pacific links with Texas Pacific to form Second Transcontinental Railroad.
1885 1st cable car line—2nd St. Railway.
1885 1st engine of Santa Fe Railroad enters town; third Transcontinental Railroad completed.
1885 1st major "land boom"—LA wealth doubles while land values increase five times.
1886 1st electric trolley car line—Charles H. Howland.
1886 1st special train loaded exclusively with LA oranges.
1887 1st avocado trees.
1887 1st iron works: Llewellyn Company.
1887 1st double-track streetcar lines.
1888 1st swimming pool: "the LA Natatorium—a Swimming Bath."
1888 1st woman police officer: Lucy Gray.
1888 1st permanent Chamber of Commerce.
1889 1st Tournament of Roses sponsors chariot race, greased pole climbing, parade of carriages—"The Battle of Flowers."
1892 1st LA oil well dug by Edward L. Doheny with a shovel.
1897 1st hydroelectric power.
1897 1st orchestra west of the Rockies: LA Symphony founded by L. E. Behymer.
1897 1st golf course—9 holes (tin cups) at Pico and Alvarado Street.
1897 1st LA automobile built by E. E. Erie and S. D. Stugis.
1897 1st kinetoscope parlor opened by T. L. Tally.
1897 1st elevator: Nadeau Hotel.
1897 1st fish cannery: albacore—later sold under LA-coined name of "tuna."
1898 1st LA Country Club—formed by Ed Tufts and Joseph Sartori.
1898 1st solar water heaters.
1898 1st basketball game.
1899 1st bicycle squad formed by LAPD.
1899 1st elevated roadway for bicycles, LA to Pasadena.

1900 1st internal combustion automobile manufactured in LA: the "Tourist."

1901 1st discovery of La Brea fossils by Union Oil.

1902 1st movie house in the world: "The Electric Theatre."

1902 1st local skyscraper: Brady Building soars to 14 stories.

1903 1st baseball league formed: Pacific Coast. Two baseball teams—LA Angels and Hollywood Stars.

1904 1st film of city shot in Chutes Park of Roy Knabenshue's dirigible.

1904 1st auto parade: 210 cars.

1904 Mount Wilson Observatory founded.

1905 Venice-of-America founded by A. Kinney.

1905 1st directional traffic signs erected by Southern California Automobile Club.

1906 1st LA yacht race (LA to Honolulu).

1906 1st Rose Bowl football game—declared too dangerous to repeat by Tournament Committee.

1906 1st height ordinance limits LA buildings to 13 stories, or 140'.

1906 1st escalator: Bullocks.

1907 California Institute of Technology founded.

1907 1st major moviemakers in Los Angeles: Francis Boggs and Thomas Perkins start 1st local film company.

1907 1st caterpillar tractors in operation in 1st major landgrading project at LA Harbor.

1907 1st black graduate of USC: Dr. Sommerville, born in Jamaica.

1908 1st movie completed in LA: William N. Selig's "The Count of Monte Cristo."

1908 1st movie completely shot in LA: Selig's "In the Sultan's Power."

1910 1st cowboy movies: Bronco Billy and Tom Mix.

1910 1st chief engineer of highways: auto registration totals 20,000.

1911 1st movie studio: David and William Horsley form Nestor Film Company.

1911 1st Lockheed plane.

1912 1st cafeteria: "Boos Brothers."

1912 1st gas station located at Grand Ave. and Washington Blvd.: 8 cents/gallon.

1912 1st dirigible passenger service in Pasadena started by Roy Knabenshue.

1913 1st multireel film: Jack London's "She-Wolf" shot by Hobart Hosworth.

1913 1st water from Owens Valley Aqueduct.

1914 1st Panama Canal ship welcomed by city.

1914 1st "bohemian" meeting place—John Brink's Saddle Rock Restaurant.

1914 1st Southwest Museum founded by Charles F. Lummis.

1915 1st female public defender in US: Mabel Walker Wildebrant.

1915 1st movie premiere in Clunes Auditorium: D. W. Griffith's "Birth of a Nation."

1917 1st million dollar movie contract signed by Mary Pickford.

1917 1st Forest Lawn memorial park created by Dr. Hubert Eaton.

1918 University of California opens Southern Branch—later renamed UCLA.

1918 1st air passenger line in world: San Pedro to Catalina.

1921 1st airmail and air passenger service connects LA with NY.

1921 1st of the Watts Towers completed by Simon Rodia.

1922 1st summer "Symphonies Under the Stars" as Hollywood Bowl opens.

1922 1st shopping center: A. W. Ross buys 18 acres of bean fields on Wilshire Blvd.; begins "Miracle Mile."

1922 1st radio stations: KFI and KHJ.

1922 1st studio premiere: "Robin Hood" in Grauman's Egyptian.

1923 1st local Rose Bowl victory: USC over Penn State 14-3.

1923 1st Chinese admitted to the Bar.

1925 1st motel.

1925 1st tours of movie stars' homes.

1927 1st footprints at Grauman's Chinese Theatre: Norma Talmadge.

1927 1st boysenberries: Rudolph Boysen crosses Logan, Black, and Raspberries.

1927 1st supermarket: Ralph's.

1927 1st sound musical: "The Jazz Singer."

1928 1st Mickey Mouse.

1928 1st national air races.

1931 1st tourist "theme park": Olvera Street opens.

1933 1st Phillip Marlowe: Raymond Chandler begins mysteries about LA detective.

1933 1st drive-in movie: Pico Blvd (between Overland and Westwood Blvds).

1933 1st "in-flight movie": "The Crooked Circle" broadcast by experimental television station.

1933 1st TV broadcast of a breaking news story: rapid-fire filmclips of Long Beach earthquake.

1934 1st Nisei Week celebration in "Little Tokyo."

1936 1st Boulder Dam hydroelectric power reaches LA over then world's largest transmission line.

1936 1st DC-3 built by Douglas Aircraft.

1938 1st drive-in restaurant.

1940 1st freeway, Arroyo Seco Parkway.

1942 1st Japanese-Americans leave LA for evacuees' city at Manzanar.

1943 1st American ship honoring a black man: *S.S. Booker T. Washington* launched in LA Harbor.

1943 1st acute air pollution: visibility reduced to 3 blocks; termed "gas attack," "smoke nuisance," or "daylight dimout."

1944 1st use of the word "smog."

1945 1st Baskin Robbins.

1946 1st smog-control ordinances.

1947 1st commercial TV broadcasting—W6XYZ becomes KTLA Channel 4.

1947 1st faster-than-sound flight—Chuck Yeager.

1948 1st TV sports contract—UCLA and USC sign with CBS.

1948 1st Rolls-Royce dealer in the US: Peter Satori.

1949 1st "Emmy" awards.

1950 1st regular TV news programming.

1951 1st color broadcast—KTTV (CBS).

1953 1st LA Catholic Cardinal: Rev. John MacIntyre.

1953 1st ICBM production.

1954 1st McDonald's franchise sold by Ray Kroc.

1955 1st LA child receives Salk polio vaccine.

1958 1st LA "skyscraper": California Bank.

1959 1st LA World Pennant: Dodgers 4-2 over Chicago.

1959 1st Barbie Doll manufactured by Mattel.

1962 1st person to receive Nobel Prize twice: Linus Pauling.

1962 1st black appointed to City Council— Gilbert W. Lindsay.

1973 1st black LA Mayor: Thomas Bradley.

1980 1st approximation of ethnic ratio of civic founding fathers: minorities outnumber former white majority.

1981 1st yearlong Bicentennial Celebration.

1981 1st LA resident elected U.S. President.

Los Angeles entered recorded history in 1542 when navigator Juan Rodriguez Cabrillo noted the bay of San Pedro, which he called Bahia de los Fumos (Bay of the Smokes) because of the numerous campfires in the hills.

The owners of the campfires, the Gabrieleno Indians, had been in the Los Angeles Basin for over one thousand years at the time of Cabrillo's discovery, living peacefully as they gathered acorns from the live oaks covering the golden land. Although the Spanish claimed the territory, they did not explore it until 1769, when Gaspar de Portolá, Governor of the Californias, led a charting expedition through the area. Using maps drawn by Portolá and Fr. Juan Crespí, Mission San Gabriel Arcángel was founded in 1771 by the Franciscan order to secure title to the region through occupation and bring Christianity to the Indians. Fertile soil, benevolent climate, ample water, and a large supply of Indian laborers quickly brought prosperity. This success encouraged the Spanish government to sponsor a pueblo on the banks of the Porciúncula River, noted as a promising spot by Fr. Crespí. On September 4, 1781, a band of 44 settlers founded El Pueblo de la Reina de los Angeles (the Town of the Queen of the Angels). The pueblo flourished, and by the end of the 18th century, was producing and raising more grain, cattle, sheep, and horses than any other place in California. Generous grants of ranch land were made to retired soldiers by the governor of the Californias, and soon the colony was divided into mission, pueblo, and rancho.

In 1810, Fr. Hidalgo's "Grito de Delores" started the Mexican War of Independence from Spain. The Mexicans were victorious in 1821 and declared the Republic of Mexico in 1823. California was made a territory of the Republic in 1825. During Mexican rule, from 1825 to 1847, the rancheros were self-sufficient—with wealth from trade in hides, tallow, wine, and brandy—and merry, enjoying a round of barbecue parties that often lasted for days. Labor was provided by Indians under the direction of Mexican and Californio vaqueros. The property of the missions was redistributed from 1834 to 1836, which vastly enriched the rancheros.

By the late 1840s, Los Angeles was the largest town in California. Yankee traders made contacts with the Californios during this period, drawn by low prices for hides and otter skins. Some adventurous Yankees married the daughters of the rancheros, began business enterprises and soon almost monopolized the finance and commerce of the region. Los Angeles was the prize of the western theater during the Mexican-American War. On August 13, 1846, Captain John C. Frémont entered the pueblo and declared it an American territory. The Californios put up a spirited resistance that culminated with their defeat at the Battle of La Mesa by the forces of General Stephen W. Kearny and Commodore Robert F. Stockton. The Treaty of Cahuenga ending the war was signed on January 13, 1847.

A period of great prosperity began soon afterward: the discovery of gold in Northern California resulted in a flood of hungry treasure hunters. Southland cattle, formerly prized only for their hides and tallow, suddenly looked delicious and fortunes were made shipping meat to the miners. The introduction of a cash economy to replace the barter economy of the Mexican era forced the rancheros to mortgage their land to obtain money; by 1865, four-fifths of the ranchos were in American hands. Los Angeles grew slowly and steadily from 1865 to 1885. An exhibit in the East of irrigation-grown Southern California fruit provoked interest in local agriculture. Journalists touted the therapeutic climate and invalids came seeking health. In 1869, the Southern Pacific completed the transcontinental railroad at San Francisco and triggered a small land boom in the early 1870s. In 1886, the Santa Fe completed its LA link of the transcontinental railroad, breaking the Southern Pacific monopoly. In the ensuing rate war, the price of a St. Louis-LA ticket dropped at one point to $1. A land boom exploded, formulated from huge tracts of available land, cheap transportation, delirious publicity, and hordes of Midwesterners eager to retire from snowy winters to a place where, as advertising had it, they could grow 19-foot tomato plants year round. By 1889, the boom had abated, but now Los Angeles was a household word.

1890 to 1900 could be called the Era of Great Beginnings. The most remarkable thing about the growth of this era is that it was brought about almost entirely through the will of the leading citizens. Lacking water, a natural harbor, fuel, and resources that historically have led to the development of great cities, but endowed by immigration with a group of men who possessed foresight and furiously entrepeneurial spirits, LA created the things that were needed. A public transport system was inaugurated, water supplies enlarged, oil discovered, the harbor improved. A newly formed Chamber of Commerce promoted Southern California, especially in the Midwest. Communities outside the original 28-square-mile land grant were annexed to the City of Los Angeles, initiating a pattern that would ultimately increase its area by almost 200%. LA was a tourist town from 1900 to 1920. Hundreds of thousands came annually as visitors, and many stayed as new residents. Water was brought 250 miles from the Owens Valley via a huge aqueduct and was used as a lure for further annexation of surrounding communities: in 1915, the San Fernando Valley joined the city, more than doubling its area. The wave of immigration between 1920 and 1940 has been characterized as the largest internal migration in the history of the United States. The automobile became the Calistoga wagon of the new pioneer. The Depression did nothing to abate the flow, as unemployed workers flocked in looking for opportunity. New industry enriched the economy: airplanes, clothing, and tires joined oil, movies, and oranges as made-in-LA products. Colorado River water was brought 392 miles to slake the city's omnipresent thirst.

Since 1940, LA has become a major metropolitan center, the attractions of climate and terrain augmented by the presence of profitable industry. It has the second largest population in the United States spread out over the largest municipal area in the nation. After 200 years, the vitality that fed the growth from pueblo to metropolis is undiminished.

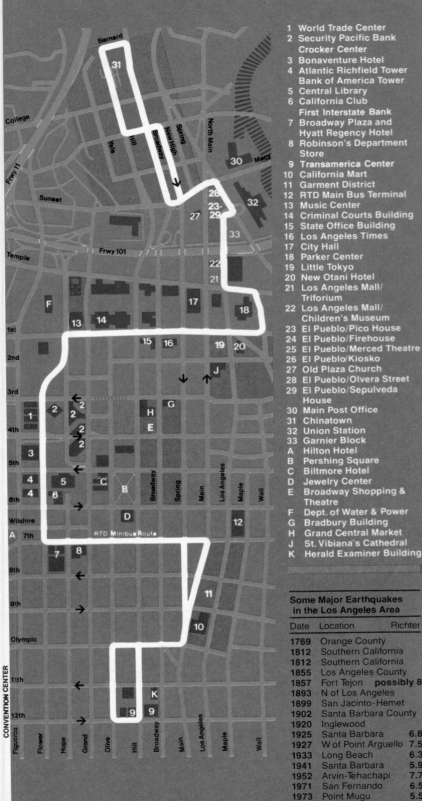

1 World Trade Center
2 Security Pacific Bank
  Crocker Center
3 Bonaventure Hotel
4 Atlantic Richfield Tower
  Bank of America Tower
5 Central Library
6 California Club
  First Interstate Bank
7 Broadway Plaza and
  Hyatt Regency Hotel
8 Robinson's Department
  Store
9 Transamerica Center
10 California Mart
11 Garment District
12 RTD Main Bus Terminal
13 Music Center
14 Criminal Courts Building
15 State Office Building
16 Los Angeles Times
17 City Hall
18 Parker Center
19 Little Tokyo
20 New Otani Hotel
21 Los Angeles Mall/
   Triforium
22 Los Angeles Mall/
   Children's Museum
23 El Pueblo/Pico House
24 El Pueblo/Firehouse
25 El Pueblo/Merced Theatre
26 El Pueblo/Kiosko
27 Old Plaza Church
28 El Pueblo/Olvera Street
29 El Pueblo/Sepulveda
   House
30 Main Post Office
31 Chinatown
32 Union Station
33 Garnier Block
A Hilton Hotel
B Pershing Square
C Biltmore Hotel
D Jewelry Center
E Broadway Shopping &
  Theatre
F Dept. of Water & Power
G Bradbury Building
H Grand Central Market
J St. Vibiana's Cathedral
K Herald Examiner Building

Some Major Earthquakes in the Los Angeles Area

Date	Location	Richter
1769	Orange County	
1812	Southern California	
1812	Southern California	
1855	Los Angeles County	
1857	Fort Tejon	possibly 8
1893	N of Los Angeles	
1899	San Jacinto-Hemet	
1902	Santa Barbara County	
1920	Inglewood	
1925	Santa Barbara	6.8
1927	W of Point Arguello	7.5
1933	Long Beach	6.3
1941	Santa Barbara	5.9
1952	Arvin-Tehachapi	7.7
1971	San Fernando	6.5
1973	Point Mugu	5.5
1978	Santa Barbara	5.1

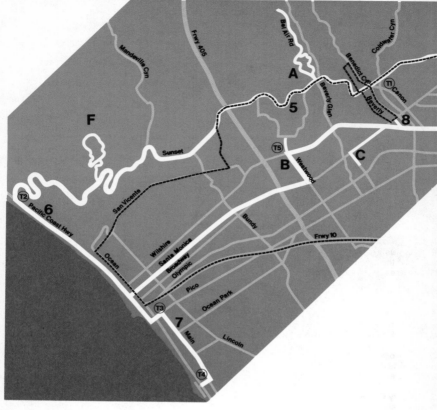

■■■Gray Line Tours for information call 481-2121

1. Pershing Square. This park is located in the center of the city's financial and commercial activities. Refer to areas **2** and **3**.

2. City Hall/Civic Center. Most of the city's governmental functions take place within this quadrant of municipal offices and courtrooms. Refer to area **1**.

3. El Pueblo de Los Angeles. The historic center of the city, where small shops and stalls recall the lifestyle of the founders. Refer to area **1**.

4. Sunset Strip. The adult playground of Los Angeles, with a concentration of nightclubs, restaurants and billboards. Refer to area **5**.

5. UCLA. One of the finest educational institutions in the world, UCLA is a major academic center of the southland. Refer to area **7**.

6. Palisades Park. The precipitous bluffs of the Palisades are the western edge of the city. The view from this spot is always impressive. Refer to area **8**.

Time: 6-8 hours
Mileage: approximately 50 miles
Area: A loop from city center and back via two major boulevards, Sunset and Wilshire. The tour includes the main commercial, civic, historic, entertainment, educational and cultural centers of Los Angeles, and may be taken by bus or car.

7. Main Street, Santa Monica. This stylish street is a preview of what's upcoming in clothes and furniture, with some nostalgia added to sweeten the mix. Refer to area **8**.

8. Rodeo Drive. One of the finest shopping streets in the world, a center of luxury and focus of fashion. Refer to area **6**.

9. County Museum of Art/La Brea Tar Pits. An excursion through history and art. The past, present and future meet on the edge of the tarry pits. Refer to area **4**.

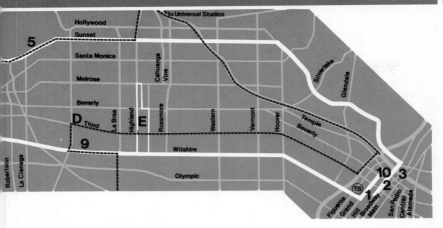

10. The Music Center. Focus of the music and theater of the city, symbol of the cultural life of Los Angeles. Refer to area **2.**

Detours

A. Bel Air. A community of the rich and famous with most of the homes discreetly veiled by greenery. Refer to area **7.**

B. Westwood Village. Small shops and restaurants combine in a people-scaled, urbane experience. Refer to area **7.**

C. Century City. A planned complex of theatres, shops and restaurants with a decidedly 21st century atmosphere. Refer to area **6.**

D. Farmer's Market. Relax and enjoy luscious sights and tastes in a homey, sun-dappled setting. Refer to area **4.**

E. Hancock Park. Location of some of the stateliest mansions in town, most of which are visible from the street. See area **4.**

F. Will Rogers State Park. 31-room house with the country philosopher's original Indian and Western decor/artifacts. 186-acre park has hiking and nature trails, picnic area (no fires). *Oct-Feb 8AM-5PM, Mar-Apr 8AM-6PM, May-Sept 8AM-7PM. House opens 10AM. Fee. 14253 Sunset Blvd. 454-8121*

Automotive mobility is the birthright of Angelenos.

Although the city had existed for over 100 years before the first rubber wheels cut ruts in the dirt streets, LA took to the car more quickly and enthusiastically than any other city. The decentralization that has been the pattern since the very beginning encouraged the use of the auto, both by need—the distances between communities were great and the public transport system sparse in outlying areas—and by accommodation, because the sporadic early building had left large open spaces suitable for use as parking lots and garages. Freeways have come to be identified with LA so strongly that it is a shock to realize that they have been here for a relatively short time. The first freeway was the Arroyo Parkway, later rechristened the Pasadena Freeway, which opened in 1940. A program of national highway construction began in the 1950s and resulted in almost 700 miles of well-maintained freeways that now bind together the various municipalities of the County of Los Angeles. The auto reigns as the economic, social, and psychic energizer in the Southland. Distances are measured in time rather than miles, and the password of the true Angeleno is the reply "thirty minutes" to the question, "How far to the airport?"

Cars are venerated as indicators of wealth, class, political beliefs, taste, and personal habits. The personalized license plate, a California invention, becomes the ultimate public telegram in Los Angeles, condensing love, wit, and pride down to seven letters. The following rules of the road will help the visitor ease into the LA life on wheels:

• Do not stop on the freeway. If you have a mechanical problem, take the nearest exit or pull over to the right shoulder of the road. Yellow call boxes are located at frequent intervals along the highway; you are allowed one free call for help.

• Entry lanes on to the freeway are used to integrate into the flow of traffic. The entering vehicle does not have the right of way.

• Slower vehicles to the right. Honking the horn is not an LA custom; if you are driving at a speed that impedes the flow of traffic, other drivers will quietly perform death-inciting maneuvers to pass you.

• Right-hand turns are allowed on a red light unless prohibited by sign. Make a full stop first to determine that the way is clear.

• Pedestrians have the right of way anywhere. A combination of this law and a conviction that anyone on foot is suicidal will lead drivers to screech on their brakes when they see a jaywalker.

• Pedestrians should use marked crosswalks Jaywalking is illegal and tickets are issued to those who defy the law.

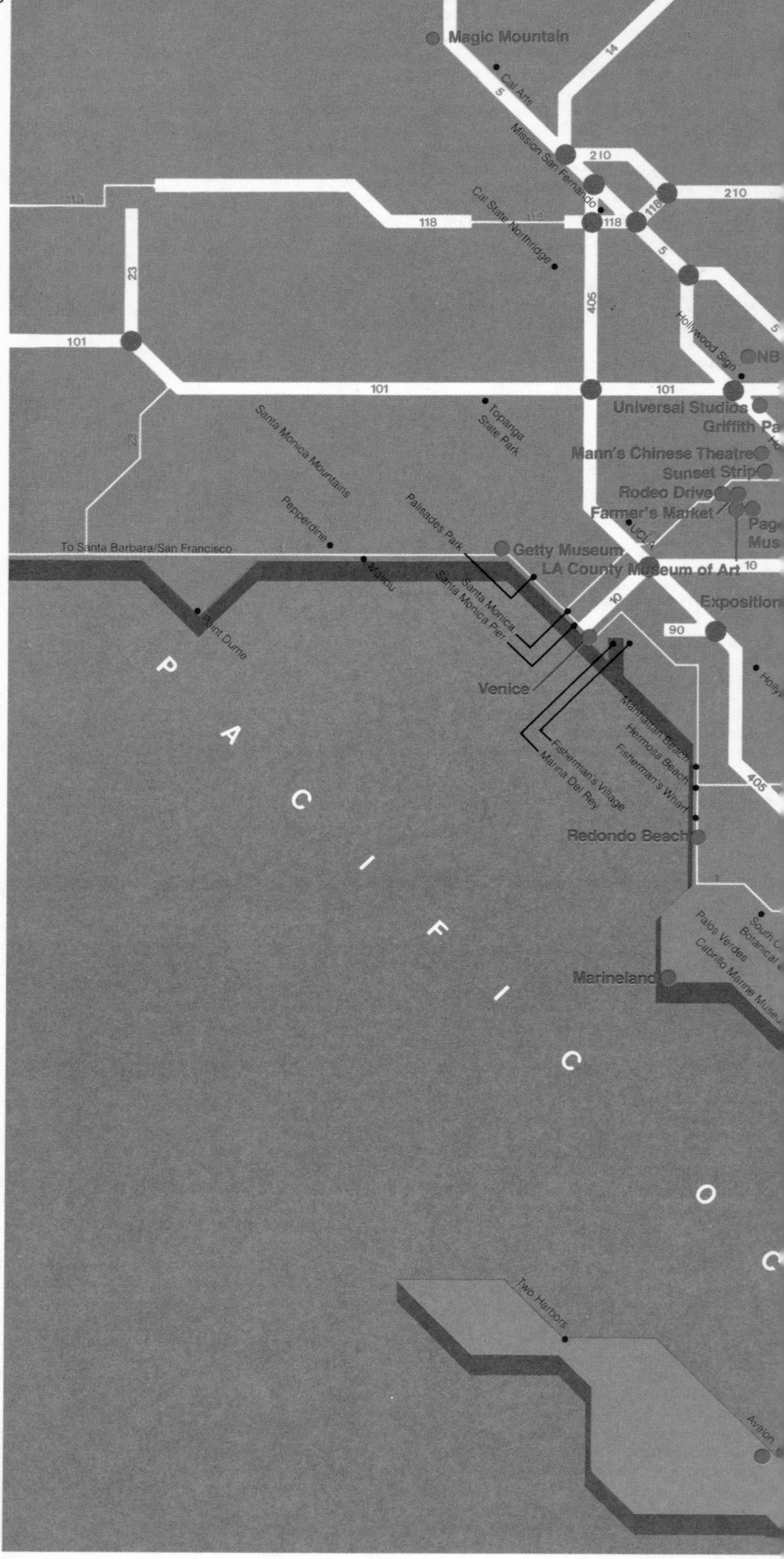

LA/GRAND TOUR

Magic Mountain

14

Cal Arts

5

Mission San Fernando

210

210

118

118

118

118

118

5

23

Cal State Northridge

Hollywood Sign

101

NB

405

Universal Studios

Griffith Pa

101

101

Santa Monica Mountains

Topanga
State Park

Mann's Chinese Theatre

Sunset Strip

Rodeo Drive

Farmer's Market

Pepperdine

Pag
Mus

To Santa Barbara/San Francisco

Palisades Park

Getty Museum

UCLA

Malibu

Santa Monica

Santa Monica Pier

LA County Museum of Art

10

Point Dume

10

Exposition

90

Holly

Venice

Manhattan Beach

Hermosa Beach

Fisherman's Village

Fisherman's Wharf

405

Marina Del Rey

Redondo Beach

P A C I F I C

South
Botanical

Palos Verdes

Cabrillo Marine Muse

Marineland

O

C

Two Harbors

Avalon

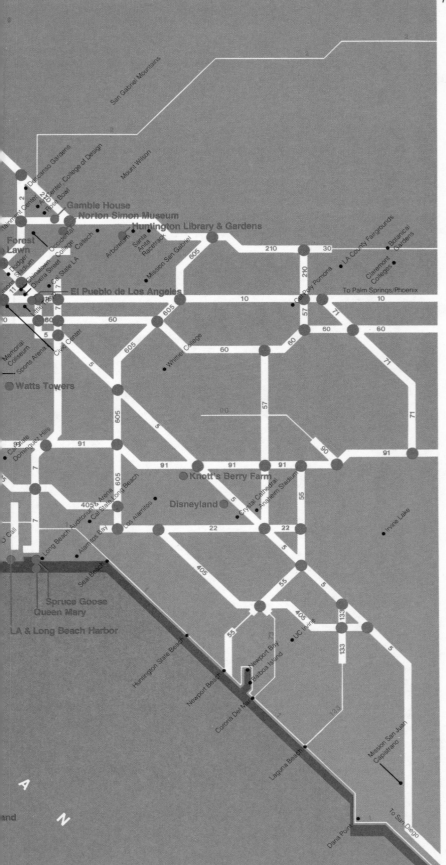

San Gabriel Mountains

Mount Wilson

Descanso Gardens
Art Center College of Design
tainment Center
Rose Bowl
Gamble House
Norton Simon Museum
Huntington Library & Gardens
Occidental College
Caltech
Arboretum
Santa Anita Racetrack
Mission San Gabriel
Forest Lawn
Dodger
Stadium
Chinatown
Olvera Street
Cal State LA
El Pueblo de Los Angeles
Little Tokyo
Memorial
Coliseum
Sports Arena
Civic Center
Watts Towers

210
30
LA County Fairgrounds
Botanical Gardens
Claremont Colleges
Cal Poly Pomona
To Palm Springs/Phoenix
210
605
10
10
57
60
71
71
605
60
605
5
Whittier College
60
80
60
605
57
90
91
Cal State
Dominguez Hills
91
91
91
91
91
Knott's Berry Farm
91
605
5
90
91
405 & Arena
Cal State Long Beach
Disneyland
Crystal Cathedral
Anaheim Stadium
5
55
22
Los Alamitos
22
22
5
405
55
5
Long Beach Auditorium &
Alamitos Bay
5
55
405
133
133
Spruce Goose
Queen Mary
Seal Beach
405
LA & Long Beach Harbor
53
133
Huntington State Beach
UC Irvine
Irvine Lake
Newport Beach
Newport Bay
Balboa Island
Corona Del Mar
Mission San Juan Capistrano
Laguna Beach
N
Dana Point
To San Diego

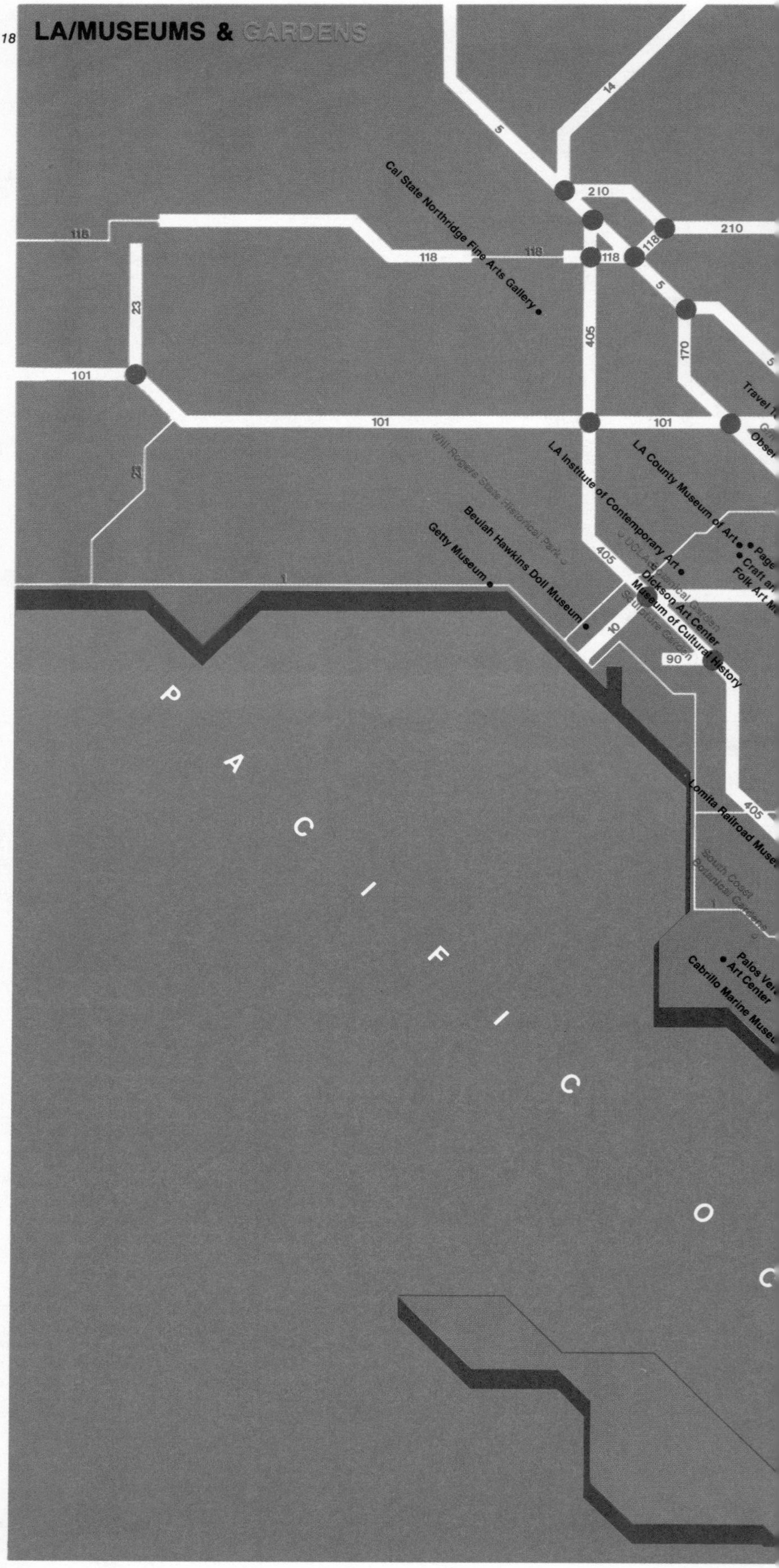

14

5

210

210

118

118

118

118

118

5

23

170

101

5

405

Travel T

101

101

C

Obser

Will Rogers State Historical Park

LA Institute of Contemporary Art

LA County Museum of Art

Dickson Art Center

Page

Cal State Northridge Fine Arts Gallery

405

Craft a

Folk Art M

Beulah Hawkins Doll Museum

Museum of Cultural History

Getty Museum

Sculpture Garden

10

90

Lomita Railroad Museum

405

South Coast Botanical Garden

P

A

C

I

F

I

C

Palos Ver

Art Center

Cabrillo Marine Museu

O

C

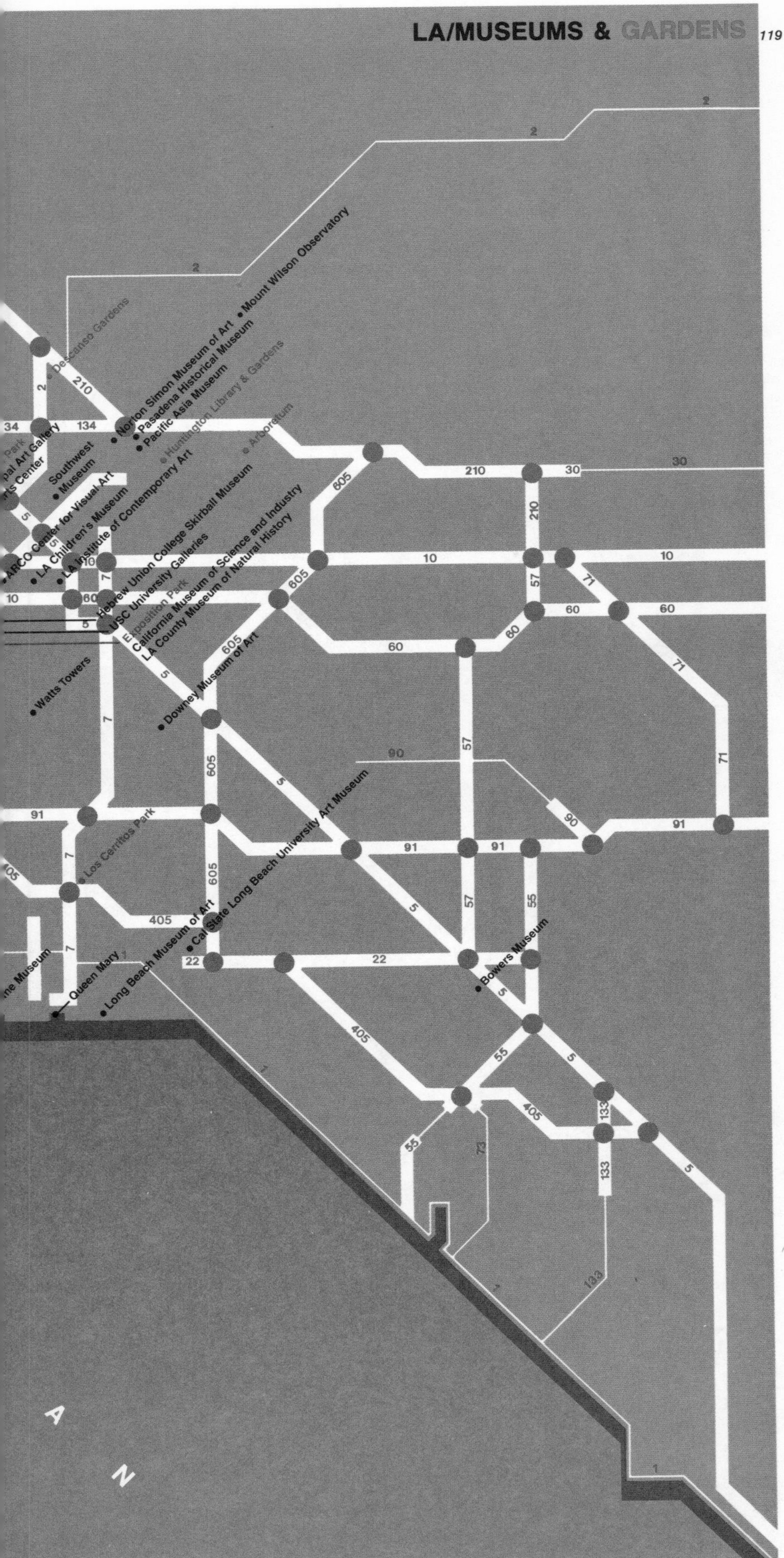

2

2

2

Descanso Gardens

34

210

34

Norton Simon Museum of Art • Mount Wilson Observatory
• Pasadena Historical Museum
• Pacific Asia Museum

134

al Art Gallery

rs Center

• Southwest
  Museum

• Huntington Library & Gardens

• Arboretum

5

• ARCO Center for Visual Art

• LA Children's Museum

• LA Institute of Contemporary Art

Hebrew Union College Skirball Museum

USC University Galleries

Exposition Park

California Museum of Science and Industry

LA County Museum of Natural History

• Watts Towers

• Downey Museum of Art

10

210

30

30

605

210

210

10

10

10

60

57

71

60

60

60

80

71

60

7

5

5

90

57

71

605

605

7

91

57

90

90

91

• Los Cerritos Park

91

91

91

55

405

605

Long Beach University Art Museum

Cal State Long Beach

5

57

405

7

• Queen Mary

Long Beach Museum of Art

22

22

Bowers Museum

ne Museum

22

5

405

55

5

55

73

5

133

133

133

A

N

55

133

1

LA/KIDS' AMUSEMENTS/SPORTS

Lake Casitas (Canoeing; Rowing)

• Magic Mountain

14

5

210

210

118

118

118

118

5

23

Pierce College Working Farm •

Mann's Chinese Theatre

LA County Museum of Art

170

Merry-

Travel Town
Griffith Park
Universal Studios •

101

Renaissance Pleasure Faire •

Malibu Creek State Park Nature Walk •

101

101

23

Malibu Municipal Pier •

Topanga State Park

Citizen's Savings Athletic Foundation & Museum

405

Pag

10

Santa Monica
Municipal Pier

Corral State Beach

Malibu Surfrider State Beach

Las Tunas State Beach

Topanga State Beach

Will Rogers State Beach

Venice Municipal Pier

10

UC

Loyola Marymount Un

Zuma County Beach

Santa Monica State Beach

Point Dume State Beach

P

A

C

Dockweiler State Beach

El Segundo

Manhattan Beach

Hermose Beach

Redondo Beach

Torrance

Palos Verdes

405

Railroad Mus

Redondo Beach
Municipal Pier

I

Bicycling

Surfing

Beaches

Cabrillo Marine Mus

Marineland

Sou

Botani

Gardens

Cabrillo

F

Abalone Cove

I

C

O

C

Catalina Island

• Mt. Waterman

2

2

• Krakta Ridge

• Mt. Baldy

2

• Rose Bowl (Football)

• Olvera Street — Chinatown   • Mt. Wilson Skyline Park & Children's Zoo

• Southwest Museum

• Union Station

• Plaza de La Raza   • Huntington Library & Gardens

• Raymond Alf Museum

134   134

• Arboretum

dall Park

nicipal Art Gallery

r Arts Center

• State Anita Park (Equestrian)

39

11

210

30

• CSU Los Angeles (Judo)   • East LA College

• LA Children's Museum   • Little Tokyo

210

Snow Summit
Snow Valley
Arrowhead Lake
Big Bear Lake

• El Mercado

• LA Times Press Room

• Grand Central Market

• Shrine Auditorium

5

• Exposition Park

• California Museum of Science & Industry

• LA County Museum of Natural History   • Whittier Narrows Nature Center

57   71

10

60   60

805

• Watts Towers

7

605

60

71

91   91

605

5

• CSU Dominguez Hills (Cycling)

91

90   57

• California Alligator Farm

• CSU Fullerton (Handball)

91   91

90

91

71

• LA & Long Beach Harbor

• Los Alamitos Racetrack

• Queen Mary

• Knott's Berry Farm   • Disneyland

• Anaheim Stadium

55

• Maritime Museum

405   7

• Ports O' Call

• El Dorado Park (Archery)

• Long Beach Convention Center/Arena (Volleyball)

• Long Beach Marina (Yachting)

22   22

• Alamitos Bay

• Huntington Harbor/Anaheim Bay

• Anaheim Convention Center (Wrestling)

• Bowers Museum

5

Coto de Caza
(Modern Pentathlon)

• Huntington Beach Pier

405

55

5

• Bolsa Chica State Beach

55

• Huntington State Beach

• Newport Bay/Balboa Park

• Newport Dunes Aquatic Park

• Balboa Ferry

133

• Lion Country Safari

• Coal Canyon
(Shooting)

133

"Day before yesterday, as men measure
growth of cities, she was a baby, mewling and
puking; only yesterday her voice was
changing; today she bellows in a baritone;
tomorrow her basso profundo will be
heard around the world; for unless all signs
fail, Los Angeles is marked to be
one of the biggest cities in this hemisphere."

Irvin S. Cobb
1926

• Corona del Mar
State and City Beach

• Laguna Beach

• Dana Point

• Doheny
State Beach

135

Time: 3-6 hours

Mileage: 53 miles round trip from the intersection of the Santa Monica Freeway (10) and the Pacific Coast Highway (1)

Area: A drive up and down the Pacific Coast Highway past some of the loveliest beaches in Los Angeles County.

Take the Santa Monica Freeway (10) to its end at Santa Monica, where it will merge into Pacific Coast Highway (1). Go north on this road for the tour. Although much of the beachfront is public, you will notice numerous private homes; many are elaborate residences of the rich and famous. Almost all the beaches are free and open to the public. A parking fee is charged in lots adjoining beach areas. On summer weekends, parking may be difficult to find. Getting across Pacific Coast Highway on foot or turning around in a car is dangerous; extreme caution is advised.

1 The first major public beach is **Will Rogers Beach State Park,** named for the famous cowboy humorist. This beach stretches for several miles along the Coast Highway and is well provided with parking, facilities and volleyball areas. Surfers congregate along the area opposite Sunset Blvd.

You may detour up Sunset Blvd. to visit
2 **Will Rogers State Historic Park** or the
3 **Self Realization Foundation Lake Shrine.** Refer to area 7.

At the corner of Coastline Drive is the
4 **J. Paul Getty Museum.** Refer to area 9.

At Topanga Canyon Blvd., a right turn will take you on a detour to the semi-rural
5 community of **Topanga, Topanga Canyon**
6 **State Park,** or a drive to the **San Fernando Valley** over a winding and scenic canyon. Refer to area 9.

7 **Malibu** is a long stretch of beach with homes pressed against the ocean edge and dotting the chapparal-covered hills. The area on the right side of the Coast Highway is subject to landslides; you will notice retaining walls holding back the earth. This is the site of Big Rock, a well-publicized episode that occurred when a keystone rock was removed, causing a series of landslides which closed the Coast Highway for several months. The area is now stabilized with concrete and steel bolts. **Malibu** is one of the most famous of the seaside communities, as much for its residents as for its scenery.

8 **The Malibu Sportfishing Pier,** located about ten miles along our route, is a charming spot for surfer-watching and reviving breaths of ocean air.

Surf Riders State Beach, located just east
9 of **Malibu Point,** is a favorite with surfers.

About twelve miles out, you may take a detour right on Malibu Canyon Road, which traverses the Santa Monica Mountains to the San Fernando Valley, following the edge of a colorful and rugged canyon with some fine vista turn-outs along the way. **Malibu**
10 **Creek State Park** is located beside this
11 road. This is also the road to **Pepperdine College.**

12 **Paradise Cove** is located just east of **Point Dume,** approximately 16 miles along our route. It is a sheltered beach with white sand, tumbled sandstone cliffs, and fishing and boat launching facilities. Admission is charged.

13 **Zuma Beach** is on the west side of **Point Dume.** This broad, flat beach is one of the most popular, offering volleyball, facilities, easy parking, miles of smooth sand, and good body and board surfing.

14 **Leo Carillo Beach** is pretty and secluded, located in a wide cove that is slightly sheltered by rocks at either end. The northern portion of the beach is popular with surfers. Swimmers should go to the center of the cove to avoid underwater rock formations. This area has had very little development so far, giving a feel of how it looked when the Indians were the only inhabitants of the beachfront.

Across the Coast Highway, approximately
15 26 miles from our start, is **Pt. Mugu State Park,** an expanse of rolling hills and sycamore-shaded canyons that is a perfect spot for an easy hike or a picnic. Refer to area 9.

To return, retrace your route on Pacific Coast Highway back to the Santa Monica Freeway.

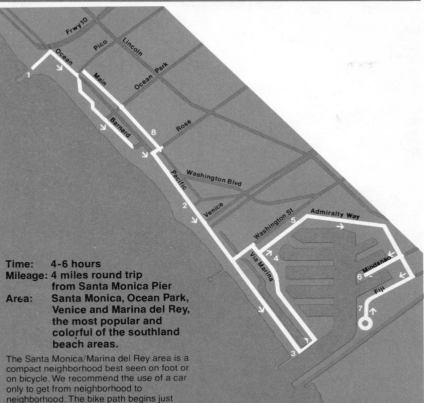

Time: 4-6 hours
Mileage: 4 miles round trip from Santa Monica Pier
Area: Santa Monica, Ocean Park, Venice and Marina del Rey, the most popular and colorful of the southland beach areas.

The Santa Monica/Marina del Rey area is a compact neighborhood best seen on foot or on bicycle. We recommend the use of a car only to get from neighborhood to neighborhood. The bike path begins just north of the **Santa Monica Pier** and parallels the beach south to **Palos Verdes**, a distance of some 30 miles. A short ride through the Marina to Playa del Rey is highly recommended. The best walking and skating sites are on **Oceanfront Walk** between the Santa monica and **Venice Piers**, and along Main Street.

1 Begin at the **Santa Monica Pier** at Colorado and Ocean Avenues in Santa Monica. You might want to stop here for a carrousel ride to get you into the proper playful mood for the tour. Take Ocean Ave. south to the intersection with Pico where the road forks. Take the right hand fork that parallels the ocean: this is Bernard Way. Follow Bernard around to the left until it rejoins the former Ocean Ave., which has been rechristened Neilsen Way. Turn right at Neilsen and continue. Surprisingly, the street changes names again in the next block as you enter Venice and becomes Pacific Ave.

Continue down Pacific past the corner of
2 **Windward**, the last remnant of old Venice, Abbot Kinney's glorious dream of a renaissance for Southern California. Roller skate rental stands abound in this area.

At Washington St., a short stroll takes you to the **Venice Pier** for views, fishing, people watching and snacks. There are several bicycle rental shops along this street. Continue down Pacific. You are now
3 entering **Marina del Rey**, about three miles from the Santa Monica Pier. The Marina section of Pacific takes you past frayed relics of the old Venice: canals, bridges, and a few disguised oil wells.

At the end of Pacific where it abuts on Via Marina is a small promenade area and jetty looking out over the Marina del Rey entrance channel. This is a fine place to stop and watch the sailboats glide by. The

air at the tip of the jetty is always brisk and refreshing. Via Marina curves around the entrance channel and enters a densely-built area of apartments and condominiums until it reaches Admiralty Way.

At the corner of Admiralty Way and Via
4 Marina is a public park with facilities and a small protected beach with a children's swimming area.

Turn right on to Admiralty. At five and a half
5 miles you will pass the **Bird Sanctuary** on the left and the **Marina City Towers** on the right.

Follow Admiralty to Mindanao Way and turn right. Continue to the end of the street where you will find the entrance to **Burton**
6 **Chace Park.** The well-maintained park has picnic areas, soft grassy knolls, facilities, and a tower to climb and watch the boats in the marina.

Return to Admiralty and turn right to the next peninsula: Fiji Way. Go right again to
7 **Fisherman's Village**, a place for shopping and strolling.

Follow Fiji back to Admiralty and go left. At the corner of Admiralty and Via Marina, go right. Go to Washington St. and turn left. Go a few blocks to Pacific and turn right. At Rose Ave. (12½ miles), turn right, go one
8 block to **Main St.** and turn left.

8 **Main St.**, beginning near Marine St. and continuing almost to Pico is a delightful small shopping and dining area. Park in the city lots to the west of Main St. To return to downtown LA on the Santa Monica Freeway (10), follow Main St. to Pico, turn right, and at Lincoln Blvd., turn left. The freeway intersects Lincoln in two blocks.

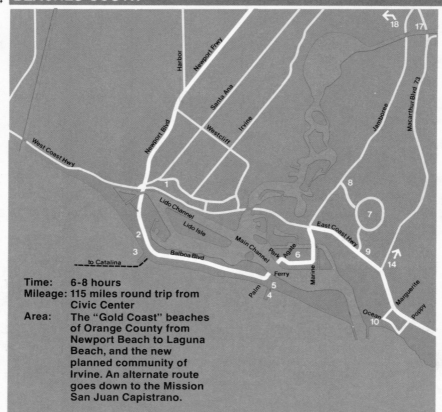

Time: 6-8 hours
Mileage: 115 miles round trip from Civic Center
Area: The "Gold Coast" beaches of Orange County from Newport Beach to Laguna Beach, and the new planned community of Irvine. An alternate route goes down to the Mission San Juan Capistrano.

Take the Santa Ana Freeway (5) south from Civic Center. An alternate route is the San Diego Freeway (405). At 34 miles, take the Newport Freeway (55) south. Go to the end of the freeway, where it becomes Newport Blvd., a four-to-six lane street. Continue
1 straight through Costa Mesa, into **Newport Beach.**

At 44 miles, get into the left lane and go
2 over the bridge on to the **Newport Peninsula.** You'll notice the yacht anchorage in the **Lido Channel** on your left as you pass over the bridge. Continue on Newport Blvd., which curves to the left as it follows the peninsula. Opposite the
3 **Newport Pier,** Newport Blvd. becomes Balboa Blvd.

At Palm St., turn into the parking lot for a
4 visit to the **Balboa Pier** to enjoy the ocean view and a breath of air. You can also rent roller skates here.

Walk across Balboa Blvd. into the **Fun Zone** for some snacking and playing and a visit to
5 the **Balboa Pavilion.**

6 To get to the ferry to **Balboa Island,** follow the signs from the parking lot to the crossing. The fare for the three minute cruise across the **Main Channel** across the **Main Channel** aboard the *Admiral, Commodore,* or *Captain* is 60ᶜ for autos, 15ᶜ for pedestrians. When you disembark at Agate, continue straight for two blocks to Park. Go right and travel through a neighborhood of ship-shape homes to Marine. Go left on Marine, through the center of the business district, and over Back Bay Channel on a little bridge. Continue straight a short distance to Bayside Dr., veer left and continue up the hill to East Coast Highway. Go right, past
7 the **Fashion Island Shopping Center.**

8 For a detour to shop or to visit the **Newport Harbor Art Museum,** go left at Newport Center Drive.

Continue straight on East Coast Highway,
9 past the **Sherman Foundation Gardens,** and turn right on Marguerite. Go through beautifully manicured residential streets to Ocean. Turn left and park near the hilly knoll
10 that tops **Corona del Mar State Beach.** This is a beautiful seaside area, rocky on the south, sandy cove on the north, with a superb view. There is excellent swimming in the northern waters that are protected by the east jetty of the Newport Harbor entrance.

Follow Ocean to Poppy and turn left back to East Coast Highway. Turn right on to the Coast Highway and continue south. The stretch between Poppy and Laguna Beach has rolling golden hills coming down to meet the undeveloped beach, giving a last glimpse of what the coast was like prior to
11 the Twentieth Century. **Cameo Cove,** just north of Laguna Beach city limits, is a breathtaking scene of dark rock promentory and emerald green water.

At approximately 55 miles, you enter
12 **Laguna Beach,** an area known for beautiful scenery and scenic artists. Go left at Forest Ave. Park to spend some time strolling down pleasant, shop-lined streets, or cross the Coast Highway to follow the Pacific along the boardwalk.

To return to Los Angeles from this point, go north a short distance on Coast Highway to Broadway. Go right to Laguna Canyon Road (133), and then to the San Diego Freeway (405).

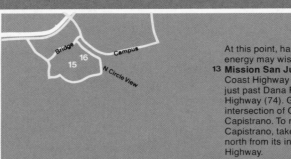

At this point, hardy souls with unflagging energy may wish to continue south to

13 **Mission San Juan Capistrano.** Follow Coast Highway down to Obispo St., which is just past Dana Point. Go left to Ortega Highway (74). Go right to the mission at the intersection of Ortega Highway and Camino Capistrano. To return to Los Angeles from Capistrano, take the San Diego Freeway (5) north from its intersection with Ortega Highway.

14 To continue back up to **Irvine** from Laguna Beach, return north on Coast Highway to MacArthur Blvd. (73). Go right.

Lovers of trees, education and/or architecture may wish to detour to the

15 **University of California at Irvine.** From MacArthur, go right on University to Campus. Go right on Campus to Bridge. Go right on Bridge to North Circle View Drive;

6 then turn left. **The Administration Building** and **Visitor Center** are located on the right-hand side of North Circle View Dr.

Meanwhile, the future may be taking shape

17 in the **Irvine Industrial Park,** located on both sides of MacArthur Blvd. The simple, monolithic shapes of these new structures contain business concerns whose product is invisible in many cases: computer software, technological systems, and other forms of up-to-the-minute-know-how.

18 **John Wayne Airport,** located on the left of the Boulevard, is one of the busiest small craft airports in the nation.

To return to Los Angeles, go to the San Diego Freeway (405) on MacArthur Blvd. and head north.

Southern California's population forecast is out for the remainder of the Twentieth Century, and it looks like a storm may be brewing. Three million newcomers are expected to swell outlying areas until these compete with the city of Los Angeles in size. Some predictions put the total regional population at nearly *15 million* by the turn of the century. While early reports pinpointed areas such as Downtown LA to Santa Monica and Anaheim/Santa Ana as major growth centers, new figures indicate that the influx of people will spread throughout Los Angeles, Orange, Riverside, San Bernardino, Ventura and Imperial counties. The growth forecasts are creating a flurry of activity among local urban planners and city managers. No one is sure whether the 140 cities included in the report can accommodate such rapid growth, or the consequences if they can't.

Take the Harbor Freeway (11) south toward San Pedro. The land extending on either side of the road is the "shoestring strip" of the City of Los Angeles, a narrow stretch in the middle of unincorporated County territory that extends down to the Port of Los Angeles.

At the intersection of the Harbor Freeway and the San Diego Freeway (405) continue straight toward San Pedro on the Harbor Freeway. You'll notice the Palos Verdes hills on the right.

To get to the **Banning Museum**, exit on Pacific Coast Highway (1) and go left. The Museum is located on "M" Street, one block south of Pacific Coast Highway, just past Avalon Blvd. Turn right on Eubank Ave., and go right on "M" St. Surrounded by a grove of mature trees, the symmetrical, three-story Greek Revival style building has been restored to its condition ca. 1865-1885 when it was the home of General Phineas Banning, father of the Los Angeles Harbor. This mansion vividly illustrates the life style of the first wave of industrious Yankee entrepreneurs who immigrated to the southland.

To continue the journey, go back to the Harbor Freeway and continue south when the freeway ends at Gaffey St. Go through the center of San Pedro to 37th Street where you'll see the tile-roofed pavillion of the **Korean Bell of Friendship** rising above the horizon. Make a right turn into the unmarked gate opposite 37th St. The huge bell was a gift from the people of

Korea to the people of the United States for the U.S. Bicentennial in 1976. It was made in Korea and is the largest bell cast in that country since the 8th century. Angels' Gate Park, the site of the bell, offers a superb view of the coastline, from the Palos Verdes Peninsula on the north to Alamitos Bay on the south. The park takes its name from the entry gap in the nine mile breakwater of the Port of Los Angeles, which is on your left as you gaze out over the Pacific. Point Fermin is located directly in front of you.

Go back down 37th St. to Pacific Ave. and turn left, then right at 36th St., which turns into Stephen M. White Dr. Continue down Stephen M. White Dr., bear left past the large black anchors, past the guard kiosk, around the little turn-about surrounding the statue of Cabrillo, and into the parking lot of the **Cabrillo Marine Museum**. The striking modern structure of the museum, an amalgam of oblique white stucco angles and a cyclone-fence superstructure, houses an exhibit hall which interprets the California marine environment and includes 32 salt water tanks containing various forms of local sea life. The Point Fermin Marine Refuge is located behind the Spanish style boathouse which formerly housed the Cabrillo Marine Museum. These natural tidepools make for a fascinating stroll at low tide, when the small anemones, starfish, crabs and other creatures are most clearly visible in their rocky homes.

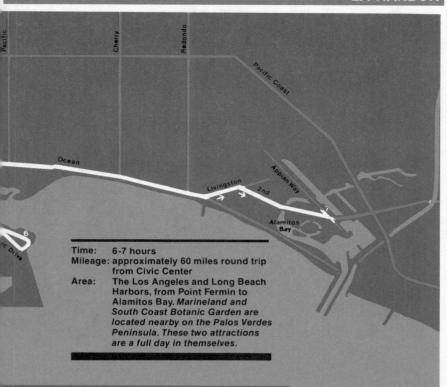

Time: 6-7 hours
Mileage: approximately 60 miles round trip from Civic Center
Area: The Los Angeles and Long Beach Harbors, from Point Fermin to Alamitos Bay. *Marineland and South Coast Botanic Garden are located nearby on the Palos Verdes Peninsula. These two attractions are a full day in themselves.*

Go back to Stephen M. White Dr., right to Pacific Ave. and right again on 22nd St. Drive toward the Main Channel of the harbor, passing the East and West Channels which are used for yacht anchorage. At the Signal St. stoplight, turn left over the little cement bridge in front of the Terminal Fisheries. Follow a small jog and go left in front of the fishing fleet anchorage. Turn right on to Harbor Blvd., in front of the Fisherman's Cooperative Association Building, parallel the Main Channel for a short distance, and then go right into the parking lot for **Ports O' Call Village**. Stop to stroll among the New England style shops, eat at one of the snack bars, ascend to the top of the 317 foot Sky Tower Crow's Nest for a panoramic view, take a Harbor Helicopter ride, or a one hour harbor cruise from the Village Boat House.

To continue, go right on Sampson Way, the street between the parking lot and Ports O' Call Village, to the **Los Angeles Maritime Museum**, located in the pale green building that formerly housed the Terminal Island Ferry. In front of the museum is the prow of the USS Los Angeles, a naval cruiser. Inside you'll find a pictographic history of the LA Harbor, and numerous fine models of ships and marine artifacts. The left gallery on the main floor retains the hoisting equipment from the old ferry, as well as the bridge of the USS Los Angeles. Opposite, on Terminal Island, and to the left, you'll see some of the container loading facilities, where towering cranes effortlessly lift 40 foot long sea containers.

Continue right on Harbor Blvd., past the passenger ship terminals and the Catalina terminal, toward the graceful turquoise arc of the Vincent Thomas Bridge. Follow the signs which direct you left to the bridge, and then experience a breath-taking moment of what

feels like free flight as you soar over the Main Channel at an altitude of 185 feet. There is a toll station at the end of the bridge; the fee is 25¢.

You are now on Terminal Island. Continue straight on Seaside Ave., which turns into Ocean Blvd. when you enter Long Beach. The Long Beach Naval Shipyards are located on your right. Cross over the Gerald Desmond Bridge, and continue straight on Ocean Blvd. until you see signs directing you to turn right on to Harbor Scenic Dr. to visit the **Queen Mary** and the **Spruce Goose**. Stop off at the Queen Mary for a shipboard stroll, a visit to the Living Sea exhibit, or a meal. The Spruce Goose, the largest wooden airplane ever built, is scheduled to open to the public in the parking lot across from the Queen Mary in Summer of 1982.

Return to Harbor Scenic Dr. and go back to Ocean Blvd. Turn right toward **Naples**, the last stop on the tour. Along Ocean Blvd. you'll pass some of the finest early-20th century homes in Long Beach. The Long Beach Museum of Art is located on Ocean Blvd. just before the Belmont Pier. Go left on Livingston Dr., opposite the Belmont Pier, and then right on to Second St. Continue straight on Second over the Alamitos Bay Bridge to Appian Way. Turn left and park in the public beach parking lot. Get out to stroll around the beautifully maintained homes of the lanes, walks and canals of Naples. You might walk south down Appian Way toward the Long Beach Marina for a sea and sail view; or cut back down Naples Plaza toward The Toledo, turn right and meander across the Rivo Alto Canal toward the Colonnade. As the sun sets over the Pacific, you can savor a quiet moment on the edge of the world.

Time: **Minimum tour: 2½-3 hours, maximum tour: 8 hours**

Mileage: **Minimum: 47 round trip from Ocean Ave. and Pacific Coast Hwy. in Santa Monica, Maximum: 100 miles with alternate routes round trip from Ocean Ave. and Pacific Coast Highway.**

Area: **Some of the most scenic but easily driven coastal mountain routes, showing rugged mountains, and beautiful ocean views.**

Begin at Pacific Coast Highway where the Santa Monica Freeway ends near the Santa Monica Pier. Follow Coast Highway north for 5.5 miles to Topanga Canyon Road.

Turn right on Topanga Canyon road. The narrow two-lane highway winds past a sycamore shaded creek at the base of chaparral-covered cliffs. As the road ascends into the hills you will see spectacular rock formations and abruptly tilted cliffs.

1 At about 10 miles is the main part of the rustic community of Topanga. The narrowness and sinuous winding of the road sometimes slows traffic—particularly on weekends.

At 15.2 miles the road descends to a panoramic view of the San Fernando Valley, and the Simi and Chatsworth Hills. This is a good place to stop and appreciate the huge expanse of the Valley's wide territory.

2 At 16.9 miles turn left on Mulholland Drive. A great deal of housing construction is going on in this once rural area.

At this point, carsick travelers or those who wish to make only a short trip can continue straight on Topanga Canyon Blvd. to Woodland Hills and the Ventura Freeway (101), which takes you back to Los Angeles.

At 17.5 miles make a left near the Woodland Plaza Shopping Center to continue onto Mulholland Highway. The road widens to 4 lanes near Daguerre Road, but narrows back to two soon afterwards.

At about 19 miles the intersection of Old Topanga Canyon Road and Mulholland Highway is confusing, but continue straight ahead and soon a sign will appear confirming that you are indeed on Mulholland Highway.

3 Steep rock, jagged hills and abrupt terrain become an interesting backdrop for the road around 23.7 miles.

Breathtakingly beautiful scenery and rock formations with all the drama of an old western movie—probably because many were filmed out here—begin around 25.5 miles.

Rich grazing lands and horse pastures appear at around 27 miles.

At 27.0 miles is a stoplight intersection for Las Virgenes Road. Turn left. The two lane highway passes rugged wide-open vistas of classic western scenery and horseback riding trails.

4 At 28.7 miles is Tapia Park, a wilderness park along Malibu Creek with great hiking paths through field and wooded areas. This is an ideal place for picnicking and relaxing.

At about 30 miles a series of geologically wondrous gorges and steep valley formations begin. Many turnouts provide a chance to stop and examine the intricate stratification of rock layers, all tilted upwards in various directions.

5 At 32.5, several Palm trees announce the Hughes Research Laboratories, where the first practical laser was built. The lab is at the peak of a hill and just at the other side is a spectacular ocean view.

6 The road to Pepperdine College soon appears. The Intersection of Pacific Coast Highway and Las Virgenes is at 33.4 miles. Turn left to return to Santa Monica.

Alternate Tours include:
At the intersection of Las Virgenes and Mulholland Highway, continue straight on
7 Mulholland and go west past Malibu Lake
8 and Lake Enchanto.

At the intersection of N9 or Kimberley Canyon Road and Mulholland Highway, a detour can be made through the rugged
9 scenery of Latigo Canyon by going south or left a short while on N9 and then turning left on Latigo Canyon Road.

Mulholland Highway (23) loses its state
10 Highway designation to Decker Road. You can follow Decker (now state 23) south to
11 the ocean from their intersection, or continue west on Mulholland, skirting the Ventura County line until Mulholland takes you into Pacific Coast Highway (1) at Leo
12 Carrillo State Beach.

Follow Pacific Coast Highway back south to Santa Monica.

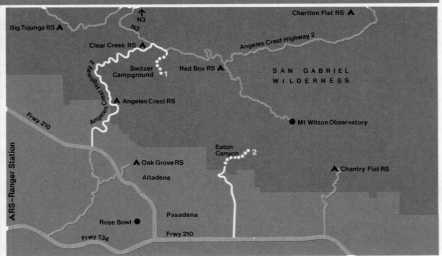

The San Gabriel mountains tower above the city to the north. A century ago; John Muir described them as among the "most rigidly inaccessible" he had ever trod. Today, these guardians are laced with trails and roads. The visitor who tours by car will see spectacular vistas from the Angeles Crest and Angeles Forest Highways, but the serenity and majesty of the range is revealed only to those who explore on foot. Fire is a danger in these mountains for half the year. *From June 1 to December 15, the trails on the portion of the slopes below 4,000 feet require an entry permit. The main roads are unrestricted year round, snow permitting; call the ranger station during the winter for snow conditions. Free entry permits may be obtained at the U. S. Forest Service Information Center in the Pasadena Hilton, 150 South Los Robles (telephone: 684-0350), or at the Oak Grove Ranger Station, in Oak Grove Park off Oak Grove Drive in La Canada (telephone: 790-1151). Trail maps, road maps, and information are also available at these locations, which are open Monday through Friday from 8:00 AM to 4:30 PM.*

Visitors should bring water. Don't touch the shiny clusters of trilobed (three) serrated leaves; they are poison oak. The rattlesnakes that live in this wilderness strike only to protect themselves. The foregoing cautions are given not to frighten, but in the belief that it is easiest to enjoy when you're prepared.

Time: 8 hours
Mileage: 60 miles by car from the intersection of Routes 210 and 2 to the intersection of Routes 14 and 210; 4 miles on foot.
Area: A vigorous driving and hiking expedition that traverses the San Gabriels from La Canada to the Antelope Valley. The hike visits the Arroyo Seco Cascades.

From the Foothill Freeway (210), take the Angeles Crest Highway (2) north into the mountains for 10½ miles. At approximately ½ mile past the intersection of Route 2 and the Angeles Forest Highway (N3), turn right off Route 2 at the Switzer Campground sign. Follow the road a winding ¼ mile and park near the picnic area. The tree shaded trail leads out of the picnic area, following the stream for 1 mile to the Commodore Switzer Trail Camp. The trail then crosses the stream, whose waters abruptly drop off into a 50 foot fall. Follow the trail uphill to a fork. Take the left branch of the fork into the gorge beneath the falls. To return, retrace your steps. Drive back to the intersection of Route 2 and Angeles Forest Highway (N3). Go right for 30 miles to the intersection with the Antelope Valley Freeway (14). Go west to the Foothill Freeway (210), a distance of 20 miles.

² **Time:** 2-8 hours
Mileage: 30 miles by car round trip from the Foothill Freeway (210); ½ to 16 miles by foot
Area: Hikes within Eaton Canyon, ranging from the ⅛ mile Arroyo Nature Trail, through the natural rock pools of Upper Eaton Canyon, to a 16 mile overnight jaunt to Mt. Wilson.

The starting point may be reached by car or bus:
Bus: Take #432 from Olive St. in downtown Los Angeles to the intersection of Huntington Dr. and Sierra Madre Blvd. Transfer to #431. Get off at New York Ave. and Altadena Dr. Walk one block north on the east side of Altadena to the gate of Eaton Canyon Park.
Car: From the Foothill Freeway (210), go left on Altadena Dr. to 1750, which is the entrance to Eaton Canyon Park. Go through the gates to the McCurdy Nature Center, ¼ mile down the path. The Center has brochures for the self-guided Arroyo Nature Trail, as well as information on the other trails in the Park and Canyon. Among the possibilities are: a ½ mile hike to Eaton Falls; a 3 mile climb to the Henninger Flat Campground and Ranger Station; a 3 mile excursion to the natural stone pools in upper Eaton Canyon; and for those who bring their pajamas, a 16 mile overnighter to Mt. Wilson.

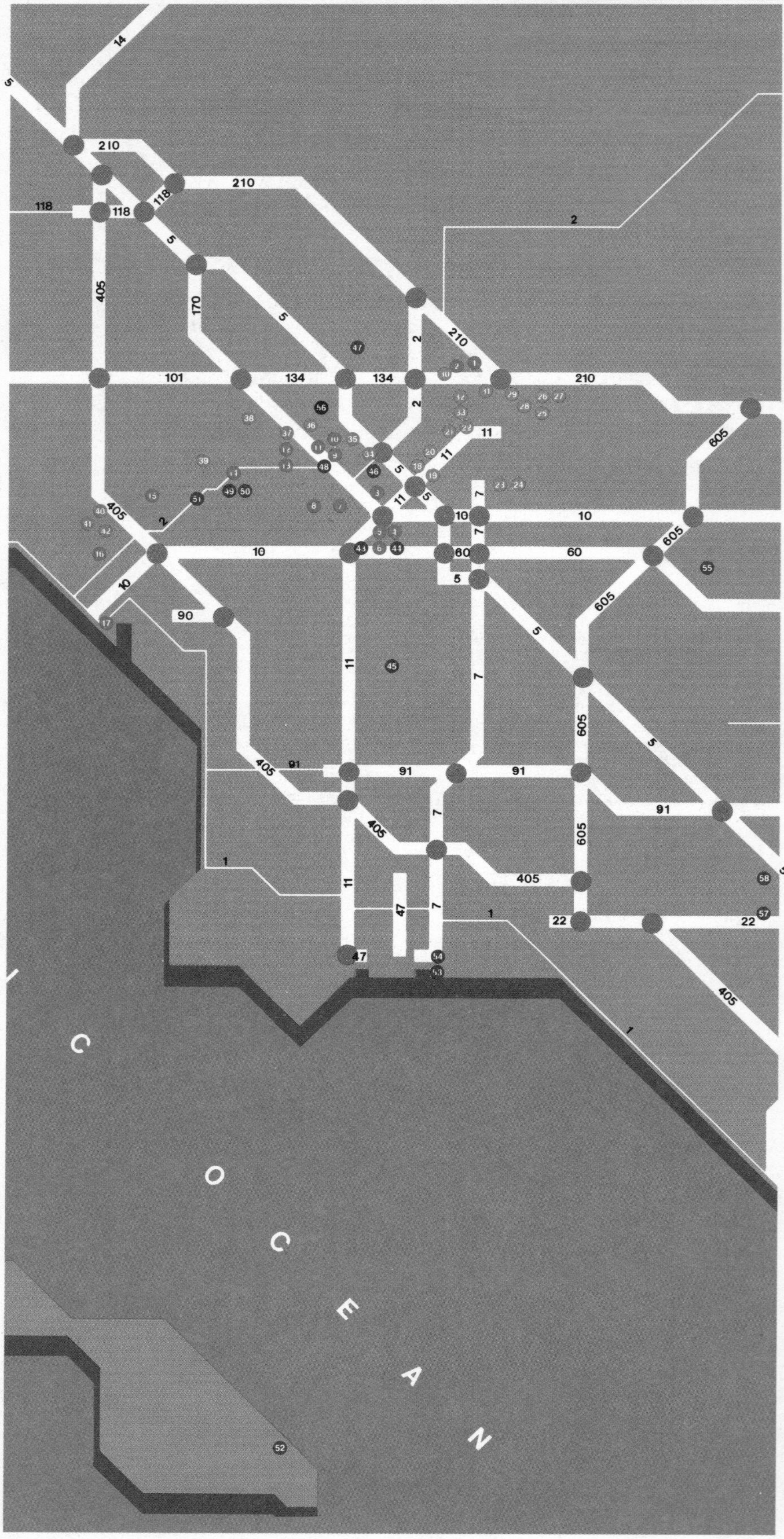
OCEAN

The architectural heritage of Los Angeles is rich and varied. This day-long pilgrimage will take you in a broad sweep of the area to see some of LA's best architectural landmarks.

It is a rewarding journey and one during which—in typical LA fashion—you hardly have to leave your car. The tour is approximately 46 miles long and takes at least five hours. **Private residences should be viewed only from the street.** Begin in Pasadena, an area rich in fine, turn-of-the-century domestic architecture. Slightly north of the exchange of the Long Beach (#7) and the Ventura (#134) Freeways or north from the Orange Grove Boulevard exit

1 of the Pasadena Freeway (#11) is the **Gamble House** (1908), 4 Westmoreland Place, a large vacation bungalow by Pasadena Craftsman architects Charles and Henry Greene. *(Open Tu and Th, 10AM-3PM, and first Su of each*

2 *month, 12-3PM).* All along **Arroyo Terrace**, the street to the left of the Gamble House, other houses by Greene and Greene can be seen. Take Orange Grove Boulevard south to the Pasadena Freeway (#11). Go south on the freeway. Stay to the right and connect with the Hollywood Freeway (#101). Exit at Echo Park-Glendale Boulevard and turn right at the end of the exit onto Bellevue Avenue. Turn left (north) on Edgeware Road and turn left again

3 on Carroll Avenue. This is the **Carroll Avenue Historic District**: the 1300 block of Carroll Avenue, lined with late 1880s Victorian homes. Take Edgeware south to Temple Street, turn left (east) and continue into downtown. Turn right on Spring Street. At Third Street turn right and

4 park nearby, because the Victorian **Bradbury Building** (1893) at the corner of Third and Broadway (304 S. Broadway) must be seen from the inside to appreciate its interior court. Continue on Third and turn left (south) on Figueroa Street. You will pass the glamorous

5 mirror-glass **Bonaventure Hotel** (1977-78) by John Portman on the left at 350 S. Figueroa St.

6 Continue on Figueroa. The **Linder Plaza** (1977), 888 W. Sixth St., is a superb contemporary complex in gray metal by Honnold, Reibsamen and Rex. Take Figueroa to Wilshire Boulevard and turn right (west) to see some Moderne commercial buildings. Visible at a distance is the tan terra cotta and green copper-trimmed

7 tower of the **Bullocks Wilshire Department Store** (1929), 3050 Wilshire Blvd., by John and Donald B. Parkinson. Further west is the

8 **Wiltern-Pellisier Building** (1930), 3790 Wilshire Blvd., a zigzag Moderne complex of turquoise terra cotta which includes a theatre, shops, and offices. Turn right (north) on Western Avenue and turn right (east) at Hollywood Boulevard. Enter Barnsdall Park on the right, before the intersection with Vermont Avenue. Here is Frank Lloyd Wright's first Los

9 Angeles project, the **Hollyhock House** (1917-20). *(Open Tu, Th, first Sa of each month, 10AM-2PM.)* Another Frank Lloyd Wright house from a slightly later period is nearby. Return to

Hollywood going right (east) and immediately turn left at Vermont. Cross Los Feliz Boulevard and, where Vermont forks, go to the left on Glendower Avenue. At 2607 Glendower Avenue is Wright's stunning concrete-block

10 **Ennis House** (1924) with its spectacular setting in the hills. Return to Vermont and at Franklin Avenue turn right (west). On the right at 5121

11 Franklin is the dramatic **Sowden House** (1926) by Lloyd Wright. Continue on Franklin following the jog to the left at Highland Avenue. Three blocks past Highland Avenue turn left (south) on Orange Drive and come up the back way to

12 Meyer and Holler's extravagant **Grauman's** (now **Mann's**) **Chinese Theatre** (1927), 6925 Hollywood Blvd. Turn left onto Hollywood Boulevard for a better view. Turn right (south) onto Highland and turn left (east) on Sunset Boulevard. At 6671 Sunset Blvd. is the

13 **Crossroads of the World**—international theme shops designed by Frank Derrah in 1936 as a tourist attraction. Turn right (south) on Cahuenga Boulevard and right again (west) on Santa Monica Boulevard. Continue on to San Vicente Boulevard and turn left (south). The

14 **Pacific Design Center** (1975) is the large blue glass structure at the corner of San Vicente Boulevard and Melrose Avenue. The building with an interior court and shops was designed by Cesar Pelli for Victor Gruen and Associates. Return to San Vicente going north to Sunset and turn left (west). Continue on Sunset, past UCLA, and turn left at Veteran Avenue. At the first street, turn right on Cashmere Street and right again on Greenfield Avenue. Rudolph

15 Schindler's unique **Tischler House** (1949) with its angular facade is at 175 Greenfield Ave. Take Greenfield to the end of the block and turn left (west) on Sunset. At Bundy Drive turn left (south) and at Montana Avenue turn left. Turn left again on 22nd Street. At Washington

16 Avenue and 22nd Street is the unusual **Gehry House**, 1002 22nd St., a 1977-78 remodeling of an older house using corrugated steel, wood, and glass, by architect Frank Gehry. Go north on Washington Avenue to 26th Street and turn right. At Broadway turn right and at Ocean Avenue (Neilson Way) turn left. In order to enter the one-way street of Hollister Avenue, turn right on Wadsworth Avenue, circling the block, making right turns at Barnard Way and Hollister Avenue. To conclude the tour, view the white

17 cubistic **Horatio West Court Apartments** (1919), 140 Hollister Ave., by Irving Gill, one of California's leading architects of the modern movement. (To get back to the Santa Monica Freeway take Ocean Avenue [Neilson Way] left [west] to Pico Boulevard and turn right. At Fourth Street turn left and you will see signs for the Santa Monica Freeway toward downtown.)

Los Angeles living has been established in style by trendsetting architects. This tour is a sampling of the finest houses designed by modern architects with the addition of a few excellent revival-style homes found from Silverlake west through Hollywood to Santa Monica.

The tour is approximately 37 miles long and takes at least 3 hours. **Private residences should be viewed only from the street.** Turn north on Reno Avenue from Sunset Boulevard

onto Silverlake Boulevard. (Silverlake cannot be entered directly from Sunset.) Follow Silverlake to the right around the lake. At 2300 Silverlake

34 Boulevard is the **Neutra House** (1933; rebuilt

1963), an International style house by Viennese immigrant architect Richard Neutra. Private residence. Down the street are a number of other houses by Neutra at 2250, 2242, 2240, 2238, 2226, 2218, 2210, and 2200. Private residences. Continue north on Silverlake and turn left at its end onto Glendale Boulevard. At the fork go left on Rowena Avenue and at Los Feliz Boulevard turn left. Two blocks further, at Commonwealth Avenue, turn right (north). Turn left at the third block on Dundee Drive. At the

35 end of the street is Neutra's **Lovell House** (1929), 4616 Dundee Drive, a classic International style house cantilevered on a hillside. Private residence. Return to Los Feliz and turn right (west). At Vermont Avenue turn right and veer to the left to take Glendower Avenue. Winding up the hill you will reach Frank Lloyd Wright's spectacular concrete-block

10 house, the **Ennis House** (1924), 2607 Glendower Avenue.Private residence. Return to Vermont and turn right at Hollywood Boulevard. On the left is Barnsdall Park. See Frank Lloyd Wright's first Los Angeles project, the

9 **Hollyhock House** (1917-20). *(Open Tu, Th, first Sa of each month, 10AM-2PM.)*

Return to Hollywood and turn left. At Normandie Avenue turn right (north) and at Franklin Avenue turn left (west). Lloyd Wright's dramatic

11 concrete and stucco **Sowden House** (1926) is at 5121 Franklin Avenue. Private residence. Continue on Franklin and turn right (north) on Western Avenue. Take it to its end where it veers left connecting with Los Feliz. Get in the left lane in preparation to turn left at the first street, Fern Dell Drive. Turn left again on Black Oak Drive. Turn left on E. Live Oak Drive and right on Verde Oak Drive. Veer to the left on Valley Oak Drive. At 5699 Valley Oak Drive is Lloyd Wright's spacious copper-trimmed

36 **Samuels Novarro House** (1922-24). Private residence. Retrace back to Los Feliz and at Western turn right (south). At Franklin turn right and continue on Franklin past the jog to the left at Highland Avenue. Three blocks past Highland turn right on Sycamore Avenue and

37 drive up to the **Yamashiro Restaurant**, 1999 N. Sycamore Avenue. The restaurant, designed as an authentic Chinese palace by Franklin Small in 1913, was formerly the home of art dealers Adolphe and Eugene Bernheimer. Return to Franklin, turn right (west) and continue to its end. At Sierra Bonita turn left (south) and at Hollywood turn right (west). At the end of this street you will automatically enter Laurel Canyon Boulevard by turning right (north). Take the winding Laurel Canyon up to Mulholland Drive and turn right (east). At Torreyson Place turn right and from this location you can see the

38 **Malin House,** known as the "Chemosphere" house, a private residence designed by John Lautner in 1960. Return to Mulholland and turn left (south) on Laurel Canyon. When you reach Sunset turn right (west). At the intersection of Cory Avenue and Sunset, take the small street to the right on Sunset Boulevard, going straight

39 onto Doheny Road. The **Doheny Mansion** is located at 510 N. Doheny Road. Its major entrance is on the right side on Loma Vista. An expansive English Tudor mansion, designed by Charles Kauffman in 1923 for oil millionaire Edward Doheny, it is owned by the City of Beverly Hills.

Return to Loma Vista and go south, turning left. At Mountain Drive veer left and turn right (west) at Sunset. Continue on Sunset and pass UCLA. Turn left on Veteran Avenue and turn left at the first block, Cashmere Street. Turn right on Greenfield Avenue and see Viennese immigrant architect Rudolph Schindler's ingenious

15 **Tischler House** (1949) at 175 Greenfield Avenue. Private residence. Continue north on the street to return to Sunset and turn left (west). At the Bundy Drive-Kenter Avenue intersection turn right onto Kenter, and at the second block on the right, Skyeway Road, turn right. Frank Lloyd Wright's redwood and stucco

40 **Sturgis House** (1939) is at 449 Skyeway Rd. Return to Sunset and turn right (west). One block past Mandeville Canyon, turn right at Riviera Ranch Road. Here, and on Old Oak

41 Road, are architect **Cliff May's original "ranch houses"** popularized throughout America during the 1940s and 1950s. Return to Sunset and turn left (east). Turn right at Rockingham Road. Across 26th Street and after a slight jog to the left, Rockingham becomes La Mesa Drive. From 26th to 19th Streets, La Mesa is draped by huge Moreton Fig trees, and in the 2100 to 1900 block of La Mesa are a number of

42 **Spanish Revival homes by John Byers** from the 1920s-30s. They can be seen at 2153, 2101, 2034, and 1923 La Mesa Drive. Private residences. At the end of the road is San Vicente Boulevard. Take it to the left one block and continue on 20th Street, jogging left at Montana Avenue. Turn left at Washington Avenue. At 22nd Street you will see an unusual

16 house on the southeast corner, the **Gehry House,** 1002 22nd St., which will conclude the tour. The Dutch Colonial house was remodeled in 1977-78 as if by intuition, not logic, by architect Frank O. Gehry, using corrugated metal, wood, and glass. Private residence. (You can return to the Santa Monica Freeway by going south on Washington. At 20th, turn right to connect with the freeway.)

The strongest cultural influence on Los Angeles architecture has been the Spanish tradition. This tour views a number of Spanish Colonial, Mexican, and Spanish Mission Revival buildings. It also concentrates on the Craftsman Movement from the turn of the century.

The Pasadena area abounds in fine architecture of many styles, but the English-based Arts and Crafts movement found one of its strongest American outlets here. This tour is approximately 19 miles long and takes at least 4 hours. **Private residences should be viewed only from the street.** Begin this tour at a location adjacent to the Pasadena Freeway (#11). On the west side of the Freeway at Avenue 43 exit

18 is the **Lummis House** (1898-1910), 200 E.

Avenue 43. The boulder home was built by Charles F. Lummis, enthusiast of the Spanish, Mexican, and Indian heritage of Southern California. *The house is open for tours Su-F,*

19 *1-4PM.* Across the freeway, **Heritage Square** is a bright cluster of Victorian mansions in various stages of renovation. Take Avenue 43 left (west) to Figueroa Street and turn right. At 4603

20 N. Figueroa St. is the **Casa de Adobe,** a 1917 reconstruction of a Mexican adobe house. *Open W, Sa, Su, 2-5PM.* Continue on Figueroa

going northeast to Arroyo Glen and turn right.

21 At 6211 Arroyo Glen is the **San Encino Abbey** (1909-1925), a private residence built by Clyde Brown in a combination of Spanish Mission and European Gothic styles. Return to Figueroa and turn right, continuing northeast. At York Boulevard turn right (east) and at Avenue 66

22 turn right (south). The **Judson Studios** are located at 200 S. Avenue 66. These turn-of-the-century studios are famous for their Craftsman glass- and mosaic-work production. Return to York and turn right. Continue on as the road becomes Pasadena Boulevard and then Monterey Road. At Huntington Drive jog left and turn right (south) on San Marino Avenue. Continue on San Marino and at a fork in the road go to the right onto Santa Anita Street. At the corner of Santa Anita and Mission

23 Drive is the **Mission Playhouse** (1927), 320 S. Mission, designed by Arthur Benton to appear similar to the Mission San Antonio in Monterey

24 County. Go east one block to visit the **San Gabriel Mission**, 537 W. Mission Dr., the fourth mission established by Fr. Serra. The restored Mission was originally built between 1791 and 1805. *Open daily, 9:30AM-4PM.* Go north on Serra Drive and turn left on San Marino Avenue.

25 Turn left on **Lombardy Road** and notice the Spanish Revival homes, all private residences, in the 1700 to 2000 blocks, especially 1750 by architect Roland Coate, Sr., 1779 by George Washington Smith, at the corner of Allen Street, 665 Allen St., another Smith house, and two Wallace Neff houses at 1861 and 2035. Turn right (north) on Sierra Bonita and go one block to California Boulevard. Before you is the

26 campus of **California Institute of Technology.** The oldest buildings, from the 1930s, were designed by Gordon Kauffman in the Spanish Renaissance and Spanish Baroque styles. Note

27 especially the **Atheneum Club** facing Sierra Bonita and the adjacent dorms seen as you turn left (west) onto California Boulevard. Continue on California to El Molino Avenue and turn right (north). At 37 S. El Molino Ave. is the Spanish

28 Colonial **Pasadena Playhouse** (1924-25) by architect Elmer Grey. Turn left at the corner on Colorado Boulevard and at Raymond Avenue turn left. One block away is Green Street. Turn left and you will be in front of the large, turretted

29 Spanish Colonial **Green Hotel** (1890-99) by architect Frederick Roehrig. Turn left on Arroyo Parkway and at Colorado Boulevard turn left (west). Turn right on Orange Grove Boulevard. Just past Walnut Street you will see a small street flanking Orange Grove Boulevard on the left. This is Westmoreland Place. At #4 is the

1 **Gamble House** (1908) by famous Pasadena Craftsman architects Charles and Henry Greene. *(Tours on Tu and Th, 10AM-2PM, first Su of each month, 12-3PM.)* To the left of the

2 house is **Arroyo Terrace**, which has a number of Greene and Greene houses. All are private residences. Especially note 368, 370, 400, 408, 424, and 440, built between 1902 and 1913. Return to Orange Grove Boulevard and turn right. At Holly Street, one block away, turn left (west). At Linda Vista Avenue turn left and go

30 one block to El Circulo; turn left. At 65 and 95 El Circulo are two rural Spanish Revival homes designed by amateur architect Edward Fowler in 1927. Backtrack to Linda Vista Avenue. Turn right (north) to Holly Street and turn right (west). At Orange Grove Boulevard turn right (south). Turn right at California Boulevard and see the

31 **Cheesewright House** (1910) at 686 W. California Boulevard, a Craftsman house appearing like an English snuggery with its thatch roof. At Arroyo Boulevard turn left

32 (south). See the **Batchelder House** (1909), 626 S. Arroyo Blvd., built by Ernest Batchelder, Pasadena craftsman and renowned tilemaker. Conclude this tour with the finest example of a Spanish Monterey Revival house, the home at

33 850 S. Arroyo Blvd. (1927) by Donald McMurray. Private Residence. (To return to the Pasadena or Ventura Freeways, turn left at Grand and again on Bellefontaine to get to Orange Grove. From Orange Grove you can connect with the Pasadena Freeway [#11] by turning right, and with the Ventura Freeway [#134] by turning left.)

This tour is a sampling of some of LA's fantastic architecture that ranges from the serious to the whimsical.

A bit of fantasy abounds on almost every street of LA, so along the way you might note additional constructed visions that have adopted the styles of other areas and other cultures, or which present straightforward indulgence and delight in commercialism, futurism, and personal eccentricities. The route is around the city in an extremely broad sweep from downtown to Watts, and north to Glendale, ending in Beverly Hills. The tour is approximately 52 miles long and takes at least 4 hours. **Private residences should be viewed only from the street.** In downtown LA the shimmering futuristic apparition at 350 S.

5 Figueroa St. is the **Bonaventure Hotel** (1977) by architect John Portman. Take Figueroa south to Olympic Boulevard and turn left at Hill Street.

43 Turn right to see the **Mayan Theatre**, 1040 S. Hill St. The now brightly painted pre-Columbian facade was designed by Morgan, Walls and Clements in 1927. Continue on Hill to Pico Boulevard and turn left (east). At the end of Pico you will come to Central Avenue and the

44 ship-like **Coca-Cola Building** (1935-37), 1334 S. Central Ave., with its enormous Coke bottles at the entrance to the plant. Turn right onto Central and follow the signs on the right to enter the Santa Monica Freeway (#10) going west (to Santa Monica). After a short distance connect with the Harbor Freeway (#11) south (headed to San Pedro). Turn off at the Manchester Avenue exit and go left (east). (Manchester turns into Firestone Boulevard.) At Elm Street turn right (Elm turns into Wilmington Avenue), and at the intersection of 107th Street, turn right. There

45 you will see the unique monument, the **Rodia Towers** (1921-54), 1765 E. 107th St. These are a personal vision made of broken tile, glass and debris erected by an Italian immigrant tilelayer, Simon Rodia. Retrace back to the Harbor Freeway and go north on the freeway (to LA-Pasadena) and connect with the Hollywood Freeway. Take the Hollywood Freeway and get off after a short distance at the Echo Park-Glendale Boulevard exit. Take Echo Park north to Baxter Street and turn right. At Avon Street turn left (driving the streets around here is like taking a rollercoaster ride). You will want

to park and walk on the right (east) side of Avon to Avon Park Terrace. There you will see what seems to be an authentic Indian pueblo, the

46 **Atwater Bungalows,** 1431-33 Avon Park Terrace (1931), by Robert Stacy-Judd. Return to your car and at Baxter turn right. At Alvarado Street turn left and at Glendale turn right. Take Glendale to San Fernando Road and turn left. At Grandview Avenue turn right and take it to its end.

At the intersection of Mountain Street and Grandview you will enter the Brand Library,

47 formerly the **Brand House** (1902), an exotic East Indian and Moorish mansion now a public library. Return to Grandview and at San Fernando turn left. At Los Feliz Boulevard turn right. Turn left at Vermont Avenue and right onto Sunset Boulevard. You will pass the East Indian

48 **Self-Realization Temple** at 4860 Sunset Blvd. and the **Crossroads of the World,** 6621 Sunset Blvd.; the 1935 tourist attraction presents a ship sailing into a courtyard of shops representing various European countries. In the brief span on Sunset is the opportunity to see the Occident and the Orient, mysticism and commercialism. At Highland Avenue turn right and at Hollywood Boulevard turn left. At 6925 Hollywood Blvd.

12 you will see **Grauman's** (now **Mann's**) **Chinese Theatre,** an extravagant and exotic Chinese design from 1927. Continue west on Hollywood and at La Brea turn left. At Santa Monica Boulevard turn right and at La Cienega Boulevard turn left (south). Along La Cienega is the famous Restaurant Row. Look for the enormous fishmouth entrance of the **Fish**

49 **Shanty Restaurant,** at 8500 Burton Way, and at the intersection of La Cienega and Beverly

50 Boulevards is the **Tail-o-the-Pup** hotdog stand, 311 N. La Cienega Blvd. Turn right on Wilshire Boulevard and continue west on it into Beverly Hills. Slightly before the intersection of Wilshire and Santa Monica Boulevards turn right on Linden Drive. At Carmelita turn left. At the corner of Walden Drive and Carmelita is the

51 **Spadina House,** 516 Walden Dr. (1921), a fairyland thatch-roof cottage that was actually a set for a Willot Productions film. (From Wilshire going west you can connect with the Santa Monica Freeway.) This tour by no means covers all the fantasy architecture in Southern California.

Interested viewers should also make it a point to see: **Avalon Casino,** 52, **Queen Mary,** 53, **Spruce Goose,** 54, **Drive-Thru Donut,** 55, **Hollywood Sign,** 56, **Crystal Cathedral,** 57, and **Disneyland,** 58.

Los Angeles Conservancy Tours. A series of excellent walking tours and changing programs available to the public. *849 S. Broadway, Suite 1225. 623-CITY*

This is a city where a home is a castle and a castle is a home.

Huge expanses of available land, ease of transport, a city plan that encouraged horizontal development, a healthy economy, and a fervent belief in the fundamental right of home ownership have combined to make LA the city of the largest concentration of single family residences in the world. There is an intense awareness of real estate: financing of loans is more widely discussed than any other topic and even renters are knowledgeable about current interest rates. The occupancy of single-family residences persists even as the persistance of the single-family unit diminishes: single Angelenos now account for a large percentage of the home-buying market. The words house and home are used interchangeably, perhaps reflecting the frequency of sale and the lack of rootedness in a particular locale.

The first settlers built simple, one-story homes of adobe, sun-dried blocks made of a mixture of clay, sand, water, and weeds or straw. The more luxurious dwellings of the rancho period reflected the growing prosperity of the region. The import of wood and manufactured appointments allowed the construction of a new style called Monterey, which featured a broad second-story balcony with a fancy wooden balustrade. The Yankees who began to arrive in sizable numbers during the last half of the nineteenth century built in Eastern architectural styles. By 1850, bricks were being made locally, and soon after, the enlargement of the harbor and improvement of the rail system resulted in the import of large quantities of lumber from the Northwest. Greek Revival, Italianate, Gothic Revival, Queen Anne, and Colonial Revival structures sprang up from this new abundance of construction material.

At the turn of the century, the Craftsman style was developed as one of the first uniquely Californian building modes. Features such as river stone foundations and fireplaces, exposed roof rafters, shingle or stucco siding and pitched roofs that overhung wide porches seemed perfectly in harmony with the warm climate and casual customs of the area. Many thousands of these low structures, often called bungalows, were built in the period between 1900 and 1930, especially in Pasadena, Hollywood, and South Central Los Angeles. Mission Revival and Spanish Colonial Revival, two extremely popular styles that emerged toward the beginning of the century, took traditional Spanish forms as their stylistic source. Characterized by stucco walls, red tile roofs, arches, and ironwork ornament, these romantic structures appealed to a growing sense of the city's unique Latin heritage.

Beginning in the 1920s, a number of architects built homes here which have changed the nature of domestic architecture. Frank Lloyd Wright and his son Lloyd Wright designed homes of theatrical contrasts that seemed monumental and ageless through their use of simplified forms. Residences by R. M. Schindler and Richard Neutra used extensive areas of glass, innovative materials, and intersecting planes to merge indoors with outdoors. Their successors continued to refine this mode and produced buildings that are dramatic in their lightness and spatial arrangement, yet unobtrusive in their allegiance to the contours of the land. The most contemporary architects have developed a style that emphasizes the elements of construction and uses prefabricated industrial parts.

We have tried to include a sampling of LA restaurants that will enable the reader to find a good meal anywhere. Our choices cover a wide range of price, type of food, and location. We have chosen restaurants that we enjoy, and hope that our purely subjective opinions will be shared. Houses, prices and even existence of restaurants change frequently and we suggest that you call ahead. Reservations are advisable at $$$ and $$$$ restaurants. Acceptable dress almost everywhere tends toward the casual; most places welcome tieless male diners. The cost of a meal can vary dramatically depending on the choice of beverage. We have based our dollar signs on a one-cocktail, or non-vintage bottle of wine meal for one person. The dollar signs translate into the following:

$ inexpensive
$$ moderate
$$$ expensive
$$$$ very expensive

★　　　　　★　　　　　★

☆☆☆ These aim for perfection in food, decor, service, and ambience (and have prices to match).

pg
15 Bernard's at the Biltmore
30 La Toque
32 L'Ermitage
32 L'Orangerie
47 Les Anges
32 Ma Maison
48 Michael's
15 Rex
31 Spago

★　　　　　★　　　　　★

☆☆ Important restaurants, some elegant, some casual-chic, with a definite personality, and worthy of an evening out.

pg		pg	
38	Bistro	38	Mandarin
38	Bistro Garden	45	Mangia
33	Chasen's	8	Mon Kee
31	Chianti	33	Morton's
35	Excelsior	24	Pacific Dining Car
36	Jimmy's	33	Palm
68	Katsu	46	Peppone
36	LaBella Fontana (Beverly Wilshire)	21	Perino's
100	La Cuisine, Dana Point	31	Ristorante Chianti
38	La Scala	36	Romeo & Juliet
85	La Serra	31	Scandia
30	Le Dome	32	Studio Grill
52	Le Gourmet (Sheraton La Reina Hotel)	17	Tower
29	Le St. Germaine	33	Trumps
48	Ma Facon	49	Valentino
		48	Verdi

★

☆ Distinctive food experiences.

pg		pg		pg	
45	Adrianos Restaurant	10	Horikawa	33	Michel Richard
45	Cafe Four Oaks	36	Homer & Edy's Bistro	38	Mr. Chow
102	Capistrano Depot	32	Hugo's	33	Pasta, Pasta, Pasta
80	Chez Sateau	46	Hymie's Fish Market	31	Nucleus Nuance
74	Chronicle	13	Inagiku	14	Pavan
30	Cock & Bull	33	Ivy and LA Desserts	31	Rex's Fishmarket
30	Dar Mahgreb	33	Kathy Gallagher	24	Regina's
30	Emilio's	36	La Famiglia	63	Saint Estephe
36	Englander's Wine Bar	69	LA Nicola	99	San Dimas Mansion
33	Entourage	31	La Petit Maison	39	Stellini's
84	Fung Lum	72	Lawry's California Center	85	Teru Sushi
32	Gardenia	55	La Scala Malibu	10	Thousand Cranes
31	Guiseppe!	38	L'Escoffier (Beverly Hilton)	38	Trader Vic's
15	Grand Avenue Bar	81	Mauro's		

Angels live on manna, but Angelenos dine on a wide variety of foods.

A much-abridged dictionary of favorite LA foods includes:

Tortilla—an unleavened bread in the form of a pancake, made of wheat flour or cornmeal.

A Chile—a pod-like fruit which is an essential ingredient of Mexican cooking, ranging in spiciness from the mild chile poblano to the incendiary chile jalapeño.

B Quesadilla—a folded tortilla enclosing melted cheese and green chile.

C Taco—a tortilla fried then folded in half and filled with shredded meat, beans, tomato, shredded lettuce, and cheese.

D Burrito—beans, meat, cheese, and chiles wrapped in a large flour tortilla.

Salsa—a spicy mixture of chiles, tomato, onion, and cilantro, used to liven up food.

E Huevos Rancheros—a tortilla topped with a fried egg and salsa.

F Tamale—cornmeal dough filled with a meat and chile mixture, wrapped in a corn husk and steamed.

Mexican beer—our Southern neighbor is one of the finest brewers in the world. Among the many delicious brands are: Dos XX, a dark beer; Superior, a light beer; Tecate, served with a lime and salt.

Tequila—a liquor distilled from the juice of the Agave cactus.

Margarita—a cocktail of tequila, triple sec, and lemon juice, blended to a froth with ice and served in a salt-rimmed glass.

Tequila Sunrise—a cocktail of tequila, grenadine, and orange juice.

G Avocado—a thick-skinned fruit with a buttery yellow flesh, used in salads, omelettes, and innumerable other dishes.

Guacamole—a thick sauce made of mashed avocado, tomato, and chile; often used as a dip for small fried triangles of tortilla.

Health food—generally, any food that contains sunflower seeds, soybeans, alfalfa sprouts, or which stresses the use of organic ingredients.

Salad—Angelenos love salads and eat a lot of them. The custom of serving salad before entree started here. There is evidence that the salad bar may also be a local invention. Salad bars are found everywhere, even in fast-food franchises.

H Abalone—a single-shelled gastropod native to the Pacific; it is pounded until tender, dipped in egg batter and sauteed.

I Sand Dab—a small flounder-like fish native to the Pacific.

Wine—The California coast produces wines that rival those of Europe. Wines are named for their varietal grape rather than the region of production. Many restaurants sell wine by the glass as well as by the bottle.

J Sushi—raw fish topping a bite-sized marinated rice ball. These are created in front of the diner at a sushi bar.

K Sashimi—sliced raw fish.

L Tempura—pieces of shrimp, chicken, or vegetables, dipped in a delicate rice batter and deep fried.

M Teriyaki—chicken, fish, or meat grilled in a soy-based sauce that has a touch of sweetness.

N Sukiyaki—meat and vegetables simmered in broth, often at the table. .

Sake—a rice wine, usually served warm and drunk from thimble-sized cups.

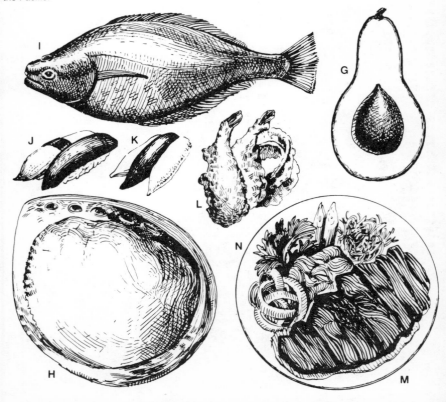

EMERGENCIES

FIRE	MAIN NUMBERS
	384-3131
	262-2111
AMBULANCE	MAIN NUMBER
	483-6721
PARAMEDICS	MAIN NUMBERS
	262-2111
	677-1181
POLICE	625-3311
COAST GUARD	590-2225
HIGHWAY PATROL	736-3374

Emergency Only Call Operator "0"
and ask for "Zenith 1-2000"

CHILD ABUSE HOTLINE	989-3157
and Emergency Shelter	
SUICIDE PREVENTION	
HOTLINE	381-5111
RAPE HOTLINE	262-0944
Spanish and English	
ALCOHOLICS	
ANONYMOUS	387-8316
LA JAILS	680-9600
FBI	272-6161
SECRET SERVICE	688-4830

SOME 24 HOUR PHARMACIES

Thrifty Drugs	381-5257
3rd & Vermont	
Kaiser Permanente Pharmacies:	
Area 5	667-8301
4867 Sunset Blvd.	
Area 10	539-1650
1050 W. Pacific Coast Hwy	
Area 17	920-4211
9400 E. Rosecrans	
Hope Hospital Pharmacy	1-714-645-8600
Area 19	
301 Newport Blvd.	
Santa Ana Tustin	
Community Hospital	1-714-953-3396
Area 19; 8A-11P Daily	
1001 N. Tustin Ave.	

GENERAL INFORMATION

Directory Assistance: Local	411
Long Distance	1-Area Code-555-1212
Phone Repair	611
Time	853-1212
Weather	554-1212
Highway Conditions	626-7231
National Parks	888-3770
State Parks	620-3342
LA County Parks	738-2961
Passport Agency	824-7070
Senior Citizens Information	738-3281
LA Public Library	626-7461
Dept. of Water & Power	481-4211

BUSES: TOUR AND INTER CITY

Grayline Tours	481-2121
Greyhound	620-1200
Starline Tours	463-3131
Trailway	742-1200

PUBLIC TRANSIT: SEE PAGE 120

TAXIS

City Cab	870-3333
Independent Cab	385-8294
Red Top Cab	395-3201
United Independent Cab	653-5050
Yellow Cab	481-2345

CAR RENTAL

American International	674-478
Avis	481-200
Aztec	776-541
Bob Leech	673-272
Budget	627-134
Hertz	800-654-313
National	626-855
Thrify	645-188

TRANSIT TERMINALS

AMTRAK/Union Station	800-252-947

AIRPORTS, LOS ANGELES AREA

LA International Airport	646-525
Santa Monica	397-261
John Wayne, Orange Cnty.	714-834-240
Long Beach	421-829
Hollywood/Burbank	840-884
Ontario	714-785-883
Van Nuys	873-138

AIRPORT BUSSES SEE PAGE

AIRLINES

AEROLINEAS ARGENTINAS	800-327-027
AEROMEXICO	380-603
AIR CAL	627-540
AIR CANADA	776-700
AIR FRANCE	625-717
AIR NEW ZELAND	776-879
AIRSPUR	417-535
AMERICAN AIRLINES	935-604
ASPEN AIRWAYS	800-525-025
AVIANCA AIRLINES	800-327-989
BRITISH AIRWAYS	272-886
BRITISH CALEDONIAN	800-231-027
C & M AIRLINES	714-377-444
CAAC	384-270
CANADIAN PACIFIC AIR	625-013
CAPITOL AIRWAYS	986-844
CHINA AIRLINES	624-116
CONDOR AIRLINES	646-801
CONTINENTAL AIRLINES	772-600
DELTA AIR LINES	386-551
EASTERN AIR LINES	380-207
ECUATORIANA AIRLINES	800-328-236
FINNAIR	800-223-570
FRONTIER AIRLINES	617-360
GOLD COAST AIR	973-378
GOLDEN WEST AIRLINES	930-220
IMPERIAL AIRLINES	800-542-615
INLAND EMPIRE AIRLINES	800-648-376
JAPAN AIR LINES	620-958
KLM ROYAL DUTCH AIRLINES	646-440
KOREAN AIR LINES	484-190
LACSA	
(Airline of Costa Rica)	800-327-770
LAN CHILE	800-327-361
LTU	
(Luft Transport Unternehmen)	640-194
LUFTHANSA GERMAN AIRLINES	800-645-388
MEXICANA AIRLINES	646-950
NORTHWEST ORIENT	380-151
PACIFIC COAST	800-322-888
PACIFIC EXPRESS	202-808
PACIFIC SOUTHWEST AIRLINES	776-012
PAN AMERICAN WORLD AIRWAYS	776-071
PHILLIPPINE AIRLINES	800-652-155
QUANTAS AIRWAYS	800-622-085
REPUBLIC AIRLINES	772-510
SCANDINAVIAN AIRLINES SYSTEM	655-860
SINGAPORE AIRLINES	655-927
SUN AIRE LINES	800-472-439
TEXAS INTERNATIONAL AIRLINES	680-115
TRANSAMERICA AIRLINES	772-269
TRANS WORLD AIRLINES	484-224
U.T.A. FRENCH AIRLIENS	625-717
UNITED AIRLINES	772-212
VARIG AIRLINES	800-223-5720
WESTERN AIRLINES	776-231
WINGS WEST AIRLINES	800-252-001
WORLD AIRWAYS	646-940